Louisa May Alcott and "Little Women"

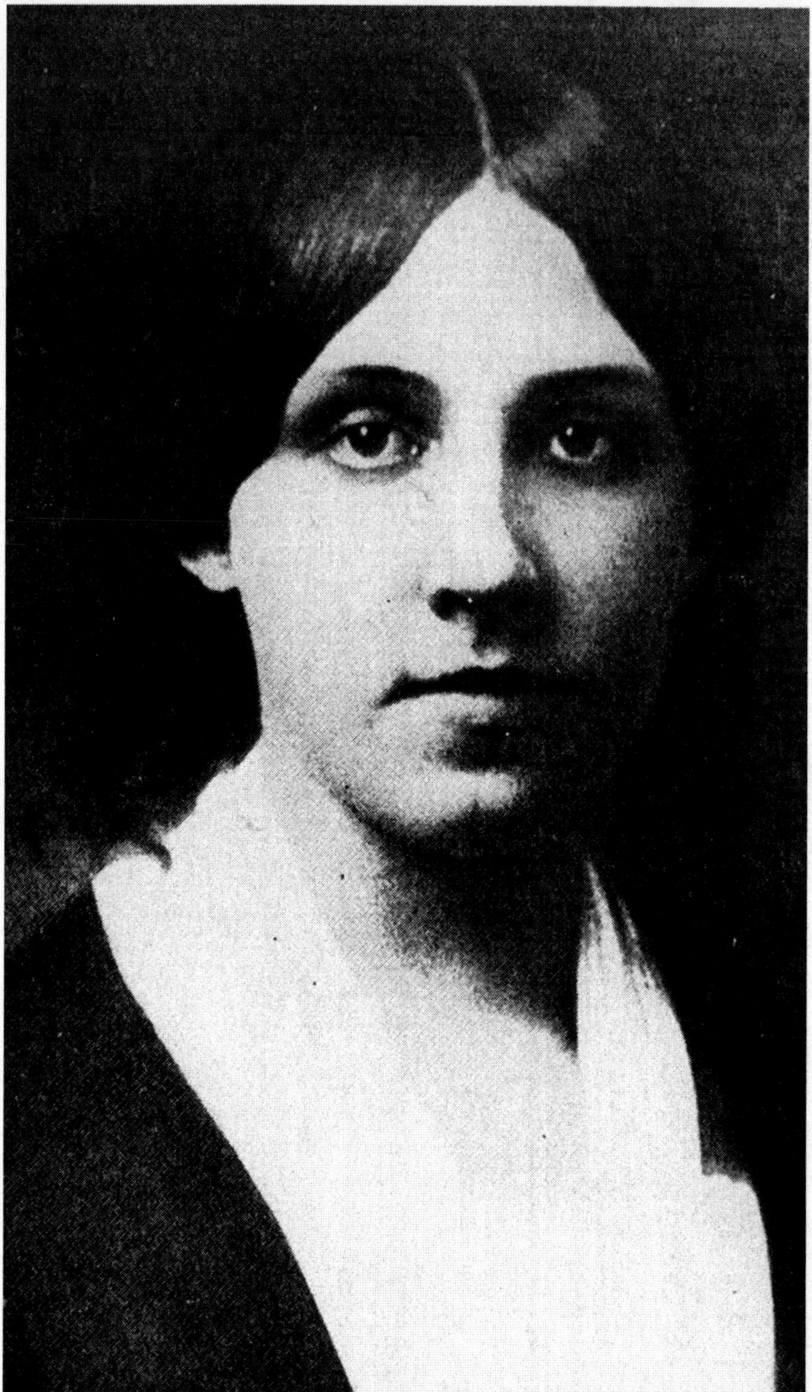

Louisa May Alcott and "Little Women"

*Biography, Critique, Publications, Poems,
Songs and Contemporary Relevance*

by
Gloria T. Delamar

AN AUTHORS GUILD BACKINPRINT.COM EDITION

Louisa May Alcott and "Little Women":
Biography, Critique, Publications,
Poems, Songs, and Contemporary Relevance

All Rights Reserved © 1990, 2001 by Gloria T. Delamar

No part of this book may be reproduced or transmitted in any form
or by any means, graphic, electronic, or mechanical, including photocopying,
recording, taping, or by any information storage or retrieval system,
without the permission in writing from the publisher.

AN AUTHORS GUILD BACKINPRINT.COM EDITION

Published by iUniverse.com, Inc.

For information address:
iUniverse.com, Inc.
5220 S 16th, Ste. 200
Lincoln, NE 68512
www.iuniverse.com

Originally published McFarland and Company

ISBN: 0-595-18722-6

Printed in the United States of America

Also by Gloria T. Delamar

Children's Counting-Out Rhymes, Fingerplays,
Jump-Rope and Bounce-Ball Chants and Other Rhythms:
A Comprehensive English-Language Reference *(McFarland, 1983)*

Rounds Re-Sounding: Circular Music for Voices and Instruments;
An Eight-Century Reference *(McFarland, 1987)*

Mother Goose: From Nursery to Literature
(McFarland, 1987)

to
William Delamar
whose loving presence encouraged the writer
and
Louisa May Alcott
whose spirit inspired the writing

Acknowledgments

No biography and study of an individual's life and works can be done without the help of many others.

There were many books by other writers that were very valuable to me: books about all the people I had to know about; books by many of the others in Louisa's life; books about the Germantown, Boston, and Concord areas; books about the culture of the times; and of course, Louisa May Alcott's own books. I thank all who have gone before—especially Louisa.

There were the many "book-houses": the libraries in Boston and Concord; the university libraries who lent their hard-to-find books; the Free Library of Philadelphia where I was permitted to photocopy from rare editions and where the nameless, faceless voices at the other end of the reference phone lines were ever helpful and courteous in providing details; and in particular, there was the Elkins Park Library in Cheltenham Township, Pennsylvania, where Joyce Bauer and Claire Borits skillfully directed the staff and interlibrary loan network to locate those hard-to-find resources and to bring them within a mile of my desk—and who took a personal interest in my progress and needs that was far beyond the call of duty. My debt to all is deep and the appreciation heartfelt.

There were knowledgeable curators and guides at the places associated with the Alcott family circle, especially Jayne Gordon of Orchard House. And there was Gene Navias at the Unitarian-Universalist Association who, in response to a phone call from a stranger, went into his personal archives and sent invaluable material about two of Louisa's hymns.

There were those who gave permission to use materials: "A Little Kingdom I Possess" and "Oh, the Beautiful Old Story" from *Singing Our History (Tales, Texts and Tunes from Two Centuries of Unitarian and Universalist Hymns)*, by Eugene B. Navias, copyright 1975 by the Unitarian Universalist Association, used by permission of the Unitarian Universalist Association; "Parody on 'The Graves of a Household,'" used by permission of the Louisa May Alcott Collection, Special Collections, the Jean and Alexander Heard Library, Vanderbilt University; "The Attic Philosopher," used by permission of the Houghton Library, Harvard University; "For the Attic Philosopher, Parody on 'The Graves of a Household,'" "Love," "To My Brain,"

"The Last of the Philosophers," and "Last Years," used by permission of William F. Kussin on behalf of Louisa May Alcott's heirs. The indoor photographs at Orchard House were taken through the courtesy and with the permission of the Louisa May Alcott Memorial Association.

There were the people who responded to my questions about their reading of *Little Women*. There were the 15 people who took time out of their busy lives to send comments about the relevance of *Little Women* today for Chapter 20.

There were the friends who went out of their way to search out resources. There was the interest from other writers in such groups as Writers' Connection, Writers' Manuscript Review, and Writers Out to Lunch.

And last, but certainly not least, there was my supportive family, who, when I was engrossed in research, communing with my muse at the computer, or reluctant to pull myself away from my involvement with Louisa for meals or other routines, were unfailingly uncomplaining, for they understood that Louisa and I had a destiny to bring to fruition.

I thank them all.

Note: All of the events in the biography section of this reference are true. Quotations are mainly from Louisa's letters and journals, and the recorded comments of her friends. Only minor changes or additions necessary to grammar, tense, or narrative were made. Louisa's mother, Abigail (May) Alcott, was addressed primarily as "Abba," but also, at times, as "Abby"; to be consistent, I've used "Abba" throughout, as well as, of course, the maternal designation of "Marmee." The youngest sister, Abigail May Alcott Nieriker, was called "Abby" as a young child, but decided she preferred "May"; to avoid confusion, I have referred to her as "May" throughout this text.

Table of Contents

Acknowledgments vii
List of Illustrations xi
Foreword xiii

Louisa May Alcott — Her Life

    Chapter 1. Late 1832–Mid-1843: A New Spirit   3
    Chapter 2. Mid-1843–1847: The Fledgling Writer   18
    Chapter 3. 1848–1855: Breaking into Print   31
    Chapter 4. 1856–Late 1862: Independence   43
    Chapter 5. November 1862–Mid-1863: Real Life   58
    Chapter 6. Mid-1863–Early 1868: The Door Opens Wider   71
    Chapter 7. Spring 1868–1869: *Little Women*   83
    Chapter 8. 1870–Mid-1874: Fame   95
    Chapter 9. Late 1874–Mid-1879: Travels and Causes   110
    Chapter 10. Mid-1879–Early 1888: Dreams   122

Little Women — The Book

    Chapter 11. 1868–Now: Reviews and Critical Analyses   145
    Chapter 12. 1868–Now: *Little Women* and Alcott in Polls and Lists   164
    Chapter 13. 1868–Now: Adaptations   171
    Chapter 14. 1868–Now: On Foreign Ground   189

Louisa May Alcott — The Legacy

    Chapter 15. 1855–Now: The Range, Dimension, and Legacy of Alcott's Works   201
    Chapter 16. 1845–1887: Louisa's Lyrics to Songs   207

Chapter 17. 1888–Now: Alcott as the Subject of Literary Studies   226
Chapter 18. Now: Alcott Sites as Literary Mecca   239
Chapter 19. Now: The "Little Women" of Today   249
Chapter 20. Now: The Relevance Today of *Little Women*   253

Appendix A: Biographical Sketches of People in the Alcott Circle   265
Appendix B: Chronology   275
Appendix C: Time-line Chronology   287
Chronological Bibliography of Louisa May Alcott's Works   299
Reference Bibliography   323
Index   333

List of Illustrations

Frontispiece: Louisa May Alcott
Amos Bronson Alcott   4
Abigail May Alcott   11
The Fruitlands farmhouse   19
Hillside   26
Velvet breeches and russet boots   32
Illustration from Flower Fables   39
Orchard House with Alcott family   45
Elizabeth Sewall Alcott and her melodeon   50
Louisa May Alcott, 1862   59
Tribulation Periwinkle and Baby Africa from Hospital Sketches   69
Louisa May Alcott's handwriting, 1865   72
Louisa May Alcott's handwriting, 1880   79
Louisa's half-moon writing desk   84
Illustration by May Alcott from Little Women   90
Anna Bronson Alcott (Pratt)   96
Frontispiece from Little Men   101
Abigail May Alcott (Nieriker)   112
Thoreau-Alcott-Pratt House   116
Louisa's cottage at Nonquit, Massachusetts   124
Dunreath Place   134
Louisa May Alcott's grave   141
Advertisement for Little Women, *from* Little Men   146
Bas relief of Louisa M. Alcott   153
Jo and the Professor from Little Women   161
Louisa May Alcott postage stamp   165
Scene from 1913 Little Women *Broadway production*   176
The "little women" and Marmee, from Little Women   179
Illustration from Good Wives   191
Title page illustration and verse from Aunt Jo's Scrap-Bag II   198
Louisa May Alcott, 1886   202
The Marches at the piano, from Little Women   208
Louisa May.Alcott (engraving)   228
Frontispiece from The Children's Friend   232

20 Pinckney Street, Boston 241
"Mood pillow" and living room at Orchard House 246
Bust of Louisa May Alcott 250
Taking the breakfast, from Little Women 254
Jo in a vortex, from Little Women 259
School of Philosophy 266
Advertisement for Little Women, *from* Louisa May Alcott: Her Life, Letters, and Journals 276
"Tessa's Surprises" from Aunt Jo's Scrap-Bag I 283
Advertisements for Alcott's works from Louisa May Alcott: Her Life, Letters, and Journals 289
Louisa May Alcott (crayon drawing) 301
"My Boys" from Aunt Jo's Scrap-Bag I 309
"The Autobiography of an Omnibus" from Aunt Jo's Scrap-Bag IV 317
Orchard House, today 325

Foreword

Long ago, as a girl, I was given a complete set of the Alcott books. They have remained my favorite keepsakes. Even before starting this study I had reread several as an adult. Especially in *Little Women,* Louisa May Alcott captured the nuances that still move me to laugh and cry over Meg, Jo, Beth, and Amy March.

As a writer, I have learned to separate personal preferences and emotions from critical evaluation. The persona of Louisa May Alcott has achieved a literary longevity that has nothing to do with *my* reading habits. But my interest in her books does have something to do with my writing this reference book about Louisa's life and legacy.

There's an adage that posits that the biographer does not choose the subject—the subject chooses the biographer. It is a neat phrase, but somewhat specious perhaps. The writer is in control. At least, the writer ought to be. There is, however, one phenomenon with which even the diligent researcher becomes afflicted as the work progresses—the feeling that one knows exactly what the subject would have done or said under particular circumstances. And here the writer must beware. And be aware.

When one "just knows" that the subject reached into the left-hand desk drawer to withdraw a certain letter, one has to get out of the skin of the subject and back into the reality of the task at hand.

There are several ways to write a biography. The first is to write a recollection of one's acquaintance with the subject; this method, of course, is only available to those who actually knew the subject, and is certainly ruled out for those who write a biography a century later. There is the detailed academic approach, which documents every comment with footnotes or afternotes, the notes ultimately occupying almost as much space as the biography itself. In the hands of the skilled writer, this treatment can be quite readable; in the hands of the less skilled, it can become a mere listing of facts. Regardless, the notations will be of use to those who follow. Another approach is that of the psychological interpretation. With the same facts, the writer here attempts to analyze the subject's actions; it is at most a dubious approach, fraught with the pitfalls of drawing conclusions without knowing the real dynamics or issues; as such the result is often questionable as a reliable picture of the biographee.

Another way of dealing with the subject (one frequently used when writing for juveniles) is for the biographer to take the facts and fictionalize what the subject would have done or said; this frequently makes for more informal reading, but can hardly be said to be true nonfiction, which biography presumably is. (And this is not meant to discount the fact that most people want their biographies in casual doses.) Finally, a biography can be a synthesis of carefully researched and documentable (rather than documented) events, authentic dialogue, and fiction techniques. I have chosen this last approach. Using the language of familiarity that the subject would have used evokes immediacy, provided the biographer refrains from author-intrusion.

Fortunately for this biographer, Louisa May Alcott left journals and letters from which to cull quotations and dialogue. A number of her contemporaries wrote recollections from which to draw additional dialogue as well as the little details that make the subject come alive. The recollections in themselves dealt primarily with only a small portion of Louisa's life, but when collated, they fill the patchwork with delightful and sometimes surprising incidents.

As Louisa moved in a circle of people who themselves were notable, there were their letters and journals to draw upon, with Alcott quotations along with their own. Books about them, and other books about Louisa, along with Louisa's own works, helped to complete the fund of research.

As a compulsive researcher, I have tried to remain true to documented material; as one who prefers to draw my own conclusions and assumes the reader has the same predilection, I have avoided questionable psychological interpretations. I immersed myself in the available materials about her life, and then chose those aspects which seem most clearly to show the character of the subject and those around her. (All biographies, in the end, come down to what the writer has chosen to include, and to exclude.) I hope the reader will find the biography section readable, and most importantly, will have a sense of the person who was Louisa May Alcott.

Louisa's poetry ranges from clever doggerel to serious poems. It seems important to incorporate a generous selection of her work and intimations of personality, and also to detail her interactions with the people around her and her reactions to the events of her time.

When a subject stays in the public memory as long as Alcott has, the matter of latter-day assessments becomes significant. I've always thought that biographies ought to bring things up to date in some way that does not intrude upon the telling of the life. In Louisa's case, one book has been the primary star to which her immortality has been hitched. Although a number of her other works have also remained in print, and as she has become the object of contemporary study more have been reissued, *Little Women* still stands out as her major accomplishment. It seems appropriate and important that its history be documented.

I have treated the legacy, studies, and sites connected with her and

Alcott's relevance today as separate issues. This allowed for the fuller treatment that would go beyond biography and make this a reference book.

A reference work on any author should include a comprehensive bibliography of that individual's works, as well as a record of other studies of the subject. In that vein, I hope that readers will welcome the comprehensive lists and appendixes.

As work on this book proceeded, I began to feel the mystique that brings writer and subject to an understanding — to a fulcrum. (Added to which are some personally pleasing coincidences: we share the same middle name, May; both stand at 5'10", with blue eyes and long chestnut brown hair; both grew up determined to write; and we have both even experienced chronic writer's cramp. It seems right that I read and now write about Louisa, with whom I am comfortably on a first-name basis.)

The whole has been an experience of an intensive coming-together. If Louisa May Alcott had not *been*, and I had not *been*, this particular book about her would not have been written. In that same sense, the circle is completed with those who have chosen to read this book and, I hope, gain something in the reading.

> Gloria T. Delamar
> *Melrose Park, Pennsylvania*

Far away there in the sunshine
  are my highest aspirations.
I may not reach them,
    but I can look up
      and see their beauty,
        believe in them,
and try to follow where they lead.

L. M. Alcott.

I.
Louisa May Alcott — Her Life

Chapter 1

Late 1832–Mid-1843: A New Spirit

Louisa May Alcott was, in real life, her own most famous fictional character. Her readers will recognize events and real people who were main characters in Little Women, *and in other books and stories she wrote.*

Into Little Women *she put her own family. Her own dear mother was Marmee to the Alcotts as well as to the fictional Marches. Her older sister, Anna, was seen as the domestic "Meg." Louisa herself, the strong-willed aspiring writer, was topsy-turvy "Jo." Their gentle Beth was the sweet, frail "Beth" of the story, and her youngest artistic sister, May, was shown as the charming, but annoying "Amy." Louisa's own father, an aloof philosopher, was sketched in as the seldom-seen but loved Mr. March. Even Anna's husband and sons appeared with counterparts in the books, as did other real people in the Alcott circle.*

Throughout Louisa's life, she had the good fortune to know other remarkable and accomplished individuals. The names of many of those people are familiar.

The Alcott family's early years were difficult. They were poor. They were creative people who struggled for recognition. Their strength was in their family love and their spirit.

Louy, like all people, had dreams. With determination, she set out to attain them. By the time of her death, she had realized all of them. She attained financial success, achieved independence, and was accorded fame.

She was a loving and devoted daughter, sister, aunt, and family supporter. She filled roles as seamstress, housemaid, teacher, army nurse, traveling-companion, amateur actress and monologist, fledgling writer, and finally as professional author.

As an advocate of human rights, she actively participated, in her century, as an abolitionist and suffragist. She was a feminist before there was a word for it. Her spirit could go to its final rest in peace, for her life had heart and meaning.

In her books, drawing on "real life," she touched a wellspring of human understanding that spanned the centuries. One thing she gained was something she never dreamed of: Louisa May Alcott achieved immortality.

***

From her letters and journals and from records left by others who knew her, it's possible to share her adventures and hear the actual words used by Louisa, her family, and others. Her story, here, is drawn "from real life."

Louisa May Alcott was born into a family that loved books and writing. Even as a toddler, Louy loved them, too. She loved to have her father and

Amos Bronson Alcott. Portrait by Caroline Hildreth, 1857.

mother read to her, and she wanted to write in a journal as she saw them do. She made up her mind, early on, to practice.

One day, standing on tiptoe, little Louy reached up to the shelves and pulled down her father's big dictionaries and heavy philosophy books. When he discovered her, she had a stubby pencil in her hand, and there was dark scribbling on the once-blank flyleaves of his precious books. When those bright

A New Spirit

eyes and that earnest face turned to him, her father hadn't the heart to reprimand her.

Mr. and Mrs. Alcott rarely punished their children for their little adventures. Mr. Alcott was far too gentle a man. Mrs. Alcott was so warm that even when her quick temper made her speak out sharply, her arms reached in a hug.

These two had found soul mates in each other. Abigail "Abba" May (of the well-connected Sewell and May families of Boston) was a strong-minded and artistic woman who taught school for a while. Amos Bronson Alcott (son of poor farmers from Spindle Hill, Wolcott, Connecticut) was a former pedlar who became a genuine scholar and a dedicated teacher.

After a three-year courtship of letter-writing and sharing of journals, they were married on May 23, 1830, at King's Chapel in Boston. He was 30 and she was 29.

Seven months later, they moved to Germantown, Pennsylvania, because Mr. Alcott's new educational ideas were to be sponsored there by a wealthy Quaker, Reuben Haines, with some additional help from Roberts Vaux, the Quaker famous for prison reform. They arrived in "The City of Brotherly Love" by paddleboat in December 1830. The Philadelphia port was full of clipper ships, and the northern part of the city was already industrialized with plants that produced drugs, chemicals, leads, paints, and all manner of textiles: cloth, lace, wool, and carpets. The hosiery and knits produced near the area where the Alcotts settled were known all over as "Germantown goods."

Germantown had become a suburban retreat for the rich who wanted to escape the stale air of the city. It was renowned for its mica-flecked limestone houses, separated by streams, hilly fields, and stone fences. Its gardens were envied—hyacinths, tulips, and roses predominated, and exotic imports from Europe provided horticultural competition for the landowners.

Mr. Alcott was to take in pupils to try out his teaching methods. His dear friend, William Russell, who had also come to Germantown, would teach the female academy and he would teach the boys. They hoped his new ideas would rejuvenate the stodgy remains of the old Germantown Academy that had been founded in 1759. He began teaching in January 1831.

Their first home was a rooming house; it was in a Germantown rooming house that the Alcott's first child, Anna Sewall Alcott, was born on March 16, 1831. Soon after, the Alcotts were settled on a piece of Haines's property on Germantown's busy, hard-dirt main street, the Germantown Road. It was a mile down the road from Haines's own fine rose garden and estate, Wyck. The Alcott's piece of land had raspberries, currants, and gooseberry bushes. A serpentine path wove through the property, lined with pines, firs, cedars, apple, pear, peach, and plum trees. A long cedar hedge ran from the front to the back of the property. Amidst flower and vegetable gardens sat the cottage that Haines had called "Rookery Cottage," but Mrs. Alcott renamed "The Little Paradise of Pine Place."

She felt attracted to the city where the husband of her Aunt Dorothy Quincy Hancock, the illustrious John Hancock, had been the first signer of the Declaration of Independence. In addition, they were to live in Germantown, where Aunt Dorothy's acquaintances had been—President George Washington and his wife, Martha, had lived a short way up the road, and both George Washington and General Lafayette were known to have walked the very road on which they were settled.

Although Haines was generous, the Alcotts had spent too much money furnishing their new home and acquiring books. They took in some students to help defray expenses.

One was a precocious eight-year-old, Elizabeth Lewis, with whom he eventually began a correspondence, discussing such erudite topics as religion, self-improvement, and the development of the soul. The scholar had a tendency to use long, overblown words, but by the sixth letter, little Elizabeth had asked him to write in "clear and simple words." He did, and learned a lesson therefrom. In all, they wrote 26 letters.

Unfortunately, what had started so full of hope was suddenly interrupted when Reuben Haines died in October 1831. Mr. Alcott determined to keep the school going.

A year later their second daughter, Louisa May Alcott, was born on Bronson Alcott's own 33rd birthday, November 29, 1832. She was named after her mother's dearest sister, Louisa May Greele, who had died four years before. On the day of this infant's birth, her father wrote: "Abba inclines to call the babe *Louisa May,*—a name to her full of every association connected with amiable benevolent and exalted worth. I hope *its present possessor* may rise to equal attainment, and deserve a place in the estimation of society."

Mr. Alcott, with a growing family to support, was worried about the school's future. Reuben Haines had paid the tuition for not only his own large family, but for many of the others as well. His widow could not afford to continue this generosity. Finally, after struggling along for so many months, the school had to close.

The Alcotts were forced to borrow money from Abba Alcott's father, the Revolutionary War Colonel, Joseph May, and from her brother, the Reverend Samuel May. In desperation, they moved to the center of Philadelphia and Mr. Alcott tried to get another school established at 222 S. Eighth Street. As always, his favorite book, *Pilgrim's Progress,* was presented to his students.

In April of 1834, needing more time to study, Mr. Alcott made the decision to find rooms for his wife and daughters in Germantown. On weekends, he walked the six miles to Germantown to be with his family. From his own room in the area behind the city's library, he had easy access to the library and he set about an intensive reading and self-education program. From this, and the earlier interchanges with the erudite William Russell, who had by now returned to Boston, he began to further develop his philosophy.

Alone all week in Germantown, still a stranger to the community, Abba Alcott, now Marmee to her little ones, was lonely and tired from caring for two babies. Although Anna was a quiet child, Louisa was already showing signs of a strong will. The parents recognized their own temperaments in the little ones. Pale, blue-eyed, dark brown-haired Anna was much like her placid father. Louy, with her ruddy complexion, flashing blue eyes, and chestnut brown hair, had the same determination and fire as her mother.

Abba Alcott had joined the Philadelphia Female Anti-Slavery Society which was founded by Lucretia Mott in 1833. It was the first significant organization for women and Mrs. Alcott felt strongly about its precepts, but now found that her family burdens and financial worries kept her from attending meetings.

Her one adult female friend continued to be Jane Haines. Marmee and her little girls spent many happy days at Wyck. The big house, built in 1690, was simply kept. Beyond the huge uncurtained glass doors of the "great room" was the Wyck farm with its ducks, pigs, and cows. The garden was a glorious place of damask roses where little Louisa toddled happily.

There were occasional walks to the wooded Wissahickon River, where Anna and Louy could romp. Sometimes they went as far as the steep slopes of the Schuykill River, where Marmee would let them pick the violets and mayflowers that grew under the gray trunks of the beech trees.

Almost overnight, the Philadelphia experiment came to a halt. The Alcotts were deeply in debt, the school enrollment was dwindling, and Marmee suffered a miscarriage in May.

Marmee made up her mind that this Philadelphia experiment had gone on long enough. They already owed money. She and the children saw husband and father only on weekends. She finally told him that they must go to Boston where they had relatives and friends, and where their little family could be together. Father agreed.

By July 10, 1834, the destitute family had accepted the help of their lifelong friend and financial and emotional supporter, Ralph Waldo Emerson, and moved back to Boston. The trip itself was not without adventure. At one point Marmee and Father discovered that their little Louy had wandered off. After a flurry of concern and searching, they found her in the engine room of the boat, happily exploring.

For Louisa, the Germantown of her birth was only a told-to experience. It was in Boston that her own memories and observations of life began. The family's first Boston home was a tall, narrow boardinghouse, one of the many such row houses with common walls. It was close to the fifty-acre parkland known as the Common. Louisa and Anna ran joyfully past the tall trees and around the park's Frog Pond.

One day, Louisa accidentally slipped on the bank and tumbled in. The ducks scattered, quacking, as she struggled in the mud and weeds to keep her head above water. As she gasped for breath, frightened and realizing she might drown, a pair of black arms reached down, grasped her firmly, and pulled her back to solid ground. Then, after a flash of a smile from a black boy's face, her brave, unknown rescuer was gone. Louisa, young as she was, knew the memory of that friendly, helping face would forever hauntingly remain—a sign to her of the humanity of the black race.

She had already heard about the black people in the southern states who were slaves. She knew that her mother, dear Marmee, and Marmee's good friend, Lydia Maria Child, were members of the Female Anti-Slavery Society. Her father and her uncle Sam went to lectures given by their friend, William Lloyd Garrison. With emotion and fire, Garrison would cry out, "Our enslaved black brothers and sisters must be set free." In the Alcott house, Louisa could overhear the men talking until midnight. Her uncle Sam told Garrison, "I am sure you are called to do great work, and I mean to help you." Her father also said he would join this anti-slavery abolitionist cause. Louisa listened attentively, wishing that she were old enough to help.

Near the Common, Bronson Alcott had opened his Temple School. It was decorated according to his belief that children appreciated beautiful things and should be exposed to them in order to learn "refinement of soul." There were busts of Plato, Socrates, and Shakespeare, engravings and pictures on the walls, large and handsome furnitured, multi-colored rugs on the floors and tinted glass in the windows. His favorite book, a beautiful English edition of *Pilgrim's Progress,* was displayed in a place of honor.

He also believed that learning could be fun. As time went on, Louy wished she could go to the school along with Anna, but she wasn't old enough yet at four. Her father began to teach her at home. Parading around the room, or collapsed on the floor, he demonstrated the letters of the alphabet with his body. He spread his arms and legs so that his body formed an *X*. To make an *I* he stood stiff and straight. When it came to *Y*, he stood on his head and spread his legs. Her scholarly father might look peculiar, but gymnastic alphabets were fun.

In the meantime, her father's Temple School went well at first. His assistant, Elizabeth Peabody, also had many new ideas about how young children should be taught. Together, they delighted in nurturing the children's minds. Soon they began to write a book about their educational experiments. Elizabeth's sister, Sophia Peabody, helped by drawing some illustrations.

Elizabeth became a close friend to the family, as well as a coworker. When a third daughter was born to the Alcotts on June 24, 1835, they named her Elizabeth Peabody Alcott.

To celebrate their joint birthday in 1835, Father and Louy met with their own family and Father's pupils at the Temple School a day early, as the real birthday fell on Sunday. Father told tales about their lives to entertain everyone. The birthday two were crowned with laurel wreaths, and then it was time for the treats. Louy, turning three, was allowed to stand on a table to hand out the cakes to everyone, but as the last child in the procession came up, she noticed that there was only one cake on the plate — there would be none left for her. It was her birthday — she clutched the cake tightly, till her mother said gently, "It is always better to give away than to keep the nice things; so I know my Louy will not let the little friend go without." Reluctantly, Louy passed over the "dear plummy cake" and received a kiss from Marmee in exchange.

Life went back to normal. But soon the family was aware that Mr. Alcott and Miss Peabody were having difficulties with the work on the book. They had different ideas about what should be included and how it should be written. As they argued about the book, it became harder to work together in the school. Finally, Miss Peabody quit the school and left Mr. Alcott to finish the book by himself.

His next assistant was Dorothea Dix. This young woman's real interests, however, were in mental health reform and nursing, rather than in working with children. After a short term of teaching, she left.

The bouyant, liberal, feminist Margaret Fuller took the job. Sometimes Bronson Alcott found her, as he said, "a little hard to take," as she was very outspoken. He shook his head at the odd ways she dressed. Clothing meant little to her, and she was as apt to have her blouse on backward as frontward. He admired her quick mind, nevertheless, and they found that they worked well together.

When Mr. Alcott's book *Conversations on the Gospel* was published in 1837, attendance at the Temple School began to dwindle. Bostonians didn't believe that young children could have anything important to say about the Bible. Keeping the school going was getting more and more difficult as tuition money for students dropped off. The Alcotts moved from one boardinghouse to another. Their clothes were threadbare, and they had only the simplest food for the table. Anna and Louisa were now old enough to be aware that they were poor. They certainly knew that they were often hungry. Sometimes the family stayed with relatives when their mother took jobs to bring in a little money. There never seemed to be money for even the barest needs. The girls often heard their parents speak in desperation of The Alcott Sinking-Fund. That meant that money was running out and some miracle was needed to fill it again. More often than not, the miracle came in the way of gifts.

The girls adored their crotchety grandfather, Joseph May, who always had treats for them and envelopes of cash for Marmee. They knew that he was disgusted with their father for not supporting his family properly, and that he and his daughter, Abba, had many harsh words about this philosopher husband of hers. Father said that the Colonel was "rather too old-fashioned.... He is contemplating the physical fluctuations of things. I am observing the moral and intellectual changes. He is recollecting and relating the *past* — I am looking upon the present and anticipating the *future*."

The girls knew that Marmee would always mourn for her own beloved mother, which was why she and Grandfather's second wife, Mary Ann Cary, could not get along with each other. Nevertheless, visiting Grandfather's house at the corner of Washington and Oak streets was always fun. He told them tales of his adventures, gave them treats of sweet cakes and prunes, and sometimes even gave them pretty frocks.

As soon as she was able to write, Louisa was given a journal in which she could record her thoughts and experiences. This was a custom she and her sisters continued all their lives, just as their parents did. The journals were not secret diaries. Their parents frequently read what was written and often added comments for the girls to read. Louisa began the habit of writing about her life, adventures, and achievements at an early age. "I drove my hoop round the Common without stopping today. As I'm only six, everyone said I was the youngest girl to ever do so." Sometimes her adventures had unhappy endings. She was strong-willed and unafraid. She thought nothing of wandering away on her own to see new things. Once the town-crier had to ring his bell and send out the call, "Hear ye, hear ye ... little girl lost ... six years old, in a pink frock, white hat, and new green shoes." Louisa, who had joyfully played with some Irish children, shared their potatoes cooked over ashes, and then fallen asleep in a doorway with her head on the warm body of a stray dog, was surprised to recognize herself. "Why, that's me." That time, she was punished. Her mother tied her to the sofa where everyone could see her, that she might learn she was not to wander.

Sometimes she created her own punishment. She liked to follow the older children around, especially the boys, who seemed to do such daring things. They soon learned that Louy Alcott couldn't resist a dare. Poor Louisa—on one occasion she rubbed red pepper in her eyes and on another jumped from a high beam, spraining both ankles. Anna comforted her younger sister, but could never quite understand. "Oh Louy, why don't you act like a girl?"

"I wish I were a boy," she answered. "They have more fun." "Anyway," her blue eyes flashed, "no boy can be my friend till I beat him in a race, and no girl if she refuses to climb trees, leap fences, and be a tomboy." She paused to think. "I think I must have been a deer or a horse in some former state, because I love to run."

Marmee's stepmother, as she was dying in 1838, tried to reunite Grandfather and Marmee, and the two families visited each other in June. When Mary Cary May died in February 1839, Marmee wrote to Grandfather, "This new attitude in which this death places me both in regard to yourself and the world embarrasses me exceedingly but it shall be my continual effort to do what is right.... I am confident that the remnant of your days cannot be embittered by a reunion with me, my husband, and children."

As the summer came, Louisa and Anna were worried about Marmee's poor health. She hadn't been well since April 1839 when their baby brother was

A New Spirit

Abigail May Alcott

born dead. He was buried in the little cemetery in the Boston Common, but the girls were taught to speak of him as though he was one of the family.

Both girls wished that Father's school would do better, but instead, matters got worse. The final blow to the school came when Mr. Alcott admitted a young black girl as a student. Even the anti-slavery North wasn't quite ready for that. Though they might be abolitionists in theory, having a black child in the same classroom as their children was a situation they did not accept. The wealthy Bostonians who had enrolled their children in Bronson Alcott's progressive school reacted by withdrawing them.

In mid-1839, the Temple School had to close and most of its beautiful decor was sold to pay the debts it had incurred. This was a sad day for the Alcotts. They managed to save the busts of Plato and Socrates, but little else. Father took to giving "Conversations," but his lectures brought in very little money. The family recognized that a pattern had begun — moving from place to place with Mr. Alcott frequently off lecturing or "experiencing" and Mrs. Alcott borrowing or working to support the family. Happily, they were such charming people that their friends and relatives were moved to help them, sometimes with money, often with food or clothing, and many times with the offer of a roof over their heads.

Mr. Alcott's friend, Ralph Waldo Emerson, persuaded the family to move to Concord, where he himself lived. His generosity with money made it possible for them to do so. In the spring of 1840, the Alcotts, with their trunks, piled onto the Boston-Concord stagecoach. They were moving again, this time twenty miles across the green slopes and stone-cropped byways of Massachusetts.

Just a few months later, on July 16, a fourth sister, Abigail May Alcott, was born into the family. Although this child was blue-eyed as the others were, she had neither the dark brown hair of Anna, the chestnut brown hair of Louisa and Marmee, or the light brown hair of Beth. This sprite had golden yellow hair like her father. The girls adored her.

Life was different from busy Boston in the country atmosphere of Hosmer Cottage. The girls could see the Monadnock and Wachusett Mountains and run in the woods. The brown house was big enough to accommodate the pillow fights they so loved before hopping into bed for the night. There was a barn beside the house where they could play and act out stories.

Next door were the five Hosmer children. One time, Cyrus Hosmer was down in the fields with some men who were hoeing potatoes, when Louisa came along. The men were chewing tobacco, and Louy, curious and never afraid, asked for a quid. When they gave it to her she chewed it so vigorously that Cy had to carry her home in a wheelbarrow. Though Cy was a year younger than she, they were good friends.

Anna had more or less adopted Henry Hosmer as her special friend. Lydia Hosmer was Beth's playmate; another quiet, gentle girl. These two preferred to be the audience and let the others put on the performances.

Lydia was particularly intrigued by the novel method that the Alcott girls had of taking a bath. Whenever it rained, they took a natural, beautifying, rain shower on the back piazza, facing the grove and modestly hidden from view.

The Alcott sisters enjoyed their frolics, as did those who merely observed them. Once Mr. Emerson and Margaret Fuller were visiting the Alcotts. Miss

Fuller challenged, "Well, Mr. Alcott, you have been able to carry out your education methods in your own family, and I should like to see your model children." She did in a few moments, for a wild uproar announced the arrival of a wheelbarrow holding baby May as queen, Louisa as horse, bitted and bridled, and Anna as driver. Beth played dog and barked as loud as her gentle voice permitted. Seeing the group of adults, Louy tripped and down they all went in a giggling heap. Her mother, laughing, waved her hand dramatically and declared, "Here are the model children, Miss Fuller." Miss Fuller was enchanted, and later told this, as well as other anecdotes about what she called "the charming family." They found playmates to share their fun—the children of the Channings and Emersons.

The people around them and the town of Concord offered new and exciting visions and experiences. Just a short distance away, on the other edge of town, was the little hump-backed bridge where the first shot of the Revolutionary War had been fired 75 years before on April 19, 1775. It was a time Louy already knew about. Her mother often talked about Louy's "Great-Aunt Hancock," her mother's Aunt Dorothy, who had been married to the great John Hancock, first signer of the Declaration of Independence and first governor of Massachusetts. It was said that one of the reasons for the raid on Concord and Lexington had been to capture Hancock. Aunt Dorothy might now actually be Madam Dorothy Quincy Hancock Scott, but to the Alcott girls she would always be "Great-Aunt Hancock" for whose marriage to the great man Chinese red wallpaper had been put on her parlor wall.

It was exciting to stand where history had been made. One of the children's favorite spots was under the bridge, where the Concord River flowed. The "Concord" which meant "peace" had been called the "Musketaquid" for "grass-ground" by the Indians who had lived in the area before the town was founded in 1635. Mr. Emerson told them about the area's Indians of so long ago. He spoke of Squaw Sachem who had insisted upon ruling after the death of her Indian chief husband. "It was perhaps the first example in Massachusetts of woman asserting and maintaining her rights," he said. Louisa admired that determined Indian woman.

She also admired some of the grown-ups around her. So many of them were writers. Mr. William Ellery Channing was a poet. Their friend Mr. Ralph Waldo Emerson was an essayist and philosopher. She could understand that philosophers thought a lot and talked a lot, after all, her father was a philosopher, too.

There was another special new friend. He was a poet and writer by the name of Henry David Thoreau. It was a pleasure to tramp the woods and swamps with him. Although he liked to be alone, he never minded when the children joined him. This man of nature knew the secrets of the owls and otters, and could lure a thrush with a sweet whistle. He could make a birch bark into a container, and then find the sweetest berries to fill it with. As he told about the creatures and plants, he would people the woods with made-up fairies and play upon his flute in floating notes.

Summer went quickly with all these new experiences. Soon the brilliant yellow, red, and chestnut foliage of a Massachusetts autumn came. It quickly went and winter set in. With winter came word that Grandfather May had died. It was the first death of someone close to Louisa. He had left some money to Marmee which helped pay off some of their debts. He had also left some books from his library. And of course, Mother had the lovely Colport china with its clear white center and jade green border, with fine lines of gold running through the jade.

One cold morning, as spring came again, Anna and Louy found a half-starved robin in their garden which they warmed and fed. Louisa, eight years old, was inspired to write her first poem. Her mother was delighted with it. "Louisa, she said, "you could grow up to be a second Shakespeare if you keep writing." Louisa was pleased. "Could I, Marmee?"

To the First Robin

Welcome, welcome, little stranger,
Fear no harm and fear no danger;
We are glad to see you here,
For you sing "Sweet Spring is near."

Now the white snow melts away;
Now the flowers blossom gay;
Come dear bird and build your nest,
For we love our robin best.

Pleased at the compliments about her effort, she went on to write more poems about such things as dead butterflies, lost kittens, and the baby's eyes.

The days were not filled with only play and poems though. In an effort to earn a living for his family, Mr. Alcott not only tilled his own little farm, but hired himself out to his neighbors. He tilled and plowed and chopped wood. Marmee took in sewing, and taught her girls to sew, that they might eventually have the necessary skills. They also helped with the housework, hard work for such little girls. Louisa didn't enjoy helping with the cooking because she didn't like what they had to eat. Mr. Alcott insisted on a vegetarian diet, so they prepared vegetables, rice, other grains (some boiled and some baked into husky bread) and nuts and fruits. Mrs. Alcott insisted that the children must have milk, but that was the only animal product they were permitted. Certainly, no meat, chicken, fish, eggs, or butter ever passed their lips.

Even with their meager larder, however, they frequently knew of families even poorer than they and gladly sent meals to them. Poor they might be, but the Alcotts were ever generous with such as they had. It was not unusual for them to have two scanty meals a day and yet send food to another family. Even when their woodpile was low and snow covered the ground, they shared their wood so that others might not be cold.

Discipline came in less charitable ways, especially from Father. If he was displeased, a daughter might be made to go without dinner; even worse was when he induced guilt by letting them know how much he was upset by rising from the table and going without dinner himself.

In her free time, Louy continued to poke around and observe. One day she found a black man hidden in the barn's huge oven. Surprised, she slammed the door and ran to tell her parents. They had to confide in her. He was a runaway slave, a "contraband." They explained that many of the Concord families did this. They would hide him until it was safe for him to continue North. It was called the underground railroad. She nodded, happy to keep this secret so that the man might be free. She remembered the black boy who had saved her from drowning in Frog Pond.

She knew a lot about the antislavery movement. Both Father and Marmee thought it was right. Uncle Sam May, a Unitarian minister, always talked about the movement on his visits, or when they visited with him at his summer place on the Scituate beach. Dear Mr. Emerson, who had once been a Unitarian minister but now kept to his lecturing and writing, was also active as an abolitionist. She listened to many conversations between her father and these learned men, forming her own ideas.

Not all her thoughts were formed from overheard conversations, sermons, or books, however. Her intuition was strong. One summer morning she ran over the hills at dawn and paused to rest in the woods. Later she wrote in her journal: "And I *got religion* there. I saw the sun rise over river, hill and wide green meadows. It was lovely and I was in a happy mood. And it seemed to bring my soul very near to God. I'll never forget it."

Her father's educational ideas were applauded in England, where the Alcott House School was established and named for him. Mr. Emerson, anxious to help his friend get back into teaching, offered the money for Mr. Alcott to take a trip to Europe, that he might see how his ideas were being developed. Mr. Alcott left in May of 1842. Marmee and the girls stayed in Hosmer Cottage with Mr. Alcott's brother, their sickly Uncle Junius, to keep them company.

When Mr. Alcott returned in October he brought with him several people, including Mr. Charles Lane and his ten-year-old son, William. Marmee and the girls were startled to learn that these people were to live with them in the little house. They cooked and cleaned for all these people, while a great Transcendental communal-living experiment was planned. They would find even more people, and everyone would live together as one family. They called it a Consociate-Family, and talked about establishing a "New Eden," or a new paradise. "The Newness," they called it.

"The Newness" affected their entire daily routines. They had to rise at six and be ready for breakfast at seven. There wasn't much to eat—set out on napkins, they had unleavened bread, and perhaps an apple or potato, along with water. After that, they had singing lessons with Mr. Lane, followed by reading, writing, and arithmetic, to which Father added conversations. The noon meal was similar to the morning's. In the afternoons Mr. Lane conducted lessons in geography, geometry, and drawing. Supper was a repeat of the other meals. After supper there might be more conversations or another singing lesson. At eight, the girls went to bed. Marmee and Mr. Lane were obviously not fond of each other; Marmee worried that her family was malnourished, and Mr. Lane thought her sense of family was too strong.

In January, Marmee invented the Household Post Office to lighten the days a bit for the girls. At first they could deposit little notes and packages in the basket by the door; later Marmee created a "Bon-Box," into which they could put their names at the end of the day if they had been good. Louy was to write the code word "Bon" and add three crosses, but she found it hard most days to earn her "Bon," for she had to admit to herself that she was not feeling kindly toward the new routines.

The house was filled with talk and people. William Ellery Channing, who wrote poetry, had moved nearby and came often to join the conversations. The girls liked him, but found him a creature of whim, sometimes gentle and other times rough.

In the meantime, Father and Mr. Lane looked around for a place where "The Newness" of the "New Eden" could settle and become a community.

On Louy's tenth birthday, Marmee gave her the pencil case she had wanted and told her, "I have observed that you are fond of writing, and wish to encourage the habit." Marmee also gave her a picture that showed a daughter taking care of her aged mother saying, "Dear Louy, keep it for my sake and your own, for you and I always liked to be grouped together." Louisa put the picture in her journal. Seeing her mother work so hard made Louisa determined to see that some day Marmee could have an easier life. She promised herself she would take care of her. One day, she opened her journal to look at the picture Marmee had given her on her tenth birthday and wrote a poem under it.

To Mother

I hope that soon, dear mother,
    You and I may be
In the quiet room my fancy
    Has so often made for thee,—

The pleasant, sunny chamber,
    The cushioned easy-chair,
The book laid for your reading,
    The vase of flowers fair;

A New Spirit

>   The desk beside the window
>   Where the sun shines warm and bright:
>   And there in ease and quiet
>   The promised book you write;
>
>   While I sit close beside you,
>   Content at last to see
>   That you can rest, dear mother,
>   And I can cherish thee.

It was many months before a suitable piece of land for the "New Eden" was found near Harvard, Massachusetts. It had 90 acres, 14 of which were wooded. There were some fruit trees, plenty of nuts and berries, and the necessary water. A dilapidated house and a barn stood on the property. As soon as the house could be made livable, the newly formed Consociate-Family would move into this new home called Fruitlands.

Chapter 2

Mid-1843–1847: The Fledgling Writer

On June 1, 1843, the Consociate-Family, in a large wagon drawn by a small horse, moved 15 miles westward to Fruitlands. The seven-room red house was larger than the Concord cottage, but still crowded for 11 people. Now there were the Alcotts, the two Lanes, and three other men. Joseph Palmer soon joined them, and later Miss Anna Page, who gave the children music lessons.

Both Mr. Emerson and Mr. Thoreau supported the idea of the community, but neither joined it. Mrs. Alcott had her own doubts about the experiment, but wanted her husband to have the chance of building his "New Eden," so had agreed to move her family again.

The busts of Plato and Socrates were placed in the downstairs library and shelves were installed for all of Mr. Alcott's books. The Alcott girls had their beds in the sloped-roof attic. Although it was so low that even they had to stoop so as not to bump their heads, Louisa liked it. "The rain makes a pretty sound on the roof," she said.

Being a transcendentalist wasn't easy. First Mr. Lane and Mr. Alcott had to decide what everyone could wear. Cotton was forbidden as it was grown by the sweat of slave-labor. Wool robbed the sheep. They decided to have all clothing made of linen, for the flax plant could provide acceptable material. The males wore white trousers and the females white bloomers or skirts. All wore white tunics. Everyone had broad-brimmed black hats. After great mental turmoil, they agreed to allow the use of leather shoes—mainly because they could not think of any other material that would wear as well as animal hide.

Louisa thought two things were especially good about Fruitlands. "I love cold baths," she declared, even when she had to get up at five in the morning to take one. Best of all was having "the brown boy," as she teasingly called him, for an almost-brother. William Lane was always ready to race across the meadows or climb trees with her. Anna and Beth did not like this activity very much, but little May often tried to follow, vainly trying to catch William and Louy as they exercised their young muscles. Louy loved to run in the wind and play be-a-horse.

All of them thought the place absolutely perfect for picnics. The farm

The Fledgling Writer

The Fruitlands farmhouse, Harvard, Massachusetts. Photograph by Gloria T. Delamar.

clung to the steep slope of Prospect Hill, where trees covered the summit behind them in the east. To the west, they had a magnificent view of the valley and river below, and the mountains beyond. The woods and the barn were fine for playing fairies complete with gowns and paper wings, of which Louy declared that she "flied" the highest of all. Other times they acted out dramas with crowned princes and princesses, or made plays out of Dickens's stories.

While the men set to work farming the dry, rocky land and planting vegetables and grains, the women tended to the house. That is, Marmee, with such help as Anna and Louy were able to give, tended to the cooking, laundry, and cleaning. Little Beth and baby May were too young to help. The only other woman in the new family, the music teacher Miss Page, seemed to think she was too good for such chores. Once, when asked if there were any beasts of burden on the farm, Mrs. Alcott snapped, "Yes, one woman."

In the beginning the grounds were farmed without animal-power. Later Mr. "Beard" Palmer convinced the Consociate-Family to let him bring in two oxen to help with the heavy plowing and tilling. (Rumor had it that one of these oxen was really a cow, which the long-bearded Mr. Palmer secretly milked in order to have some of the forbidden beverage.)

The "Sun" or "Solar Diet" of the Consociates was even stricter than Mr.

Alcott's former vegetarian diets had been. No animal products were permitted. Sugar, tea, coffee, and chocolate were forbidden, and even salt was not permitted. It was a dreary, flat diet for children, as well as adults. Not only that, the supply of food was meager, so they were always hungry.

Father did like to bake his simple "cottage bread" and would often make it in the shapes of animals, to make it more attractive to the children.

After dinner, with their stomachs still growling, the entire family, including the children, sat around and discussed spiritual doctrines. They had question and answer sessions about the mind of man and the meaning of the world and universal brotherhood.

The children learned: "Transcendentalism is the belief that all ideas come from spiritual inspiration." When Mr. Lane asked Anna and Louisa, "What is man?" their answers were: "A human being; an animal with a mind; a creature; a body; a soul and mind." Louisa wrote in her diary, "After a long talk we went to bed very tired." No wonder.

They had to know all about "The Newness." There was the statement of the goals of the Consociate-Family: "simplicity in diet, plain garments, pure bathing, unsullied dwellings, open conduct, gentle behavior, kindly sympathies, serene minds."

They were a strange kind of people. Some departed and others joined. One man ate only uncooked food. This wasn't so bad, but he believed that clothes kept him from his true spiritual growth. Mr. Alcott had to convince him that it would be best to exercise this naked belief in the darkness of night. Another came, proudly proclaiming that he had subsisted one whole year on crackers and then for another year ate only apples. Another man kept a vow of silence and never said a word, but as he was the only man helpful to Mrs. Alcott in the house, cooking and helping to care for the younger children, he was a welcome presence. He was certainly more welcome than the one who kept climbing the trees to shout at the top of his lungs. Several young men had the disconcerting habit of saying even the mildest things by swearing. They would nod pleasantly and gently say, "Damn you, good morning." Such was the crew of Fruitlands. Some dreaming philosophers, some earnest seekers, and some crackpots.

Almost a thousand books had been brought to Fruitlands, most about mystical philosophy; not a single book, not even a pamphlet, had been brought about agriculture. Although Bronson Alcott was a good farmer, he had to agree to the farming methods decided upon by the group. Many of those ideas were impractical; some of the colonists wanted to grow only "aspiring" vegetables that reached toward heaven and none that grew downward. This would have eliminated from the already scanty diet such staples as potatoes, carrots, beets, and other root vegetables. Fortunately, that plan was abandoned. Other suggestions were simply contrary to good farming techniques. Much of the barley, rye, and wheat, planted in long single rows, did poorly. Some crops were plowed under "to enrich the earth." As a result of some of their strange methods, crops did not grow well. This meant less food on the table. Members of the Consociate began to drift away. Mr. Lane, who had supplied most of the money for the venture, was getting discouraged. The children could not help but be aware of the beginning threat to the continuation of the communal-living experiment.

They struggled on. They worked at the farming and continued their lofty discussions. Mr. Lane and Miss Page taught the Alcott girls and William Lane, until it was discovered that Miss Page had not only kept cheese hidden in her trunk, but had been tempted by a morsel of forbidden fish while visiting a neighbor. Having committed this sin, she was asked to leave the community. The rules were harsh and strict.

From time to time they had visitors. Theodore Parker came, and Henry David Thoreau, and of course, Ralph Waldo Emerson. Occasionally someone came over from Brook Farm.

Just at harvest time, Mr. Lane and Mr. Alcott decided that it would be a good idea for them to go around giving lectures about the Consociates. Maybe more people could be persuaded to join them. While the Shaker Community's nearby Brook Farm experiment was prospering and growing, their own Fruitlands was failing. They wandered idly. Mr. Alcott always had friends in Providence so they made their way there. Still wearing the linen tunics of Fruitlands, they finally arrived in New York, where they called on Mrs. Alcott's old friend, Lydia Maria Child. "What brings you to New York?" she asked. "I don't know," Mr. Alcott told her. "It seems a miracle that we are here." They had no money when they had left Fruitlands; it seemed as though some kind of Providence was guiding them.

During their absence, Marmee heard a clap of thunder one afternoon and realized that their only field of barley, already cut, would be ruined if she and the children did not get it into the granary before the storm. "Hurry, children," she called. Three-year-old May was too young, but the others all helped, according to their strengths and abilities—Anna, Louisa, Beth, and William.

They gathered the grain hastily in baskets and aprons, dumped it into a huge Russian linen sheet, and together, dragged it into the barn. They repeated this over and over. They just managed to store and save the barley before the heavy rains began. It gave them enough grain to feed them for a few weeks at least. Marmee and the children had no help from Providence; they had made their own miracle. But even at that, food was scarce. Anna fainted one day in the kitchen. William, weak, developed a mysterious lingering illness and could not even sit up. Mr. Lane was more and more discouraged. He unreasonably blamed much of their troubles on Mrs. Alcott, whom he did not consider saintly enough. He was convinced that she cared more for her own family than for the experiment they were all living. In addition, he was, himself, celibate and made it known that he felt the lack of celibacy might be responsible for the community's failure. He began to try to persuade Mr. Alcott to separate from his family. Mrs. Alcott was so tired, she began to think it might be the best thing to do. Bronson Alcott, ever mindful of everyone's thoughts on matters, discussed with the family the question of separating. Louisa retreated to her journal to write:

> I did my lessons and walked in the afternoon. Father read to us in dear *Pilgrim's Progress*. Mr. L. was in Boston and we were glad. In the eve Father and Mother and Annie and I had a long talk. I was very unhappy, and we all cried. Anna and I cried in bed, and I prayed God to keep us all together.

To keep her own mind occupied and to cheer up the others, Louisa began to make up more and more of her own stories to add to their store. She discovered that she had a fine imagination and could make up exciting fair damsels and brave knights. She sewed pretty things for her dolly. She told Mother she liked to have her write in her book and Mother said she would write more often.

On Louisa's eleventh birthday, there was snow on the ground and they were allowed to play in it before school. That night Father asked what each considered their worst faults. Louisa said, "My bad temper."

Her prized pencils, gifts from her mother to encourage her to write, flew across the pages. She kept her journal entries. She wrote more poems. One was about the sunset. Of this, Anna said, "Oh Louy, it's so fine." Typically, Louisa replied, "I don't like it very much."

Sunset

Softly doth the sun descend
To his cloud behind the hill,
Then, oh, then I love to sit
On mossy banks beside the rill.

When Anna went to Boston to visit with a cousin, Louy missed her so much that she wrote a poem of two verses for her.

To Anna

Sister, dear, when you are lonely,
 Longing for your distant home,
And the images of loved ones
 Warmly to your heart shall come,
Then, mid tender thoughts and fancies,
 Let one fond voice say to thee,
"Ever when your heart is heavy,
 Anna, dear, then think of me."

The Fledgling Writer

>Think how we two have together
> Journeyed onward day by day,
>Joys and sorrows ever sharing,
> While the swift years roll away.
>Then may all the sunny hours
> Of our youth rise up to thee,
>And when your heart is light and happy,
> Anna, dear, then think of me.

Other poems were about elves and spirits. Losing herself in poetry and stories helped to take the threat of separation from her mind. To add to the troubles, more people wanted to come live with them. Louisa wrote in her journal, "I wish we could be together, and no one else. I don't see who is to clothe and feed us all, when we are so poor now." Feeling dismal, she went for a walk and wrote a poem.

>Despondency
>
> Silent and sad
> When all are glad,
>And the earth is dressed in flowers;
> When the gay birds sing
> Till the forests ring,
>As they rest in woodland bowers.
>
> Oh, why these tears,
> And these idle fears
>For what may come to-morrow?
> The birds find food
> From God so good,
>And the flowers know no sorrow.
>
> If he clothes these
> And the leafy trees,
>Will He not cherish thee?
> Why doubt His care;
> It is everywhere,
>Though the way we may not see.
> They why be sad
> When all are glad,
>And the world is full of flowers?
> With gay birds sing,
> Make life all Spring,
>And smile through the darkest hours.

Before November was over, most of the colonists had left Fruitlands. The only ones left were the Alcotts, the Lanes, and the faithful Joseph Palmer. Uncle Sam May, worried about his sister and her girls, offered them some rooms near him in Lexington. They all cried at the idea of separating. Finally, they knew that they must stay together as a family — as the Alcott family — not the

Consociate-Family. The Lanes left Fruitlands in December. The experiment, with its trials and troubled memories, had lasted only six months. Mr. Alcott, tired and dismayed, heartsick that his dream of a Transcendental community had failed, went to bed and turned his face to the wall, refusing to even eat. The girls tiptoed through the house, wondering if their father would ever get up again. This went on for three days. It took all of his wife's love to comfort him and make him begin to drink hot tea, and eventually eat again. She tempted him with stewed blackberries. She made arrangements for the family to move before the winter got any worse, borrowing money from Sam May again.

Joseph Palmer was going to stay on the property. He planned to farm it and to keep it as a "wayside stop" where the tired or poor could get a bite to eat or a few nights rest. On January 16, 1844, the Alcotts climbed on an ox sled and left Fruitlands behind them for their new home in Still River, Brick-Ends.

Still River meant a real school for the first time for Louisa. Every morning, grabbing the basket which held her skimpy lunch, she would urge Anna to hurry so they wouldn't be late. The red brick schoolhouse with its plank benches also meant girlfriends and the happy exchange of confidences. Annie Lawrence became Beth's playmate, Margaret Gardner was Anna's, and Louy paired off with Sophia Gardner. All of their new playmates were impressed with the Alcott girls' knowledge of historic customs, and all the children liked to gather on the grass plot in front of Brick-Ends to jump rope, toss ball, and roll hoops.

In one ceremony of tradition, Louisa and Walter Gardner were "married" in a mock wedding performed in the manner of gypsies. Louisa wore a white apron as a veil and the old woodshed served as the church. As another playmate, Alfred Haskell, served as preacher, Louisa and Walter jumped over a broomstick held in place by two attendants, thus completing the ceremony. Not long afterward, they slapped one another and parted, ending the short make-believe marriage, deciding that their tempers did not agree.

Now the little troupe had others to help in acting out Louisa's stories. There was also a new boy, whom Marmee had met on the Boston coach. When he planned to room in Still River, he had visited the Alcotts and within a few days, had accepted their offer to board with them. The tale of fourteen-year-old Frederick Llewellyn Hovey Willis's life was heartbreaking. His mother had died three days after his birth, and his father was imprisoned for debt. His grandmother had raised him, but he was on his own now. He and Louisa shared a love of books and drama, so he was immediately accepted by the young miss in charge of the local drama troupe. For it was Louisa who was author, production director, and casting director of the plays put on in the barn. Beth, as always, helped in a more quiet way, sewing on the costumes, for she loved to sew.

For Beth's eighth birthday, there was a memorable party. The Alcott sitting room was ornamented with a small tree, from the boughs of which hung gifts, not only for the birthday-girl, but for each little guest. The kitchen table was laden with little cakes and cherries, with a big birthday cake in the center. There were skits by the adults, and songs for all. Anna appeared as a Scotch lassie in bonnet and plaid as she gave a recitation. But Louisa was the hit of the party. Marmee helped Louisa stain her face, arms, neck, and legs, so that she would have the ruddy hue of an Indian girl. Her dress was made all of feathers, and feathers crowned her head. Everyone was enchanted when she burst into the room, singing the popular song, "Wild Roved an Indian Girl, Bright Alfarata." Then she strode forward, bearing a large shield, and in almost blood-curdling tones recited a passage from "Ossian," which she followed with a softer, tender rendering of the poem, "Geehale—An Indian Legend." The next day, the children all wanted to examine Louisa to see if any of the paint was left on her limbs.

Feathers had an attraction for her at that time, and she set up a little business making feathered hats for her friend's dolls. This millinery venture came to an abrupt halt when the neighbors complained that their chickens were in a constant uproar as Louy chased them about to pluck their tail feathers.

With her own dolls, Louisa had dramatic ideas. She had a lovely pale, blonde-wigged doll dressed in pastel clothes. One day, she decided that Lulu should be a widow. She dyed the doll's clothes jet black—and so Lulu remained a widow forevermore.

Her actions tended to be extravagant. Once, she bumped herself against a chair, whereupon the chair was arraigned, found guilty and immediately hanged by being suspended from a window of the house.

Louisa enjoyed the school lessons, especially when they took trips into the woods for botany. She knew she was always good there.

When she learned about the bones in the body and how they get out of order, she decided that she must be careful of hers because she climbed and jumped, and ran so much.

It wasn't long though, before their father was their teacher again, for the Alcotts were still nomads. They moved from house to house, constantly packing up the busts of Plato and Socrates, their large library of books, and their few other belongings.

When Mrs. Alcott was left some money after Grandfather May died, Emerson generously added a bit more to it for them and they moved into their first bought-home on April 1, 1845. The Concord house, right on the famous Lexington Road, was dubbed Hillside.

Mr. Alcott was not of a mind to teach or lecture yet, but as soon as he had his strength back, he busied himself using his considerable skills at carpentry and gardening. The house was practically built over. Repairs were made,

Hillside at Concord, Massachusetts (later called Wayside). Nathaniel Hawthorne added the tower rooms. The barn beyond the house is where the Alcott sisters put on plays. Photograph by Gloria T. Delamar.

a porch was added, and an extra barn building was cut in half with a half added to each side of the house. He painted the house a warm olive-brown. The house had eight outside doors, so when there was a knock the family headed in all directions to answer.

Father built a rustic bathhouse with a thatched roof on a parcel of their land across the road at the brook. The girls could use that water for their baths in warm weather. They learned to make quick dashes across the road to the brook. In winter, they would use a shower bath in the house. Cleanliness was an Alcott doctrine.

Father put a little summer house against the hillside. The vegetable garden was planted immediately, a necessity for the still vegetarian family. In his spare time, he chopped wood for nearby farmers. Mrs. Alcott was happy to be in a house of her own. She washed, scrubbed, and sewed. In order to bring a little money into the Alcott Sinking-Fund, she sewed for her neighbors. Times were still hard. The family cares and peculiar trials began to lay heavily on Louisa's mind. She began to realize that although her father was brilliant, devoted to his wife and "four little women," he was incapable of earning a good living for them.

She found comfort in writing. She had her journal, as well as an "Imagination Book" into which she put poems, "thinks," moods, and dreams. Lost in her own world of writing, she wrote, "I had a pleasant time with my mind, for it was happy." Another joy was to be among old friends again. The Emersons and Channings lived a short way down the road. Mr. Emerson, noticing that Louisa was starved for new books, allowed her free use of his own library. She could choose any book she liked and curl up in a deep chair to escape into literature. Lydian Emerson, his wife, frequently didn't even know that this earnest, ardent girl had crept in to bury herself in reading.

Thoreau, who had built a hut at Walden Pond, often walked the one and a half miles into Concord to his mother's home. It was in the woods, however, that most of their time with him was spent. He shared with them his own love of nature, and taught them more secrets of the earth—how the seed grows to be a flower—how the fish spawn—and the ways of the little insects and wild creatures.

Others they knew were present, also. Elizabeth Peabody's sister, Sophia, had married Nathaniel Hawthorne, a writer of novels. He was a handsome, shy man. Once he had lived at Brook Farm, near Fruitlands. The blue smock of the old community was his favorite garment for gardening. The girls could see him working there when they went down to the river, as the Hawthornes lived in The Old Manse, which had been built near the Concord Bridge by Ralph Waldo Emerson's grandfather. Sophia and Elizabeth Peabody had another sister, Mary. Louisa thought Mary's husband, Horace Mann, had some good ideas. She heard him say that there should be schools to train people to be teachers, instead of people just announcing themselves educated enough to teach. He also said that women deserved an education just as much as men did, and he hoped to see that they got it some day.

In addition, their mother had taken in Frederick Llewellyn Willis as a summer boarder again. It was wonderful to adopt a brother once more.

One lovely day, Father and Mother took the girls and Llewellyn for a walk out to Mr. Thoreau's hut. There was no lock on his door, nor any curtain at the window, but he did have regular furniture—his desk, a table and chairs, and a cane bed. He took the children out onto the pond in his boat, where he enchanted them with tales of the woods and the Indians who had once lived there. They listened, charmed, to the silver notes of his flute.

Hillside, too, held charms for them. It was a grand house for playing *Pilgrim's Progress.* With their mother's rag-bags on their backs as burdens, they started in the cellar, which was "The City of Destruction," and toiled up the stairs to the top of the house, "The Celestial City." Or the young Pilgrims progressed outdoors, where they marched up the ridge on the hillside in back of the house, climbing among the trees. Anna and Louisa both loved acting and wished they could go on the stage. They wrote poetry, pining to be "something great." Louy declared, "I *shall* be famous some day." Anna thought Louisa to be a genius and firmly agreed, "Yes, you will write something great one of these days, but I won't, I'll probably spend my life as a housewife." Beth at 10 was attracted to music and ached to be a fine pianist. May, only five, was happy with some paper and something to draw with.

But the happy days suddenly became more somber again when Mr. Lane reappeared. Originally only intending to leave his books at Hillside, he ended up staying most of the summer. Again, the rigid schedule was in effect; there were posted hours for everything. When Father had to go to Spindle Hill in September to tend to Uncle Junius, who was ill, Mr. Lane took over the schooling again. Louisa wrote a sample lesson in her journal:

"What virtues do you wish more of?" asks Mr. L. I answered:—

Patience,	Love,	Silence,
Obedience,	Generosity,	Perseverance,
Industry,	Respect,	Self-denial.

"What vices less of?"

Idleness,	Wilfulness,	Vanity,
Impatience,	Impudence,	Pride,
Selfishness,	Activity,	Love of cats.

They were all glad when Father came back in October. Mr. Lane left soon after. And if that was not enough, cheese and milk had been added to their diet.

In January 1845, twelve-year-old Louisa wrote a long entry into her journal:

Did my lessons, and in the P.M. mother read "Kenilworth" to us while we sewed. It is splendid! I got angry and called Anna mean. Father told me to look out the word in the Dic., and it meant "base," "contemptible " I was so ashamed to have called my dear sister that, and I cried over my bad tongue and temper.

We have had a lovely day. All the trees were covered with ice, and it shone like diamonds or fairy palaces. I made a piece of poetry about winter:—

Winter

The stormy winter's come at last,
    With snow and rain and bitter blast;
Ponds and brooks are frozen o'er,
    We cannot sail there any more.

The little birds are flown away
    To warmer climes than ours;
They'll come no more till gentle May
    Calls them back with flowers.

Oh, then the darling birds will sing
    From their neat nests in the trees.
All creatures wake to welcome Spring,
    And flowers dance in the breeze.

With patience wait till winter is o'er,
    And all lovely things return;
Of every season try the more
    Some knowledge or virtue to learn.

That winter she read Lydia Maria Child's "Philothea," which she liked very much. She made a dramatic version of it, in which she performed gloriously as Aspasia, a role perfectly suited to her fancy.

In 1845, Louisa and Anna were allowed to go to John Hosmer's school. The young teacher had been at Brook Farm at one time, so his influence was considered acceptable. The girls had the chance to make the companionship of other young people. There were playmates now, like Clara Gowing, with whom they had fun leaving notes, poems, and bouquets in the post office established in a hollowed-out stump. Though Clara was more Anna's friend, it was Clara who shared a naughty adventure once, as Louisa one morning on the way to school usurped a neighbor's horse and sleigh to take a short ride. Though Anna was too chagrined to go along, Louy took Clara for a quick jaunt before returning the team to where she had found it.

A short distance from the Lexington Road was an area that some called "Gowing's Swamp." But the girls loved the secluded little stream and pool in the woods, bordered with flowering shrubs in season. They spent many happy hours in their "Paradise."

One day, Louisa wrote a note to Marmee:

> Dearest Mother, — I have tried to be more contented, and I think I have been more so. I have been thinking about my little room, which I suppose I never shall have. I should want to be there about all the time, and I should go there and sing and think.
>
> > But I'll be contented
> > With what I have got;
> > Of folly repented,
> > Then sweet is my lot.
>
> From your trying daughter,
> > Louy.

As always, Marmee wrote back, laying the note on her pillow, to tell her how much joy the note had given her. She urged her repentant daughter to go on "trying," and said she would put a warm kiss on Louy's lips, and say a little prayer over her in her sleep.

Louy knew her parents were good people. The family had once carried their breakfast to a starving family and another time lent their whole dinner to a neighbor suddenly taken unprepared by distinguished guests. When a poor child and father stopped at their door one snowy night to beg for wood, Father had said, "Give half our stock, and trust in Providence; the weather will moderate, or wood will come." Mother had laughed, and answered in her cheery way, "Well, their need is greater than ours, and if our half gives out we can to go bed and tell stories." Later a farmer stopped by and asked if they would take his load of wood to save him the trip to Boston. He was willing to have them pay later. Father said, "Didn't I tell you wood would come if the weather did not moderate?" Louisa knew Mother's motto was, "Hope, and keep busy," and one of her favorite sayings was, "Cast your bread upon the waters, and after many days it will come back buttered."

In March, Louy's dream was answered; she was given a room of her own, and she exulted over her work basket and desk by the window, with a closet full of dried herbs to make it smell nice. She said, "I have at last got the little room I have wanted so long, and am very happy about it. It does me good to be alone."

Bronson Alcott was still aloof and despondent about the failure at Fruitlands. He spent a lot of time thinking of possible ways to start another such experiment in communal-living. Abba Alcott could not support the idea this time. She was frustrated and embarrassed about constantly borrowing from relatives and friends. Her worries began to make her sharp-tongued and moody. Although the Hillside days were happy in many respects, there was an underlying tension. The two older girls, who were growing out of childhood, could not help but notice. Louisa, in particular, brooded. The scarcity of money, the incapability of her father to earn a decent income to support the family, her mother's deep love, yet growing bitterness, and her own strong will and growing conviction of her talents, created a determination in her to aim high.

She made a vow to herself. "I shall make a plan, as I am in my teens, and no more a child . . . I am old for my age, and don't care much for girl's things. People think I'm wild and queer; but Mother understands and helps me."

She planned to make something of herself. She would not only be famous, but she would be rich. The family was not going to be poor forever if she could help it. She put her mind to work.

Chapter 3

1848–1855: Breaking into Print

Louisa May, only 15, took her destiny into her own hands. She had heard Mr. Mann say that there were no regulations about teacher-training. As long as anyone thought they could teach, and parents sent their children, a new school could be started. Having decided she had sufficient education to instruct others, Louy opened her first school. Mr. Emerson made his barn available, and her earliest pupils were some of her younger playmates, Emerson's own children, and the children of the poet Ellery Channing.

Louisa's life was full. In addition to teaching and sewing, she helped with the housework. Her family indulged her whim to have a "mood pillow," which she kept on the living room sofa. When she was in a good mood, and willing to have conversation, the pillow would be pointed up. A downward position indicated that she wanted to be left alone. It was a time of many emotional states for her. She wandered in the moonlight instead of sleeping, wrote romantic poems, and kept a "Heart-Journal."

Having done so many of Dickens's works as plays, Louisa tried her hand at creating others. She loved the "Philothea" written by her mother's friend, Lydia Maria Child, elegantly posing herself as the Greek maiden, Aspasia.

She and Anna threw themselves into the writing, directing and producing of their own plays. Louisa wrote and acted the action parts, delighting in the villains, ghosts, bandits, knights, and sorcerers. Anna was writer and actress of the romantic notions, dreamily presenting the tender maidens and gentler characters. Sometimes Beth was called upon to play a page or messenger, and May to be a fairy sprite, but usually Anna and Louy played all the parts, one rushing off stage to change costume while the other held forth with a long speech designed to accommodate this need.

In these *Comic Tragedies* they had the opportunity to use their creativity to the utmost. Their stage was either the garret or the empty barn, and their props were few. Old sheets, lights, garlands, tinsel, bits of cardboard, old furniture, and anything else they could get their hands on, were pressed into use. Relatives and friends had always given the Alcotts their cast-off clothing. Now some of the more exotic garments were passed on to them for their dramatic

The velvet breeches and "Roderigo's" russet boots Louisa wore for plays (displayed at Orchard House). Photograph by Gloria T. Delamar.

presentations. Old silk and lace gowns, velvet breeches and vests, and all kinds of hats were used over and over again for the plays. Louy's most prized possession was a pair of high soft leather russet boots. She found any excuse to work them into the plays. Tall and thin as she was, she made a dashing appearance as she strode in wearing "Roderigo's boots."

Louisa commandeered an old red and green party cloak as her "glory cloak." This she took to the attic where she wrote. She would go into what she called a "vortex" of writing, filling page after page by the hour, rarely stopping to rest or even eat. Wrapped in her "glory cloak" she had visions of herself as a rich and successful writer.

Her dear friend, the younger Ellen Emerson, was so delighted with Louy's storytelling that the budding author wrote an entire series of "Flowers Fables," for her, putting each into its own pretty, colorful cover.

She was inspired, too, by her adoration of Ellen's father, the kind, illustrious Emerson. To this friend she was deeply attached. Inspired by the romantic books of Goethe, she wrote secret love letters to Emerson which she never mailed, and left wildflowers on his doorstep. She sat in a tall cherry tree at midnight to serenade him with German love songs, sung so softly he never knew she was under his window. "He is my idol," she sighed. Besides his kindnesses to her, she knew that it was he who so frequently left discreet gifts of money on their mantle under a candlestick or tucked into a book. He had great faith in Bronson Alcott but knew how little the family had in the way of worldly goods.

They were terribly poor. At last, with deep regrets of leaving Hillside,

Breaking into Print

Mrs. Alcott decided she must take an offer of employment which had been made to her. Friends in Boston were opening a charitable society for women poorer even than the Alcotts. By offering Abba Alcott the job as city missionary, they provided her with a face-saving way of accepting their help. This was not merely a charitable gesture, however, for she was well qualified for such a job, having all her life shared her small lot and found ways to help those less well-off than she.

The difficult decision to leave Hillside was made. At first, Mr. Alcott suggested that he would stay behind alone. Louisa's heart was heavy. It was family council time again. In the end, happily, it was the entire family that left the wooded country of Concord in November of 1848, to move back to the bustle of Boston.

Tensions were running high in the family, however. Anna dutifully taught. Louisa felt cramped in their small quarters, especially as she had the household responsibilities and no privacy for pursuing her writing. She yearned to try her hand at acting, but the family frowned on this as a profession. She tried to content herself with writing plays and putting on amateur productions. Her dreams took her beyond their Boston and Concord circle. She wanted to see her birthplace in Germantown some day; she wanted to see the nation's capitol at Washington; she wanted to see New York City; she wanted to sail the Atlantic Ocean to see the old cities of Europe.

She was melancholy. "Seventeen years have I lived, and yet so little do I know, and so much remains to be done before I begin to be what I desire — a truly good and useful woman." Her sadness was not soothed by her father's withdrawal. He took rooms in another part of Boston in which to hold "Conversations," which would, with luck, earn some money. Gradually, however, he stayed at the rooms more and more often. The girls began to worry about their father's withdrawal. Their mother explained it simply. Marmee understood this genius of a husband and patiently waited out his need to be alone. It was difficult for the girls, however.

Father looked over the girls' journals and said, "Anna's is about other people, Louisa's about herself." Louisa admitted that was true, but said, "I don't *talk* about myself; yet must always think of the wilful, moody girl I try to manage, and in my journal I write of her to see how she gets on." It was an introspective time for her. She felt that Anna was so good, but that her own quick tongue was always getting her into trouble. She tried to keep down vanity about her long hair, well-shaped head, and her good nose. And it was hard not to covet the fine things she saw in shop windows. She found every day to be a battle and confessed, "I'm so tired I don't want to live; only it's cowardly to die till you have done something."

She was very depressed. In May of 1850, she said, "I know God is always ready to hear, but heaven's so far away in the city, and I so heavy I can't fly up to find Him." She wrote a poem to get her feelings out.

Faith

Oh, when the heart is full of fears
    And the way seems dim to heaven,
When the sorrow and the care of years
    Peace from the heart has driven,—
Then, through the mist of falling tears,
    Look up and be forgiven.

Forgiven for the lack of faith
    That made all dart to thee,
Let conscience o'er thy wayward soul
    Have fullest mastery:
Hope on, fight on, and thou shalt win
    A noble victory.

Though thou art weary and forlorn,
    Let not thy heart's peace go;
Though the riches of this world are gone,
    And thy lot is care and woe,
Faint not, but journey hour'ly on:
    True wealth is not below.

Through all the darkness still look up:
    Let virtue be thy guide;
Take thy draught from sorrow's cup,
    Yet trustfully abide;
Let not temptation vanquish thee,
    And the Father will provide.

Seventeen-year-old Louisa was confused. Standing a lovely, tall, five feet ten, with an attractive physique, a handsome face, clear blue eyes, and luxurious, long chestnut brown hair, she was on the brink of womanhood.

To the suitors who began to notice her, she had nothing to say. It seemed to her that a woman had to be able to take care of herself—depending on no man. "I'm not looking to be married ... not having seen very many truly happy ones." For this, she did not blame her parents. As mother and father she thought they were splendid.

Even when her father returned to the arms of his loving, welcoming family, her feelings about marriage remained unchanged. Her devotion to her family and her determination to reach financial success and fame were enough to consume her energies.

That summer, Louisa started a family newspaper, "The Olive Leaf." In it she put poems, stories, and tips on cooking or housekeeping, and other articles she thought of interest.

The Alcotts, as always, were outspoken in supporting the causes they believed in. They had concern for the city's underprivileged and continued their aid to the abolitionist movement. Three nights a week, Marmee, Anna,

Breaking into Print

and Louisa taught reading and writing to black adults in the Relief Room that Mrs. Alcott had established on Washington Street.

At the close of the Anti-Slavery Convention in Boston, a number of people had stayed over to discuss a national women's convention. Along with Quaker abolitionist, Lucy Stone, there were philanthropists and professionals among the women; the petition they circulated was signed by Bronson Alcott, William Lloyd Garrison, the Rev. Samuel May, Wendell Phillips, and the Rev. Theodore Parker. Louisa was much interested to know that the first National Women's Rights Convention was to be held in Worcester, Massachusetts, on October 23, 1850.

A bout of smallpox, which the family caught from some poor immigrants Mrs. Alcott had brought in to feed, occupied most of the summer of 1850. The girls had light cases, but their parents were very ill and required their attention for a long time. They managed without doctors and friends and all got well in time.

Louisa thought of women's rights again when they heard that Margaret Fuller, feminist and "Priestess of Transcendentalism," had tragically drowned off the Atlantic coast with her husband and baby son. This energetic, romantic figure had often urged women to demand their rights.

Louisa taught, and liked it better than she had thought, but she did find it difficult to be patient with the children at times. She said, "As a school-marm I must behave myself and guard my tongue and temper carefully, and set an example of sweet manners."

In August, her journal entry was introspective:

> ...I think a little solitude every day is good for me. In the quiet I see my faults, and try to mend them; but deary me, I don't get on at all.
>
> I used to imagine my mind a room in confusion, and I was to put it in order; so I swept out useless thoughts and dusted foolish fancies away, and furnished it with good resolutions and began again. But cobwebs get in. I'm not a good housekeeper, and never get my room in nice order. I once wrote a poem about it when I was fourteen, and called it "My Little Kingdom." It is still hard to rule it, and always will be I think.
>
> Anna wants to be an actress, and so do I. We could make plenty of money perhaps, and it is a very gay life. Mother says we are too young, and must wait. A. acts often splendidly. I like tragic plays, and shall be a Siddons if I can. We get up fine ones, and make harps, castles, armor, dresses, water-falls, and thunder, and have great fun.

By 1851, they had settled into a routine, 22-year-old Anna and 18-year-old Louisa taught. Beth, at 16, did the housekeeping. Louisa called her "Our Angel in a Cellar Kitchen." Beth objected. "Now, Louy, you know I'm only doing what I'm happiest at . . . I really like to cook and sew and make our little home neat. This, and finding time to play a piano, is all I need." May, now 11, went to school, where her happiest hours were spent in art class. Pert and self-confident, she announced, "I have artistic talent and mean to be a famous painter some day." Mr. Alcott wrote or occasionally taught classes or gave "Conversations." Mrs. Alcott continued to work at the Intelligence Agency. The family was together—still poor—but joined in love and happiness.

To make life even brighter, a momentous thing happened. First, Louisa had her very first published work; her poem "Sunlight," under the pen-name of Flora Fairfield, was printed in *Peterson's Magazine* of September 1851. Though her own name was not on it, she had finally had something published.

As she tried to think of ways to help the family, she wondered if some wigmaker would buy her long, thick hair for a goodly sum. As she brushed it, deciding whether to wear it in a snood, or piled on top of her head, the thought kept reoccurring. When she finally suggested it, the entire family was upset. She was glad they hadn't agreed to the idea, but she resolved to keep it in reserve nevertheless.

Marmee, in the meantime, had added her own intelligence or Employment Agency to her Mission work. She matched workers wanted with those who wanted to work. One day a request for a companion for his sister came from a well-dressed clergyman. When her mother asked if Louisa, now 18 years old, knew of anyone for the position she answered, "Why couldn't Miss Louisa May Alcott go, Mother?" It sounded more interesting than teaching; she would be companion to the invalid sister, read to her, and make herself useful in small ways. The clergyman promised that she would be paid handsomely, have only light work, and would be treated as one of the family. Louisa was in for a shock. She scrubbed floors, cleaned furniture, made beds, sifted ashes in the fireplace, sudsed dishes, brought water from the well, carried wood for the stove, and shoveled snow. After seven weeks, she balked. The final insult was when "the master" expected her to black his boots. Hastily packing her clothes, she demanded her pay. It was handed to her in a little purse. Grabbing it, she rushed home to the family. "I shan't go back, but at least I have earned something for us." She opened the purse to reveal a paltry four dollars. Mr. Alcott was so angry, a rare thing for the gentle, aloof man, that he himself returned the money to the clergyman, giving him a tongue-lashing in the bargain for having taken advantage of Louisa. It was a sad experience for Louy, but she determined that she might yet make some money from the adventure if she could turn it into a story. She set to work recording the incident for "How I Went Out to Service."

The following summer, their old friend, Lewellyn Willis, came to board with them before entering Harvard Divinity School. He was surprised that Louisa had not had the courage to send any of her stories out for publication. He carried one to an editor. Due to this effort, Louisa had her first story published. "The Rival Painters" appeared on the front page of the *Olive Branch Magazine* on May 8, 1852. She received $5 for it, and the satisfaction of seeing her initials listed as author.

Breaking into Print 37

In the meantime, there were other activities of interest. Louisa went to an antislavery meeting where Boston's leading abolitionist, Wendell Phillips, spoke. The people were much excited and cheered, "Shadrack and liberty," and groaned for "Webster and slavery," and made a great noise. She said, "I felt ready to do anything, — fight or work, hoot or cry, — I shall be horribly ashamed of my country if this thing happens and the slave is taken back." Later, she learned that he had been.

On her father's 52nd birthday, she wrote a poem for him.

To Father

A cloth on the table where dear Plato sits
By one of the Graces was spread
With the single request that he would not design
New patterns with black ink or red.
And when he is soaring away in the clouds
I beg he'll remember and think
Though the "blackbirds" are fair his cloth will be fairer
For not being deluged with ink.
May plenty of paper of pens and of quiet
To my dear pa forever be given
Til he has written such piles that when on the top
He can walk calmly on into Heaven.

In December, Louisa went to hear the Rev. Theodore Parker speak at the Music Hall. He spoke of women's rights — that women should have the right to vote and to be eligible for public office. His sermon, "The Public Function of Woman," fired her soul. His subject was not a new one to her. She was, after all, a *May* and an *Alcott*. And Marmee had signed the woman's rights petition.

Anna went to teach in Syracuse where Uncle Sam May had his church now, while Louisa continued to teach in Boston. Although teaching was not to her taste, she rejoiced nevertheless at the news that their old friend Horace Mann had helped establish Antioch College at Yellow Springs, Ohio. True to his goals, women as well as men were to be admitted. Louisa was glad that others, at least, would have this opportunity.

Over the summers, when schools were not in session, Louy took jobs sewing or as a "second girl" willing to do the wash and eager to earn a few extra dollars.

In mid-1853, Mr. Alcott went to the west to try his luck at lecturing. Mrs. Alcott outfitted him with all-black and all-white suits to be worn according to the season, feeling he would make a distinquished appearance thus attired. When he returned in February 1854, he had paid only his way, but no more. The few dollars he had earned had been spent to buy a shawl when his coat was stolen. He had only $1 to show for his many months away. Mrs. Alcott glad to see her husband home, declared stoutly, "Well, I call that doing *very well*." Louisa saw the incident as a "lesson of love."

Louisa never gave up writing, no matter how tired she might be from teaching or sewing. Here and there, she began to sell some of her wild adventures and romance stories for a few dollars each. She neatly rewrote her old story "How I Went Out to Service." With her heart beating wildly, she set out for The Old Corner Bookstore. The clerk, Thomas Niles, showed her to the little back room where Mr. James T. Fields reviewed manuscripts. Shyly, she handed him hers. She waited while he read it. He finally looked up at her. "Stick to your teaching, Miss Alcott," he said. "You can't write." Such a fit of depression hit her that she wandered the streets for hours. But, her old spirit asserted itself. With her shoulders back and her head up, she determined, "Just wait, Mr. Fields. I *won't* teach; and I *can* write, and I'll prove it.... And I'll write something you'll want to buy."

It wasn't long before she had reason to have her faith in her talents renewed. Her father showed some of her earlier stories, the ones written for Ellen Emerson, to a friend. They were interested in publishing them. Louy wrote an introduction to the seven stories, added a verse, "Fairy Song," and a conclusion:

Flower Fables

The summer moon shone brightly down upon the sleeping earth, while far away from mortal eyes danced the Fairy-folk. Fireflies hung in bright clusters on the dewy leaves, that waved in the cool night-wind; and the flowers stood gazing, in very wonder, at the little Elves, who lay among the fern-leaves, swung in the vineboughs, sailed on the lake in lily cups, or danced on the mossy ground, to the music of the harebells, who rung out their merriest peal in honor of the night.

Under the shade of a wild rose sat the Queen and her little Maids of Honor, beside the silvery mushroom where the feast was spread.

"Now, my friends," said she, "to wile away the time till the bright moon goes down, let us each tell a tale, or relate what we have done or learned this day... [tales]

Fairy Song

> The moonlight fades from flower and tree,
>   And the stars dim one by one;
> The tale is told, the song is sung,
>   And the Fairy feast is done.
> The night-wind rocks the sleeping flowers,
>   And sings to them, soft and low.
> The early birds ere long will wake;
>   'Tis time for the Elves to go.
>
> O'er the sleeping earth we silently pass,
>   Unseen by mortal eye,
> And send sweet dreams, as we lightly float
>   Through the quiet moonlit sky;—

Breaking into Print 39

THERE CAME A STRANGE LITTLE BOAT FILLED WITH ELVES.

Illustration from *Flower Fables*. Philadelphia: Henry Altemus, (1855) 1898.

> For the stars' soft eyes alone may see,
>   And the flowers alone may know,
> The feasts we hold, the tales we tell;
>   So 'tis time for the Elves to go.
>
> From bird, and blossom, and bee,
>   We learn the lessons they teach;
> And seek, by kindly deeds, to win
>   A loving friend in each.
> And though unseen on earth we dwell,
>   Sweet voices whisper low,
> And gentle hearts most joyously greet
>   The Elves where'er they go.
>
> When next we meet in the Fairy dell,
>   May the silver moon's soft light
> Shine then on faces gay as now,
>   And Elfin hearts as light.
> Now spread each wing, for the eastern sky
>   With sunlight soon will glow.
> The morning star shall light us home;
>   Farewell! for the Elves must go.

As the music ceased, with a soft, rustling sound the Elves spread their shining wings, and flew silently over the sleeping earth; the flowers closed their bright eyes, the little winds were still, for the feast was over, and the Fairy lessons ended.

Her excitement over the book slowly turned to despair when the printing of it took so much longer than she had thought. She confided to Anna in a letter:

> ...But my mite won't come amiss; and if tears can add to its value, I've shed my quart,—first, over the book not coming out; for that was a sad blow, and I waited so long it was dreadful when my castle in the air came tumbling about my ears. Pride made me laugh in public; but I wailed in private, and no one knew it. The folks at home think I rather enjoyed it, for I wrote a jolly letter. But my visit was spoiled; and now I'm digging away for dear life, that I may not have come entirely in vain. I didn't mean to groan about it; but my lass and I must tell some one our trials, and so it becomes easy to confide in one another. I never let Mother know how unhappy you were in S(yracuse) till Uncle wrote...."

Finally, the book was set in print. In the garret, Louisa worked on the proofs. On December 19, 1854, 22-year-old Louisa May Alcott saw her own name listed as the author of her first book, *Flower Fables*. Officially the book was copyrighted for 1855.

To her mother, she wrote a note:

> 20 Pinckney Street, Boston, Dec. 25, 1854.
> Dear Mother,—Into your Christmas stocking I have put "my first born," knowing

that you will accept it with all its faults (for grandmothers are always kind), and look upon it as an earnest of what I may yet do; for with so much to cheer me on, I hope to pass in time from fairies and fables to men and realities.

Whatever beauty or poetry is to be found in my little book is owing to your interest and encouragement of all my efforts from the first to the last; and if ever I do anything to be proud of, my greatest happiness will be that I can thank you for that, as I may do for all the good there is in me; and I shall be content to write if it gives you pleasure.

Jo is fussing about;
My lamp is going out.

To dear mother, with many kind wishes for a happy New Year and merry Christmas.

I am ever your loving daughter.

Louy

For her father, this Christmas, she wrote a verse:

For the Attic Philosopher

With wishes for a Merry Christmas from his
daughter Louisa with (A Pair of Slippers)

Santa Claus saw while passing thro' Greece
   The sandals Plato had worn,
And he thought of a certain philospher
   Whose feet they would greatly adorn.
But feeling the ancient sandals to be
   Out of keeping with modern hose
He changed them into these slippers you see,
   More fitting a land of snows.
But still they're adorned on their surface of green
   With oak leaves Plato once wore,
To remind the good sage when they garnished his feet
   Of the wise man who wore them of yore.
The leaves by good rights should have been on the head,
   But Santa Claus knew in the street
That both sages and saints wear hats and not crowns,
   So the oak leaves were best on the feet,
Thus to shield the ten philosophical toes
   From all stubs, slips, stumbles and shocks,
And to hide from the eyes of the peeping old world,
   The holy Platonic blue socks
The transmagnified slippers good Santa Claus brings
   For the "student and seers" cold feet.
The sage thinks so much of all human soles
   His own should most surely be neat,
Then long life and repose to Plato the second,
   No matter how empty his *pus*.
May he dwell undisturbed with gods, poets and saints,
   In the green groves of Acade, *mus*.

She watched for the reviews of *Flower Fables,* pleased when the *Transcript* called the tales "agreeable sketches ... adapted to the capacity of intelligent young persons." The *Gazette* mistitled the book as *Flower Tables,* but said the "little legends of faery land" were "very sweet." Although she earned only $32 from the little book, being spoken of as an author suited her. It was a beginning.

Surrounded by apples, she huddled in her garret and wrote a farce, "Nat Bachelor's Pleasure Trip." She gave it to her cousin, Dr. Charles May Windship with whom she exchanged correspondences using the names "Beaumont" and "Fletcher." He took the farce into hand, trying to place it with one of his theatre connections. Though a practicing physician in Roxbury, he had long had an interest in the theatre and knew many people. He was certain it would one day be produced, but there was no luck at the present.

In the summer of 1855, Louisa visited her Aunt Lizzie Wells in Walpole, New Hampshire, where she entertained others, while thoroughly enjoying herself, in the town theatre troupe, the Walpole Amateur Dramatic Company. Aunt Lizzie enjoyed the cheerful girl. They laughed together as Louisa used her sewing skills to redesign the hand-me-down mousseline, lace, and batiste dresses Aunt Lizzie gave her.

She wrote in her journal, "Up at five, and had a lovely run in the ravine, seeing the woods awake. Planned a little tale which ought to be fresh and true, as it came at that hour and place, — Have lively days, — writing in a.m., driving in p.m., and fun in eve. My visit is doing me much good."

In July the entire family moved to Walpole to live rent-free in another relative's house. Father could have a garden and Mother could rest. The children could have freedom and fine air. There were plays, picnics, pleasant people and good neighbors. Louisa and Anna acted in some of the plays, which played to an audience of a hundred and were noticed in the Boston papers.

Louisa wrote "The Christmas Elves" while in Walpole. May worked at making appropriate drawings to go with the story. When the book was finished, complete with May's illustrations, Louisa decided it was time for her to take on Boston alone. Mr. and Mrs. Alcott understood their daughter's need to assert herself. Her relatives would be around to keep an eye on her. Besides, they knew that there was no stopping Louisa once she had made up her mind.

With her little trunk of homemade clothes, $20 she had earned from stories sent the *Gazette,* and her manuscripts, Louisa left Walpole one rainy day, on her own for the first time.

Chapter 4

1856–Late 1862: Independence

Louisa set about trying to find a publisher for "The Christmas Elves" and learned her first lesson about book publishing. No publisher was interested in trying to print it. A Christmas book had to be in the publisher's hands many months before it was needed in print if there were to be any sales. Disappointed, but with strength of will, she made up her mind. "I won't go home." Louisa determined to find some kind of work. She arranged to stay with a Sewall cousin and found sewing work. "Sewing won't make my fortune, but I can plan my stories while I work, and then scribble 'em down on Sundays."

She decided to write a story about one year in the life of four sisters who had to earn their own livings. The inspiration came from home, for the four girls were remarkably like the Alcott sisters. "The Sisters' Trial" depicted Agnes (Anna) who wanted to be an actress, Nora (Louisa herself) who stayed at home to write, Ella (Beth) who worked as a governess, and Amy (May) who was studying art. It appeared in *The Saturday Evening Gazette* on January 26, 1856. She received $5 for it, but only her initials, L.M.A., appeared as author. She sold the *Gazette* several more stories for $5 each, and was happy to see the earnings go up to $10 as people liked them and asked who wrote the anonymously-printed tales.

She took time out in April to participate in the "parlor entertainment" of two short plays, managed by May, whose tongue-in-cheek playbill flagrantly highlighted the name of the manager and the parts played by (the misspelled) "Miss Allcott."

In May, she was distressed yet happy when Anna stopped in Boston to see her after working for several months at a mental institution in Syracuse. "I'm sick and worn out, Louy. The work was too much for me." "Never mind. We'll do some visiting about, and you'll feel better," Louisa told her. In June, they were back in Walpole to help care for Beth and May who had caught scarlet fever helping mother to nurse two poor children.

In the fall, Mr. Alcott went off on another lecture tour, and Louisa moved back to Boston. She took an attic "sky parlor" in a boardinghouse, and arranged to do some sewing for the landlady in exchange for reduced rent. Later, she added a tutoring job to her schedule.

A play that she wrote was offered to a Boston theatre for production, and although they did not accept it, she was given a pass. She also had lecture tickets and a new cloak, gifts from Aunt Lizzie Wells.

She went to hear the Unitarian minister, the Rev. Theodore Parker, speak at his church. A talk on "Individuality of Character" particularly appealed to her. At his house, she met Wendell Phillips, William Lloyd Garrison, Charles Sumner, and other great men. Sometimes the writer, Julia Ward Howe, would be there with her husband. One evening, Louy went to her corner, where she went weekly to stare and enjoy herself. Parker searched her out to say in that cordial way of his, "Well, child, how goes it?" "Pretty well, sir." "That's brave." With his warm handshake he left her feeling proud and happy, though she had trials. She explained it by saying, "He is like a great fire where all can come and be warmed and comforted. Bless him!"

Lydia Parker, too, befriended Louisa, calling on her, reading Louy's stories, and being good to her. Mrs. Parker, mindful of Louisa's need to earn money, kept an eye out for those who might need some sewing done or have a child to be tutored.

Louisa enjoyed the history of Boston. She walked to the old State House on Beacon Hill where John Hancock had been inaugurated as first Governor of Massachusetts. The Common nearby was where the Puritans once had stocks and pens for punishment, where the British mustered before the Battle of Bunker Hill, and, she remembered, where her dead baby brother was buried. She visited King's Chapel where her parents had been married, and the Old North Church where Paul Revere had flashed his lanterns. Down near the wharf, she went to Faneuil Hall, the "Cradle of Liberty," scene of many stirring gatherings during the revolutionary movement, and to the Oyster House which had once been the dry goods store where "Great-Aunt Hancock" had sewn bandages and mended clothes for the colonists. There were so many old sites to absorb and new pleasures to experience. She particularly enjoyed the Sunday sermons and Sunday evening receptions held by the Reverend Theodore Parker.

She was awed by the silver-tongued speakers—Wendell Phillips, Charles Sumner, William Lloyd Garrison—the talk of humanitarianism and freedom for the slaves inflamed her own soul. She found Mr. Parker the most impressive of all. In spite of his lofty principles and philosophy, he always found time to seek out the shy guest sitting in the corner of the room to say something like, "So, child, how goes it? And how do your worthy parents do? ... God bless you, Louisa; come again." His warm handshake gave her courage to face another anxious week.

She went to the ceremony to greet and cheer the return of Charles Sumner after the Brooks affair, watching him, pale and feeble, smiling and bowing, breaking into laughter when his friend, Theodore Parker, cheered like a boy as he pranced and shouted, bareheaded and beaming.

She wrote and sold romantic tales, beginning to feel as though she might

Independence

Orchard House with the Alcott family (old photograph).

yet stake her claim to fame. Boston stimulated her. May, too, was attracted to Boston. Louisa was proud of their "little Raphael," who arranged to stay with relatives and signed up for music, French, and drawing lessons. "I mean to be an accomplished Alcott," May declared. Louisa's reply was only slightly different. "I mean to prove that though an *Alcott* I *can* support myself . . . I like the independent feeling; and though not an easy life, it is a free one, and I enjoy it. I can't do much with my hands; so I will make a battering-ram of my head and make a way through this rough-and-tumble world."

The winter went quickly, full of sewing, tutoring, writing, and her various pleasures. In January of 1857, she was pleased to have a visit from her father who was on his way back to Walpole from another lecture tour. "Well, Louisa, there's little money, but I had a good time, and was asked to come again." "Oh, father, why don't rich people who enjoy your talk pay for it? Philosophers are always poor and too modest to pass around their own hats."

In the spring, May returned home and Louisa made a brief visit there. A delightful Sunday was spent with the Emersons where she proudly informed everyone, "I have done what I planned, — supported myself, written eight stories, taught four months, earned a hundred dollars, and sent money home."

After a visit from Grandma Alcott and the talk of her father's growing-up, Louisa got an idea for a story, saying, "The trials and triumphs of the Pathetic Family would make a capital book; may I live to do it." She could include Fruitlands, Boston, and Concord; perhaps "The Cost of an Idea" would make a good title.

She returned to Boston and her routine. In summer, Anna came to spend some time with her and they had happy times together. The only cloud over the Alcotts now was Beth's feeble health, lingering from the scarlet fever. She did not appear to be getting any stronger. Marmee was pale and exhausted with the strain of caring for her. Taking up a collection of their few financial resources, the invalid and mother were packed off to the seashore in hopes that the sea air would put color back into the cheeks of their frail and patient Beth. Anna and Louisa were left with the responsibility of packing the busts and books again. Mr. Alcott longed for Concord and his literary friends, especially Mr. Emerson. So with Emerson's repetition of financial assistance, they purchased an old house and orchard on the Lexington Road. It was just a short distance from the Emersons and next door to their old Hillside, which Nathaniel Hawthorne had bought and rechristened the Wayside. They knew they would truly be home again. The family was settled in a little "half-house" in October 1857 while their newly-acquired Orchard House was to be put in order. Mr. Alcott was happy to use his carpentry skills again, hammering and sawing to repair the old house. Anna, Louisa, and May scrubbed, dusted, papered, and painted. May put lovely painted decorations on some of the panels. Over the hearth in Louisa's bedroom she painted an owl "for our wise Louy."

Their old friend William Ellery Channing wrote a motto for Bronson Alcott's new study. Over the chimneypiece May painted the words: "The hills are reared, the valleys scooped in vain, if Learning's altars vanish from the plain."

With most of the work done, Louisa alternated between Concord and Boston in the next months. The Boston theatre still appealed to her and she flirted again with the idea of becoming an actress, but contented herself attending the plays. She did not want for attention. She declared, "It is funny to see how attentive all the once cool gentlemen are to Miss Alcott now she has a pass to the new theatre."

Louisa's low moods were usually shown only to her family. When around others, she called up her acting skills and managed to seem cheerful even when she was not. Being of a curious nature also gave her high spirits, so that she was good company. More than one fine gentleman was attracted to her, but she realized she did not love any of them and agreed with Marmee that she should not make the self-sacrifice of marrying merely to secure a position which would make her able to help her family. "Besides, you know I love activity, freedom and independence ... I do get tired of everybody and feel sure I should of a husband if I married."

There was plenty of activity and companionship. Frank Sanborn, an old friend from Theodore Parker's Sunday receptions, had opened a school in Concord. Louisa spent many happy days visiting there or attending the frequent picnics or evening games and dances. One of her favorite companions was a fair-haired boy of 15, Alfred Whitman. He and the young man at whose home he was staying, 24-year-old John Pratt (son of Brook Farm's Minot Pratt), often visited the Alcotts. Despite the difference in their ages, Louisa and Alf got along very well. Louisa called him "my boy." They performed together in the Concord Dramatic Union. Frank Sanborn, as manager, was well pleased with their performances. Everyone noticed that Anna and John Pratt were particularly radiant as they performed love scenes together.

Louisa read about the life of novelist Charlotte Bronte and daydreamed. "A very interesting, but sad life. So full of talent; and after working long, just as success, love, and happiness come, she dies. Wonder if I shall ever be famous enough for people to care to read my story and struggles. I can't be a C.B., but I may do a little something yet."

The diversions were only one side of the family's life, however. On Louisa's 25th birthday, her thoughts were of her dear ailing sister. She wrote in her journal:

> Twenty-five .. I feel my quarter of a century rather heavy on my shoulders just now. I lead two lives. One seems gay with play, etc., the other very sad—in Beth's room; for though she wishes us to act, and loves to see us get ready, the shadow is there, and Mother and I see it. Beth loves to have me with her; and I am with her at night, for Mother needs rest. Beth says she feels *strong* when I am near. So glad to be of use.

By January of 1858, Anna took over the housekeeping so that Mother and Louisa could devote all their time to Beth. Mr. Alcott returned from a speaking tour to find his daughter no better. It was difficult to accept that Beth was dying. As she often did, Louy found some solace in working out her sadness through poetry.

Our Angel in the House

Sitting patient in the shadow
   Till the blessed light shall come,
A serene and saintly presence
   Sanctifies our troubled home.
Earthly joys and hopes and sorrows
   Break like ripples on the strand
Of the deep and solemn river,
   Where her willing feet now stand.

O my sister, passing from me
   Out of human care and strife,
Leave me as a gift those virtues
   Which have beautified your life.
Dear, bequeath me that great patience
   Which has power to sustain
A cheerful, uncomplaining spirit
   In its prison-house of pain.

Give me—for I need it sorely—
   Of that courage, wise and sweet,
Which has made the path of duty
   Green beneath your willing feet.
Give me that unselfish nature
   That with charity divine
Can pardon wrong for love's dear sake,—
   Meek heart, forgive me mine!

Thus our parting daily loseth
   Something of its bitter pain,
And while learning this hard lesson
   My great loss becomes my gain;
For the touch of grief will render
   My wild nature more serene,
Give to life new aspirations,
   And new trust in the unseen.

Henceforth, safe across the river
   I shall see forevermore
A beloved household spirit
   Waiting for me on the shore;
Hope and faith, born of my sorrow,
   Guardian angels shall become;
And the sister gone before me
   By their hands shall lead me home.

On March 14, 1858, after two years of patient pain, with the entire family gathered around her, Beth died. Her last words to them, spoken a few days earlier, were spoken with a contented smile, "All here." It was her goodbye to them.

Louisa made some entries in her journal:

> ..A curious thing happened, and I will tell it here, for Dr. G. said it was a fact. A few moments after the last breath came, as Mother and I sat silently watching the shadow fall on the dear little face, I saw a light mist rise from the body, and float up and vanish in the air. Mother's eyes followed mine, and when I said, "What did you see?" she described the same light mist. Dr. G. said it was the life departing visibly.
> For the last time we dressed her in her usual cap and gown, and laid her on her bed, — at rest at last. What she had suffered was seen in the face; for at twenty-three she looked like a woman of forty, so worn was she, and all her pretty hair gone.

Ralph Waldo Emerson, Henry Thoreau, Frank Sanborn, and John Pratt carried her "out of the old home to the new one" at Sleepy Hollow Cemetery. The Alcotts were in a daze of grieving.

Later, they went through her treasures. In the last months she had frequently been busy sewing, but would never say what she was sewing. Now, they found that she had been making keepsakes for the family and friends she loved. Each little thing was carefully wrapped and marked with the name of the person for whom she had made it. Penwipers, pinblocks, and needlebooks were made from colorful silks or leathers and neatly stitched. When Lydia Hosmer saw the penwiper for Henry, the pinblock for Cyrus, and the needlebooks for her sister Sarah and herself, she knew she would always count the purple silk needlebook with its yellow lining as one of her most precious possessions.

On April 7, Anna announced her engagement to John Pratt. Louisa was moody. "Another sister gone," she mourned.

In the July heat of 1858, the Alcotts moved into their Orchard House. Because its orchard was puny, and the plain house reminded her of the lumpy dessert, Louisa nicknamed it "Apple Slump." She was happy to see her parents settled into this house, but declared that it would probably never be home to her. She had decided she didn't really like Concord. For her, Boston was the hub.

Back in Boston, Theodore Parker's sympathy helped her through the mourning for Beth. She learned, through her grief, that she was essentially strong. She had some moments of despair, especially when it did not appear that she would be able to find work, but Parker's intervention got her a position sewing. For entertainment, she went to lectures by Parker, Thomas Wentworth Higginson, and other abolitionists, or went to the theatre, happy to see Edwin Booth in *Hamlet*.

May came to stay with her, taking more drawing lessons. When her father was gone on a tour of the West, she spent some time in Concord, caring for Marmee who was ill. Her nursing skills were called into practice again, and

Portrait of Elizabeth Sewall Alcott on wall above her melodeon (dining room at Orchard House). Photograph by Gloria T. Delamar.

she wondered if she ought to be a nurse, for she liked it, and everyone said she had a gift for it.

Writing, however, remained her real endeavor. She felt that she was learning the writing craft, and "growing up to do my great book." She was learning much about plotting, the use of language, and character development, through the wild adventures and romances that were bringing in a few dollars.

In November, her story, "Love and Self-Love," was accepted by the *Atlantic Monthly* and she shouted, "Hurray," and declared, "I've not been pegging away all these years in vain. I may yet have books and publishers and a fortune of my own." The sweetest satisfaction was at having sold her work to editor James T. Fields, who had once told her, "Stick to your teaching, Miss Alcott. You can't write."

In May 1859, Frank Sanborn arranged for John Brown to appear at the Concord Town Hall. The Alcotts, Emerson, and Thoreau warmly welcomed the abolitionist. In October when they heard the news of the raid on Harper's Ferry, in which he freed slaves, they cheered. He had, however, been captured. They quickly began to gather forces to send pleas to the governor of Virginia to free him. All their Concord friends rallied. From Boston, Lydia Maria Child petitioned the governor to let her treat Brown's wounds. Elizabeth Peabody actually went to plead in person, but had no more success than anyone else. On December 2, 1859, John Brown was hanged. Memorial services were held at the Concord Town Hall, at which many impassioned speeches were made. Louisa referred to Brown's tragedy as "the execution of Saint John the Just." When she saw a rose bloom out of season on the day of John Brown's execution, she took it as a symbol, and inspired, wrote a poem in tribute to him, which was later published in the *Liberator*.

With a Rose, That Bloomed on the Day of John Brown's Martyrdom

> In the long silence of the night,
>   Nature's benignant power
> Woke aspirations for the light
>   Within the folded flower. ..
>
> Then blossomed forth a grander flower
>   In the wilderness of wrong,
> Untouched by Slavery's bitter frost,
>   A soul devout and strong....
>
> No monument of quarried stone,
>   No eloquence of speech,
> Can grave the lessons on the land
>   His martyrdom will teach. ..

Louisa was inspired to write a story about a mulatto loved by a white woman — a story about abolition; but no one would buy "M.L.," so it was put away for the time being.

In April of 1860, Horace Mann came running to Orchard House to tell them that Frank Sanborn had been collared, handcuffed, and dragged out of his house on Sudbury Street by 11 officers who were charging him with aiding and abetting John Brown with the plans at Harper's Ferry. He was tried and acquitted, which set the bells of Concord ringing in celebration. In more serious response, however, they held a meeting in the Town Hall, at which Louisa was elected to serve with others on a Vigilance Committee.

The year 1860 was happier for the Alcotts. Mr. Alcott was appointed superintendent of schools in Concord, and May returned home in April.

Louisa had a tale to relate:

> I had a funny lover who met me in the cars, and said he lost his heart at once. Handsome man of forty. A Southerner, and very demonstrative and gushing, called and wished to pay his addresses; and being told I didn't wish to see him, retired, to write letters and haunt the road with his hat off, while the girls laughed and had great fun over Jo's lover. He went at last, and peace reigned. My adorers are all queer.

On May 4, her farce was finally produced at the Howard Athenaeum on Howard Street. The main attraction was a full-length benefit performance of *The Romance of a Poor Young Man,* but Louisa's after-sketch followed. "Nat Bachelor's Pleasure Trip" was listed on the playbill as "a New Local Sketch by the Popular Authoress, Miss Louisa Adcott." In addition to having her name misspelled, Louisa felt that the production was not very well done, but she'd had the pleasure of sitting in a private box seat and of being handed up a "bouquet to the author" by Charles Windship, who made as much as he could of a small affair. One review said, "It is a creditable first attempt at dramatic composition, and received frequent applause." Another critic simply said, "It proved a full success." The management seemed to agree with the author, however, for the announcement in the next day's paper was that no aftersketch would follow the featured production.

Anna and John Pratt were married at Orchard House on May 23, the Alcott's own anniversary. Uncle Sam May performed the ceremony for his niece, just as he had for his sister 30 years before. Louisa said, "The house is full of sunshine, flowers, friends and happiness." Friends danced on the lawn in German fashion under the Revolutionary elm tree.

At the end of her journal entries about the wedding, Louisa added, "Mr. Emerson kissed her; and I thought that honor would make even matrimony endurable, for he is the god of my idolatry, and has been for years."

Mr. Emerson, indeed, had invited Louisa to join the "learned ladies" in his classes on "Genius." She felt honored. Besides Mr. Emerson, her own father also gave some of the lectures, earning a few dollars, most of it contributed by Mr. Emerson himself.

May was progressing with her art, and Louisa began another vortex of writing with work on an adult novel, *Moods.*

One sad experience marred the year. Louisa regarded Ralph Waldo Emerson and Theodore Parker as the two men who had given her the best part of her education. The death of Theodore Parker on May 10, in Florence, saddened her. His memory would be a rich legacy to Boston. She said, "I am glad to have known so good a man, and been called 'friend' by him."

She found much more enjoyment with the younger people who frequented Frank Sanborn's school. One of her favorites was young Julian Hawthorne. His sisters Una and Rose were nice girls, his mother a friend and admired amateur artist, and his father a writer whose work she liked. As she and Nathaniel Hawthorne both had the habit of walking alone in the moonlight, they frequently silently passed each other in the dark on the ridge that ran behind their houses. Fourteen-year-old Julian was a boy who liked frogs, dances, and the Alcott girls, even though they were quite a bit older than he. He whirled them in schottisches, lancers, and waltzes. He appeared at the Alcott teas, and spent many a Sunday evening playing cards, such as longwhist, euchre, or old-maid, with them. Together, they laughed over the homemade root beer and deep dish pies they consumed.

On one memorable occasion Julian, Louisa, and May went on the river at dawn to see the water lily open, as Thoreau had told them it would. They tumbled into three feet of water and had to race home with their dark flannel throat-to-ankle swimsuits soaking wet, hoping no early risers would see them.

Another time, Julian, who was rather smitten with May, came down the road to find her flirting with a dashing young man. For weeks, the Alcott sisters had been hinting about this impending visitor. On being introduced, the "English Gentleman" began to treat Julian most patronizingly. He twirled his cane, caressed the ends of his thin, black mustache, and drawled, "My dear child, do you know, I find you quite amusing." Julian bristled. "Child!" He was about to hit this fop when the visitor pulled off his hat—Louisa's dark hair fell down her back—and she and May laughed and danced about, pleased with their prank. Teasing Julian with May's supposed courtship was one way of dealing with romance. For herself, Louisa rejected romantic relationships.

But she realized that romantic stories would sell. Drawing on the idea of Anna's romance with John Pratt, she wrote a story about three sisters, which she called "A Modern Cinderella." Anyone reading it could tell that the young ladies in the story were based on the three living Alcott sisters; there was a sweet dutiful homemaker called Nan (clearly Anna) who quietly pined for the hardworking and gentle John Lord (obviously John Pratt). The younger sister, called Laura (this sister was just like May), a pretty, pert, somewhat spoiled artist, was also in love. And Louisa? All those who knew her knew immediately that she appeared in the story as "Chaos Di," the sister who always had her nose buried in a book and wanted to be a writer.

The story's Di said the very things that Louisa so often wrote in her diary or told family and friends, "I'll turn my books and pen to some account, and write stories full of dear old souls like you and Nan; and some one, I know, will like and buy them, though they are not 'works of Shakespeare.' I've thought of this before, have felt I had the power in me; now I have the motive, and now I'll do it."

In the end the two sisters who had let Nan do most of the work learned to be more helpful and cheerful, and rejoiced as Nan agreed to marry John. For this story, Louisa gave Laura (May) a romance, but her own independent "Chaos Di" was not linked to any man. "A Modern Cinderella" was published in *The Atlantic Monthly* in October 1860.

By now the independent Louisa had told her family, "I would rather be a free spinster and paddle my own canoe." She had no inclination for married life.

In fall, the Concord Lyceum, the town's self-supporting public education forum, administered by volunteers, began another series of lectures; the village, and the Alcotts, had the good fortune of hearing some of the best speakers of the day—Emerson, Sumner, Higginson, and others.

September had seen a new fad in Concord. Dr. Dio Lewis, a hygiene and gymnastics instructor, arrived in the quiet town to give workshops in physical fitness. Dumbbells, clubs, wands, and flailing arms and legs moved to the accompaniment of music. Louisa wrote a letter to her aunt, Mrs. Bond, in which she described the events:

> ...This amiable town is convulsed just now with a gymnastic fever, which shows itself with great violence in all the schools, and young societies generally. Dr. Lewis has "inoculated us for the disease," and it has "taken finely"; for every one has become a perambulating windmill, with all its four sails going as if a wind had set in; and the most virulent cases present the phenomena of black eyes and excoriation of the knobby parts of the frame, to say nothing of sprains and breakage of vessels looming in the future.
> The City Fathers approve of it; and the city sons and daughters intend to show that Concord has as much muscle as brain, and be ready for another Concord fight, if Louis Napoleon sees fit to covet this famous land of Emerson, Hawthorne, Thoreau, Alcott & Co. (May) and I are among the pioneers; and the delicate vegetable productions clash their cymbals in private, when the beef-eating young ladies faint away and become superfluous *dumb belles*.

In real life, May had much the same fierce independence as Louisa. Her real aim was to succeed at her painting. In the meantime, there was a living to be made. In December, May went to Syracuse to teach, her first flight alone in the world.

Christmas was a lonely time, as well as a hard one financially. Louisa had been thinking about writing about "the pathetic family" again, though saying it was also "a happy family." As the year ended she wrote in her journal:

> ...A quiet Christmas; no presents but apples and flowers. No merry-making; for Nan and May were gone, and Beth under the snow. But we are used to hard times, and, as Mother says, "while there is famine in Kansas we mustn't ask for sugar-plums."

All the philosophy in our house is not in the study; a good deal is in the kitchen, where a fine old lady thinks high thoughts and does kind deeds while she cooks and scrubs.

In February of 1861, Louisa spent three weeks at work on *Moods*, donning a green silk cap with a red bow along with the old green and red party wrap she wore as her "glory cloak." She scarcely took time to eat or sleep. Marmee kept her supplied with hot tea, and Father brought his best red apples and hardest cider. At the end of her session, she was exhausted but elated. Having read the manuscript to her family, she was ready for their comments. Mr. Alcott was fascinated. "Emerson must see this. Where did you get your metaphysics?" Louisa had not known she had any. Mrs. Alcott pronounced it "wonderful," and Anna laughed and cried as always saying, "My dear, I'm proud of you." Louisa basked in their admiration. Publishers were not as complimentary as her family. They judged the book to be too solemn and far too long. Louisa went into a fit of depression. But world events soon turned all thoughts elsewhere.

All Concord was in an uproar at the declaration of war between the North and the South in April 1861. Louisa said, "I've often longed to see a war, and now I have my wish." Even Mr. Alcott and Mr. Emerson saw the cause as good reason for fighting. Although she hated keeping house, Louisa interrupted her story writing for it when the two daughters of John Brown, Anne and Sarah, came to board with them. Their presence, and the Concord boys marching off to be soldiers, brought the war close to home.

Yet, despite Civil War concerns, the rest of life was normal. May returned to Concord to teach in Frank Sanborn's school and Louisa took a vacation with cousins in New Hampshire. She recorded her adventurous ride to Mount Washington in a letter to Alf Whitman with whom she continued to correspond regularly.

Concord life held little to interest Louisa, and she headed for Boston again in January of 1862, this time with the offer of a teaching post. The family's old friend, Elizabeth Peabody, invited her to observe her teaching techniques. She had opened a new "Kindergarten" patterned after children's classes in Germany, in 20 Pinckney Street, a house which had once been the Alcott's home. After viewing Miss Peabody's methods, Louisa was ready to open her own school in a room at the Warren Street Chapel. James T. Fields, whose second wife was Louisa's cousin, Annie Adams, made a loan of $40 to sponsor the school that started out with twelve pupils, including Fields's nephew.

Annie Fields invited Louisa to spend a month at their home. The Fields home was a virtual literary salon. Annie Fields, a writer herself, was a popular hostess in Boston. Louisa recorded some of her impressions:

Saw many great people, and found them no bigger than the rest of the world, — often not half so good as some humble soul who made no noise. I learned a good deal in my way, and am not half so much impressed by society as before I got a peep at it. Having known Emerson, Parker, Phillips, and that set of really great and good men and women living for the world's work and service of God, the mere show people seem rather small and silly, though they shine well, and feel that they are stars.

She enjoyed the opportunities which Boston offered to hear lectures and attend the theatre. She was invited out but found some of these invitations tedious, writing, "Hate to visit people who only ask me to help amuse others, and often longed for a crust in a garret with freedom and pen. I never knew before what insolent things a hostess can do, nor what false positions poverty can push one into."

Despite having published her work, Mr. Fields, as she always called him, still felt she should "stick to her teaching." Although the teaching went well and the children loved her gay spirit and bright imagination, it did not pay enough, especially as she had been made to have an assistant she did not want. The main thing was that she still did not like teaching.

May agreed to take her place for the last month of the semester so the school would not have to close, and Louisa retired to her desk. She wrote another story. She was pleased to find that she received more money for it than she had for teaching. "My teaching days are over," she announced to her family. She was absolutely certain she could write. Noticing that "blood and thunder" tales were popular in the gazettes, she indulged her wild fancies in ideas of murder, brutality, and revenge. She felt the style "easy to compose" and was attracted by the fact that they paid better than moral romantic stories.

Back in Concord, she joined with the village to pay last respects to dear Henry David Thoreau, who on May 9, 1862, at the age of forty-four, quietly passed away. Her old friend of the woods of Walden Pond, would play his flute no more. Louisa wrote to tell Alf Whitman:

> ...Mr. Channing wrote an Ode, Mr. Emerson made an address, and Father read selections from Henry's own books, proving that though he didn't go to church he was a better Christian than many who did. A party of great people from Boston came up, the church was full and though he wasn't made much of while living, he was honored at his death.

Other men of Concord were gone too. The dusty Lexington Road was almost a parade-ground of boys who answered the call of their country. Julia Ward Howe had written a stirring poem called "The Battle Hymn of the Republic," which was being sung to the same tune as "John Brown's Body."

Louisa had applied to teach contrabands at Port Royal, South Carolina. These were black slaves who had escaped from the Southern-held territory or who were otherwise now within the Union lines. She and another young woman had been chosen from Concord before word came that unmarried

Independence

women were forbidden. She heard that there was to be a school in Washington for the blacks, and determined that if she were asked she would go, as she liked the plan.

Frustrated, Louisa fretted that she was not doing her part. Believing in the cause was not enough. There must be something she could do.

Chapter 5

November 1862–Mid-1863: Real Life

Louisa found herself with an important decision to make in the winter of 1862. All Concord was excited about the progress of the Civil War. As it progressed, the Lexington Road in front of Orchard House was almost a parade-ground of boys who answered the call of their country. In Boston there were recruiting tents on the Common. She had heard that Alf Whitman was in the quartermaster's department. In June, after being captured and imprisoned since July 1861, Cyrus Hosmer, to whom she had pledged her affections at the age of nine, had finally been released, along with others she knew from the Concord regiment. From the village, Frank Sanborn reported that his students were leaving their studies to join in the adventure of war.

The young men marching away to fight for the antislavery cause had been sent off to the whistles of fifes and rat-a-tat rolling of drums. The Massachusetts women, like many others, busied themselves making bandages, and sewing shirts, blue flannel jackets, and other needed items.

The Alcott living room was the scene of much of this activity, as neighbors gathered for the patriotic work of Sewing Bees and Lint Picks. As always, Marmee was at the forefront of setting up aid. Louisa dutifully helped. But she raged, longing to be a man so she could see the war. When she heard bad news of the war she said, "Anxious faces, beating hearts, and busy minds. I like the stir in the air, and long for battle like a war-horse when he smells powder. The blood of the Mays is up!" She felt a great need to fight for what she believed in and to be useful. Only one way seemed to be open to her.

Their old friend, Dorothea Dix, was now Superintendent of U.S. Army Hospitals. According to circulars she issued from Washington, mature and healthy women were sorely needed as nurses in the District of Columbia army hospitals. Among the requirements were that a woman should be strong, healthy, of good character, and of serious disposition. A minimum commitment of three months of service was expected. The "pay" amounted to free room and board, free travel to and from the assigned hospital, and 40¢ a day.

"Help needed, and I love nursing, and *must* let out my pent-up energy in some way," Louy said. "I want new experiences and am sure to get 'em if I go." So, shortly before her 30th birthday on November 29, Louisa sent off her application. The coveted call-to-service came on December 11th.

Louisa May Alcott, 1862

As the required black, brown, or gray clothing was exactly what her usual wardrobe consisted of, packing her bags was an easy matter. "Nurses don't need nice things, thank Heaven," she declared, as she neatly mended her old clothes. Her brass ink bottle and copper teakettle were packed in among the garments. In addition, she tucked in some games and copies of Dickens's books, which she intended to read to her soldier patients.

Just before leaving the heart of her beloved family, she suddenly realized she had taken her life in her hands and might never see them again. She rushed into Marmee's arms. "Shall I stay, Mother?" She got a hug in response. "No go! And the Lord be with you!" As Louisa left, accompanied by May and Julian Hawthorne, Marmee stood at the doorstep waving her wet handkerchief. Louy felt as if she were the son of the family going off to war.

On Friday the 12th, she ran all over Boston to get her pass, get a tooth filled, and buy a veil, her only purchase. From relatives, she received some old clothes, some money, and lots of love and help. At the station she bid goodbye to the tearful faces saying, "I'm full of hope and sorrow, courage and plans." The slow, bumpy, cumbersome journey by train—boat—train again—and finally carriage—gave her plenty time to think. She had ample time to make some journal entries:

> A most interesting journey into a new world full of stirring sights and sounds, new adventures, and an ever-growing sense of the great task I had undertaken.
> I said my prayers as I went rushing through the country white with tents, all alive with patriotism, and already red with blood.
> A solemn time, but I'm glad to live in it; and am sure it will do me good whether I come out alive or dead.

Louisa arrived at the Georgetown Union Hotel Hospital on December 14, 1862. Guards were stationed at the doors of the old building, and the Union flag, with its 13 stripes and 34 stars, flew proudly before it. With patriotism and determination to guide her, she was set to succeed at her duty.

Louisa's previous nursing experience was for her own family in the clean rooms at home. She had tended Beth during her long illness. That, and even her reading of Florence Nightingale's instructions on nursing, were no preparation for the filth, stuffiness, rotten straw-beds, foul odors, and overcrowded conditions of this war hospital converted from an old three-story run-down tavern-hotel. She was put to work immediately. Her first two days were a confusion of meeting doctors, nurses, supervising attendants, caring for patients, carrying trays, and fetching bandages and other supplies. Already she had seen a man die at dawn, and sat between a man who had been shot through the lungs and a boy with pneumonia. When she covered the boy with her mother's old black shawl, he smiled, panting for breath, and said, "You are real motherly, ma'am." Although that made her feel as if she was "getting on," she tried to look "motherly" to comfort him.

The meals were plain and generally badly cooked. Breakfast might be "uninvitable" fried beef, salt-butter, husky bread, and "washy" coffee. Dinner and supper were soup, meat, potatoes, and bread. This was new fare for someone who had been raised a "vegetarian product." Between meals, she poked up fires, joked, coaxed, and commanded. The orderlies were sent to fetch clean bed linens. She pursued her crusade for fresh air, opening closed windows, though the men grumbled and shivered, not fully understanding the pestilence that would breed without better ventilation. Conscientiously, she moved around the former ballroom, now filled with rickety beds and thin, dirty mattresses. At day's end, she fell exhausted into her iron bed in the small curtainless, dusty-windowed room she shared with two other nurses.

On December 16, the wounded of the Battle of Fredericksburg descended on the hospital. There were 40 full ambulances of moaning, groaning soldiers. In addition, many trudged in on foot, the "walking-wounded." Many had makeshift bandages torn from dirty rags wrapped around their bleeding limbs. The first task was to clean the filthy, mud-caked, bloody men, so their wounds could be seen. The nurses had a job to do. Louisa undertook hers stoically.

One of her favorite patients was a 30-year-old, tall, handsome, mortally-wounded Virginia blacksmith, John Sulie. She called him "the prince of patients," and said that though he was what one called a "common man of education and condition," he had "a heart as warm and tender as a woman's, a nature fresh and frank as any child's." She felt indignant that such a man should be so early lost. It was painful watching him wait for the release of death. Life as an army nurse wasn't quite what Louisa had thought it would be. Her days were full. She kept a record in her diary:

> Up at six . . . a more perfect pestilence-box than this house I never saw, —cold, damp, dirty, full of vile odors from wounds, kitchens, wash-rooms, and stables. . . . Till noon I trot, trot, giving out rations, cutting up food for the helpless "boys," washing faces, teaching my attendants how beds are made or floors are swept, dress wounds, take Dr. F.P.'s orders (privately wishing all the time that he would be more gentle with my big babies), dusting tables, sewing bandages, keeping my tray tidy, rushing up and down after pillows, bed-linen, sponges, books, and directions, till it seems as if I would joyfully pay down all I possess for fifteen minutes' rest."

At twelve the dinners arrived, and at five, supper set everyone to running that could run. It was not until nine in the evening that the bell rang signaling the end of the day shift.

Despite some homesickness and continued longing to "follow the fighting," the tall, athletic "Miss Alcott" quickly became a favorite, for she was warmly cheerful and full of fun. In addition to her regular duties for her patients, she wrote letters for them, read to them from her beloved Dickens, gaily performed "Mrs. Sairey Gamp" skits, and comforted their pain and loneliness.

When she had night duty, she was free to spend part of her days walking around the hills of Georgetown and into Washington itself. She went up and down the streets in all directions, her long skirt sweeping through the cluttered trash. The streets were always full of chattering people, both white and black, and of soldiers wearing all manner of colorful uniforms. There was an abundance of Union Army blue, with an assortment of gold lace on the officers' uniforms. She thought the ladies, with their elaborate flower-bedecked hats, were dressed in the worst possible taste, and walked like ducks. The men too, in her opinion, were overdressed with vanities, making Washington look like a mammoth masquerade.

The city was a constant succession of army wagons, each pulled by six mules, to whom Louisa assigned human characteristics and stances, from coquettish, melodramatic, and jovial, to pathetic and moral. She was fascinated by the curious mixture of mansions and shacks set beside each other. Cats, dogs, and pigs roamed freely, adding to the congestion. She noted the unfinished white dome of the capitol and wished for a glimpse of Mr. Lincoln. It was exciting to see and sniff the flavor of the nation's capital.

Ever the writer, her mind was alert to the story possibilities in her new surroundings and in these strange brave men under her care. She wrote about them in her journals and in her letters home:

> When dinner is over, some sleep, many read, and others want letters written. This I like to do, for they put in such odd things, and express their ideas so comically, I have great fun *interiorally*, while as grave as possible *exteriorally*. A few of the men work their paragraphs well and make excellent letters, John's was the best of all I wrote. The answering of letters from friends after some one had died is the saddest and hardest duty a nurse has to do.

She found the staff conversations at meals comical:

> ...listen to the clack of eight women and a dozen men, — the first silly and stupid, or possessed of one idea; the last absorbed with their breakfast and themselves to a degree that is both ludicrous and provoking ... the conversation is entirely among themselves, and each announces his opinion with an air of importance that frequently causes me to choke in my cup, or bolt my meals with undignified speed lest a laugh betray to these famous beings that a "chiel's amang them taking notes."

She enjoyed using Cockney phrases from Dickens, and frequently followed a custom of signing her letters "Sairey Gamp" when she was away from home. Those dramas, in which Anna had played Betsy Prig and she had been Sairey Gamp, seemed so far away. They enjoyed recalling them by calling each other by their "Dickens" names. Now Louy called upon her dramatic skills to cheer the patients, glad to introduce them to her beloved Dickens, but feeling underneath the passion of the life and death dramas going on all about her.

In her journal, she recorded the sad as well as the humorous events of the days. There was the pain and courage of the men, their adjustments to the loss of arms or legs, and their various ways of facing death. There were the many "helpers" who pretended to give attention to the men, while "helping themselves" to the men's belongings.

There was much about nursing to learn. For every soldier who was wounded, there were two who were suffering from measles, pneumonia, typhoid, diphtheria, bronchitis, rheumatism, or chronic diarrhea. Many of the nurses and doctors came down with the diseases to which they were exposed.

In the midst of the ever-present suffering, Christmas arrived. The holiday was certainly unlike those at home. Some evergreen boughs, some wreaths, and some red bows were all the decoration they had. The holiday dinner was not much different from the everyday greasy fare. Louisa and the other nurses did their best to provide some entertainment and festivity. A sprig of evergreen adorned the usual red knitted, scarf-like rigolette she wore around her head to keep her long hair out of the way. Although she missed her family very much, and was fatigued as usual, Louisa kept her spirits up for the sake of the wounded soldiers.

New Year's Day brought firecrackers and jubilant shouts of "Glory, Hallelujah" from the contrabands. They celebrated noisily, calming down only to hear the reading of "Father Abraham's" Emancipation Proclamation.

On that 1863 New Year's Day, she found time to write some thoughts in her journal:

> I never began the year in a stranger place than this: five hundred miles from home, alone, among strangers, doing painful duties all day long, and leading a life of constant excitement in this great house, surrounded by three or four hundred men in all stages of suffering, disease, and death. Though often homesick, heartsick, and worn out, I like it, find real pleasure in comforting, tending, and cheering these poor souls who seem to love me, to feel my sympathy though unspoken, and acknowledge my hearty good-will, in spite of the ignorance, awkwardness, and bashfulness which I cannot help showing in so new and trying a situation. The men are docile, respectful, and affectionate, with but few exceptions; truly lovable and manly many of them....

In early January, after only three weeks of work, Louisa began to notice that she was so tired she could hardly lift the trays, so tired in fact, that even the writing she enjoyed was too much for her. Within a few days, she too was ill and delirious with the fever, coughing, dry and swollen tongue, raw throat, and headaches of typhoid pneumonia. She thought of home and wondered if she was going to die at the hospital, as Mrs. Ropes, the matron from Boston, had.

Dorothea Dix came to see her and wanted to move her to another hospital to care for her. Louy stubbornly refused. When she did not appear to be recovering, her father was informed, that he might come to take her back home. He arrived on January 16. At first, she was angry because she knew she would have to go; nevertheless, she was glad to see him.

By January 21, "feeling very strangely and dreading to be worse," she had to make the soulful decision to go home. Dorothea Dix brought a basket full of bottles of wine, tea, medicine and cologne, besides a little blanket, a pillow, a fan, and testament, and wished her a safe journey. She was dimly aware that quite a flock of her patients came to see her off, sorry to see her go. Louisa was so weak and ill that she barely was aware of the travel transfers. With her father beside her, she finally reached Concord. She vaguely saw May's shocked face at the depot, and Marmee's bewildered one at home. It was January 23, 1863, and though she thought the house had no roof, she was home.

Back in her own bed, she gave herself up to the loving care of Marmee, May, and Anna. In her delirium, she kept seeing a stout, handsome Spanish spouse, dressed in black velvet, with very soft hands, and a voice that kept saying, "Lie still, my dear." Not recognizing the shadow figure as Marmee tending her, she was in utter terror of it. The apparition was always coming after her, appearing out of closets, in at windows, or threatening her dreadfully all night long. She appealed to the Pope, startling the family as she actually got up and made a touching plea in what was evidently meant to be Latin.

In one nightmare she thought she had gone to heaven, and found it a twilight place, with people darting through the air in a queer way—all very busy, and dismal, and ordinary. Miss Dix, W.H. Channing, and other people were there; but she thought it dark and slow, and wished she hadn't come. Among other fancies were that of a mob at Baltimore breaking down the door to get her, being hung for a witch, burned, stoned, and otherwise maltreated. She dreamt that she was tempted to join some of the Union Hospital staff in worshipping the devil, and that she had to tend millions of rich men who never died or got well.

May tried to soothe her, softly singing her favorite songs. Marmee used all her nursing skills; the doctor was certain that Louisa was going to die. Anna's John understood that his wife, though expecting their first child, was needed at the Alcott house. Someone was with Louisa all the time, as they took turns sitting up through the night. Eventually, to their relief, the horrible nightmares, chills and fever stopped. After three weeks of delirium she had recovered her senses, and was told she had had a very bad typhoid fever, had nearly died, and was still very sick. All of this seemed very strange to her, for she remembered nothing of it. But the worst was over and the family breathed a sigh of relief. Louy was going to recover.

For her army service, she was paid $10.

The medical treatments of calomel left her with sore gums and a hoarse throat. For a time, her family kept from her the information that the calomel, which contained a mercury compound, had caused mercury poisoning of her system. As a result, she would have lingering illness and weakness for the rest of her life.

When she looked in the mirror she found a queer, thin, big-eyed face and didn't know herself at all. When she tried to walk she couldn't and cried because her legs wouldn't go. Sadly, her mass of beautiful hair, a yard and a half long, was not only thinned, but had been cut, lost in the service of her country. She was unconsolable at first, but eventually her sense of humor returned. She "went into caps like a grandma," saying she "felt badly about losing my one beauty. Never mind, it might have been my head and a wig outside is better than a loss of wits inside." She saw her pallid face and the dark rings about her eyes and said, "I don't suppose it is going to kill me, but I shall never get over it. I go to bed at nine o'clock and think steadily of the wood-box in order to keep my mind from more serious subjects."

Slowly, Louisa began to recover her health. As she felt somewhat stronger, she sat up for longer periods and read a great deal. "No end of rubbish, with a few good things as ballast." She couldn't write yet, but said, "I think out sketches of stories and put them away in little pigeon-holes in my brain for future use." In March, her first little job was characteristic; she cleared out her piece-bags and dusted her books, though it made her as tired as if she had cleaned the whole house. March 22 was the red-letter day on which she was finally able to leave her room.

On March 28, Father came home snowy and beaming, crying out, "Good news! Good News! Anna has a fine boy." Marmee cried, May laughed, and Louisa declared, "There, I knew it wouldn't be a girl!" Everyone enjoyed the joke, for all knew that Louisa had made a pincushion with the initials *L.C.* for "my niece, Louisa Caroline." In due time, and despite Louy and May's idea that the boy be named Amos Minot Bridge Bronson May Sewell Alcott Pratt, so that all the families would be suited, he was named Frederick Alcott Pratt.

Soon, as she was able to sit up for longer periods of time, Louisa began to think of writing again. She got out a poem in tribute to Thoreau that she had composed one night at Georgetown while on watch at the hospital. Here and there, she wrote new lines.

She was able, also, to take stock of the good things that had begun to happen. Her miscegenation story "M.L." had been published in the January issue of *The Commonwealth*. Her first "blood and thunder" tale, written just before going off to serve as a nurse, was printed in the February issue of *Frank Leslie's Illustrated Newspaper*. The editor, Frank Leslie, had informed her that "Pauline's Passion and Punishment" won the $100 prize, and she realized she could begin to earn a steady income from other stories like it. After thinking it over, she decided to use the pen name of A.M. Barnard for these lurid tales, as she was not at all sure her family would want the Alcott name associated with them. They were not, after all, "good literature."

In April, she was well enough to go to Boston to see "our baby." At the time of Freddy's birth, she had predicted that she would "fall down and adore" when she first saw the mite; now she noted that she "thought him ugly, but promising." Nevertheless, she agreed with Anna, "that of all splendid babies, he was the king."

The poem she had written in memory of Henry David Thoreau, "Thoreau's Flute," was published. One evening, while "taking the air," she had slipped it under the Hawthornes' door to share it with them. When Julian found it, he passed it on to his mother, Sophia, who was so impressed with it that she sent it to Mr. Fields. He bought it and printed it. Louisa had to admit that she was pleased to have shown him, again, that she could indeed write.

Thoreau's Flute [words later changed]

We sighing said, "Our Pan is dead;
   His pipe hangs mute beside the river;
   Around it wistful sunbeams quiver,
But Music's airy voice is fled.
Spring [came to us in guise forlorn;]   [mourns as for untimely frost;]
   The bluebird chants a requiem;
   The willow-blossom waits for him;—
The Genius of the wood is [gone.]   [lost.]

Then from the flute, untouched by hands,
   There came a low harmonious breath:
   "For such as he there is no death;—
His life the eternal life commands;
Above man's aims his nature rose.
   The wisdom of a just content
   Made one small spot a continent,
And [turned] to poetry life's prose.   [tuned]

Haunting the hills, the stream, the wild,
   Swallow and aster, lake and pine,
   To him grew human or divine,—
Fit mates for this large-hearted child.
Such homage Nature ne'er forgets,
   And yearly on the coverlid
   'Neath which her darling lieth hid
Will write his name in violets

To him no vain regrets belong
   Whose soul, that finer instrument,
   Gave to the world no poor lament,
But wood-notes ever sweet and strong.
O lonely friend! he still will be
   A potent presence, though unseen,—
   Steadfast, sagacious, and serene;
Seek not for him—he is with thee.

Unfortunately, her name did not appear as the author of the poem, as it was the custom of the prestigious *Atlantic Magazine* not to print the names of the writers. That custom provided her some warm pleasure when Father told her that the poet Henry Wadsworth Longfellow had credited the illustrious Ralph Waldo Emerson with the beautiful poem. With a thrill to have her father correct him, telling him that his own Louisa had written it. She exulted. "It was printed, copied, praised, and glorified; also *paid for,* and being a mercenary creature, I liked the $10 nearly as well as the honor of being 'a new star' and 'literary celebrity.'"

She began to take walks and said, "I feel as if born again, everything seems so beautiful and new. I hope I was, and that the Washington experience may do me lasting good. To go very near to death teaches one to value life, and this winter will always be a very memorable one to me."

Marmee and May tried to teach others to value themselves. It was always the custom for the Alcotts to open their home to those who needed help, treating it somewhat like a halfway house. When indigents came by, May and Marmee would lecture them on temperance and the evils of sloth, feed them, and try to find them jobs.

Friends were more apt to be led in conversations by Father. Monday evenings, weather permitting, were the Alcott at-home times when neighbors and friends would come to call. Nathaniel Hawthorne confided to Bronson Alcott that he would have come more often, except that he found it hard to take Abba Alcott's booming voice.

Some of the boys from Frank Sanborn's school were frequent visitors, eager to join the evening of poker-sketches and talk with the ladies. Marmee enjoyed quiet games of chess with some older person in a corner. Louisa usually sat by the fireplace, knitting rapidly with an open book in her lap. Young Frank Stearns noted that she only pretended to be quietly resigned when asked to join in a game, for soon her love of fun would break forth and her bright flashes of wit would play about the heads of all who were in the room. Just after ten, the philosopher would come in with a dish of handsome apples and his wife would produce some ginger cakes. After a lively chat of 15 or 20 minutes, the guests would walk home.

Feeling so much better now, Louisa also had the pleasure of getting a new set of furniture for her room, a long-delayed dream, as well as a new carpet and new paper. May took on the task of painting and papering the parlor. When Marmee went away to Anna's they gave the house a full sweep so that she came home to a clean, fresh house.

Louisa wrote a few short tales which she sold, making her happy that her winter bore visible fruit. She kept her hands busy, too, with sewing shirts and gowns for her "blessed nephew, who increased rapidly in stature and godliness."

Three of the "Hospital Sketches" Louisa wrote were published by the *Commonwealth Magazine,* where her old friend, Frank Sanborn, was now an editor. These were based on some of her letters home. As a result of their warm acceptance by readers, she was asked to write a few more and form them into a book. To her surprise, two publishers, Roberts Brothers and James Redpath, offered to publish the sketches. She chose Redpath, largely because he was, like herself, an ardent abolitionist.

Her agreement with Redpath was that for each copy sold at fifty cents, the orphan fund would receive ten cents and she would receive four; for each paperbound copy for army reading, the orphan fund would receive five cents and she would receive two. In preparing the advertisement for the book, the publisher wrote, "...besides paying the Author the usual copyright, the publisher has resolved to devote at least five cents for every copy sold to the support of orphans made fatherless or homeless by the war.... Should the sale of the little book be large, the orphans' percentage will be doubled." Louisa wished she could give all her share, but the finances of the Alcott Sinking-Fund dictated that she be more prudent.

The result of the combined letters and her additional material was a slim volume of six chapters. Louisa made herself the fictional heroine, Nurse Tribulation Periwinkle, writing with wit and pathos about her adventures as an army nurse at Hurlyburly House, and the men who were her charge. Having described the washings, feedings, racket of dishes, and utensils, "Nurse Trib" concluded that it "made most inspiring music for the charge of our Light Brigade." Author Alcott inserted a parody at this juncture:

Beds

Beds to the front of them,
Beds to the right of them,
Beds to the left of them,
  Nobody blundered.
Beamed at by hungry souls,
Screamed at with brimming bowls,
Steamed at by army rolls,
  Buttered and sundered.
With coffee not cannon plied,
Each must be satisfied,
Whether they lived or died;
  All the men wondered.

The letters had wit and humor, for she had tried to tell of the fatigue, sadness, and horror without being maudlin. She added a "poetical gem" upon the "untimely demise of Nurse Periwinkle":

Tribulation Periwinkle's Epitaph

Oh, lay her in a little pit,
With a marble stone to cover it;
And carve thereon a gruel spoon,
To show a "nuss" has died too soon.

As she had received inquires from "various friendly readers" of the letters first printed in magazine form, she added chapter six in the form of a postscript

Nurse Tribulation Periwinkle and Baby Africa. Illustration from *Hospital Sketches*. Boston: Roberts Brothers, (1863) 1869

which tried to answer questions about the hospital, the patients, and general administration. She ended the postscript with words that left no one in doubt as to her sympathies:

> ...The next hospital I enter will, I hope be one for the colored regiments, as they seem to be proving their right to the admiration and kind offices of their white

relations, who owe them so large a debt, a little part of which I shall be proud to pay.
>Yours,
>With a firm faith
>In the good time coming,
>Tribulation Periwinkle.

When complimented on *Hospital Sketches*, she demurred, pleased that the stories were commended, in particular one that she liked best herself. "'Night' was much liked, and I was glad; for my beautiful 'John Sulie' was the hero, and the praise belonged to him."

The public accepted *Hospital Sketches* eagerly, and Louisa May Alcott was acknowledged as an author of note. It was a new feeling for her. She now had two books to her credit. She mused: "This is a sudden hoist for a meek and lowly scribbler, who was told to 'stick to her teaching,' and never had a literary friend to lend a helping hand! Fifteen years of hard grubbing may be coming to something after all; and I may yet 'pay all the debts, fix the house, send May to Italy, and keep the old folks cozy,' as I've said I would so long, yet so hopelessly."

She was surprised at the flood of letters that the stories evoked. Included among them was one from Henry James, who complimented her and sent along a copy of his own book, *Substance and Shadow*.

In writing *Hospital Sketches*, Louisa for the first time wrote "from real life." All her previous stories had been fairy tales or romances. And it was in real life stories that her true talent lay. Although she might add bits of fiction, her simple, warm handling of real events and real people was wonderful. The Sketches might not earn much money, but, she said, "they showed me my style, and taking the hint, I'll go where glory awaits me."

But the money to be made from blood and thunder stories was greater, so she knew she would have to consider that. The family was as poor as ever, and the financial support she might be able to add was crucial. It was distressing that she still felt so weak. She had never been ill before this time, but it looked as though she might never be well afterward.

Chapter 6

Mid-1863–Early 1868: The Door Opens Wider

The success of *Hospital Sketches* opened publishing doors for Louisa. She went into a great vortex of writing, trying to supply all she could, happy to know that most of her manuscripts would now be printed.

Her hand ached from the long writing sessions. Her crabbed backhand was difficult to read, and even she sometimes had trouble making out the hastily written words when the time came to copy them over neatly. Whether her hand and head ached or not, she must keep on. The Alcotts had many debts. There were still doctor bills from Beth's long illness, and new ones for Louisa's treatments.

She wrote the "blood and thunder" stories demanded by readers of such gazettes as *Frank Leslie's Illustrated Newspaper* and *The Flag of Our Union*, content to have the money and let the stories be credited to the pseudonym of A.M. Barnard. At the same time, she began work on a fairy story which she intended to do as a book, *The Rose Family*.

She was delighted to pause in her writing activity when, in September 1863, a Concord company of returning soldiers came marching down the Lexington Road in their army-blue uniforms. News of their coming had preceded them, so the neighbors along the road had set up boards on sawbucks to serve as tables and brought carefully protected ice. Julian Hawthorne said, "Lemonade enough has been made to flavor Walden Pond."

Excited, Louy pulled out her old red rigolette, her nurse's headdress. The rolling drums and the high piping of the fifes abruptly stopped in front of Orchard House. The men had halted in their parade. For a little while, they mingled with the milling neighbors. Louisa moved among them, chatting. She, too, had experienced the blood and tragedy brought by war. Her time at the Union Hotel Hospital gave her a bond with these young men who had been on the battlefields. Just before they went on their way again, the 60 men — caps waving in the air — shouted and cheered for Miss Louisa Alcott. Louy, standing in a dark dress, a replica of her former uniform, with the red rigolette on her head, stood proud. She had served her country. She had been a soldier for the cause of freedom. The tribute of the men touched her heart

Louisa May Alcott's handwriting, 1865

and she struggled to control the moisture welling up in her eyes; it was one of the few times anyone ever saw Louisa shed a public tear.

For the present, though, there were other concerns. She sifted through all her old experiences, thought of all the people she had known, searching her memories for story materials. She wrote some more stories based on her hospital service. She wrote short romance stories of various kinds; "Enigmas," for instance, was mild enough to appear over her own name; "V.V.: or, Plots and Counterplots," was just lurid enough, to her mind, to warrant the A.M. Barnard byline. At one point she told Anna, "You ask what I am writing. Well, two books half done, nine stories simmering, and stacks of fairy stories moulding on the shelf."

With some of her earnings she was able to pay for May's advanced art lessons; May would travel back and forth from Boston to Concord to take anatomical drawing from Dr. William Rimmer. With other money, she was able to begin to pay small amounts on the family's debts.

But she was depressed when publishers held stories too long, and paid for them slowly saying, "If I think of my woes I fall into a vortex of debts, dishpans, and despondency awful to see. So I say, 'every path has its puddle,' and try to play gayly with the tadpole in *my* puddle, while I wait for the Lord to give me a lift, or some gallant Raleigh to spread his velvet cloak and fetch me over dry shod."

She fretted over having "one dollar, no bonnet, half a gown, and a discontented mind." With her dollar, however, she purchased a simple bonnet and then dug into "the Widow Cruise's oil bottle," her ribbon box which, she said, was "the eighth wonder of the world, for nothing is ever put in, yet I always find some old dud when all other hopes fail." This time, she found some old white ribbon and a bit of black lace from which she made a "dish," serving up the ribbon in bows, "like meat on toast."

In December, Louisa dramatized six scenes from Dickens for the Sanitary Fair in Boston. She went in on December 14th, acting for six nights. The production was not at all satisfactory to her, but people seemed to like it anyway. They made $2500 for the fair, and she was satisfied with that.

Family responsibilities often interfered with time to write. She confided to Anna, "I feel very moral to-day, having done a big wash alone, baked, swept the house, picked the hops, got dinner, and written a chapter in *Moods*. May gets exhausted with work, though she walks six miles without a murmur.... I can't do much, as I have no time to get into a real good vortex.... These extinguishers keep genius from burning as I could wish, and I give up ever hoping to do anything unless luck turns...."

Unfortunately, *The Rose Family* did not do very well when it was published; but Louisa knew there were many more stories in her head still to be written. Some of them had just come out together in *On Picket Duty, and Other Tales*—two books from Redpath in 1864. She would yet pay off the debts, buy nice things for Mother and Father, and support the family through her own talents.

Louisa May Alcott, author, was becoming known; A.M. Barnard, in the meantime, was helping to pay the bills. She said, "I can't afford to starve on praise, when sensation stories are written in half the time and keep the family cosey." Life was beginning to look a bit easier.

Burying old friends was never easy, however. Another of Concord's literary talents passed from the scene when Nathaniel Hawthorne died. He joined Thoreau and Beth in Sleepy Hollow Cemetery.

Louisa reworked *Moods* again and finally saw it published in 1865. *Moods* was not quite what the public expected from the author of *Hospital Sketches* and light romances. Although the first sales were brisk, the reviews were not very favorable with one review stating, "Miss Alcott should write about something she knows something about." She snapped, "My next book shall have no *ideas* in it, only facts, and the people shall be as ordinary as possible; then critics will say it's all right."

She was depressed that *Moods* was called "transcendental literature." Some critics declared the relations of the characters impossible, while at the same time a woman asked her how she had known. She didn't know how she knew—it had just come to her, but she groused, "It was meant to show a life affected by *moods*, not a discussion of marriage, which I know little about, except observing that very few are happy ones." There were good reviews as well, and she had letters from Lydia Parker, Frank Sanborn, Thomas Wentworth Higginson, and some others. All were friendly and flattering.

She was soothed by words she had heard Mr. Emerson thunder at her father, "Write!" he had shouted, "Let them hear or let them forbear. The written word abides until, slowly and unexpectedly, and in widely sundered places, it has created its own church." The great man spoke about the kind of books she hoped to write some day saying, "I would have my book read as I have read my favorite books, not with explosion and astonishment, a marvel and rocket, but a friendly and agreeable influence stealing like a scent of a flower, or the sight of a new landscape on a traveler...."

She was asked for a poem for the great album at the St. Louis Fair and sent "Thoreau's Flute" as her best. She also received a letter from the Philadelphia managers asking for contributions for the paper to be printed at their fair.

When asked for a photograph and sketch of her life, she respectfully refused. Father and she were invited to a Fraternity Festival on June 3, where, much to her amazement, she found her "umble self made a lion of, set up among the great ones, stared at, waited upon, complimented, and made to hold a 'layvee' whether I wanted to or no." She was introduced till she was tired of shaking hands and hearing the words "Hospital Sketches" uttered in every tone of interest, admiration, and respect. She concluded, "I liked it, but think a small dose quite as much as is good for me; for after sitting in a corner and grubbing *a la* Cinderella, it rather turns one's head to be taken out and treated like a princess all of a sudden."

On the Fourth of July, she approached Frank Stearns with a twinkle in her eye and said, "A few of us are going to have a picnic tomorrow at Conantum Bluff—and Mrs. Austin and I have engaged a boat for the occasion and are now looking for a muscular heathen to row it. Will you come?" He said that nothing could please him more. Louisa, her friend Jane G. Austin, and Louisa's sister May, settled in the boat. Young Frank found the crooked Concord River hard rowing in a head wind with a rudderless boat and exclaimed, "This is the darnedest boat I ever pulled." "Frank," said Louisa, "never say darn. Much better to be profane than vulgar. I had rather live in hell than in some places on earth. Strong language, but true. Here, take some cold tea." With Conantum in sight, Louisa and May decided to get out at the next bridge to walk the rest of way. Jane and Frank neglected to watch over the bottle of tea, and the cork came out, spilling the tea. Frank explained to her what had happened, as he knew she needed the tea, not being really strong enough yet for an all-day picnic. She joked with him, partly relieving and partly concealing her vexation, saying, "Don't talk to me. I know you college boys. That cork never came out by accident. You drank the tea yourself, and now in what way I am going to punish you for it I cannot tell."

In August, Louisa and May went to Gloucester for a fortnight, where they had a jolly time boating, driving, charading, dancing, and picnicking. In her journal she wrote, "One mild moonlight night a party of us camped out on Norman's Woe, and had a splendid time, lying on the rocks singing, talking, sleeping, and rioting up and down. Had a fine time, and took coffee at all hours. The moon rose and set beautifully, and the sunrise was a picture I never shall forget."

Back in Boston, she went to hear Father lecture at the Fraternity, and met Henry James, Sr. there. He and Mrs. James called upon her later. In January 1865 they invited her to dinner, treating her like the Queen of Sheba. Henry, Jr. had written a review of *Moods*, on the one hand saying the author knew little of human nature, and on the other admitting that few except Miss Alcott could write an above-average novel. At dinner, however, he was very friendly, giving her advice, which Louisa thought somewhat humorous, he being a literary youth of only 21 acting as though he were 80 and she a girl. She decided that her curly crop made her look young, though she was 31.

She received a letter from Annie Lawrence, a voice from the past of Still River. In answering it she recalled the mock-gypsy wedding with Walter Gardner saying, "Those *were* jolly times, and I never think of them without a laugh ... I rather think my prejudices in favor of spinsterhood are founded upon that brief but tragical experience." She said, "I also have been a schoolmarn for ten years, but I don't like it and prefer pen and ink to birch and book, for my imaginary children are much easier to manage than living responsibilities."

She acted in some public plays for the New England Woman's Hospital and had a pleasant time. When asked to write for a new paper, she agreed provided she would be paid beforehand. When the editor agreed she cheered, "So, here's another source of income and Alcott brains seem in demand, whereat I sing 'Hallyluyer' and fill up my inkstand." But Louisa had a lot to think about.

When Richmond, Virginia, was taken by the Northern forces on April 2, she went to Boston to enjoy the "jollification." She saw Edwin Booth again in *Hamlet* and thought him finer than ever. She also had a pleasant walk and talk with Wendell Phillips.

Concord, like all the North, went into a week of celebrating at the news of the Southern General Lee's surrender to General Grant at Appomattox on April 9, 1865. The Civil War was over!

Five days later, the nation was in mourning because President Abraham Lincoln had been assassinated by John Wilkes Booth. Louisa wrote in her journal: "I am glad to have seen such a strange and sudden change in a nation's feelings. Saw the great procession, and though few colored men were in it, one was walking arm in arm with a white gentleman, and I exulted thereat."

That spring, Louisa discovered that the fame she had desired could be a trial. Letters came which she had no time to answer; people stared and pointed at "the author" when she went out. She had lost her treasured privacy. She got "porcupiny" and pleaded, "Admire the books but let the woman alone, if you please, dear public." With her health and energy returning, she was able to help at Anna's house when the Pratts had their second son, John, on June 24, 1865. The baby had been born on Beth's birthday.

A sudden offer of a trip to Europe brightened Louisa's mood. It was something she had always wanted to do. Hearing of her nursing ability, the wealthy invalid Miss Anna Weld, three years younger than she, wanted her as a traveling companion. The thought of the exotic scenes she could note, and of the new characters she might meet and experiences she could have, made any doubts melt away. Her family said, "Go." On July 19, 1865, she and Miss Weld boarded the steamship *China*, with Anna's half-brother George, who was to go as far as Liverpool with them.

They reached Liverpool ten days later, "heartily glad to set feet on solid earth." Louisa kept her pocket-diary at hand that she might record the sights and sounds about her. They spent several dull, drizzly days in London, where she saw Westminster Abbey and some of the famous streets of literature. She said, "I felt as if I'd got into a novel while going about in the places I'd read so much of." The English weather she thought abominable.

After London came the green country of Dover, the quaint old city of Brussels, and the picture-book countryside of Cologne—the city, however, was "very hot, dirty, and evil-smelling." They saw the Cathedral, bought cologne, and "very gladly left after three days." They were happy to begin the lovely voyage up the Rhine which Louisa found almost too beautiful to describe. She was enamored with the moonlit river at Coblentz, and even more charmed with the rest of the way along the Rhine, which she said filled her head with pictures that would last all her life. They passed through a queer Dutch town, and finally reached their first resting place, Schwalbach, Germany.

After a few weeks of slow walks, mineral baths, reading, and "quiddling about," they moved on through Weisbaden and Frankfurt, where Louisa thrilled to statues of Germany's literary giants, Goethe, Schiller, and Gutenberg. She stared at Goethe's house, remembering how his story of a young girl's infatuation for an older man had inspired her extravagant behavior toward Mr. Emerson. They went next to the castle at Heidelberg, chateau and Cathedral of Baden-Baden, Basle, Berne, the lake at Lausanne, and finally to their destination, the charming Pension Victoria at Vevey, Switzerland.

In November, they made the acquaintance of a tall, thin, 18-year-old Polish boy, who was in Vevey to rest after an illness. As Ladislas Wisniewski was anxious to learn English, they taught him while he helped them with their French. Louisa alternately called him Laddie or Laurie, as they went about taking walks, talking, and sailing on the lake.

Her 33rd birthday was spent with Laurie and Anna Weld. Anna gave her a painting, and Ladislas promised her the notes to the Polish National Hymn and played his sweetest airs as a present after wishing her, "All good happiness on earth, and a high place in Heaven as a reward." It was a happy day, but she could not help thinking of her father celebrating his 65th birthday in Concord with all the happy family she missed around him.

She found Laurie "interesting and good," and enjoyed walks and talks

The Door Opens Wider

with him in Vevey. They enjoyed the chateau garden and a sail on the lake, with much laughter over the exchange of English and French lessons.

In December, Ladislas went with them as far as Lausanne and then kissed their hands in parting, as Louisa and Anna Weld traveled on to Nice where they took pleasant rooms. Despite the shops full of curious things, the castles, towers, and blooming flowers, Christmas was quiet and Louisa felt homesick.

She managed occasionally to get away by herself to walk among the vineyards and olive trees or down into the queer old city. She avoided the hours of the "fashionable Promenade," where everyone was on exhibition, preferring to go before or after to enjoy the sea and sky in solitude.

She wrote a little on three stories which came into her head and worried her until she "gave them a 'vent.'" She wrote letters and always felt happy when the mail brought letters from home. She also played around with simple poems which she dedicated to her nephews. For baby John she bought some little blue stockings, and though he was too little to appreciate the verse, there would be others at home who would.

For Johnny

Two pair of blue hose,
For Johnny's white toes,
So Jack Frost can't freeze em,
So pretty and neat
I hope the small feet
Will never go wrong,
But walk straight and strong,
The way father went.
We shall be content,
If the dear little son
Be a second good John.

As Fred's birthday approached in March 1866, she wrote out a ditty for him. It was labeled with the instruction, "To be sung by Marmar with appropriate accompaniment of gesture, etc."

A Song for Little Freddie
On His Third Birthday

Down in the field
Where the brook goes,
Lives a white lammie
With a little black nose.

He eats the grass so green,
He drinks the "la la" sweet,
"Buttertups" and daisies,
Grow all about his feet.

The "birdies" they sing to him,
The big sun in the sky,
Warms his little "Toe-toes,"
And peeps into his eye.

He's a very gentle lammie,
He never makes a fuss,
He never "saps his marmar,"
He never says "I muss."

He hops and he runs,
"Wound and wound" all day,
And when the night comes,
He goes "bye low" on the hay.

In a nice little barn,
Where the "moo-moos" are;
Freddie says "Good night,"
But the lammie he says "Baa!"

Although her tasks as traveling-companion were not heavy, they were a strain for Louisa's still-low store of energies. Besides, she itched to see more of Europe. She tried to content herself with visiting the cathedral, attending the theatre, and taking frequent walks through Valrose, a villa almost buried in roses. Anna would only go for an outing in the woods if Louisa tempted her with books and lunch and hired a wheelchair for her and a man to draw it. It was getting tedious. Anna wanted her to stay, but Louisa was tired of it, and as Anna was not going to travel, Louisa felt her own time was too valuable to be wasted.

In May she left Miss Weld in the care of a sister and a servant and went on to Paris where Laurie helped her get settled into her room. In spite of the differences in their ages, they had a warm friendship. He called her "Little Mama," and she called him "My Boy." They spent a laughing two weeks before she left for London.

London, with its literary history, was thrilling. She saw the houses of Milton, Johnson, Lamb, Thackeray, Bacon, and the inn where Charles Dickens wrote. She even went to hear Dickens read. With the introductions she had, she was invited to dinner parties, went to the theatre, and was hospitably shown around. The resourceful Miss Alcott even managed to talk a London publisher into reprinting *Moods*. Her journals and diaries were full of notes. Her brain reeled with ideas and stories based on all she had seen. It was almost a year since she had seen her family. It was time for her to return home.

After a two-week seasick sail across the Atlantic, the sight of John Pratt waiting for her on the wharf renewed her spirits. The *Africa* docked on July 19th, exactly a year after she had left. She slept on board, and the next day, wrote in her journal, "Reached home at noon to find Father at the station, Anna and the babies at the gate, May flying wildly round the lawn, and Marmee crying at the door. Into her arms I went, and was at home at last."

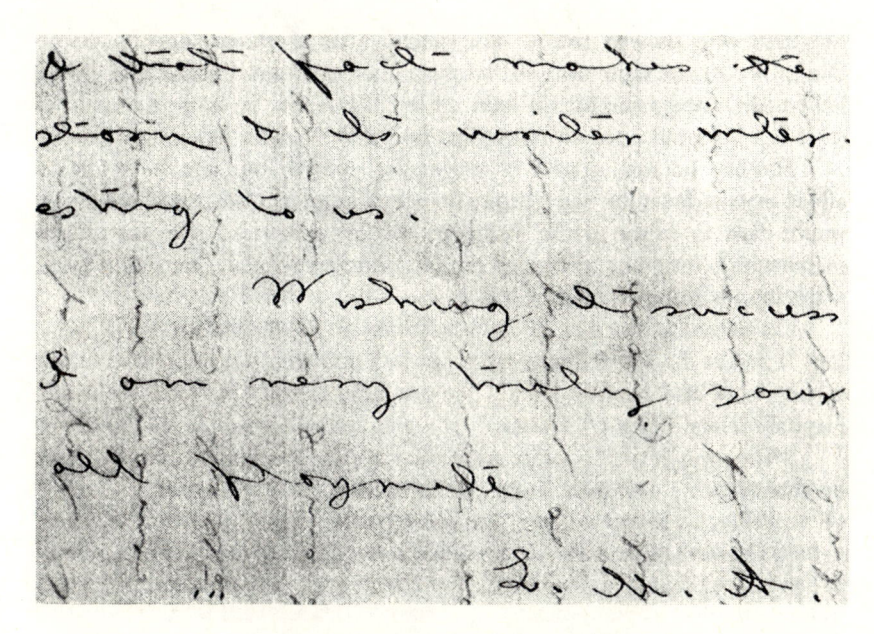

Louisa May Alcott's handwriting, 1880

She found also that she must fall to work immediately on some stories "for things were, as I expected, behindhand when the money-maker was away." In addition, the last two months of her trip, without Anna Weld's financial support, had caused the family to borrow, that she might have the experience. She was distressed to see how old, pale, weak, and tired Marmee looked. It was up to her to put money back in the Alcott Sinking-Fund, and to care for the dear mother who had spent her life caring for all of them.

She went into a vortex of writing. With apples at her elbow and the "glory cloak" around her shoulders, one story after another poured from her pen. Just the process of getting the stories neatly hand rewritten on paper was exhausting. Her hand ached, and in January 1867, she wrote in the journal, "I am sick from too hard work.... Got to work again ... for bills accumulate and worry me. I dread debt more than anything." Although the dollars for the stories were welcome, she knew that her health was fragile and that she could not keep up the present pace much longer.

A new interest appeared in the form of Lucy Stone's Appeal for Woman's Right to Suffrage. She was pleased that her father signed the petition. She was determined to be independent. If she could support herself, and hopefully her family as well, certainly she ought to have the right to vote. Here she was, almost 35 years old, and it was time to make her mark in the world. In September, Mr. Thomas Niles, a partner of Roberts Brothers, asked her to write a girls' book. This was the same Mr. Niles who, so many years ago, had been the clerk who showed her to Mr. Fields's little room at The Old Corner Bookstore. At the same time she received his suggestion, Horace Fuller asked her to edit a magazine for children, *Merry's Museum*. To both she said, "I'll try." She began at once on both jobs, but said, "I don't like either."

She had no real interest in writing for children but felt she could not afford to turn down the opportunity for a regular salary. The steady money she would earn as editor of the magazine was an attraction. She was to read manuscripts, write one story each month, and an editorial. She would wait a while before doing the girls' book.

On October 28, 1867, she rode to Boston on her load of furniture declaring, "I feel as if I was going to camp out in a new country; hope it will prove a hospitable and healthy land." She playfully called her small room at 6 Hayward Place, "Gamp's Garret."

With enough time to write additional stories, she figured that she would be able to earn a nice sum. Truly, she knew that she was a writer. The rest of the world began to know it too. She wrote home, "I am pretty well, and keep so busy I haven't time to be sick. Everyone is very clever to me; and I often think as I go larking round, independent, with more work than I can do, and a half-a-dozen publishers asking for tales, of the old times I went meekly from door to door peddling my first poor little stories, and feeling so rich with $10." She took an account and realized she had earned $1000, paid her own way, sent home some, paid up debts, and helped May.

It was a busy winter, especially as she acted Dickens's Mrs. Jarley nine times for charity, always giving life and variety to the representation. She enjoyed the acting and it was one way to contribute though she had no money.

On New Year's Day, 1868, her first hyacinth bloomed, white and sweet, — "a good omen," she thought, — "a little flag of truce, perhaps." On the 15th, she went to the theatre and on to a supper afterwards. She was off to one side when Oliver Wendell Holmes found her out and affably asked, "How many of you children are there?" As she was looking down upon his illustrious head, she thought the question was funny, but she answered the little man with deep respect, "Four, sir." He seemed to catch her naughty thought, and asked, with a twinkle in his eye, looking up as if she were a steeple, "And all as tall as you?" She uttered a mental, "Ha! Ha!"

She spent time with Father when he was in town, saw May a lot, as she gave lessons in drawing, and visited Anna, John, and the children when she could. She was glad to see her sister so happy. It made her think, "I sell *my* children; and though they feed me, they don't love me as hers do." It made her sad when she thought of Freddy and Johnny's sweet voices and that Anna could not hear them as they were, for they had to speak through the ear-trumpet to their mother.

On January 22nd, she went to the Club with Father to hear him lecture on "The Historical View of Jesus." It amused her to see how people listened

The Door Opens Wider 81

and applauded *now* what was hooted at 20 years ago. In the evening, she attended the Antislavery Festival declaring, "I'm glad I have lived in the time of this great movement, and known its heroes as well. War times suit me, as I am a fighting *May*."

At the Radical Club she ran into Frank Stearns and took the opportunity to draw him into a corner to get some information. She told him that she was planning to write a book for young people and would like to know about the game of cricket. Frank recalled the time she had said, in her father's presence, "It requires three women to take care of a philosopher, and when the philosopher is old the three women are pretty well used up." But she had also said, "To think of the money I make writing this trash, while my father's words of immortal wisdom only bring him a little celebrity."

On the 24th, her second hyacinth bloomed, pale blue, like a timid hope, and she took the omen for a good one. She enjoyed the little spring the little flower made for her.

At the beginning of February she began arranging the tentatively retitled, *Hospital Sketches and War Stories*. "By taking out all Biblical allusions, and softening all allusions to reb., the book may be made 'quite perfect,' I am told. Anything to suit customers."

On Valentine's Day, her third hyacinth bloomed a lovely pink. She spent most of the day sewing and writing, then went out to collect some debts owed her and to fetch a squash pie for her lonely supper. No one paid, and she had wanted to send some money home. She felt cross and tired as she trudged back at dusk. Her pie turned a somersault, a boy laughed — and so did she — and she felt better.

On her doorstep she found Mr. Robert Bonner who asked if Miss Alcott lived there. She took him up her winding stair; he handed her a letter out of which fell a $100 bill. With that bait, he lured her to write "one column of Advice to Young Women," for *The New York Ledger*, as several other women writers were doing.

She planned her article as she ate her dilapidated squash pie. She aimed to call it "Happy Women," and it would be about old maids. There would be L., the physician; M. the music teacher; S. the home missionary; and A., a writer. Here, in A., was herself. She had a podium in this article.

> . . .A. is a woman of strongly individual type, who in the course of an unusually varied experience has seen so much of what a wise man has called 'the tragedy of modern married life,' that she is afraid to try it. Knowing that for one of a peculiar nature like herself such an experiment would be doubly hazardous, she has obeyed instinct and become a chronic old maid. Filial and fraternal love must satisfy her, and grateful that such ties are possible, she lives for them and is content.
>
> "Not lonely . . not idle . . . not unhappy. . . .
>
> "My sisters, don't be afraid of the words, 'old maid,' for it is in your power to make this a term of honor, not reproach. . . ."

She wrote in her journal, "...liberty is a better husband than love to many of us. This was a nice little episode in my trials as an authoress, so I record it. So the pink hyacinth was a true prophet." She went to bed a happy millionaire. It was especially nice to get paid for writing about what she believed in.

Louisa soon found that the task of editing *Merry's Museum* was taking more and more time. She was, in fact, writing the entire issues. To her surprise, she enjoyed writing for young people. She wrote a story, "Poppy's Pranks," which was a retelling of her own childhood experiences so long ago in Boston, when she had been lost, and when she had fallen into Frog Pond. As "Aunt Wee," she wrote tales of childhood, weaving in many of the bits of nature lore she had learned from Thoreau. Many of the stories were founded on real events which had happened to her family. She used the same techniques she had used so successfully five years before in *Hospital Sketches*. That had been for adults. Now she remembered, and observed life anew for children's material, putting it down in her own honest, clear, and simple style. She wondered if a career could be built on writing juvenile stories.

Chapter 7

Spring 1868–1869: *Little Women*

In the spring, she returned to Concord as she was needed at home. In May, Mr. Niles again suggested that he would like a girls' book from Louisa. Father had been to see him about the publication of his own book, *Tablets*, and he carried the message to her. Several writers had written successful and popular books for boys and for girls as well. Mr. Niles wanted a domestic novel for Roberts Brothers. The experience of writing for *Merry's Museum* had shown her new dimensions of her talents. She had already written tales using many of the Alcott adventures. What could she write in book form that girls would like?

For many years she had played with an idea about a story that she thought of as "The Pathetic Family." She remembered the editorial she had written for her debut in the January 1868 issue of *Merry's Museum;* in "Merry's Monthly Chat with His Friends" she told about Nan, Lu, Beth, and May, who gave up their breakfast for a poor family—this might make a warm episode near the beginning of the book. There was also the story she had written in 1856; "The Sisters Trial" had told about a year in the lives of four sisters—the four Alcott girls. And too, there was the romantic story she had written in 1860 called "A Modern Cinderella"; that had been about Anna and John ("Nan" and "John"), with May ("Laura"), and herself ("Di")—just the three sisters, for Beth had died in 1858. Maybe this time she could write a whole book—make it even truer to life—with the childish pranks she and her sisters had shared—and the sisterly squabbles. She would include Beth so all four of them would be in the book.

She put on her "glory cloak" and pulled her chair up to the little half-moon desk Father had built for her between the two front windows of her bedroom in Orchard House. On the vertical frame in front of her were the lovely flower designs May had painted. Outside was the Lexington Road. Louisa May Alcott, author, began to write...:

"Christmas won't be Christmas without any presents," grumbled Jo, lying on the rug.

"It's so dreadful to be poor!" sighed Meg, looking down at her old dress.

"I don't think it's fair for some girls to have lots of pretty things, and other girls nothing at all," added little Amy, with an injured sniff.

The half-moon desk at which Louisa wrote *Little Women*, with mural by May Alcott (Louisa's bedroom at Orchard House). Photograph by Gloria T. Delamar.

"We've got father and mother, and each other, anyhow," said Beth, contently, from her corner....

Gazing out of the window at the whispering pine trees, Louisa collected her thoughts. From her fertile brain, the parts of her story began to take shape.

The title for her book came from her father's term for his four daughters—his "little women." In discussing this with Mr. Niles, she speculated that "Little Women" or something of that sort, might be used for No. 1, and *if* there were to be a No. 2, it might be called "Young Women."

The home she put her "March" family into was the home of her happy childhood—Hillside. It still stood next door, ready to help invoke memories of *Pilgrim's Progress,* plays in the barn, and other interactions of the Alcott girls' growing-up years.

Her own dear Marmee would be portrayed as the dear, sweet, ever-helpful, and loving mother that she was in real life. Her father she found harder to depict. As a result, Mr. March spent most of the book away recuperating from an illness contracted in the war. When he reappeared, he was distinguished by his scholarship.

Her main characters were the four Alcott-March sisters, much like their real-life counterparts. Within the first few pages, through their choices of Christmas presents and their comments to each other, she gave each of the characters a strong identity. Anna could be recognized in the oldest sister, "Meg"—pretty, domestic, and just a little envious of riches.... Louisa was the aspiring writer, "Jo"—independent, brash, and of passionate temperament.... Dear Beth kept her own name and gentle and courageous personality—for her memory could not be otherwise.... May appeared as the hopeful artist, "Amy,"—a little spoiled, but nevertheless charming and loving.... Anna's beloved, John Pratt, was drawn as the good and earnest John Brooke, the name chosen because the Pratts were from "Brook Farm."

Additional characters had to be invented. She created them, however, from among the familiar circle of friends and relatives. The personality of the boy next door came to her as she remembered two boys, both of whom she had called "my boy." Ladislas Wisniewski, the sparkling Polish boy she had met in Europe, was combined with Alf Whitman, the dependable friend. Even the name was manufactured out of a combination. She had called Ladislas "Laurie." Alf was from Lawrence, Kansas. Therefore, Theodore "Laurie" Laurence was the perfect name for her young hero. "Theodore" was a quiet tribute to the Reverend Parker. Laurie's grandfather she patterned after the remembered, kind, dignified images she carried of her grandfather, Colonel Joseph May, and his son, her dear Uncle, the Reverend Sam May.

She admitted that she had drawn Laurie and Mr. Laurence from these real people, but stoutly maintained that the others were made up. "Aunt March" was not the most sympathetic of characters, and Louisa had sensitivity. Some of that character's generous, but haughty behavior however, was highly reminiscent of the long-ago tales about the magnificent "Great-Aunt Hancock." The kindness of Aunt Lizzie Wells and other relatives also appeared in similar characters who exhibited charitable actions toward the fictional Marches.

Into the story Louisa wove the domesticities Mr. Niles wanted. The girls cleaned house, helped the poor, went on picnics, fought with each other, wrote and acted plays, and played at *Pilgrim's Progress,* just as the Alcott girls had done. Meg fell in love, Jo longed to be a famous and wealthy writer, Beth, though frail, patiently calmed the others, and Amy manipulated and charmed to get her own way.

Louisa sent the first twelve chapters to Mr. Niles; both he and she thought they were dull. But she said, "I'll work away and mean to try the experiment; for lively, simple books are very much needed for girls, and perhaps I can supply the need." In her heart, she felt that she could write the simple words, the uncomplicated grammar, and the real home life experiences that girls would enjoy reading.

The character Louisa knew best, of course, was Jo. Carefully, she tried to be honest about this Josephine March, her own mirror-image. Jo was Louy all over again—full of moods—with a hot temper—aiming to be cheerful—and always, determined to succeed. She even decided to use the Dickensian name of "Jo" that she occasionally used to refer to herself.

In the book, she included a few verses. One was given as a "pome" from "Topsy-Turvy Jo," written to amuse her father. It was a funny mixture of "Louy-Jo's" humor and preachiness, with a clever twist at the end.

A Song From the Suds

Queen of my tub, I merrily sing,
   While the white foam rises high;
And sturdily wash and rinse and wring,
   And fasten the clothes to dry;
Then out in the free fresh air they swing,
   Under the sunny sky.

I wish we could wash from our hearts and souls
   The stains of the week away,
And let water and air by their magic make
   Ourselves as pure as they;
Then on the earth there would be indeed
   A glorious washing-day!

Along the path of a useful life,
   Will heartsease ever bloom;
The busy mind has no time to think
   Of sorrow or care or gloom;
And anxious thoughts may be swept away,
   As we bravely wield a broom.

I am glad a task to me is given,
   To labor at day by day;
For it brings me health and strength and hope,
   And I cheerfully learn to say,—
"Head, you may think, Heart, you may feel,
   But Hand, you shall work alway!"

Louy relived the childhood days when the Alcott sisters wrote and acted melodramas. She still had the russet-leather boots and velvet doublet and breeches she had adored, and now they became Jo's treasures. "Roderigo's boots" were resurrected as the March sisters acted out Jo's play for their friends — and "the spirit" in the play was called up to bring a love philter — and answered:

Magic Spell

Hither, hither, from thy home,
Airy sprite, I bid thee come.
Born of roses, fed on dew,
Charms and potions canst thou brew?
Bring me here, with elfin speed,
The fragrant philter which I need;
Make it sweet, and swift and strong;
Spirit, answer now my song!
   Hither I come
   From my airy home,
Afar in the silver moon;
   Take the magic spell,
   Oh, use it well!
Or its power will vanish soon!

A replica of the Alcott girls' family newspaper went into the book. This time the members of the "Pickwick Club" were Meg, Jo, Beth, and Amy, instead of Anna, Louisa, Beth, and May.

To add the emotional pitch necessary to the telling of a story, she added bits of fiction to the real experiences. Louisa had been willing to sell her hair to help her family, but instead had lost it in the service of her country; Jo March actually carried out the plan of selling her long, full, chestnut hair to a wigmaker. Other incidents were shaped to make the story line stronger. The sisters' ages were altered to suit the needs of the tale. The story would start with Meg at 16, Jo at 15, Beth at 13, and Amy at 12. She planned to end the story with the March sisters a year older and Meg engaged, foretelling brighter futures for all. Deliberately, Louisa wove together fact and fiction to create a story that had "heart" and "spirit."

She worked steadily, and on July 15th, after a vortex of only six weeks, had filled 402 hand-written blue-lined pages. The chapter titles were patterned on the trials of *Pilgrim's Progress,* and the preface as well:

Preface to *Little Women*

Go then, my little book, and show them all
That entertain, and bid thee welcome shall,
What thou dost keep close shut up in thy breast;
And wish what thou dost show them may be blest

> To them for good, may make them choose to be
> Pilgrims better, by far, than thee or me.
> Tell them of Mercy; she is one
> Who early hath her pilgrimage begun.
> Yea, let young damsels learn of her to prize
> The world which is to come, and so be wise;
> For little tripping maids may follow God
> Along the ways which saintly feet have trod.
> — Adapted from John Bunyan

She had told much of her life story, but Louisa's instincts as a storyteller were strong. *Little Women* ended on a note that allowed for a sequel if the book should be successful:

> So grouped, the curtain falls upon Meg, Jo, Beth, and Amy. Whether it ever rises again, depends upon the reception given to the first act of the domestic drama called "Little Women."

Her task was done. The next step was waiting to see how the book would be received by the publisher. Roberts Brothers were not at all certain that Miss Alcott's tale would catch the public's fancy. Fortunately, the editor, Thomas Niles, a bachelor, did not trust his own judgment in the juvenile field. He asked his 20-year-old niece to read the story. Even after her enthusiastic endorsement (she could scarcely put it down, she was so intrigued with it), he asked several of her friends to read it. They all thought it the best book for girls they had ever read.

The author had good feelings about it too. She had had poems published — stories for young people — romances — "blood and thunder" tales — and four books. Something told her that this was the best thing she had ever written.

She was relieved and delighted when the decision was made to set it into print. Mr. Niles made an offer for the story, but at the same time advised her to keep the copyright. If the book was a success, she would receive royalties, rather than a flat sum. If it was very successful, she could expect to earn quite a bit of money from it. She said, "It is simple and true, for we really lived most of it; and if it succeeds that will be the reason of it." After seeing it in print, she felt pleased, for it read even better than she expected.

Little Women; Meg, Jo, Beth, and Amy. The Story of Their Lives. A Girls' Book, by Louisa M. Alcott, was offered to the public on September 30, 1868. The enthusiastic reaction to the book was far more than any of them could have hoped. Everyone loved it. The four illustrations by May Alcott were universally considered bad, but the story by Louisa found instant success.

Mr. Emerson, in giving his judgment of Louisa's talent, said, "She is a natural source of stories.... She is and is to be, the poet of children. She knows their angels." The young girls for whom it was intended were delighted. Even their parents read the tale of the March family, laughing and crying over the misadventures. Louisa began to get letters from her readers. They wanted to know more about the "Little Women." Especially, they wanted to know if Jo ever married Laurie. Roberts Brothers asked her to write a sequel.

On November 1, she began the second part, but declared firmly, "I *won't* marry Jo to Laurie to please any one."

She set up her schedule, figuring that she could do a chapter a day, and be finished in a month. She would start with Meg, Jo, Beth, and Amy three years older. She said, "A little success is so inspiring that I now find my Marches sober, nice people, and as I can launch into the future, my fancy has more play."

She considered not having Jo marry at all, saying "marrying isn't the only end and aim of a woman's life." Her story-sense guided her, however, and she invented Professor Friedrich "Fritz" Bhaer as a romantic interest for Jo. He bore a surprising resemblance to the gentle and understanding Mr. Emerson, whom Louisa had idolized in early girlhood. He was German, like Goethe, the 17th-century author whose romantic notions she had once imitated, and whose *Faust* she considered one of the finest novels ever written. She had two Teutonic memories to help her mold the characterization, Dr. Reinhold Solger who had lectured at Sanborn's school, and Dr. William Rimmer, May's former drawing teacher.

Louisa worked in a vortex again. Thomas Niles informed her that Roberts Brothers wanted the second volume for spring.

She took time out on November 16 for a change, as she had written like a steam-engine since the first. She went to hear a paper on "Woman's Suffrage" and enjoyed the "good talk afterward," as she lunched with "the poetess of the Isles of Shoals" Celia Thaxter and others. Louisa and Celia had several things in common: they had both been schooled primarily by their fathers, though Louisa's had been far the better education; they both had views on religion that were based more on their own views of "living" Christianity than on church doctrine; the illustrious James T. Fields had suggested that Louisa couldn't write and had wanted Celia to change some of her poetry — both women heartily rejected Fields's suggestions; and there was also the connection to Annie Fields, Louisa's cousin and Celia's close friend. They had a pleasant lunch.

The next day, Louisa finished chapter 13. She was so full of her work that she couldn't stop to eat or sleep, or do anything but take a daily run.

When the work on the second part of the book was partly done, Louisa felt the need to get back to Boston. Father was away on a tour of the West, giving lectures, and Marmee would be happy to spend some time at Anna's. In December, Louisa and May turned the key on "Apple Slump," as Louy still called Orchard House, and they treated themselves to a stay at the new Bellevue Hotel on Beacon Hill.

Illustration by May Alcott from *Little Women or, Meg, Jo, Beth, and Amy*. Boston: Roberts Brothers, 1868.

May would be busy taking art lessons from William Hunt. It was nice to have her company for occasional walks and talks, though.

As Miss Alcott, the author of *Little Women*, had become something of a celebrity, she received numerous invitations to receptions and dinners. At one of the dinners, she was seated beside Henry James. Later, she regaled the family and Julian Hawthorne with an account of their conversation. Her sense of humor may have prompted some exaggeration of the situation, but Julian highly enjoyed it.

According to the account, as retold by Julian, "Henry, who took his

Little Women

literature seriously, almost prayerfully, felt the obligation laid upon him to warn and to command, more than to comfort, his contemporaries in the venerated craft. He had probably never read *Little Women,* but he would have, as it were, scented it, and his conscience compelled him to let Louisa know that he was unable to join in the vulgar chorus of approval. He was silent during the early stages of the dinner, and his gravity deepened as he overheard the compliments which Louisa was absorbing with her wonted humorous discrimination ... success to her was a happy accident, and laudation nine-tenths whipsillabub. She laughed and smiled, hoped her good luck might continue, and was resolved to do her best to be not undeserving of it. At length Henry, from the height of his five-and-twenty winters, felt that it was time to act. He bent toward her and spoke thus: 'Louisa—m-my dear girl—er—when you hear people—ah—telling you you're a genius, you mustn't believe them; er—what I mean is, it isn't true!' Then he relapsed, spoke no more, and—er—declined the pudding."

Louisa continued the story of the Marches in the same style which had proved itself so successful. She detailed the domestic life of Meg and John, the literary pursuits of Jo, and the artistic hopes of Amy. She shared with her reader the sadness of Beth's death. In the story, Amy, instead of Jo, took the European trip that Louisa had once taken, for she felt that this suited her story plans better. Laurie grew to manhood as the three girls matured. The story had its share of "lovering," which she knew the young readers would like, even if some of their elders might not.

From her store of published poems, she brought out one that had been printed in *The Flag of Our Union* in March 1865. Then, it had been about Nan, Lu, Bess and Amy. Now it was made to fit the March sisters; it would work nicely to bring the romance of Jo and Professor Bhaer to a culmination.

In the Garret

Four little chests all in a row,
   Dim with dust, and worn by time,
All fashioned and filled, long ago,
   By children now in their prime.
Four little keys hung side by side,
   With faded ribbons, brave and gay,
When fastened there with childish pride,
   Long ago, on a rainy day.
Four little names, one on each lid,
   Carved out by a boyish hand,
And underneath, there lieth hid
   Histories of the happy band
Once playing here, and pausing oft
   To hear the sweet refrain,
That came and went on the roof aloft,
   In the falling summer rain.

"Meg" on the first lid, smooth and fair,
   I look in with loving eyes,
For folded here, with well-known care,
   A goodly gathering lies —
The record of a peaceful life,
   Gifts to gentle child and girl,
A bridal gown, lines to a wife,
   A tiny shoe, a baby curl.
No toys in this first chest remain,
   For all are carried away,
In their old age, to join again
   In another small Meg's play.
Ah, happy mother! well I know
   You hear like a sweet refrain,
Lullabies ever soft and low,
   In the falling summer rain.

"Jo" on the next lid, scratched and worn,
   And within a motley store
Of headless dolls, of school-books torn,
   Birds and beasts that speak no more.
Spoils brought home from the fairy ground
   Only trod by youthful feet,
Dreams of a future never found,
   Memories of a past still sweet;
Half-writ poems, stories wild,
   April letters, warm and cold,
Diaries of a wilful child,
   Hints of a woman early old;
A woman in a lonely home,
   Hearing like a sad refrain, —
'Be worthy love, and love will come,'
   In the falling summer rain.

My "Beth!" the dust is always swept
   From the lid that bears your name,
As if my loving eyes that wept,
   By careful hands that often came.
Death canonized for us one saint,
   Ever less human than divine,
And still we lay, with tender plaint,
   Relics in this household shrine.
The silver bell, so seldom rung,
   The little cap which last she wore,
The fair, dead Catherine that hung
   By angels borne above her door;
The songs she sang, without lament,
   In her prison-house of pain,
Forever are they sweetly blent
   With the falling summer rain.

Upon the last lid's polished field —
   Legend now both fair and true —

> A gallant knight bears on his sheild,
>   "Amy," in letters gold and blue.
> Within the snoods that bound her hair,
>   Slippers that have danced their last,
> Faded flowers laid by with care,
>   Fans whose airy toils are past—
> Gay valentines all ardent flames,
>   Trifles that have borne their part
> In girlish hopes, and fears, and shames.
>   The record of a maiden heart,
> Now learning fairer, truer spells,
>   Hearing, like a blithe refrain,
> The silver sound of bridal bells
>   In the falling summer rain.
>
> Four little chests all in a row,
>   Dim with dust, and worn by time,
> Four women, taught by weal and woe,
>   To love and labor in their prime.
> Four sisters, parted for an hour,—
>   None lost, one only gone before,
> Made by love's immortal power,
>   Nearest and dearest evermore.
> Oh, when these hidden stores of ours
>   Lie open to the Father's sight,
> May they be rich in golden hours,—
>   Deeds that show fairer for the light.
> Lives whose brave music long shall ring
>   Like a spirit-stirring strain,
> Souls that shall gladly soar and sing
>   In the long, sunshine, after rain.
>   "J.M."

Just at the end of the book, Jo speaks of establishing Plumfield, a school for boys, where they would be taught kindly and thoughtfully. Thus, Louisa gave a tribute to her father's educational theories.

On New Year's Day, 1869, she turned over the completed sequel to the publisher. At one time Louisa had thought that the title could be "Young Women," but now suggested to Mr. Niles that other possibilities might be "Little Women Act Second" or "Leaving the Nest. Sequel to Little Women," but declared that she did not approve of the pun suggested by a friend, "Wedding Marches." None of these was deemed right by the editor. But, upon its publication, with professional illustrations, *Little Women or Meg, Jo, Beth, and Amy. Part Second* was as popular as Part One had been.

Louisa was almost too exhausted to enjoy her success. Her head ached constantly, and she felt quite used up. "Don't care for myself," she said, "as rest is heavenly even with pain; but the family seem so panic-stricken and helpless when I break down, that I try to keep the mill going."

She wrote to Alf Whitman in January:

> ...Don't you ever think old Sophy forgets her Dolphus! Why bless your heart, I put you into my story as one of the best and dearest lads I ever knew! "Laurie" is you and my Polish boy "jointly." You are the sober half, and my Ladislas (whom I met abroad) is the gay whirligig half; he was a perfect dear.
> All my little girl friends are madly in love with 'Laurie' and insist on a sequel, so I've written one which will make you laugh, especially the pairing-off part. But I didn't know how to settle my family any other way. I wanted to disappoint the young gossips who vowed that "Laurie" and I *should* marry. Authors take dreadful liberties but you won't mind being a happy spouse and a proud papa will you?...

With the book finished, she had time to catch up with her mail. Horace Fuller wanted Louisa to write the entire *Merry's Museum* magazine. This seemed a bit too much for her to undertake, but she did manage to write a couple pieces.

Throughout the year, the sales for *Little Women* changed the Alcott fortunes. Roberts Brothers issued Parts I and II as one fat book, and *Little Women* established Louisa May Alcott as an author. She was grateful that she had found an honest publisher who urged her to keep her copyright, for now it made all the difference in the income she was receiving.

She wrote to her publishers:

> After toiling so many years along the uphill road, always a hard one to women writers,—it is peculiarly grateful to me to find the way going easier at last, with pleasant little surprises blossoming on either side, and the rough places made smooth by the courtesy and kindness of these who have proved themselves friends as well as publishers.

Louisa knew she had found her writing form; the juvenile field. At first, Louisa wondered if she had used up all of the events she might draw upon, but when she put her mind to it, was able to find more and more ideas welling up in her. She had also found her style; simple, true, with characters who talked like real people. She would write "from real life." She felt confident of her ability. She did not feel confident about her physical capability to carry on. She was seeing the ninth doctor now, saying, "I haven't a bit of faith in any of them; but my friends won't let me gently slip away where bones cease troubling, so I must keep trying.

Besides the headaches, dizziness, and aching bones, she got terrible writer's-cramp when she copied over her manuscripts neatly for submission. Sometimes she had to study over the original words to make sense of them. The publisher and print-setter would have the same trouble. She would have to accept the problem and manage somehow, for write she must. The Alcott Sinking-Fund needed the money. Her family needed nice things. And she was still feeling driven. But she was afraid to fall into a vortex lest she fall in.

Chapter 8

1870–Mid-1874: Fame

Louisa was very tired. Although it was wonderful to have the Alcott Sinking-Fund in good shape, she was afraid to let it get low again. She got out some of her old stories and sent them off to be published. Gratefully, she admitted, "The success of 'little women' helps their rejected sisters to good places where once they went a-begging."

She decided to give up writing the "blood and thunder" A.M. Barnard stories. Although the tales were nothing she need be ashamed of, she felt that even their mild violence and emotions were not in keeping with the image her young readers had of their favorite author.

She had another novel for children in mind. Despite the loss of her voice, and a severely sore throat that had to be "burned" by the doctor every day, she set to work. As always, once she got herself into a vortex of writing, she didn't know how to stop. She worked 14 hours a day, going with little sleep and little food. Even when not writing, she paced in agony, or tossed and turned restlessly in her bed.

Her mind was full of the plot of her story. This time she would place her honest, hearty heroine in the home of fashionable and pretentious people, and through their domestic drama show what was of value in life. *An Old-Fashioned Girl* was ready for publication in March of 1870. Louisa sighed in relief and declared, "I wrote it with left hand in a sling, one foot up, head aching, and no voice. Yet, as the book is funny, people will say, 'Didn't you enjoy doing it?' I certainly earn my living by the sweat of my brow."

Marmee and Father were worried about her health. When May was invited to accompany a friend to Europe on the condition that her famous sister go along, they told their daughters to go. May begged to go. With such urging, Louisa felt free and happy to take the trip. This time, she was to make "the grand tour" in style. There would be no invalid to cater to. Instead, the celebrated 37-year-old author was to travel with the lively company of her 27-year-old sister, and their younger companion, the 24-year-old Alice Bartlett. Having Alice with them would make traveling much easier. This sophisticated young lady spoke both French and Italian. As she had been to Europe before, she would be most helpful with the problems of travel.

John Pratt escorted the girls to New York. The train-boy, hoping to sell

Anna Bronson Alcott (Pratt)

his wares, put a copy of *An Old-Fashioned Girl* into Louisa's lap. She told him, "No thank you, I don't care for it."

He exclaimed with surprise, "Bully book, Ma'am! Sell a lot; better have it."

John, smiling, told the boy that Louisa had written the book, whereupon the young man stared at the author, declaring in astonishment, "No!"

The book was in the hands of little girls on their steamer, the French *Lafayette*. Many of them visited Miss Alcott, seasick in her berth, done up like a mummy. They landed at Brest, in April 1870, spent some weeks in Brittany, and went from there to Dinan, Vevey, and Bex. Somewhat concerned about the talk of war between France and Russia, they decided to go to Italy for the winter. May's desire for Rome decided the destination for them. "I pine for the artist's paradise," she said.

As their talents inclined them, they recorded their journey. May sketched the turreted castles, colorful countrysides, and quaint markets. Louisa, in her journal, described the white-capped women, queer little deep-dish cakes, and meadows full of blue hyacinths and rosy daisies.

Louisa and May both wrote fat letters to the folks at home, keeping them up to date on their adventures. Louisa had met an army surgeon. He had many of the same bone problems Louisa had. He too, had been given calomel medications, and had never gotten the poison out of his system. Upon his advice, she proceeded upon a three-month treatment of iodine of potash, which she declared, "Is simple, pleasant, and seems to do something to the bones that gives them ease; so I shall sip away and give it a good trial."

In addition to letters from Anna, Marmee, and Father, Louisa received occasional letters and checks from her publisher. She exulted, "A neat little sum for 'the Alcott's who can't make money!' With $10,000 well invested, and more coming in all the time, I think we may venture to enjoy ourselves, after the hard times we have all had." She went on, "The cream of the joke is, that we made our own money ourselves, and no one gave us a blessed penny. That does soothe my rumpled soul so much that the glory is not worth thinking of."

Nevertheless, they tried to be careful with their traveling money and went second class most of the time. Their spirits were merry, and after a few months, Louisa even began to feel better. She wrote home: "My bones are so much better that I slept without any opium or anything, — a feat I have not performed for some time."

More letters followed her to Europe. Editors wanted more stories, more verses, more words, from the mind and pen of the popular Louisa May Alcott. Louisa, however, was determined to rest. Still more requests came. It was tempting to write something; she would never have enough money. Her sense of humor finally impelled her to write a long verse — wherein she wrote about herself as the goose who laid the golden egg. Her father, "a mild Socratic bird," appeared, as did James T. Fields as "great cock-a-doodle . . . great chanticleer," and a pun on the name of Mr. Niles himself. This she sent back to America, asking Mr. Niles to send it on to another editor who had promised to pay for anything at all that she wrote.

The Lay of a Golden Goose

Long ago in a poultry yard
  One dull November morn,
Beneath a motherly soft wing
  A little goose was born.

Who straightway peeped out of the shell
  to view the world beyond,
Longing at once to sally forth
  And paddle in the pond.

"Oh! be not rash," her father said,
  A mild Socratic bird;
Her mother begged her not to stray
  With many a warning word.

But little goosey was perverse,
    And eagerly did cry,
"I've got a lovely pair of wings,
    Of course I ought to fly."

In vain parental cacklings,
    In vain the cold sky's frown,
Ambitious goosey tried to soar,
    But always tumbled down.

The farm-yard jeered at her attempts,
    The peacocks screamed, "Oh fie!
You're only a domestic goose,
    So don't pretend to fly."

Great cock-a-doodle from his perch
    Crowed daily loud and clear,
"Stay in the puddle, foolish bird,
    That is your proper sphere."

The ducks and hens said, one and all,
    In gossip by the pool,
"Our children never play such pranks;
    My dear, that fowl's a fool."

The owls came out and flew about,
    Hooting above the rest,
"No useful egg has ever hatched
    From transcendental nest."

Good little goslings at their play
    And well-conducted chicks
Were taught to think poor goosey's flights
    Were naughty, ill-bred tricks.

They were content to swim and scratch,
    And not at all inclined
For any wild-goose chase in search
    Of something undefined.

Hard times she had as one may guess,
    That young aspiring bird,
Who still from every fall arose
    Saddened but undeterred.

She knew she was no nightingale,
    Yet spite of much abuse,
She longed to help and cheer the world,
    Although a plain gray goose.

She could not sing, she could not fly,
    Nor even walk with grace,
And all the farm-yard had declared
    A puddle was her place.

But something stronger than herself
    Would cry, "Go on, go on!

Remember, though an humble fowl,
  You're cousin to a swan."

So up and down poor goosey went,
  A busy, hopeful bird.
Searched many wide unfruitful fields,
  And many waters stirred.

At length she came unto a stream
  Most fertile of all *Niles*,
Where tuneful birds might soar and sing
  Among the leafy isles.

Here did she build a little nest
  Beside the waters still,
Where the parental goose could rest
  Unvexed by any *bill*.

And here she paused to smooth her plumes,
  Ruffled by many plagues;
When sudddenly arose the cry,
  "This goose lays golden eggs."

At once the farm-yard was agog;
  The ducks began to quack;
Prim Guinea fowls relenting called,
  "Come back, come back, come back."

Great chanticleer was pleased to give
  A patronizing crow,
And the contemptuous biddies clucked,
  "I wish my chicks did so."

The peacocks spread their shining tails,
  And cried in accents soft,
"We want to know you, gifted one,
  Come up and sit aloft."

Wise owls awoke and gravely said,
  With proudly swelling breasts,
"Rare birds have always been evoked
  From transcendental nests!"

News-hunting turkeys from afar
  Now ran with all thin legs
To gobble facts and fictions of
  The goose with golden eggs.

But best of all the little fowls
  Still playing on the shore,
Soft downy chicks and goslings gay,
  Chirped out, "Dear Goose, lay more."

But goosey all these weary years
  Had toiled like any ant,
And wearied out she now replied,
  "My little dears, I can't.

"When I was starving, half this corn
   Had been of vital use,
Now I am surfeited with food
   Like any Strasbourg goose."

So to escape too many friends,
   Without uncivil strife,
She ran to the Atlantic pond
   And paddled for her life.

Soon among the grand old Alps
   She found two blessed things,
The health she had so nearly lost,
   And rest for weary limbs.

But still across the briny deep
   Couched in most friendly words,
Came prayers for letters, tales, or verse,
   From literary birds.

Whereat the renovated fowl
   With grateful thanks profuse,
Took from her wing a quill and wrote
   This lay of a Golden Goose.

Louisa celebrated her 38th birthday in Rome. Weeks later she learned that John Pratt had died suddenly, the day before her birthday. He too, had once had calomel treatments; after years of pain, the aftereffects brought death before he had lived out a normal life span.

Shortly after, she received a note from Mr. Niles asking, "Are you dead?" It seemed that there were rumors flying about that she had died of diphtheria; men, women, and children, with tears in their eyes, were coming into the Roberts Brothers publishing office to find out if it was true. That provided some humor to the European travelers.

Louy immediately started to work on a new book. She told May and Alice, "I shall write *Little Men,* that John's death may not leave Anna and the two dear little boys in want. In writing and thinking of the little lads, to whom I must be a father now, I find comfort for my sorrow."

She felt responsible for all of them—for Father and Marmee—for May with her desire to improve her drawing—and now for the widowed Anna and her two little boys. There was, after all, no one else to support them.

She carried the new manuscript with her on their outings and on their little trips around Italy. She could write a few pages in odd moments, and frequently had an entire chapter at the end of the day.

Into the tale she put the main characters of *Little Women,* continuing the story of the March family. Out of what she knew about Father's early Germantown school, about his Boston Temple School, and about Frank Sanborn's Concord Academy, she created the ideal school for boys, Plumfield. Here they

Frontispiece from *Little Men: Life at Plumfield with Jo's Boys*. Boston: Roberts Brothers, 1871.

would be treated with love, and taught the values of education, courage, and determination. She called the book, *Little Men: Life at Plumfield with Jo's Boys*. Satisfied with her efforts, she packed the manuscript off to Mr. Niles.

The trio went to London, where Louisa enjoyed showing her companions her favorite places and people. Now that she had money to spend on some luxuries, she bought some lovely Colport china pieces to match what Marmee had inherited from Grandfather May. On May 11, Alice Bartlett sailed for home, and Louisa began to make preparations for her own departure on May 25th.

May yearned to take more drawing lessons. Louisa was glad they had come for she felt it had been a very useful year for May. Generously Lousia offered May the chance to stay in Europe another year to study and told her, "Be happy and free to follow your talent."

When Louisa arrived in Boston Harbor on June 6, 1871, she was greeted by her father and Thomas Niles. Smiles lighting up their faces, they had pinned to the carriage a huge red placard announcing the publication of *Little Men* by Louisa May Alcott.

Her old friends in Concord were glad to welcome her back. Most of the villagers had known Louy long before she was "the famous Miss Alcott," and though happy for her success, did not fawn on her as strangers did. She could easily stroll down the Lexington Road, along Main Street, or out Sudbury Road to have pleasant talks with Laura Whiting Hosmer. Here was one widowed woman who used her maiden name professionally, for the physician and friend was known about as Dr. Whiting.

On July 1, dear Uncle Sam died. Louisa mourned with the family, knowing they had lost an irreplaceable friend. In her journal she wrote: "Peace to his ashes. He leaves a sweeter memory behind than any man I know."

On July 3, she wrote to Mr. Fields to return the $40 he had once lent her saying she could return it when she had made "a pot of gold."

Later, she said she told him that she found writing paid so much better than teaching that she thought she would stick to her pen. Louisa said he laughed and admitted he'd made a mistake.

She and Marmee felt that Father had made a mistake. William Ellery Channing had offered him some gratuitous advice in July, at which Father had ordered Channing from the house. He still came to visit Marmee, but they both knew it would probably take a couple years before the rift was mended between the philosopher and the poet.

In a letter to Louisa Wells, she indulged her wit in yet another verse, "suggested by my late afflictions with my teeth":

Parody on "The Graves of a Household"

They grew in beauty side by side,
   They filled one mouth with glee,
Their graves are severed far & wide
   By mount & stream & sea.
The same fond toothbrush went at night
   O'er each fair pearly row,
It had each perfect one in sight,
   Where are those *toothies* now?
One sleeps in the forests of the West,

> For in old Concord's shade,
> It was the first that openly confest
> The ruin *Calomel* had made.
> The sea, the blue lone sea has one —
> It lies where pearls lie deep.
> Nuts aboard ship that deed hath done,
> I think of it & weep!
> One snapped at Milan; to me, bereaved,
> No splendors can atone,
> We asked for bread & we received it
> At *St. Marc's* hands a stone.   (*name of our hotel)
> One crumbled like the Roman towers
> That tottering round us stand,
> It perished mid Italia's bowers
> The last of that bright band.
> And parted thus they rest who stood
> Together in one gum,
> Whose chomping mingled as they chewed
> Life's sweet or sour plum.
> Farewell my teeth! of thee bereft
> I know no peace nor mirth;
> Alas for me, if there were left
> No dentists upon earth!

The letter concluded:

> I think this plaintive gem may make you laugh & will do you good. My mouth is now fair to see, for the ruins are gone & a choice collection of china-ware gleams before the eye. They tumble out now & then, but I am learning to rattle them in with an unmoved face, & in time won't know which are my own & which my "store teeth." I only want a wig to be quite beautiful. Gray hair is the fashion however so I shall wait a while.

Her poor health, the damp air, and her preference for solitude, led her to the decision to leave Concord again for Boston. She hired two girls to help at Orchard House, and in October moved to a refined boardinghouse at 23 Beacon Street.

After a few letters back and forth across the Atlantic, May returned from Europe in November, realizing that Louisa was too tired to care for the family at Orchard House. Louisa arranged for the installation of a furnace, for fireplaces had provided their only warmth. It was such a joy to be able to heat the old house at last, so the family could be cozy.

In Boston, she went to meetings about the woman's suffrage movement, adding her voice to the others. This was one issue in which she disagreed with her publisher, Mr. Niles. When she asked if he would donate books for the Great Fair to make money for the cause, he refused.

In January of 1872, mysterious bouquets came from some unknown admirer or friend. She had no idea who sent them but said, "I enjoyed them very much, and felt quite grateful and romantic as day after day the lovely great nosegays were handed in by the servant of the unknown."

Boston offered a number of diversions. She went to a series of lectures by learned men, but reacted thoughtfully, "Much talk about religion. I'd like to see a little more really *lived.*"

She was made much of at literary teas. To her surprise and pleasure, she was evidently as much of a literary figure as Julia Ward Howe, Mary Mapes Dodge, and Harriet Beecher Stowe. Out in public, she noticed that many Bostonians were beginning to recognize THE Miss Alcott by sight.

She wrote some tales based on her European travels, remarking, "All is fish that comes to the literary net. Goethe put his joys and sorrows into poems; I turn my adventures into bread and butter."

There was much to do in Boston, and there were many more stories she could write. Concord had its attraction, too, for the family was there.

When she went back to Orchard House in June of 1872, she sat at her little desk between the windows and wrote in her journal: "Twenty years ago, I resolved to make the family independent if I could. At almost forty that is done. Debts all paid, even the outlawed ones, and we have enough to be comfortable. It has cost me my health, perhaps; but as I am still alive, there is more for me to do, I suppose."

She was charmed when a letter came from Allegheny County, Pennsylvania, from five sisters, Carrie, Maggie, Nellie, Emma, and Helen Lukens, the oldest 17 years old. They were starting a little newspaper, just as the March sisters had put out the "Pickwick Portfolio." So far, they had only written them in manuscript form, but their Papa was getting them a small printing press. They wondered if Miss Alcott wanted to subscribe. Louisa remembered the "Olive Leaf" that the Alcott sisters had put together in 1849. On August 3, she wrote them that she would gladly subscribe to their paper, telling them that Freddy and Johnny were very impressed that the girls were getting out a "truly paper." Louisa told them, "I admire your pluck and perseverance, and heartily believe in women's right to any branch of labor for which they prove their fitness."

The Lukens sisters wrote back to ask about the prices paid for stories. Louisa gave them some accounts of what some magazines had paid her, then told them, "For you, I will, if I have time, write a tale or sketch now and then for love, not money, and if the name is of any use you are very welcome to it. I remember the dear little 'Pickwick Portfolio' of twenty years ago, and the spirit of an editor stirs within me prompting me to lend a hand to a sister editor. I like to help women help themselves, as that is, in my opinion, the best way to settle the woman question. Whatever we can do and do well we have the right to, and I don't think any one will deny us. So best wishes for the success of 'Little Things' and its brave young proprietors."

Fame

Fame had come to "topsy-turvy Louisa." Letters came from fans asking her advice. Children brashly or shyly tried to see the author. One said mournfully, "Oh, I thought you would be beautiful." Probes into her private life were distasteful to Louisa. The nosey reporters who were told by the plainly dressed "servant" that Miss Alcott was not at home, never knew that the servant was Miss Alcott, dodging their inquiries.

"People *must* learn," she said, "that authors have some rights; I can't entertain a dozen a day, and write the tales they demand also. I'm but a human worm, and when walked on must turn to self-defence. Reporters sit on the wall and take notes; artists sketch me as I pick pears in the garden; and strange women interview Johnny as he plays in the orchard. It looks like impertinent curiosity to me; but it is called "fame," and considered a blessing to be grateful for, I find. Let 'em try it." She worked out her frustration in verse. Sometimes Louisa took her "jingles" to the Concord Woman's Club, to enliven the ritual of the club-teas. When she wrote about the trials of the town's sought-after literati, Maria Porter thought the piece ought to be called, "A Wail Uttered in the Woman's Club." Louisa read it to them with her usual dramatic elocution.

Fame

God bless you, merry ladies,
   May nothing you dismay,
As you sit here at ease and hark
   Unto my dismal lay.
Get out your pocket-handkerchiefs,
   Give o'er your jokes and songs,
Forget awhile your Woman's Rights,
   And pity author's wrongs.

There is a town of high repute,
   Where saints and sages dwell,
Who in these latter days are forced
   To bid sweet peace farewell;
For all their men are demigods, —
   So rumor doth declare, —
And all the women are De Staëls,
   And genius fills the air.

So eager pilgrims penetrate
   To their most private nooks,
Storm their back doors in search of news,
   And interview their cooks,
Worship at ev'ry victim's shrine,
   See halos round their hats,
Embalm the chickweed from their yards,
   And photograph their cats.

There's Emerson, the poet wise,
   This much-enduring man,

Sees Jenkinses from every clime,
  But dodges when he can.
Chaos and Cosmos down below
  Their waves of trouble roll,
While safely in his attic locked,
  He woos the Oversoul.

And Hawthorne, shy as any maid,
  From these invaders fled
Out of the window like a wraith,
  Or to his tower sped —
Till vanishing from this rude world,
  He left behind no clue,
Except along the hillside path
  The violet's tender blue.

Channing scarce dares at eventide
  To leave his lonely lair;
Reporters lurk on every side
  And hunt him like a bear.
Quaint Thoreau sought wilderness,
  But callers by the score
Scared the poor hermit form his cell,
  The woodchuck from his door.

There's Alcott, the philosopher,
  Who labored long and well
Plato's Republic to restore,
  Now keeps a free hotel;
Whole boarding-schools of gushing girls
  The hapless mansion throng,
And Young Men's Christian U-n-ions,
  Full five-and-seventy strong.

Alas! what can the poor souls do?
  Their homes are homes no more;
No washing-day is sacred now;
  Spring cleaning's never o'er.
Their doorsteps are the strangers' camp,
  Their trees bear many a name,
Artists their very nightcaps sketch;
  And this — and this, is fame!

Deluded world! your Mecca is
  A sand-bank glorified;
The river that you see and sing
  Has "skeeters," but no tide.
The gods raise "garden-sarse" and milk
  And in these classic shades
Dwell nineteen chronic invalids
  And forty-two old maids.

Some April shall the world behold
  Embattled authors stand,

> With steel pens of the sharpest tip
>   In every inky hand.
> Their bridge shall be a bridge of sighs,
>   Their motto, "Privacy";
> Their bullets like that Luther flung
>   When bidding Satan flee.
>
> Their monuments of ruined books,
>   Of precious wasted days,
> Of tempers tried, distracted brains,
>   That might have won fresh bays.
> And round this sad memorial,
>   Oh, chant for requiem:
> Here lie our murdered geniuses;
>   Concord has conquered them.

Louisa was in Boston on November 9, 1872, when the Great Boston Fire burned over sixty acres of Boston's business district. Like many others, she had left her room to stand at the steps of the Granery Cemetery to watch the blaze below. She was up all night, grateful that her place had been spared. She described the fire as a "very splendid and terrible sight."

More and more stories flowed forth from Louisa's experiences. Two of Boston's top editors, Harriet Beecher Stowe and her brother Henry Ward Beecher, told her they would print almost anything she wrote.

Her old adult story, *Success,* was still in her mind, and she began to rework it, now calling it *Work*. It was an expanded version of her experiences as a breadwinner, drawn from her trials as a servant, actress, seamstress, and traveling-companion. It had a strong feminist theme; how could Louy *not* write about independence? The year was 1873.

The story brought her new fans. Whether in Boston or Concord, other women who were trying to make a living said how much she had inspired them. The book was not, however, the kind of success that her books for young people were, having only a mild flow of sales.

From time to time, Louisa returned to Concord to tend family needs. She nursed Anna through pneumonia, and nursed Marmee through dropsy of the brain. Anna was so ill they thought she was dying, and she gave her boys to Louy, who was finally glad to declare, "The dear saint got well, and kept the lads for herself. Thank God!" In general, Louisa spent most of her time in Boston, with summers devoted to quiet times with the family in Concord at Orchard House.

Mary Mapes Dodge, who was to be editor of a new magazine for young people, *St. Nicholas,* wanted Louisa to write a serial story for the magazine, but Louy declined, being too busy caring for the family and not really caring much for the serial style. Celia Thaxter was to be in the first issue as well as other poets and writers for young people. Perhaps this would be a market for Louisa's stories.

On September 30, she wrote to the Lukens sisters again, glad they had received her photograph and thanking them for the five they sent, which she said made "a very pretty 'landscape,' as Jo used to say, all in a group on my table." She wrote, "You may like to know that my Polish boy, Laddie (or Laurie), has turned up in New York alive and well with a wife and 'little two daughters' as he says in his funny English. He is coming to see me, and I expect to find my romantic boy a stout papa, the glory all gone. Isn't it sad?"

Earlier, when Ladislas Wisniewski had lost all his money in the Vienna crash, she had sent him money; now she got Roberts Brothers to give him $400, for after all, he partially inspired the fictional Laurie for the book that had made her fortune, as well as contributing to theirs.

Laurie's other persona, Alfred Whitman, was living happily in Lawrence, Kansas. When Louisa and he wrote to each other they always used the names of "Sophy" and "Dolphus," after the parts they had played so long ago in the Concord Dramatic Union. Anna and May also wrote to him for they had all remained fond of the shy Alf.

She was busy with *Work*, writing three pages at once on impression paper, as Beecher, Roberts, and Low of London all wanted a copy at once. She never liked to complain when there was money to be made, but the difficulty of the writing caused a disabling paralysis of her thumb.

Father was away much of the time, for now that he was the "Grandfather of *Little Women*," he was much in demand as a lecturer. How good it was to see him happy, and earning money for his "Conversations" about the literary personages of his circle. Included in his talks were such people as Margaret Fuller, Henry David Thoreau, Nathaniel Hawthorne, his dearest friend Ralph Waldo Emerson, and his daughter, the author Louisa May Alcott.

Marmee was tired and feeble, but safe from any pressures to work. Anna, though now so deaf that she had to use an ear trumpet all the time, was comfortably housed with her two boys, Frederick and John. Johnny, in particular, had become a favorite of Louisa's. May was aching to return to Europe to finish drawing lessons, so Louisa sent her back.

Louisa kept herself busy by writing still more stories to keep the Alcott Sinking-Fund afloat. She was ready now to write for Mary Mapes Dodge and the new *St. Nicholas* magazine for children, glad to have another editor eager for her stories.

When she was criticized for not attending a women's rights meeting, Louisa wrote to Lucy Stone to explain that she was too busy proving "Woman's Right to Labor" to have time to help prove "Woman's Right to Vote."

She was supporting the family on income now, and they were able to keep a good amount in savings. Marmee, Anna, and the boys came to Boston to spend the winter with Louisa, while Father made another lecture circuit of the West.

After his return, Marmee and Father visited King's Chapel, where they had been married almost 50 years before, and where a tablet had been put in memory of Marmee's father (Louisa's Grandfather May). Marmee broke down, thinking of all the times past, and her family and so many friends, now, in 1874, almost all gone. She cried saying, "This isn't my Boston; all my friends are gone. I never want to see it any more."

Louisa met the clergyman and novelist, Charles Kingsley, in February, and declared him "a pleasant man." His book for children, *The Water-Babies,* had just come out the previous year. She said, "His wife has Alcott relations and likes my books. Asked us to come and see him in England; is to bring his daughters to Concord by and by."

When Maria Porter was elected to the school committee of Melrose, Louisa wrote to congratulate her:

> I rejoice greatly thereat, and hope that the first thing that you and Mrs. Sewall propose in your first meeting will be to reduce the salary of the head master of the High School, and increase the salary of the first woman assistant, whose work is quite as good as his, and even harder; to make the pay equal. I believe in the same pay for the same good work. Don't you? In future let woman do whatever she can do; let men place no more impediments in the way; above all things let's have fair play, — let *simple justice* be done, say I. . . .

By March, May was ready to return, and the family made preparations to reopen Orchard House. May's pictures were hung, as she planned to stay with her parents for a while.

Louisa, exhausted, almost never able to sleep without morphine, returned to Boston alone, knowing that it was imperative that she rest.

Chapter 9

Late 1874–Mid-1879: Travels and Causes

Louisa no longer had to settle for a Boston "sky parlor" in a narrow, row boardinghouse. She took two rooms at the elegant Hotel Bellevue, overlooking the north end of the Common. The second room was for May, who was to come from Concord once a week to give art classes.

Throughout the winter of 1874, Louisa worked on a new novel for girls, *Eight Cousins,* much amused and delighted that several publishers clamored for the right to publish it. In this novel she would place one girl cousin amidst seven boy cousins, and through their domestic adventures, write about the advantages of sun, fresh air, and exercise.

In January 1875, Father wrote, "I am flourishing about the Western cities, riding in Louisa's chariot, and adored as the Grandfather of *Little Women.*"

In February, Louisa was invited to attend the tenth anniversary of Vassar College. She found some of the speeches long-winded and was amused when some had to put away their papers without having the chance to deliver them. She had no intention of speaking herself, but when pressed, agreed to turn slowly so all her Vassar admirers could see her. There were groups of "Little Women" Clubs, with a Meg, Jo, Beth, and Amy. One group had encompassed the entire March family and friends, saying they called each other by those names as readily as by their real ones. They planned to have a group photograph taken, in costume, and would send it to Miss Alcott. Louisa and her sisters had pretended so many times to be various Dickens' characters; now girls were enacting the characters of her own book.

On Fred's twelfth birthday in March, Aunt Louisa wrote him a verse; though it was mainly idle patter, she did not refrain from including in it Fred's attachment to the watch that had belonged to his father who had passed away in 1870.

F.A.P.

Who likes to read a fairy tale,
Or stories told of sword and sail,
Until his little optics fail?
        Our boy.

Travels and Causes

>Who loves his father's watch to wear
>And often draws it out with care
>Upon its round white face to stare?
>>Our boy.
>
>Who rather proud of his small feet
>When wearing slippers new and neat,
>And stockings red as any beet?
>>Our boy.
>
>Who in his pocket keeps his hands
>As round the house he "mooning" stands
>Or reads the paper like the mans?
>>Our boy.
>
>Who likes to "boss" it over Jack,
>And sometimes give a naughty whack,
>But get it heartily paid back?
>>Our boy.
>
>Who likes to have a birthday frolic
>And eats until he has a colic,
>That for the time is diabolic?
>>Our boy.
>
>Who is the dearest little lad,
>That aunt or mother ever had,
>To love when gay and cheer when sad?
>>Our boy.
>
>May angels guard him with their wings,
>And all brave, good and happy things,
>Make nobler thou than crowned kings.
>>Our boy.

Back in Concord, plans were underway for a centennial celebration of the Battle of Lexington and Concord, complete with minutemen reenactments and the unveiling of Daniel French's handsome new bronze Minute Man Statue. The grand 100th anniversary took place on April 19, 1875. Louisa was there to take part in it. Marmee wanted her to go to the centennial costume ball as "Great-Aunt Hancock." Louisa flatly refused. The evening's ball, though she went, had little appeal for her after the maddening events of the day.

The women of Concord had been asked to wait on the sidelines, well out of the way, while Ulysses S. Grant, President of the United States, paraded by with the Marine Band. While the women meekly waited for their "escorts" to lead them to the Oration Tent, the celebration went on without them. At last, they linked arms and marched themselves to the tent. On reaching it, they found they had to stand, as no chairs had been provided for them. Louisa was outraged. When the platform holding the dignitaries collapsed, it seemed as though justice had been done. Louisa, in a flash of wit, remarked, "It probably collapsed because they left out the Women's Suffrage Plank."

Abigail May Alcott (Nieriker)

She determined to see if Concord might not be stirred up a bit. Lucy Stone had appeared there on behalf of the suffrage movement, only to be received coldly. "The Lucy Stone Leaguers" — women like Lucy who married but refused to give up their maiden names — found little sympathy with their cause in Concord.

Mary Livermore, another leading suffragist, had come to speak at the Concord Lyceum. She and Louisa stayed up almost all night talking. Now Louisa was inspired to set up a town meeting for the purpose of airing voting rights for women. Round and round the little town she drove in her wicker pony cart pulled by a white horse, trying to arouse interest in the meeting. To her dismay, those who were *opposed* to women's right to vote turned out at the meeting full force. They had come to create a nuisance with loud catcalls and other noises. It came near to being a riot.

Other ventures she got involved in were of a quieter nature. Her uncle Samuel Sewall served as her investment advisor. She generally left decisions in his capable hands, but in September of 1875, she heard of Dr. Rhoda Ashley Lawrence. The doctor was in need of additional financial support to help establish a homeopathic convalescent home.

A large house in Roxbury, just outside Boston, would serve admirably for

Travels and Causes 113

the boarding-type nursing home. Louisa wished to help, so asked her uncle to make several thousand dollars available as an investment in the experiment. Her own opposition to strong drugs, grown out of her terrible lingering weakness because of the treatments given her so many years ago, made her inclined to the simple, natural herbs and cures advocated by homeopathy. With Louisa's help, her friend could establish the nursing home at Dunreath Place.

In October, she went to the Woman's Congress in Syracuse, New York. Here she listened avidly to the impassioned speeches and heard Julia Ward Howe deliver "The Battle Hymn of the Republic." Mary Livermore was there and introduced the famous Miss Alcott to the assembly. They fell upon her pleading for autographs. Describing her reception she said, "Write loads of autographs, dodge at the theatre, and am kissed to death by gushing damsels." Although she did not like being idolized, she did feel the excitement of the suffrage movement. The experience affected her deeply. In particular, she was humbly pleased at the honor bestowed upon her of membership in the National Congress of the Women of the United States.

After viewing the mighty Niagara Falls, she went in November and December to Dr. Eli Peck Miller's Bath Hotel in New York. At this Hygienic Institution, for a modest payment, she had a pleasant, comfortable room, food based on a "hygienic diet," (no pickles, spices, tea, or coffee) and access to the comforts of vapor, hot air, electric, Russian, Turkish, or Roman baths or Swedish massage. She found that the other guests were intelligent people with some of her own concerns for the education and better treatment of former slaves.

Here, she put aside her writing for the most part, and enjoyed a vacation, being careful not to drive herself beyond her strength. What she liked about New York were the visits arranged by friends—to the hospital and orphan institution at Randall's Island—to the Newsboys' Home—and to the prisoners at The Tombs.

She had been invited to go to Randall's Island on Christmas Day, where the waifs put on a program in the chapel. She was particularly amused when one bright lad in gray, with a red band on his arm, recited the poem she had given to William Gill for inclusion in his *Horn of Plenty*, "Merry Christmas," by Louisa May Alcott.

Merry Christmas

Rosy feet upon the threshold,
Eager faces peeping through,
Wish the first red ray of sunshine,
Chanting cherubs come in view;
Mistletoe and gleaming holly,
Symbols of a blessed day,
In their chubby hands they carry,
Streaming all along the way.

No one knew her, so she had the joke to herself, and found afterward that she had been taken for the mayoress, who was expected.

They went on to the hospital where they handed out gifts and candy. Louisa wrote home, "There the heartache began, for me at least, so sad it was to see these poor babies, born of want and sin, suffering every sort of deformity, disease, and pain ... it was simply awful and indescribable."

From there they went to the home for the mentally ill where she wondered how the teachers, so ladylike and devoted, could lead such a life and not go mad themselves.

In a letter home she wrote, "I got home at five, and then remembered that I'd had no lunch; so I took an apple till six, when I discovered that all had dined at one so the helpers could go early this evening. Thus my Christmas day was without dinner or presents, for the first time I can remember. Yet it has been a memorable day, and I feel as if I'd had a splendid feast seeing the poor babies wallow in turkey soup, and that every gift I put into their hands had come back to me in the dumb delight of their unchild-like faces trying to smile."

Frivolity did not suit her when there was compassion and help to be given out. The new experience and the New York climate suited her, and she looked better, and felt better, and was in less pain than she had been for a long time.

Her friendships with Mary Livermore and Julia Ward Howe helped her gain entry into intellectual circles, which she found invigorating. She was intrigued by their Association for Advancement of Women, a group which advocated that women drop Miss or Mrs. from their names in the interest of eliminating feminist discrimination. The talk of writers, editors, and artists at the dinners and parties she attended was, to her, high-minded and attractive. She even felt gay enough to care about what she wore, making more effort than usual to dress in fancy clothes and adorn herself with jewelry.

Her vacation ended with a visit to her birthplace. Long ago, even as a child, she had hoped to visit here one day. In January, Philadelphia was already making preparations for the 1876 Centennial celebration. Her cousin Joseph, son of dear uncle Sam May, was being installed as minister of the First Unitarian Church in Philadelphia, the Frank Furness–designed edifice at 2125 Chestnut Street. After attending the services, she agreed to give a talk at the Germantown Academy. This was the school which had taken new life from the teachings of the little school her father had begun. The babe who had been born here 43 years before was now cheered lustily as she came up School House Lane.

She spent some time with Elizabeth Lewis, now in her fifties, who as a child had had the precocious correspondence with Father. At her hostess's home, she received both girls and boys, eager with questions about the real lives of the Alcott-March family depicted in *Little Women*. She signed autographs until her hand ached and kissed all those who pined for a warm touch from this famous author who had been born in their own Germantown.

She visited Wyck, still owned by the Haines family, but the rose garden where she had toddled as a child was in its winter bareness. She went down the road to see the place where she had been born — Marmee's "Little Paradise of Pine Place." But the house had been torn down the year before; she felt an end put to any ties to Germantown.

She returned to Boston and Concord, making many trips between the two towns as she was frequently needed at home to help care for the ailing and very depressed Marmee. Summer, as always, was spent at Orchard House.

The summer of 1876 was the centennial year for the United States. There was to be an Exposition in Philadelphia. Briefly, she wondered if she might go to see the exhibition of kindergarten work that Elizabeth Peabody and Mary Peabody Mann had designed for the Centennial Exposition. Truly, though, she had had enough of centennial celebrations with the Lexington-Concord excitement of the year before. In her journal, she wrote: "Exposition in Philadelphia; I don't care to go. America ought to pay her debts before she gives parties."

Although her own debts had long ago been paid, she always felt pushed to write when publishers offered such nice amounts for her work. She lamented, "The mill must be grinding.... My brain is squeezed dry, and I can only wait for help."

By summer's end, she had an idea, and began work on the sequel to *Eight Cousins,* although she hated sequels. In *Rose in Bloom,* Rose would return from the grand tour of Europe to find her seven boy cousins as much grown as she herself. As they matured, romances would develop and Rose would eventually choose her own life's mate. The story was quickly written, and at Mr. Niles suggestion, Louisa refrained from making the tale heavily moralistic, although she did manage to insert her feelings about temperance and women's rights. Both before the book and after, she wrote more stories. They appeared regularly in Boston publications, keeping the Alcott Sinking-Fund in constant fulfillment. The family was financially comfortable, and Louisa was able to provide them with extras, as well.

In September, May was once again sent abroad for a year in London or Paris. Louisa felt May had done her share of nursing and deserved a reward. She could only get the art help she needed abroad and was always happy and busy in her own world over there.

Anna longed for a separate house for herself and her sons. Although she was very close to her parents, she felt a need to establish her own home. "Louisa has her writing," she said, "and May has her art. I have my two boys. That's all." Father understood her feelings. "The boys are better than anything else, Anna," he told her. "Cherish them." As the money left from John Pratt's estate was not enough for the $4,500 purchase, Louisa made a gift of the $2,500 balance needed. The home Anna bought was the house in which their friend of nature, Henry David Thoreau, had lived and died.

The Thoreau-Alcott-Pratt House in Concord, Massachusetts. Photograph by Gloria T. Delamar.

Louisa's next book, *Under the Lilacs*, reflected her nephews' love of animals, as well as her own. She "studied at the circus," so that the performing dog, Sanch, would seem real. In addition to the novel, she wrote yet more short tales for young people.

Ever since rereading Goethe's *Faust* a year before, she had been toying with an idea for a modern adult story of the devil promising riches in return for a soul. When Mr. Niles asked if she would like to write a story for the No Name Series to be published by Roberts Brothers, she told him yes immediately, and set to work on *A Modern Mephistopheles*.

Secure in her room in the Bellevue Hotel, Louisa was once again A.M. Barnard, writing a lurid tale of romance, heroines, heroes, villains, and treachery. Her pen flew in the change from the simple and moral tales for the young she had been writing. When it was finished, Anna and a friend copied it for her, so that even Mr. Niles's assistant would not recognize her handwriting and know that she was the author. When the book was finally published in 1877, she was secretly delighted when friends, trying to guess who the author might be said, "I know *you* didn't write it, for you can't hide your peculiar style." Those few who knew the secret laughed with her at the many guesses as to who the author might be. Among those to whom it was attributed was her friend, Julian Hawthorne, who had now made his own entry into the field of writing. The book was praised a little and criticized a lot. Louisa decided that she would never acknowledge it as one of her works. Marmee, however, thought it one of the best things that Louisa had ever written, and read it over and over again.

May wrote from Paris that she had looked up Ladislas Wisniewski, who was living there with his mother. He had taken her shopping, just as he had Louisa ten years before. To add to the family pride, May told them that one of her paintings had been accepted and admired in the Salon exhibition at the Palais des Champs-Elysees and that another painting had been sold for a nice sum. Mr. Alcott, too, was having a successs, for his book, *Table-Talk,* was published to good reviews.

As Marmee's health failed more and more, Louisa feverishly tended her and worked on a collection of stories. The novel, *Under the Lilacs,* was still not quite finished. She recorded in her journal: "Brain very lively and pen flew. It always takes an exigency to spur me up and wring out a book. Never have time to go slowly and do my best."

She was very concerned about her mother, who clung to her saying, "Stay by Louy, and help me if I suffer too much." She wound up becoming ill herself, and for a week was in danger of her own life. She told Anna, "I mustn't go before Marmee. I must pull through so that I can get up and help her die." They were both taken to Anna's new home, where Louisa showed a little renewed strength.

A week later, on November 25, 1877, Mrs. Alcott spoke her last words to her husband of so many years, "You are laying a soft pillow for me to go to sleep on." To all of them gathered around her, she smiled, saying "A smile is as good as a prayer." As Louisa held her in her arms, she breathed her last breath, and two days later was buried in Sleepy Hollow Cemetery at sunset, beside Beth, who had been alone so long.

Louisa felt that she could not wish her back, for the last days had been so hard, but a warmth had gone out of her own life, and she said that she had no motive to go on. Both she and her father were in a daze for many weeks, and to Anna fell the task of cleaning out Orchard House, for none of them had the desire to return to it. It was too full of memories of Marmee.

The family had purposely not called May from Europe, feeling that it was best. Fortunately, the artist had a new-found friend to comfort her. Half a year later, on March 22, 1878, May was married to a young Swiss banker, Ernest Nieriker. She was 38 and he 23. Their marriage was idyllic. They adored each other. May wrote home that if her life were to end soon, it would have been worth the happiness she had had with Ernest. Louisa knew that May would never live in Concord again. She thought about traveling to Europe to see May and her new husband, but was still too desolate to make plans. She and Father went through Marmee's journals and letters, and Louisa thought about writing a biography of her mother's life. Frank Sanborn had recently written a magazine biography of Louisa called, "Miss Alcott, the Friend of Little Women and Little Men." Now he offered to publish her story of Marmee. The memories were too painful, however, and she abandoned the idea.

She was moved to write a poem in her mother's memory. It had been a long time since she had time to indulge in this form of expression, but the sadness that had overtaken her impelled her to poetry. When she later showed it to her father, he felt it was one of her best efforts.

Transfiguration
In Memoriam

Mysterious death! who in a single hour
  Life's gold can so refine,
  And by thy art divine
Change mortal weakness to immortal power!

Bending beneath the weight of eighty years,
  Spent with the noble strife
  Of a victorious life,
We watched her fading heavenward, through our tears.

But ere the sense of loss our heart had wrung,
  A miracle was wrought;
  And swift as happy thought
She lived again,—brave, beautiful, and young.

Age, pain, and sorrow dropped the veils they wore
  And showed the tender eyes
  Of angels in disguise,
Whose discipline so patiently she bore.

The past years brought their harvest rich and fair;
  While memory and love,
  Together, fondly wove
A golden garland for the silver hair.

How could we mourn like those who are bereft,
  When every pang of grief
  Found balm for its relief
In counting up the treasures she had left?—

Faith that withstood the shocks of toil and time;
  Hope that defied despair;
  Patience that conquered care;
And loyalty, whose courage was sublime;

The great deep heart that was a home for all,—
  Just, eloquent, and strong
  In protest against wrong;
Wide charity, that knew no sin, no fall;

The spartan spirit that made life so grand,
  Mating poor daily needs
  With high, heroic deeds,
That wrested happiness from Fate's hard hand.

We thought to weep, but sing for joy instead,
  Full of the grateful peace
  That follows her release;
For nothing but the weary dust lies dead.

> Oh, noble woman! never more a queen
>   Than in the laying down
>   Of sceptre and of crown
> To win a greater kingdom, yet unseen:
>
> Teaching us how to seek the highest goal,
>   To earn the true success, —
>   To live, to love, to bless, —
> And make death proud to take a royal soul.

As she began to take stock of her family, Louisa realized that her father, "dear old Plato," still needed her. With heart heavy, she wondered what was to happen with the rest of her life.

After the holidays, she retreated again to the Bellevue Hotel in Boston. She wondered what the year 1879 would hold in store. In January, she got into costume once again for the Author's Carnival, to play Mrs. Jarley at the Wax Works at the Music Hall. Her old friend Maria Porter, who was in charge of "The Old Curiosity Shop," thought Louisa was fine, but Louy felt that the old aches and pains affected her performance. She said, "A queer time; too old for such pranks. A sad heart and a used-up body make play hard work, I find."

To ensure that Freddy and Johnny would get an education, she set up education funds for them.

Much to her surprise, she received an invitation from the Papyrus Club, the group who liked to be considered the most "Bohemian" literary club. They wanted to honor a group of female authors. On February 15, as she entered the Revere House, Louisa was greeted by Dr. Oliver Wendell Holmes, who escorted her to her table. To her further surprise, she was seated beside the club's president, for she and Frances Hodgson Burnett had been declared the guests of honor. Mary Mapes Dodge was there, for many of the lady authors present were writing for *St. Nicholas* which she edited. Mrs. Dodge was meeting her contributor Celia Thaxter for the first time, each anxious to meet the other. Louisa had known both for many years, as she had Fanny Burnett. It was interesting to have in one place so many of the women who were writing for children, all appearing at some time in the pages of *St. Nicholas:* Mary Mapes Dodge, Frances Hodgson Burnett, Helen Hunt Jackson, Elizabeth Stuart Phelps, Nathaniel Hawthorne's daughter Rose Hawthorne Lathrop, Harriet Prescott Spofford—the most published of them all, Celia Thaxter, and of course, Louisa herself. In describing it later Louisa said, "Dr. Holmes was very gallant, and *Little Women* often toasted with more praise than was good for me."

Back in Concord, she had pleasant times with Dr. Laura Whiting Hosmer, whom she called her "rainy-day friend." Laura was a great comfort to her, with her healthy common sense and tender patience, aside from skill as a doctor and beauty as a woman. Louisa said, "I love her much, and she does me good."

As always Mr. Emerson was on hand to offer moral support. The Alcotts no longer needed financial help from him, but his steady friendship proved a continuing boon. With the help of Frank Sanborn, Emerson urged Bronson Alcott to set up the longed-for School of Philosophy of which he had long spoken. As the Alcotts were living with the Pratts (Anna and her two boys) the Orchard House might offer the space needed for such lofty discussions. How could "dear Plato" fail to respond to this fulfilled desire? Plans were made for a summer of philosophic discussions, with Mr. Alcott finally in his element. The School of Philosophy was an unexpected success. The first lecture was on Father's beloved Plato. While Father served as dean, Frank Sanborn took over the responsibilities of secretary and treasurer.

Even the townspeople rejoiced, for as visiting students and philosophers flocked into town, they needed beds and food, and other sundry articles. The visitors roamed all over the town, wandered out to Walden Pond, and paid calls, hoping to mingle more with the elite. To Anna and Louisa fell the task of cleaning and decorating Orchard House for the seminars and lectures, and preparing food and tea for the "guests." When Father asked why Louisa and Anna did not attend the lectures, Anna showed him a list of 400 names of callers, and he said no more.

With Father safely in the hands of his colleagues and his transcendental thoughts, Louisa thought that she might be able to leave Concord again for Boston. But first it fell upon her to tend Anna, who had broken a leg, and to manage the Alcott-Pratt household.

On Marmee's birthday, almost a year since her death, Louisa and her father went to Sleepy Hollow Cemetery on a cold, dull day, to quietly lay red leaves and flowers on her grave. For Louisa, there was a note of finality in the action. She resolved to set her fertile mind to work on the activity she liked best—it was time to start writing again. As always, she preferred Boston so she settled once again in the Bellevue Hotel. The ideas began to flow freely, and she started two books, one of them a continuation of the March family. Deliberately, she held herself back. She "dared not get into a vortex for fear of a breakdown."

She forced herself to go about and be with people. Once again, she performed skits from Dickens for a fair and the Author's Carnival, but neither her heart nor body were in her performance. She had long ago decided that dark clothes suited her best, always dressing in black or browns; now they matched her somber attitude. She found, for the first time, that Boston's hubbub was too much for her. After years of fleeing from Concord, she was happy to go back to its restful atmosphere. Her health was bad, and although the homeopathic treatments provided some relief, she never felt quite well. But she felt comfortable in the new house and even invited Frances Hodgson Burnett and Mary Mapes Dodge to lunch. "Most agreeable women," she said.

She bought a phaeton so she could drive about, as walking was now too much for her. The carriage provided an additional pleasure in that Father could use it to take his guests around the town.

A singular pleasure occurred on July 14, 1879. Louisa wrote in her journal with a flourish: "Was the first woman to register my name as a voter." She tried to stir up the women about suffrage, but found them "timid and slow." But she would yet stir up "the sacred sandbank, Concord."

As the Orchard House stood empty most of the year, they decided to rent it out. Beth had never seen it—Anna had established her family away from it—Marmee would never warm its hearth again—and May would never brighten it—only Father and Louisa remained, neither of whom had any desire to live in it again. Anna's home was now theirs. They realized that if they rented it out, space would be needed for the School of Philosophy; generous friends contributed to the building of a wooden chapel-like structure in the side yard of Orchard House, set back just a little from the house against the hillside. Here, Bronson Alcott could live out his dream. In this little schoolhouse-of-philosophy appeared some of the best minds of the day: Ralph Waldo Emerson, Frank Sanborn, Elizabeth Peabody and others. And those long gone, from Plato and Socrates to Henry David Thoreau and Margaret Fuller, were talked about. Amos Bronson Alcott held forth, and on one or two occasions, even Miss Louisa May Alcott. Nevertheless, the continuing stream of philosophy-seekers amused Louy, who wrote a verse to capture her vision of them.

The School of Philosophy

Philosophers sit in their sylvan hall
And talk of the duties of man,
Of Chaos and Cosmos, Hegel and Kant,
With Oversoul well in the van;
All on their hobbies they amble away,
And a terrible dust they make;
Disciples devout both gaze and adore,
As daily they listen and bake.

Maria Porter heartily agreed with this, saying she knew from experience while attending the sessions in the School of Philosophy, that the "sylvan hall" was the hottest place in historic old Concord.

When fall arrived, Louisa, somewhat refreshed, was planning a new book, *Jack and Jill*. Vaguely, she worked together a boy, a girl, and a sledding accident. The young people of Concord and their doings would round out the action.

She told the family, "After two years of rest, I am going to try again, it is so easy to make money now, and so pleasant to have it to give. A chapter a day is my task, and not that if I feel tired. No more fourteen hours a day; make haste slowly now." This was a new lesson for "topsy-turvy Louisa," for "Jo" was no longer young and energetic. The tall, matronly woman, with her hair in a bun, must learn to curtail her tendency to go into a vortex of writing.

Chapter 10

Mid-1879–Early 1888: Dreams

Louisa, Anna, and Father kept up a steady correspondence with May. Louisa found some of May's letters so fascinating that she arranged for a packet of them to be published as *An Artist's Holiday*. As one of Roberts Brothers best money-makers, Louy had some influence with them. They were persuaded to publish a little booklet, *Studying Art Abroad: How to Do It Cheaply*, also by May Alcott Nieriker.

Their artistic May was awaiting the birth of her first child. Louisa felt again the urge to go to her youngest sister, away from the center of the family. After considering it, she realized her poor health might make her a burden to May. She decided to try Boston again and retreated to the Bellevue Hotel to continue work on *Jack and Jill*. While there, she learned that a daughter had been born to May and Ernest Nieriker on November 8, 1879.

Louisa gave up the room in Boston and returned to Concord for more rest— rejoicing in May's happiness but with a sense of foreboding troubling her. She felt that she ought to be by May's side. On December 28, after weeks of fever, May Alcott Nieriker died. Mr. Emerson carried the telegram to the Alcott-Pratt house, tears streaming down his face. As he approached Louisa he spoke compassionately, "My child, I wish I could prepare you, but alas, alas!" She knew without looking what the telegram said. "I am prepared," she told him, and thanked him. It was for her to wait for Anna's return from Boston and Father's return from errands to tell them the sad news. May's only requests were that she be buried where her beloved husband could visit her, and that her little daughter be given over to the arms of her Aunt Louy, for whom she was named.

Ernest Nieriker abided by his adored wife's wish for her daughter to be brought up by Louisa, and agreed to send little Louisa May Nieriker to America when she was old enough to travel safely.

Louisa and Father could not sleep. She said, "He and I make verses as we did when Marmee died. Our grief seems to flow into words." She, who for so long had been ill, again was in mourning for a sister younger than herself.

Our Madonna

A child, her wayward pencil drew
On margins of her book

Garlands of flowers, dancing elves,
Bird, butterfly and brook.
Lessons undone, and play forgot
Seeking with hand and heart
The teacher whom she learned to love
Before she knew 't was Art.

A maiden, full of lofty dreams,
Slender and fair and tall
As were the goddesses she traced
Upon her chamber wall.
Still laboring with brush and tool,
Still seeking everywhere
Ideal beauty, grace and strength
In the "divine despair."

A woman, sailing forth alone,
Ambitious, brave, elate,
To mould life with a dauntless will,
To seek and conquer fate.
Rich colors on her palette glowed
Patience bloomed into power;
Endeavor earned its just reward,
Art had its happy hour.

A wife, low sitting at his feet
To paint with tender skill
The hero of her early dreams,
Artist, but woman still.
Glad now to shut the world away,
Forgetting even Rome;
Content to be the household saint
Shrined in a peaceful home.

A mother, folding in her arms
The sweet, supreme success;
Giving a life to win a life,
Dying that she might bless.
Grateful for joy unspeakable.
In that brief, blissful past;
The picture of a baby face
Her loveliest and last.

Death the stern sculptor, with a touch
No earthly power can stay,
Changes to marble in an hour
The beautiful, pale clay.
But Love the mighty master comes
Mixing his tints with tears,
Paints an immortal form to shine
Undimmed by coming years.

A fair Madonna, golden-haired,
Whose soft eyes seem to brood

The cottage Louisa bought at Nonquit, Massachusetts (old photograph)

> Upon the child whose little hand
> Crowns her with motherhood.
> Sainted by death, yet bound on earth
> By its most tender ties,
> For life has yielded up to her
> Its sacred mysteries.
>
> So Live, dear soul, serene and safe,
> Throned as in Raphael's skies,
> Type of the love, the faith, the grief
> Whose pathos never dies.
> Divine or human still the same
> To touch and lift the heart:
> Earth's sacrifices to Heaven's fame,
> And Nature's truest Art.

The idea of having a child to bring up gave Louisa renewed hope. Having spent the early part of her life struggling to get along financially, she had aimed for and reached financial security. She had thought that she wanted fame, but now found it to be more of a burden than she had expected. She hated being stared at and being asked personal questions.

When asked for a sketch of her life for a book about famous women, she felt she did not belong there. When asked for pictures she refused, saying, "My readers don't want to see Jo as an old lady."

It occurred to her that if she were to die her journals and letters, kept throughout her life, would be ransacked for bits of fact, fancy, and gossip about her life. Systematically, she began to read through her lifelong jottings and to destroy those she did not want anyone to see. Under some of the early entries she put updated notes to show how events had affected them. But what she wished to hide forever from the prying eyes of journalists went relentlessly into the fire. Having been trained since early childhood to keep those journals, she could not bring herself to destroy the entire works. She knew how much it had meant to read Marmee's journal; her own would be ready, though edited, for Anna's boys and little Louisa May Nieriker.

Her other dream, to see women have the right to vote, was at last partially answered on March 29, 1880. For the first time ever, the women of Concord were permitted to vote for School Committee at the Town Meeting. Twenty-eight registered and twenty were able to show up at the polls. At Bronson Alcott's suggestion that it would be a nice token of respect, it was agreed to let the women vote first. Louisa filed past the ballot box, her spirit proud to participate in this right. To the women's surprise, as soon as the women had voted, the judge proposed that the polls be closed. In even greater surprise, the men agreed. The polls closed, the women of Concord having cast the only votes. Louisa exulted, "We elected a good school committee." It seemed only fair as the men had decided matters for so many years. She sent a report to *The Woman's Journal*, detailing this step forward for female suffrage. Later, it was reprinted in a number of other publications. It was only one small step. The right to vote in state and national elections would still have to be fought for. But even one small step was better than none at all. She felt in her independent and determined soul that the time would come when women would regularly and rightfully cast their votes just as men did. The emotional reaction to the Concord election sparked her spirits. Furthermore, word came that Louisa May Nieriker was to arrive in September in care of her father's sister, Sophie Nieriker.

As the time got nearer for baby Lulu's arrival, Louisa was overcome with the responsibility of taking care of so precious a thing, and knew too, that there would be interruptions in her writing. But she soon put aside her apprehensions saying, "She may have a literary turn and be my assistant, by offering hints and giving studies of character for my work."

Lulu of the blue eyes and blonde hair enchanted her Aunt Louy. The spinster, Louisa May Alcott, suddenly gifted with a child to raise, found a new dimension in her life. She reacted as any parent might — pleased with the first crawl — delighted at the first real steps — and thrilled at the emerging language of her charge. To Lulu, she was "Aunt Wee-Wee."

Although they spent some time in Concord, they lived most of the time in Boston in a townhouse at 81 Pinckney Street, across from the English-style courtyard and little park of Louisburg Square. While delighting in Lulu's development, Louisa occasionally managed to write a short story for children.

As usual, the procedure was to publish the stories in magazines and later combine several as a book.

She was saddened to hear that James T. Fields had died on May 24 — the man who had spurred her determination that she could indeed write, the friend who helped her set up a school and offered his hospitality, the editor who published her work. As his wife Annie read to him and Celia Thaxter sat nearby, he had closed his eyes in eternal sleep.

It was good to see Father when he was not away on another of his speaking tours, or to enjoy the company of Anna, Freddy, and Johnny. Her nephew, John Pratt, Louisa called "my boy," just as in years past she used the term for Alf Whitman and Ladislas Wisniewski.

While summering at Orchard House, John's 16th birthday on June 24, 1881, was an occasion for games and charades under the direction of the inimitable Aunt Louisa, and for a glorious climax there was a wonderful cake with all the 16 candles and a little verse of dedication.

> John's Sixteenth Birthday
>
> A sunshiny cake
> For a sunshiny boy,
> For him and his friends
> To eat and enjoy;
> Sixteen years hence
> When he is thirty-two
> May his friends be as many
> And his sorrows be as few.

Louisa found additional satisfaction in writing, speaking, and attending fashionable teas on behalf of the suffrage movement. It was frustrating sometimes. "Hard work to stir them up; cake and servants are more interesting." Her feminist nature impelled her to declare emphatically, "I, for one, don't want to be ranked among idiots, felons, and minors any longer, for I am none of the three."

She urged her publisher, Mr. Niles, to consider publishing manuscripts in support of the movement. She challenged him, "Do you scorn the whole thing? Better not; for we are going to win in time, and the friend of literary ladies is to be also the friend of woman generally." How could he help but respond in the affirmative? She finally won him over. For Louisa, these activities were vital. She said, "I can remember when Antislavery was in just the same state that Suffrage is now, and take more pride in the very small help we Alcotts could give than in all the books I ever wrote or ever shall write."

As a lifelong dietary purist, she also supported the Temperance movement, advocating abstinence from alcoholic beverages. Feeling that a serious drinking problem existed in Concord, she took time during the visits to help start a Temperance Society there.

With all of these reform activities, her busy life with Lulu, and her occasional writing, Louisa's life was fairly settled.

Roberts Brothers put out a holiday edition of *Little Women* in 1880, with over 200 illustrations by Frank T. Merrill, a young Concord artist. Louisa was very pleased with them, and wrote to Thomas Niles to tell him so:

> The drawings are all capital, and we had great fun over them down here this rainy day.... Mr. Merrill certainly deserves a good penny for his work. Such a fertile fancy and quick hand as his should be well paid and I shall not begrudge him his well-earned compensation, nor the praise I am sure these illustrations will earn.... The papers are great gossips, and never get anything quite straight, and I do mean to set up my own establishment in Boston. Now I have an excuse for a home of my own, and as the other artistic and literary spinsters have a house, I am going to try the plan, for a winter at least.... Come and see how cosey we are next October at 81 Pinckney Street. Miss N. will receive.

Miss N.—little Lulu—was providing Louisa with a whole new life-style. And Louisa's public was given the revised *Moods, A Novel* (1882).

In 1882, another sad experience came. On April 27th, the beloved "Sage of Concord" Ralph Waldo Emerson died. How she would miss the dear man who had encouraged her and always been a support to the family. Louisa made a yellow lyre of jonquils for the church memorial service. In her journal she wrote some of her sorrowful thoughts about him: "Our best and greatest American gone. The nearest and dearest friend Father has ever had, and the man who has helped me most by his life, his books, his society.... I can never tell all he has been to me.... Illustrious and beloved friend, good-by!"

After his burial, she stood quietly in Sleepy Hollow Cemetery. Here were buried Marmee and Beth. May too was gone, and surely her spirit had joined the others here. Just down the slope was the grave of John Pratt, with space waiting beside him for his Anna. Quite by chance, the family plots of Henry David Thoreau, Nathaniel Hawthorne, Ralph Waldo Emerson, and the Alcotts were nestled on the same knoll. Already, it was being called "Author's Ridge." Listening to the pines sing overhead, Louisa knew it would not be too many years before Amos Bronson Alcott and his daughter Louisa May Alcott would join the others.

She was glad that Father had lived to see several of his works published. In October she knew that he would write no more. Bronson Alcott had a paralytic stroke. He was put to bed. One hour a day, he was propped up in the square of Concord sunshine coming through the window. He was able to force only a few words through his lips. The father was now virtually a child. It was a difficult time for Louisa. She made Father comfortable, but knew that there was nothing else she could do for him. Concord became a more and more depressing place for her. On Beacon Hill in Boston, she was in her element. There she could always write. She spent months at a time in each place, back and forth, constantly drawn to the town she was not in.

Almost with reluctance, she returned to the idea begun in 1879, *Jo's Boys*. It was strange to be going back to the "little women" and the "little men" and to be picking up the thread of their stories. She resolved to be true to their beginnings. Mr. Niles had some objections when she told him that she intended to show how Jo was besieged by annoying literary lionhunters. After all, everyone knew that "Jo" was Louisa herself. What would her public think if she objected to her treatment as a celebrity? As always, Louisa persisted. *Little Women* had been a success because it was true to life. She had built the rest of her works on that premise. She had no intention of changing that successful pattern now.

The book went slowly, however, as her health was bad. Her throat troubled her as did her digestion. At night, she could not sleep without drugs. By day, she had energy enough for only an hour or two of work. As relief, and so that the Alcott Sinking-Fund should stay full, she took time out from the book to write more short stories, for they could be written so much faster.

By January of 1883, her father was improving, but when people came to see him he got excited, so they had to deny him the company. Louisa went to Boston for a week's rest in February and for a month in March, taking Lulu with her in March to give Anna a rest. In April, she moved back to Concord. At the April 2nd town meeting, seven women voted, Louisa and Anna among them. Louisa said, "A poor show for a town that prides itself on its culture and independence."

That summer, she went to Nonquit with Lulu and a housekeeper, happy to watch Lulu take her first bath in the sea and boldly walk off toward Europe, up to her neck. She wrote to tell Mary Mapes Dodge that 28 children had come to sit round her big chair to hear her tell stories. "Such an audience must inspire even my used up wits . . . I have an eye to business, and out of their hints, chats, and pretty ways hope for the germ of the 'forthcoming work.'"

On New Year's Day of 1884, Louisa wrote in her journal:

> New Year's Day is made memorable by my solemnly spanking my child. Miss C. and others assure me it is the only way to cure her wilfulness. I doubt it; but knowing that mothers are usually too tender and blind, I correct my dear in the old-fashioned way. She proudly says, "Do it, do it!" and when it is done is heartbroken at the idea of Aunt Wee-wee's giving her pain. Her bewilderment was pathetic, and the effect, as I expected, a failure. Love is better; but also endless patience.

On February 2nd, Wendell Phillips died and Louisa said, "I shall mourn him next to R.W.E. and Parker."

In June, the Orchard House was sold, and Louisa bought a furnished cottage at Nonquit. Louisa wrote, "Restful days in my little house, which is cool and quiet, and without the curse of a kitchen to spoil it." Meals were sent over from a nearby hotel. Freddy, Johnny, and Lulu could enjoy summers at the seashore, while Anna and Louisa took turns with each other between Nonquit with the children and Concord tending Father.

Louisa had always intended to write about her father's life some day. Her plan had never been carried out. Among her short stories had been "Eli's Education," the tale of her father's early education, and "Transcendental Wild Oats," the story of the Fruitlands months. Now, however, she knew that she could not deal with his biography.

Frank Sanborn had already edited Parker's prayers, written about Thoreau, and undertaken a biography of Emerson. She was glad to pass over her father's papers when he suggested that he and William T. Harris (who had bought Orchard House) wanted to write Amos Bronson Alcott's biography. She wondered idly if there would be any biographies written about her.

At year's end, Louisa was exhausted from work on *Jo's Boys* and forbidden to write for six months. In February of 1885, she decided to try "mind-cure" treatments, but they were of no more help in curing her physical ailments than the medicines had been. She felt restless not writing, and felt as though she might get more rest if she could get the stories out than in letting them simmer away in her head without being put on paper. So, she wrote about mind-cure for the April *Woman's Journal* explaining, "No effect was felt except sleepiness for the first few times; then mesmeric sensations occasionally came, sunshine in the head, a sense of walking on the air, and slight trances, when it was impossible to stir for a few moments."

In July, she suggested to Mr. Niles that stories that had appeared in *Harper's Young People* and *St. Nicholas* might be put together for a book. In September, she suggested stories to put together for a Christmas book.

Mr. Niles had sent her a copy of Helen Hunt Jackson's *Ramona*. Three years before, in 1881, that lady had sent to every congressman a copy of her *A Century of Dishonor*. When the nonfiction treatment of the government's base treatment of American Indians brought no change, she had turned to fiction, combining her message with a romance. *Ramona* was a popular success. Louisa wrote, "The 'H.H.' book is a noble record of the great wrongs of her chosen people, and ought to wake up the sinners to repentance and justice before it is too late. It recalls the old slavery days, only these victims are red instead of black. It will be a disgrace if 'H.H.' gave her work and pity all in vain." Of Louisa, Helen Hunt Jackson had said, "Miss Alcott is really a benefactor of households."

On October 1, 1885, all of them, the Pratts, the paralytic Bronson Alcott, Lulu, and Louisa, moved into a large rented house on Beacon Hill, on the west side of the little green park of Louisburg Square. Soon the tall author and sunny energetic Lulu were a familiar sight as they often walked back and forth between the two marble statues at either end of the square. Now Louisa could show Lulu and the boys her Boston. She showed them some of the many row-houses in which she had boarded—the State House—The Old Corner

Bookstore—Roberts Brothers Publishers—and the Common which held so many memories.

How different life was from what it had been in her early days. Then, she had struggled to earn a living, willing to teach, sew, or do housework. Now she could afford to hire such help as was needed in the house, as well as provide a nurse for Father. She was supporting them all.

She was preparing a short story for *St. Nicholas,* a delightful fantasy that defied the strict diets she had endured as a child. "The Candy Country" offered all the forbidden sweets any child could desire. This was a light story to lift her own spirits as well—no serious prayer for courage and patience. One of the poems invited all to join in the fun:

        Sweet! Sweet!

Sweet! Sweet!
Come, come to eat,
Dear little girls
With your yellow curls;
For here you'll find
Sweets to your mind.
On every tree
Sugar-plums you'll see;
In every dell
Grows the caramel.
Over every wall
Gum-drops fall;
Molasses flows
Where our river goes.
Under your feet
Lies sugar sweet;
Over your head
Grow almonds red.
Our lily and rose
Are not for the nose;
Our flowers we pluck
To eat or suck.
And, oh! what bliss
When two friends kiss,
For they honey sip
From lip to lip!
And all you meet,
In house or street,
At work or play,
Sweethearts are they.
So, little dear,
Pray feel no fear;
Go where you will;
Eat, eat your fill.
Here is a feast

From west to east;
And you can say,
Ere you go away,
At last I stand
In dear Candy-land,
And no more can stuff;
For once I've enough.
Sweet! Sweet!
Tweet! Tweet!
Tweedle-dee!
Tweedle-dee!

As her father's birthday approached, Louisa watched him get weaker every day; sadly, she worried that he would not be with them much longer. She wrote a poem to him for November 29, 1885, her 53rd birthday, and his 86th—incorporating into the tribute allusions to his beloved *Pilgrim's Progress*.

To My Father
on His Eighty-Sixth Birthday

Dear Pilgrim, waiting patiently,
  The long, long journey nearly done,
Beside the sacred stream that flows
  Clear shining in the western sun;
Look backward on the varied road
  Your steadfast feet have trod,
From youth to age, through weal and woe,
  Climbing forever nearer God.

Mountain and valley lie behind;
  The slough is crossed, the wicket passed;
Doubt and despair, sorrow and sin,
  Giant and fiend, conquered at last.
Neglect is changed to honor now;
  The heavy cross may be laid down;
The white head wins and wears at length
  The prophet's, not the martyr's, crown.

Greatheart and Faithful gone before,
  Brave Christiana, Mercy sweet,
Are Shining Ones who stand and wait
  The weary wanderer to greet.
Patience and Love his handmaids are,
  And till time brings release,
Christian may rest in that bright room
  Whose windows open to the east.

The staff set by, the sandals off,
  Still pondering the precious scroll,
Serene and strong, he waits the call
  That frees and wings a happy soul.

> Then, beautiful as when it lured
> The boy's aspiring eyes,
> Before the pilgrim's longing sight
> Shall the Celestial City rise.

Louisa felt it would be best for them to spend only the summers in Concord. Even so, when the bustle of the household was too much for her, she took a room in the Bellevue Hotel further up the hill, in order to retreat to do her writing work. Just as her mother, dear Marmee, had understood her husband's need to get away by himself, now Anna and the children bore with Louisa's withdrawal from their company.

Louisa felt poorly; editors were still anxious to have stories that would bring in money; everything seemed so difficult. And she wanted so much for Lulu. She could put her feelings into a poem of prayer:

> Courage and Patience
>
> Courage and patience, these I ask,
>   Dear Lord, in this my latest strait;
> For hard I find my ten year's task,
>   Learning to suffer and to wait.
>
> Life seems so rich and grand a thing,
>   So full of work for heart and brain,
> It is a cross that I can bring
>   No help, no offering, but pain.
>
> The hard-earned harvest of these years
>   I long to generously share;
> The lessons learned with bitter tears
>   To teach again with tender care;
>
> To smooth the rough and thorny way
>   Where other feet begin to tread;
> To feed some hungry soul each day
>   With sympathy's sustaining bread.
>
> So beautiful such pleasures show,
>   I long to make them mine;
> To love and labor and to know
>   The joy such living makes divine.
>
> But if I may not, I will not ask
>   Courage and patience for my fate,
> And learn, dear Lord, thy latest task—
>   To suffer patiently and wait.

In all, she worked on *Jo's Boys and How They Turned Out; A Sequel to Little Men*, for seven years, finally seeing it go into print in 1886. The frontispiece was a bas-relief of Louisa done by Walton Ricketson. Ricketson preferred

Dreams

softness to strength, said Louisa, thereby missing what she liked best, but all in all, she thought it made her look 10 or 15 years younger. A letter to Mr. Niles, confirmed her viewpoint:

> Sorry you don't like the bas-relief; I do. A portrait, if bright and comely, wouldn't be me, and if like me would disappoint the children; so we had better let them imagine "Aunt Jo young and beautiful, with her hair in two tails down her back," as the little girl said.

Louisa knew that *Jo's Boys* would be her last novel. There was simply no strength to do an entire book again.

Nevertheless, she continued to contribute articles on the various thoughts of Miss Louisa May Alcott to *The Woman's Journal*. She kept Mary Mapes Dodge supplied with stories for *St. Nicholas,* a steady source of income for many years now. After Dodge had paid a visit, Louisa wrote to her to say, "Wasn't I glad to see you in my howling wilderness of wearisome domestic worries! Come again."

It was Lulu who first heard the stories for young people. Louisa ordered bound volumes of *St. Nicholas* to replace those worn out from Lulu's "luggings up and down for 'more towries, Aunt Wee-Wee.'"

Aunt Wee wrote a special story for her darling girl. All the principal characters in "Lu Sing" were real people, though disguised by Chinese names; and of course the Chinese incidents were entirely fanciful. Little Lulu ("Lu Sing") could not pronounce the names of her two aunts very plainly, so Aunt Louisa became "Ah Wee" and Aunt Anna "Ah Nah." In the same way Louisa introduced Lulu's names of her two cousins as "Ef Rat" (EF for Freddie) and "Jay Rat" (JAY for John), while Julia, the name of the governess, became "Ju Huh." Lulu treasured the oriental tale, among the last her Aunt Wee wrote.

As her health got progressively worse, Louisa spent months at a time at Dunreath Place in Roxbury, outside of Boston. Many years before, she had helped supply the financial support for Dr. Lawrence's Homeopathic Treatment Center; now she was to be treated there herself.

Throughout 1886, her letters had gotten longer. Formerly, they were businesslike, except when writing to the family, when she would go on at length to regale them with her activities. Now, curtailed from writing stories, she got more chatty with Mr. Niles, Mrs. Dodge, her Auntie Bond, Laura Whiting, and even a letter to one of the Lukens sisters, who had sent her a book.

She wrote a poem to herself:

To My Brain

Rest, weary brain, thy task is done.
The burden of the day is past;
Thy wage is earned and freely paid
Thy holiday begins at last.

Dunreath Place, the nursing home Louisa May Alcott helped found and where she died

There is no need for thee to seethe
   With romance, poem, play or plot,
As when stern Duty was the spur
   That kept poor Pegasus a trot.

The world our oyster was, and we
   With patience, courage, and some wit
Delved at it till our good right hand
   Armed with a pen, did open it.

We found the pearl men call success,
   A small one, but to us how fair!
Because it set our dearest free
   From haunting penury and care.

Then be content, for it is much
   To do the task that nearest lies.
Love, not Ambition, led us on
   And hers the sweetest, noblest prize.

Rest, and rejoice in thy one gift.
   For sure it is a happy art
To conquer fate, win friends and live
   Enshrined in many a childish heart.

In the summer of 1887, Dr. Lawrence went with her to Princeton, both of them hoping the change of scenery would do Louisa some good. She contacted Sam Sewall and told him she wanted to draw up her will. Louisa put her affairs in order. So that she would have a legal heir for her copyrights, she legally adopted John Pratt. She made her will, leaving her money to Lulu, Freddy, Johnny, and Anna, naming Anna executrix. Everything was duly signed on July 10, 1887.

When "Aunt Wee-Wee" died, Lulu should return to her father in Europe. Fred and John were grown and making their own ways in the world; it was reassuring to know they were both working for Roberts Brothers, the firm that had been so good to her.

Louisa returned to Dunreath Place in September. Nearby, also in Roxbury, was the New England Hospital for Women and Children, which had been founded by another friend of Louisa's, Dr. Marie Elizabeth Zakrzewska. Louisa's own cousin, Lucy Sewall, was a doctor at this hospital. Many years before, it had been Lucy who had delivered Anna's second son John whom Louisa had legally adopted.

An idea began to form in her mind. She wrote to a friend, telling about how "real life" gave her ideas for fiction, "Any paper, any pen, any place that is quiet suit me.... Now ... I ... can write but two hours a day.... While a story is underway I live in it, see the people, more plainly than real ones round me, hear them talk.... Material for the children's tales I find in the lives of the little people about me.... In the older books the events are mostly from real life, the strongest the truest...."

She combined what she knew about the two hospitals she had helped; it was the last story she would create. "A Free Bed" was the story of two older women, the complaining Mrs. Moody, and the sick but cheerful Mrs. Cheerable. A "blessed Dr. Z." had encouraged Mrs. Cheerable to give money so there could be a "free bed" for poor people who were ill but couldn't afford to stay in the hospital. But Mrs. Cheerable did more; she kept in touch with the women, girls, and children who used the bed. By visiting them, and sending notes and little gifts, her life was enriched by the new friends she made.

On eleven and a half handwritten pages, Louisa painfully scribbled the story. Louisa herself, of course, was the Mrs. Cheerable who had found satisfaction in being able to help others.

The story was written to teach a lesson about unselfishness and helpfulness so she sent it off to a Boston minister who published a religious magazine. She was exhausted.

But still, she wrote another poem, having, "'fell into poetry,' as Silas Wegg says," (from Dickens's *Our Mutual Friend*), hers being inspired by "a little poem found under a good soldier's pillow in the hospital," which she set up as a final prayer and acceptance of the death that surely would come soon:

Last Years

I am no longer eager, bold and strong,
   All that is past;
I am ready not to do
   At last—at last.
My half-day's work is done,
   And this is all my part.
I give a patient God
   My patient heart.

Louisa's ailments were always with her; the vertigo, the dyspepsia, the lack of appetite, and the insomnia. She had an enlarged spleen and a sluggish liver. Her leg ached most of the time, and she had long ago lost the use of her right thumb and been forced to learn to write with her left hand. Now though, she had little strength to write. In fact, the doctor forbad her to do so, telling her she could live a few years longer only if she rested. Although her mind created more tales, to work them into finished stories would be too much for her frail body.

The only thing she could do was collect volumes of previously published stories to add to those already published in volume form. In all, she would now have *Kitty's Class Day* (formerly *Proverb Stories*) in which she had put a very early story "The Baron's Gloves" as "a sample of the romantic rubbish 'Jo March' wrote in the beginning"), *Aunt Jo's Scrapbag* (in six volumes), *Silver Pitchers, Spinning Wheel Stories, Lulu's Library* (in three volumes), and her latest effort, scheduled for publication soon, *A Garland for Girls*.

Over the years, her works had created warm responses in her readers. Throughout the country, she heard from many groups of four girls, telling her they had organized their own "March Family ... of Meg, Jo, Beth, and Amy." Age seemed not to matter, for the letters came from elementary school, high school, and college-aged girls.

She heard from girls, boys, and adults, many of them asking her advice about writing. When she could, she tried to share some insights into the writing process with them.

* * *

Be a great reader.

* * *

I never had a study. Any pen and paper do, and an old atlas on my knee is all I want. Carry a dozen plots in my head, and think them over when in the mood. Sometimes keep one for years, and suddenly find it all ready to write. Often lie awake and plan whole chapters word for word, then merely scribble them down as if copying.

* * *

One person's method is no rule for another. Each must work in his own way; and the only drill needed is to keep writing and profit by criticism. Mind grammer

[sic], spelling, and punctuation, use short words, and express as briefly as you can your meaning. Young people use too many adjectives, and try to "write fine." The strongest simplest words are best, and no *foreign* ones if it can be helped.

* * *

Write and print if you can; if not, still write, and improve as you go on. Read the best books, and they will improve your style. See and hear good speakers and wise people, and learn of them. Work for twenty years, and then you may some day find that you have a style and place of your own, and can command good pay for the same things no one would take when you were unknown.

* * *

I know little of poetry, as I never read modern attempts, but advise any young person to keep to prose, as only once in a century is there a true poet; and verses are so easy to do that it is not much help to write them.

* * *

I read anything that attracts me. Never study. Have no special method of writing except to use the simplest language, take every day life and make it interesting and try to have my characters alive. I take many heroes and heroines from real life — much truer than any one can imagine.

* * *

Write of things you understand. Sentiment is apt to become sentimentality; and sense is always safer, as well as better drill, for young fancies and feelings.

* * *

I give you for a motto Michael Angelo's wise words: "Genius is infinite patience."

* * *

Being mortal we cannot expect to fly, and must content ourselves with a long, slow climb, glad if each year we are one step higher than the last.

* * *

Keep hoping and trying, and be sure the strength and light will come, for no sincere effort is ever wasted.

* * *

Louisa lived mainly at Dunreath Place now. About all she could do was keep up with her correspondence — to her Auntie Louisa Caroline Greenwood Bond, who had received the first copy of a new book as Marmee's representative, Laura Whiting Hosmer, John Pratt Alcott, Mary Mapes Dodge, Maria Porter, dear sister Anna Pratt, and Ellen Emerson to whom she dedicated *Lulu's Library II* in memory of the happy old times when some of the stories were told to Ellen, Beth, and May. The new stories were told to Lulu who, according to Aunt Wee, inherited her mother's love for pen and ink sketches of all kinds.

She missed the jolly company of the household, especially of her namesake, little Lulu, who was now eight years old. As often as she could, she traveled to see them, and to visit with her father, still lying placidly in bed in the Louisburg Square house.

Early in 1888 she wrote another poem about him:

The Last of the Philosophers

Like Bunyon's pilgrim with his pack,
   Forth went the dreaming youth
To seek, to find and make his own
   Wisdom, virtue and truth.
Life was his book, and patiently
   He studied each hard page,
By turns reformer, outcast, priest,
   Philosopher and sage.

Christ was his master, and he made
   His life a gospel sweet.
Plato and Pythagoras in him
   found a disciple.
The noblest and best his friends,
   Faithful and fond, though few;
Eager to listen, learn and pay
   The love and honor due.

Power and place, silver and gold,
   He neither asked, nor sought;
Only to serve his fellow men
   With heart and hand and thought.
The world passed by, nor cared to take
   The treasure he could give,
He sat apart, content to wait
   And beautifully live.

A pilgrim still and in his pack
   No sins to burden and oppress,
But learning, morals, piety,
   To teach, to warn, to bless.
Unsaddened by long, lonely years
   Of want, neglect and wrong,
His soul to him a kingdom was,
   Steadfast, serene and strong.

Magnanimous and pure his life,
   Tranquil its happy end.
Patience and Peace his handmaids were,
   Death an immortal friend.
For him no monuments need rise,
   No laurels mark his pall.
The memory of the good and wise
   Outshines, outlives them all.

On March 1, 1888, she sat beside her father, knowing in her heart that he was soon to die. "Father," she said, "What are you thinking of?" He pointed up. "Up there; come with me." "I wish I could," she told him. He kissed her goodbye. After touching the wrinkled hand in comfort she rushed to the carriage. In her distress, she forgot to put on her shawl.

Only a short time before, she had been told that if she spent one more year in "Saint's Rest" she would surely have 20 more years ahead of her. But, in her frail condition, the cold and dampness affected her immediately and she was put to bed. Within hours, she had developed chills and fever, and sunk into unconsciousness. The doctor speculated that she had either meningitis or apoplexy. Louisa, only 55, was clearly dying. As she struggled for breath during her last days, the family kept from her the knowledge that Bronson Alcott passed away on March 4th.

Two days later, on March 6, 1888, at 3:30 in the morning, Louisa May Alcott died. She slipped peacefully into death from a deep, dreaming sleep. She and the father whose birthday she shared, were buried at Sleepy Hollow Cemetery in the family plot on Author's Ridge.

Among her papers the family found a poem obviously written some time during the last years. She, who had chosen not to marry, who had supported the family, who had written about other people's romances, had her own thoughts about love:

Love

A little maid, with eager eyes
    The fairy tale I read,
Of lovely princess slumbering
    Upon her splendid bed,
Until the prince came thro' the wood,
    Fighting his way to bliss,
The chosen one, brave, fair, and true,
    To wake her with a kiss.

I wondered, smiling as I read,
    If magic spell or art
Would ever bring a prince to wake
    My innocent young heart.
For yearning soul and busy brain
    Took the sweet story home,
And still asleep, began to ask
    "When will the lover come?"

It's sleeping yet and asking yet,
    This hungry heart of mine,
For never through the thicket came
    Passion, the prince divine.
Faces have peered above the thorns,
    Wistful and good and true,

> But dreaming heart still softly sighed,
> "I cannot wake for you."
>
> Ideal heroes flitted by,
> Faded, and were forgot;
> For never came my Galahad,
> Never my Launcelot.
> Gold could not bribe, nor pleasure win
> To any empty bliss,
> The lips that whispered, "Dear, awake!"
> Brought not the magic kiss.
>
> It is not that this heart of mine
> Is narrow, hard, or cold,
> For other loves have filled it up
> Fuller than it can hold.
> It longs to bless, to guard, to give;
> It aches for every pain;
> It strives to wash its sins away
> With pity's tender rain.
>
> Sorrow has laid a chastening touch
> Upon its willful pride;
> Pain, care, neglect, and bitter loss
> Have shown life's darker side.
> It's weary now, and longs for rest;
> Longs for its share of light,
> Before it feels that frost of age
> And says to life, "Good night!"
>
> Oh, foolish heart; Oh doubting soul;
> The sweet tale still is true.
> The hour will strike and thro' the thorns
> Great love will come to you.
> Be worthy, hope, believe, and wait;
> The long sleep soon will end
> In a divine world shalt thou
> Find the immortal friend.

Louisa had destroyed letters and parts of her journal that she wanted to keep private. To her family, she showed the vulnerable aspects of her nature. Yet, she, like the entire Alcott family, had a lifelong habit of keeping diaries and journals. Thus, she left a rich vein of material about herself.

Louisa May Alcott—as a girl, as a young lady, and as a mature woman—had many dreams. By the time of her death, she had attained financial success, achieved independence, and was accorded fame.

She was a loving and devoted daughter, sister, aunt, and family supporter. She filled roles as seamstress, housemaid, teacher, army nurse, traveling-companion, amateur actress and monologist, fledgling writer, and finally as professional author.

As a humanist, she actively participated, in her century, as an abolitionist, suffragist, and feminist.

Louisa May Alcott's grave on Author's Ridge in Sleepy Hollow Cemetery, Concord, Massachusetts. As a veteran of the Civil War, she is entitled to have the American flag permanently displayed on her grave. Photograph by Gloria T. Delamar.

Her spirit could go to its final rest in peace, for her life had "heart" and "meaning."

In her books, she touched a wellspring of human understanding that spanned the centuries. One thing she gained was something she never dreamed of—Louisa May Alcott achieved immortality.

II.
Little Women — The Book

Chapter 11

1868–Now: Reviews and Critical Analyses

It is probably a fair assumption that readers of this reference are already familiar with the story of *Little Women*. It is, however, a "girls' book." Most educated men know Louisa May Alcott's name, but few ever read any of her books when they were boys, including this classic. It may be more familiar in its several movie and television productions, where the "female story" label is less appended. (Chapter 7 details the writing of *Little Women*.)

After Louisa had finished writing the manuscript and taken it to the publisher for reaction, she recorded in her journal in August 1868, "Roberts Bros. made an offer for the story, but at the same time advised me to keep the copyright; so I shall." In a note she added 17 years later is: "An honest publisher and a lucky author, for the copyright made her fortune, and the 'dull book' was the first golden egg of the ugly duckling. 1885. —L.M.A."

Thomas Niles, editor and literary representative for Roberts Brothers, had suggested to Louisa that although he could pay her an outright sum for the book, it might be to her advantage to retain the copyright and acccept a royalty of 6.66 percent on each copy sold. (The 6.66 percent figure was calculated by Madeleine B. Stern in her 1950 biography of Alcott, based on later payments to Louisa on *Little Women*.) The outright payment for the book that took two and a half months to write would have exceeded her pay for a full year of work as editor of *Merry's Museum*. It was Mr. Niles who had persuaded Louisa to try writing a girls' book (her previous juveniles had been stories); he had faith in her; she made the decision to have faith in herself and declined the outright payment in favor of the royalty agreement.

Little Women was made available to the public on September 30, 1868, and although originally advertised at $1.25, advance interest pushed the price up to $1.50. The initial 2000 copies printed sold out very quickly, the book was declared a popular success, and the author made her name. Not all reviews were complimentary, however, and not all social commentators, throughout the years since the book's publication, have found it to be without flaws. (Full details for sources are in the related listings herein: Chronological Bibliography of Louisa May Alcott's Works; General Bibliography.)

"MAKE THEIR ACQUAINTANCE; FOR AMY WILL BE FOUND DELIGHTFUL, BETH VERY LOVELY; MEG BEAUTIFUL, AND JO SPLENDID!" — *The Catholic World.*

LITTLE WOMEN. By LOUISA M. ALCOTT. In Two Parts. Price of each $1.50.

"Simply one of the most charming little books that have fallen into our hands for many a day. There is just enough of sadness in it to make it true to life, while it is so full of honest work and whole-souled fun, paints so lively a picture of a home in which contentment, energy, high spirits, and real goodness make up for the lack of money, that it will do good wherever it finds its way. Few will read it without lasting profit." — *Hartford Courant.*

"LITTLE WOMEN. By Louisa M. Alcott. We regard these volumes as two of the most fascinating that ever came into a household. Old and young read them with the same eagerness. Lifelike in all their delineations of time, place, and character, they are not only intensely interesting, but full of a cheerful morality, that makes them healthy reading for both fireside and the Sunday school. We think we love "Jo" a little better than all the rest, her genius is so happy tempered with affection." — *The Guiding Star.*

The following verbatim copy of a letter from a "little woman" is a specimen of many which enthusiasm for her book has dictated to the author of "Little Women:"—

———— March 12, 1870.

DEAR JO, OR MISS ALCOTT,— We have all been reading "Little Women," and we liked it so much I could not help wanting to write to you. We think *you* are perfectly splendid; I like you better every time I read it. We were all so disappointed about your not marrying Laurie; I cried over that part,— I could not help it. We all liked Laurie ever so much, and almost killed ourselves laughing over the funny things you and he said.

We are six sisters and two brothers; and there were so many things in "Little Women" that seemed so natural, especially selling the rags.

Eddie is the oldest; then there is Annie (our Meg), then Nelly (that's me), May and Milly (our Beths), Rosie, Rollie, and dear little Carrie (the baby). Eddie goes away to school, and when he comes home for the holidays we have lots of fun, playing cricket, croquet, base ball, and every thing. If you ever want to play any of those games, just come to our house, and you will find plenty children to play with you.

If you ever come to ————, I do wish you would come and see us. —We would like it so much.

I have named my doll after you, and I hope she will try and deserve it.

I do wish you would send me a picture of you. I hope your health is better, and you are having a nice time.

If you write to me, please direct ———— Ill. All the children send their love.

With ever so much love, from your affectionate friend,

NELLY.

Mailed to any address, postpaid, on receipt of the advertised price.

ROBERTS BROTHERS, PUBLISHERS,
Boston.

Advertisement for *Little Women*, from *Little Men*. Boston: Roberts Brothers, 1871

Among the early comments were:

Miss Alcott's new juvenile is an agreeable little story, which is not only very well adapted to the readers for whom it is especially intended, but may also be read with pleasure by older people....

The Nation, October 22, 1868

Reviews and Critical Analysis

> ...Louise (sic) M. Alcott . . exceedingly sprightly, wide-awake volume where a graphic account of a year in the lives of four sisters is depicted.... The story of their adventures is sure to interest the class of readers for whom it is designed.
>
> *The Youth's Companion,* October 22, 1868

> ...The heroines (there are four of them) are the "little women" of the title, ranging from twelve to sixteen years years of age, each interesting in her way, and together enacting the most comical scenes and achieving most gratifying results.... The book is most originally written. It never gets commonplace or wearisome, though it deals with the most ordinary every-day life.... The writer almost promises, as the story is concluded, to follow this volume with others of similar character. We sincerely hope she will.
>
> *Arthur's Home Magazine,* December 1868

Almost universally, May Alcott's illustrations in the first edition were condemned as "indifferently executed," and the artist was charged with "the fact that she has not closely studied the text which she illustrates." Later editions carried the work of other illustrators, or had no illustrations at all.

Interesting remarks about what is actually a very moral book came from an early unknown critic (who also made some erroneous conclusions about previous "books"):

> About Part One: Louisa May Alcott is a very spritely and fascinating writer, and her sister, May Alcott, always makes beautiful pictures to illustrate the books. Their books and stories are always interesting and instructive about everyday life. They are not religious books, should not be read on Sunday, and are not appropriate for the Sunday School. This is the character of the book before us. It is lively, entertaining, and not harmful.
>
> *Golden Hours,* 1868

> Part Two: ...But it is not a story conveying any religious lesson.... The only Gospel preached is material goodness; the only God recognized is the maker of the universe, not the Author of our redemption .. it is not a book to be read on Sunday.
>
> *Golden Hours,* 1869

Other comments about Part Two are:

> . . The first series was one of the most successful ventures to delineate juvenile womanhood ever attempted; there was a charm and attractiveness, a naturalness and grace, about both characters and narrative, that caused the volume to become a prime favorite with everybody. This issue continues the delight — it is the same fascinating tale, extended without weakening, loading the palate without sickishness. The varied emotions of the young heart are here caught and transfixed so that we almost note the expression of face upon the printed page. Surely Miss Alcott has wonderful genius for the portraiture, as years ago, we knew she had for the entertainments of children.
>
> *The Commonwealth,* April 24, 1869

> ...It is enough to say that the second part perfectly fulfills the promise of the first, and one leaves it with the sincere wish that there were to be a third and a fourth; indeed he wishes he need never part company with these earnest, delightful people.... Miss Alcott could crave no richer harvest than that which is sure to come from her sowing. Thousands of young people will read her story of these healthy, happy homes, and their standard of home and happiness must in many cases be raised. This is a blessed thing to accomplish in these days of extravagance, when the highest ideal of home is more and more seldom realized.
> *National Anti-Slavery Standard,* May 1, 1869

> *Little Women, Part II,* by Louise (sic) M. Alcott, is a rather mature book for the little women, but a capital one for their elders. It is natural, and free from that false sentiment which pervades too much of juvenile literature.... But do not her children grow rather rapidly? They are little children in Part First, at the breaking out of the civil war (sic). They are married, settled, and with two or three children of their own before they get through Part Second.
> *Harper's New Monthly Magazine,* August 1869

Later the two parts of *Little Women* were published as a matched set, and eventually as a single edition. It is seen as one book today in the United States. In Canada and England it is published as two volumes, *Little Women* and *Good Wives.*

While Louisa continued to earn handsome royalty checks for *Little Women,* her career continued with more short stories, book collections of those stories, and serialization and subsequent book editions of juvenile novels. The sequels to *Little Women (Little Men* and *Jo's Boys)* did well enough, but her place in literary history is founded on the first book. As reviewers continued to comment on the book, publishers, regardless of whether the reviews were positive or negative, continued to sell their printings.

Henry James had a few words to say about Louisa's works. When *Moods* came out (1865) he had written in *The North American* that the author was ignorant of human nature. He did allow, however, that with the exception of two or three celebrated names, no one in the country except she could write a novel above the average. He could hardly have endeared himself to Louisa by referring to *Moods* as "Dumps." In 1875, James wrote a review of *Eight Cousins,* which he declared destroyed the very moral-educational values, which in fact, the book was espousing. More than one critic has concluded that James, then 32 and struggling to keep himself financially solvent, was probably jealous of Louisa, who at 43, was at the height of her success. His introductory words to the latter review sum up not only his opinion of Louisa's work, but his Old World chauvinism toward England's former territory.

> It is sometimes affirmed by the observant foreigner, on visiting these shores, and indeed by the venturesome native, when experience has given him the power of invidious comparison, that American children are without a certain charm usually possessed by the youngsters of the Old World. The little girls are apt to be pert

and shrill, the little boys to be aggressive and knowing; both the girls and boys are accused of lacking, or of having lost, the sweet, shy bloom of ideal infancy. If this is so, the philosophic mind desires to know the reason of it, and when in the course of its enquiry the philosophic mind encounters the tales of Miss Alcott, we think it will feel the momentary impulse to cry Eureka! Miss Alcott is the novelist of children—the Thackeray, the Trollope, of the nursery and the schoolroom. She deals with the social questions of the child-world, and like Thackeray and Trollope, she is a satirist. She is extremely clever, and we believe, vastly popular with infant readers...." (The rest of the review thoroughly lambasts *Eight Cousins,* comparing it unfavorably with the *Rollo* books.)

The Nation, October 14, 1875

Louisa died in 1888, having adopted Anna's son, John Pratt, so that he could legally renew her many copyrights and distribute continuing royalties among the immediate family—May's daughter, Lulu Nieriker; his mother, Anna; his brother, Frederick; and himself. Louisa's copyright protection came under the Copyright Act of 1831 which allowed for an initial twenty-eight years plus a renewal of an additional fourteen years to the author, widow, or children of the author. Thus the copyright on *Little Women* would last until 1910/11 (the book having come out in 1868 and 1869). A memorial article about Louisa in *The Ladies' Home Journal,* May 1888, was followed with an item discussing her copyrights, saying there was much speculation about them. At this point, it stated, Roberts Brothers had paid her about $300,000 for her share of profits on her book. (The comment is singular, so does not clarify if *Little Women* is meant or all of her books.) Part of the text read, "Mr. Lee, of the old publishing firm of Lee and Shepard, insists that when the present copyrights expire the works will become common property, and he acknowledges that there will be a general scramble among publishers to get out cheap editions. Messrs. Roberts Bros. objected to discussing the matter."

That same issue of *The Ladies' Home Journal* carried an item that read, "Miss Alcott's famous books for girls are now furnished in a much more expensive style of binding than formerly; never the less we continue to give any one of these volumes for only 8 subscribers, or for only 6 subscribers and 25 cents extra. see (sic) premium supplement, 16 pages, sent to any address on receipt of request for it."

After Ednah Cheney wrote *Louisa May Alcott, The Children's Friend,* the designation clung. The works of "the children's friend" continued to sell well, both previously published, and previously unpublished ones. An autobiographical piece that Louisa had written, "Recollections of My Childhood," had several publications in 1888, 1889, and 1890.

In 1893, Anna Pratt put together some of the plays she and Louisa had written as teenagers around 1848 and published them as *Comic Tragedies Written by "Jo" and "Meg" and Acted by the "Little Women."* An anonymous reviewer was not very favorably impressed:

> ...When the Alcott girls were young and dwelt in Concord, and were living through those events that afterward were narrated in *Little Women,* they were all stagestruck in a sort of rural, harmless, way, and, either in the garret or barn, they had frequent dramatic performances... Where these children got their crude knowledge of the theatrical stage and their dramatic instincts it is hard to say.... As a sort of companion to the late Miss Alcott's works, these seven amateur plays are now published. Most of them were written by Louisa Alcott herself, and they are all alike.... Blood is shed in almost every scene, the course of true love never does run smooth, and the language is appropriately stilted and bombastic. The subjects of the plays and some of their theatrical devices suggest that the girls must have had access to some bound volumes of real plays, quite apart from Shakespeare, for there is nothing at all Shakespearean in these infantile works.... This volume, at its best, is a curiosity which may attract the notice of people whose childhood was made brighter by the *Little Women* books.
> *The New York Times,* November 5, 1893, p. 19

"Lu Sing," the story that Louisa had written for Lulu Nieriker, was kept by her niece until December 1902, when it appeared in *St. Nicholas.* ("Lu Sing" is described in Chapter 10).

Although some of the better-known stories enjoyed republication, it was not until later in the 20th century that revived interest in Alcott from the scholarly point of view caused the republication of previously unpublished ones. (See Chapter 15).

It was *Little Women* that saw the most republications. Reviews and commentaries, especially on *Little Women,* continued to be written and continued to engender responsive interest. Thus is the life of a classic.

The New York Times Saturday Review of January 8, 1898, in an anonymous article titled "Books That Separate Parents from Their Children" stated, "...in a symposium of mothers, a gentlewoman was brave enough to say: 'I am sorry to be obliged to be sorry that Miss Alcott ever wrote.' It seemed a hard saying, but it was a wise one."

In response, a reader wrote to the editor:

> ...Miss Alcott's were among the condemned, notwithstanding when her charming stories were first published mothers and daughters united in reading them with pleasurable interest. She was the pioneer in the delineation of sprightly young-girl life, brim full of animal spirits, yet overflowing with a desire to be true and brave and helpful. There is a pure, healthy tone to all of her books, embodying, as they do, examples of unselfishness, cheerfulness, and hopefulness in spite of disappointments and misfortunes. I am sure no young girl could read them without a more eager desire to take up her share of life's duties, whether at the fireside or elsewhere. Certainly they are more worthy of being read than numerous other books that have been recommended in later letters upon literature for children....—M.L.S.

The New York Times Saturday Review of Books and Art, February 26, 1898, p. 142

In 1900, another unfavorable comparison was made between *Little Women* and the *Rollo* books of the 1840's.

> ...The world of *Little Women* is a far more sophisticated world than that of *Rollo*, a bigger one, a rather braver one, and just as sweet and clean. But instead of unquestioning self-respect, its personages display that rude self-assertion which has generally tainted the lower middle class of English-speaking countries. — Barrett Wendell
>
> *A Literary History of America*, 1900

Two years later, an unnamed editor came unbidden and emotionally to the defense of *Little Women* in an article bannered, "Why Miss Alcott Still Lives."

> .. Their success (Alcott's books) is one of the strongest illustrations afforded by juvenile literature that, in art as in life, it is above all character that counts. Other writers fancied, imagined, or observed the wonderful creatures whom they described, or built them from fragments gathered in a score of families. Miss Alcott, as all the world knows, grew to her noble womanhood in a home which surpassed in quaintness anything which she would or could describe. She and her sisters had every opportunity to perform giant labors, and all manner of uses for fairy wands, and she, the strongest and the cleverest, found need for all her strength and cleverness, and when she wrote of the March family she merely described life as she knew it.... It is the autobiographical quality, keenly felt, although unacknowledged, which endears her to children and makes them heedless of librarians anxious to give them "instructive" books.... They want the human giant and fairy, Jo and Meg, and Beth and Amy.
>
> *The New York Times Saturday Review of Books and Art*, January 18, 1902

G.K. Chesterton wrote "Louisa Alcott" in 1907, a typically witty essay in the Chesterton style:

> ...It is good for a man who has seen many books which he could not review because they were so silly, to review one book which he cannot review because it is so wise. For wisdom, first and last, is the characteristic of women. They are often silly, they are always wise. Commonsense is uncommon among men; but commonsense is really and literally a common sense among women.... The wisdom of women is different; and this alone makes the review of such books by a man difficult. But the case is stronger. I for one will willingly confess that the only thing on earth I am frightfully afraid of is a little girl. Female children, she babies, girls up to the age of five are perfectly reasonable; but then all babies are reasonable. Grown girls and women give us at least glimpses of their meaning. But the whole of the period between a girl who is six years old and a girl who is sixteen is to me an abyss not only of mystery, but of terror. If the Prussians were invading England, and I were holding a solitary outpost, the best thing they could do would be to send a long rank or regiment of Prussian girls of twelve, from which I should fly, screaming.... Now the famous books of Miss Alcott are all about little girls. Therefore, my first impulse was to fly screaming. But I resisted this impulse, and I read the books; and I discovered, to my immeasurable astonishment, that they were extremely good. *Little Women* was written by a woman for women — for little women. Consequently it anticipated realism by twenty or thirty years; just as Jane Austen anticipated it by at least a hundred years.... To take but one instance out

of many, and an instance that a man can understand, because a man was involved, the account of the quite sudden and quite blundering proposal, acceptance, and engagement between Jo and the German professor under the umbrella, with parcels falling off them, so to speak, every minute, is one of the really human things in human literature; when you read it you feel sure that human beings have experienced it often; you almost feel that you have experienced it yourself.... The same is true of a hundred other elements in the story.... But two things are quite certain; first, that even from a masculine standpoint, the books are very good; and second, that from the feminine standpoint they are so good that their admirers have really lost sight even of their goodness. I have never known, or hardly ever known, a really admirable woman who did not confess to having read these books.... I cannot understand this strange and simple world, in which unselfishness is natural, in which spite is easier than self-indulgence. I am the male intruder.... I back out hastily, bowing. But I am sure that I leave a very interesting world behind me.

A Handful of Authors: Essays on Books and Writers. Editor, D. Collins, 1953
from an article from the *Nation* in 1907

Little Brown & Company had taken over the rights of the Alcott books from Roberts Brothers in 1898; as they issued a 1908 special edition of *Little Women*, with a printing of 100,000 copies, the book was hailed as "Forty years of a Classic."

It was just forty years ago that that classic of American girlhood and boyhood, Louisa M. Alcott's "Little Women," made its first appearance in the world of books.... As a rule the classics of youth scarcely live beyond the immediate generation that welcomed their birth. It is a unique distinction of "Little Women," however, that it has never grown old, never appeared antiquated to the youngsters of today, who are rather prone, as a rule, to demand somewhat different literary fare from that which satisfied their elders when they in turn were in their nonage. Librarians and booksellers alike will tell the inquirer that Miss Alcott's masterpiece is still among the works most in demand.... Apparently Meg, Joe (sic), Beth and Amy are still as real as they ever were, their experiences, their griefs, and their joys still stir the youthful imagination as they did when their lovable author created them. And, as a still further tribute to the perennial charm of this forty-year-old story, it is whispered that it carries an appeal to readers of maturity who peruse its pages....

The New York Times Book Review, August 8, 1908

Probably the most snobbish comments ever made about the March family that most readers saw as "real" came from Katharine Fullerton Gerould in 1920:

...For what my friend said was simply that the people in the books were too underbred for her to get any pleasure out of reading about them. My friend was not, when I knew her, a snob ... (the) result of re-reading Miss Alcott was for me, the unexpected and not wholly pleasant corroboration of what my friend had said about her characters. They were, in some ways, underbred. Bronson Alcott (or shall we say Mr. March?) quotes Plato in his family circle; but his family uses

Reviews and Critical Analysis 153

Bas relief of Louisa May Alcott by Walter Ricketson. Frontispiece to *Jo's Boys and How They Turned Out. A Sequel to "Little Men."* Boston: Roberts Brothers, 1886.

> inveterately bad grammar ... but I suspect that (my friend) referred ... to another aspect of Miss Alcott's environment: to the unmistakable lack of the greater and lesser amenities of life. The plain living is quite as prominent as the high thinking. The whole tissue of the March girls' lives is very commonplace fabric. You know that their furniture was bad—and they did not know it; that their aesthetic sense was untrained and crude—and that they did not care; that the simplicity of their meals, their household service, their dress, their every day manners ... was simplicity of the common, not of the intelligent, kind. You really would not want to spend a week in the house of any one of them....
>
> *Modes and Morals,* 1920

Katherine Anthony responded to those charges with a charge of her own.

> .. This tone of criticism is a marked tribute to the reality of Louisa Alcott's stories. Someone is so affected by the life of the March girls, who are purely creations of Louisa's imagination, that she pricks forth like Don Quixote, if not with a sword, at least with a pen, to destroy them. Her iconoclasm is a testimonial to greatness.
>
> *Louisa May Alcott,* New York: Alfred Knopf, 1938

In 1955, Eleanor Perenyi devoted more words of an article than seems necessary to say that Louisa May Alcott's appearance was unfortunate — she was neither noble enough looking, nor hideous enough, to have the "authentic face of genius." She does, however, acknowledge a fascination with the author's works:

> ...It is curious how few children's books were, in fact, written for children.... Louisa was not alone but somewhat exceptional in that she always knew her audience. And that audience she has not lost. Her publishers still sell some six thousand copies a year of her books, and there is no telling how many people (myself included) reread her faithfully in spite of every killing change in fashion. She is astonishingly out-of-date. Sermons in stones are endless and the cliches fall like hail. One wonders that young stomachs ever digested it all, why they still do, and — as one reads unwillingly on and on — why one is oneself moving along with so much pleasure on the well-worn tracks.
>
> *Harper's Magazine,* October 1955, pp. 69–72

In a long article, "A Masterpiece, and Dreadful," Brigid Brophy went in the face of popular opinion to write about loving and hating *Little Women.*

> ..She (Louisa Alcott) is, I suppose, of all writers, the one whose name *means* sentimentality; and yet sentimentality is what she and her characters most dread ... having invoked the morality of the real world, sentimentality does the one thing neither morality nor art can stand for — it is hypocritical.... You can measure Alcott's technical skill by asking any professional novelist how he would care to have to differentiate the characters of four adolescent girls — particularly if he were confined to a domestic setting, more-or-less naturalism, and the things which were mentionable when Alcott wrote.... Alcott, of course, triumphed at it (that is why we have heard of her), turning out for one of her four, Meg, a brilliant portrait of the sort of girl whose character consists of having no character.... Try as she would to prettify and moralize, she could not help making Amy the prototype of a model which did not become numerous in the United States until the 20th century — the peroxided girl-doll-golddigger.... Beth's patience, humility, and gentle sunniness are a quite monstrous imposition on the rest of the family.... I concur in ... naming her Black Beth ... naming Marmee Smarmee.... Jo is one of the most blatantly autobiographical yet most fairly treated heroines in print. All that stands between her and Emma Woodhouse is her creator's lack of intellect. Alcott is not up to devising situations which analyze and develop, as distinct from merely illustrating her characters. And in fact, absence of intellectual content is the mark of the sentimental ...
>
> *The New York Times Book Review,* January 17, 1965

Brophy's diatribe evoked five (printed) letters to the editor, ranging in reaction. Following are excerpts from three.

>...It is the silliest bit of nonsense to appear for a long while. Miss Brophy has gone to great lengths to break a butterfly upon a wheel....
>...Such a poor, illiterate review does no credit to your newspaper....
>...I found it an illuminating, perceptive and revealing discussion....
>*The New York Times Book Review,* February 7, 1965

Three years later, as the 100th anniversary of *Little Women* arrived, Elizabeth Janeway, in "Between Myth and Morning," took on the task of examining the book, and although admitting to its faults (of sentimentality and manipulation of emotions), spoke mainly to its strengths.

>...*Little Women* does manipulate life, but it is also *about* life, and life that is recognizable in human terms today.... It must have been a heavenly relief 100 years ago to learn that one's faults were not unique. Today I suspect that it is a relief to be told to take them seriously and struggle with them; that it is important to be good. This general background of human interest makes *Little Women* still plausible, but it is hardly enough to keep it a perennial classic. The real attraction is not the book as a whole, but its heroine, Jo, and Jo is a unique creation: the one young woman in nineteenth-century fiction who maintains her indiviudal independence, who gives up no part of her autonomy as payment for being born a woman — and who gets away with it.... For this Victorian moral tract, sentimental and preachy, was written by a secret rebel against the order of the world and woman's place in it, and all the girls who ever read it know it.
>*The New York Times Book Review,* September 29, 1968
>(also reprinted: see reference bibliography)

Cornelia Meigs, who in 1933, had written the Newbery Medal–winning juvenile biography, *Invincible Louisa,* wrote a new introduction to an Alcott centennial edition of her book.

>...It can still probably be said with safety that any household of readers that does not contain a copy of *Little Women* is one in which the daughters have married and taken the battered volume away for their own children.... Since Louisa could not write fully about any group of young people without, of necessity, including some of their elders, older readers found their own problems with their children thoroughly recognized and understood by the observant Miss Alcott. Very soon the whole country was reading *Little Women,* with other countries following rapidly after. Not many had realized how they had been thirsting for something that was genuine and familiar, nor did all appreciate the fact that it calls for rare gifts in an author to reveal how vitally interesting everyday life actually is....
>Foreword to *Invincible Louisa,* 1968
>Reprinted: *The Horn Book* (Alcott theme issue), October 1968

In 1968, Sean O'Faolain wrote "This Is Your Life ... Louisa May Alcott," in which he compared the real Alcott life with what he called Louisa's "fibs" of that life, as given to the March family. Yet, he admires the book itself, and places it with *Treasure Island, Robinson Crusoe,* and *The Three Musketeers* in popularity, and as books with which one can escape honorably:

> ...If I were surprised (in my study) with *Little Women,* I could hold it up with, at most, a self-deprecating smile or an At-My-Age shrug and go on escaping, unabashed.... I will not quarrel with any reader's right to lay (Alcott's) book aside because there is too much sweetness and light in it, but I do feel that the balance she strikes between the dark and bright sides of life is more true to common experience than the opposite imbalance of our so-called realists.... Before *Little Women* there had been boys like Jo March; in her we meet for the first time a new kind of heroine, who, allowing for the changes of fashion and of morals since then, grins across the ages at many an American girl of today. So it may not be entirely through folly or sentimentality or advancing senility that I sometimes see, through the masks of so many girls I meet in your streets, campuses and subways, at least the potential of another Jo March. An admirable, if idealized, Miss America?
> *Holiday,* November 1968, pp. 18, 22, 25–26

In 1973, Leo Lerman wrote his love letter to Louisa, "*Little Women:* Who's In Love With Miss Louisa May Alcott? I Am.":

> ...I fell irrevocably in love with all of them whether they remained in their very New England nest or fared abroad, for to me, a first generation American, raised in an Orthodox Jewish household where more Yiddish was spoken than English, everything about *Little Women* was exotic. It was all so American, so full of a life I did not know but desperately hoped to be part of, an America full of promises, hope, optimisms, an America where everyone had a chance to become something wonderful like Jo March-Louisa May Alcott who (I had discovered that the Marches and the Alcotts were almost identical) did become, with this story book that I adored, world famous.... But what really makes me reread *Little Women* annually, so that it is not so much a rereading but revisiting a house I know intimately, filled with friends whose being is part of my being, is still the life Miss Alcott recreated, the happy, sad, unceasing flow.... So ... I love her, and to her, wherever she is, from this now ample-sized, gray-bearded Jewish boy who has become part of her enormous American—no—global family, the loveliest of Christmases, the brightest of New Years, dear Jo March, dear, very dear Miss Louisa May Alcott.
> *Mademoiselle,* December 1973, p. 40

Ellen Moers, in 1976, reviewed a reprint of Louisa's adult novel *Work* which she found oddly modern in its salute to a special kind of women's solidarity and their claim to the right to be working-women if they choose. Of *Little Women,* she also mentioned a curious modernity:

> ...Humble work, lower in intellectual content and social prestige than the family ambiance from which her various little women come, is the kind of work

that Louisa May Alcott describes with most spirit and conviction.... In *Little Women*, Meg works as a governess, Amy as a companion; Jo does child care and sewing for the mistress of a New York boardinghouse. All girls are unfitted for the work they do, and dislike doing it as much as they dislike the housework—cooking, sewing, cleaning—that, just as much as games, romances, and dreams, makes up the texture of a girl's life in *Little Women*. Work is handled playfully by Louisa May Alcott, but it is not confused with play. It is something real, lasting, serious, necessary, and inescapable as Monday morning, to be shouldered manfully—by women, little and big. Indeed, the importance of work in America's favorite girl-child's classic is worth pondering. A very different message, for boys, can be found in *Tom Sawyer*, published the following decade. There work is presented as something to be avoided at all costs and with all ingenuity, whether through the swindle, the ruse, or flight.

Literary Women, Garden City: Doubleday, 1976

In 1979's *"Little Women:* Alcott's Civil War," Judith Fetterley attempted to analyze just what Louisa's true style might be. She saw the Civil War setting in psychological/sociological terms, ignoring the fact that the story's setting was contemporary when written in 1868:

...The Civil War is an obvious metaphor for internal conflict and its invocation as background to *Little Women* suggests the presence in the story of such conflict. There is tension in the book, attributable to the conflict between its overt messages and its covert messages. Set in subliminal counterpoint to the consciously intended messages is a series of alternate messages which provide evidence of Alcott's ambivalence. To a considerable extent, the continuing interest and power of *Little Women* is the result of this internal conflict....

Feminist Studies, Summer 1979, pp. 369–370, 381–383

Two, more current, comments came in articles about young people's contemporary reading matter.

...If I were teaching literature for adolescents today, I would put more emphasis on the history of the field and insist on a fair amount of reading books like ... *Little Women*....—G. Robert Carlsen

English Journal, November 1984

.. Fiction written especially for young adults, from its beginnings in this country with Louisa May Alcott, has always had a strong didactic streak. Books were meant to educate, and books for people making the transition to adulthood needed to educate more than most. Young adults had to learn what roles society expected them to play, what traits would be most valued in the adult world, and how to win acceptance and approval.. .—Ellen D. Kolba

English Journal, November 1984

After all is said and done, the fact remains that *Little Women* is a classic. The comment on it and its author by Madeleine B. Stern is the best summation. Stern is probably America's consummate Alcott scholar. One of her articles was "A Writers' Progress: Louisa May Alcott at 150." In it she summarized Louisa's life and works and her place in society:

> ...While Louisa May Alcott could never be characterized as a woman of "amiable benevolence," her "place in the estimation of society" 150 years after that letter (from her father to her maternal grandfather) was written is indeed secure. She is recognized the world over as a "natural source of stories ... the poet of children" who "knows their angels"... If none of the books that followed *Little Women* quite attained the stature of that masterpiece, the eight books that comprise the Series form a composite picture of life in the 19th-century New England. The March family and the families of the companion volumes are, however, also touched with universality. In a simple and enduring way, Louisa May Alcott created a saga of 19th-century America that is unbounded by time or place. The door she unlatched to one home unlatched the doors of every home...
>
> *AB Bookman's Weekly,* November 1982

A number of reviewers compared *Little Women* favorably with Jane Austin's *Pride and Prejudice.* Many coupled it with *Huckleberry Finn* and *Tom Sawyer* as classics.

The main threads of comment about *Little Women* (in the reviews excerpted above and in others) seem to center on whether or not it is too episodic as opposed to plotted, whether or not there is too much casual grammar and too many clichés, whether or not the story is too sweet and light, whether or not it is too matriarchal or domestic, and whether or not it is too romantic. Or, as expressed in the terminology of *Little Women* itself, there is the charge that there is too much "lovering."

Beyond those themes, two others have emerged in specific. The first of these is the question of the religiousness, as it were, of the March family. The early review that said *Little Women* should not be read on Sunday seems to have been concerned with the overall perceived secularity of the story. Later ones make particular mention of the fact that the Marches do not seem to go to church. In *Modes and Morals* (New York: Charles Scribner's Sons, 1920), Katharine Fullerton Gerould wrote, "...Another point is perhaps even more interesting. There are not, I believe, any other books in the world so blatantly full of morality—of moral issues, and moral tests, and morals passionately abided by—and at the same time so empty of religion. The Bible is never quoted; almost no one goes to church; and they pray only when very young and in extreme cases...." Eleanor Perenyi (see page 154, 1955) wrote, "...Yet going to church is literally never mentioned in *Little Women.* Not even on Christmas Day, after the family has given their breakfasts to the exceptionally dreary Germans next door, do the Marches go to church. None of the girls is married in church. Mr. March is fleetingly depicted as some sort of minister, but again with no church, no parish, no religious duties...." Sean O'Faolain (see page 156, 1968) commented, "...All the 'correct' things are done during the Christmas season except one—no member of the family goes to church."

Yet, also in 1968, Lavinia Russ wrote about her reactions to rereading *Little Women* after fifty years, heading her article, "Not to Be Read on Sunday."

> ...I found out ... I loved it because Louisa M. Alcott was a rebel, with rebels for parents. I found out why other girls loved it—because Jo was a rebel, with rebels for parents. Not the rebels of destruction—they never threw a brick—but rebels who looked at the world as it was, saw the poverty, the inequality, the ignorance, the fear, and said, "It isn't good enough" and went to work to change it.... Its early reviewer was wrong about *Little Women,* because if religion is living Faith, Hope and Charity every minute of your life, the Alcott-Marches were a truly religious family.
>
> *The Horn Book* (Alcott theme issue), October 1968

Writing in 1968, in "Little Women in Russia," E.M. Almedingen had told about visiting Waloma Abbey on Ladoga Lake in Russia in 1910:

> ...The monks had a special guesthouse for women and children. In the refectory allotted to our use stood a rather clumsy white wooden bookcase: "for the enjoyment of our guests," said the monk who brought in our meals. "We have none but really good books there." I do not think it was a very large library, but an entire shelf was filled with children's books, all in Russian, of course. Imagine my surprise when I saw two tattered copies of *Little Women.* I pulled one out, and the old man smiled. "Ah, you have a treasure there. We had it read to us when I was a novice. Such a good story of a true Christian home, for all they were foreigners and not of our religion....
>
> *The Horn Book Magazine,* October 1968, pp. 673-674

England's Margery Fisher stated her assessment of the book's religious philosophy: "Meg, Jo, Beth and Amy—live a frugal, useful life in a quiet Massachusetts town. Their mother gently guides them in Christian behavior while their father is away serving as a chaplain in the Civil War.... *Who's Who in Children's Books,* London: Weidenfeld & Nicolson, 1975.

Several essays commented on the good feelings that the Marches' Christmas day engendered, and how it was believable that those girls could give up their breakfasts, yet feel happy with the Christmas spirit. They truly were the *angel-kinder* (angel children) that the Hummels called them. It's curious that that hungry German family, the Hummels, could be considered dreary. The Marches irreligious? Absolutely not. They lived their religion.

Whether they lived their religion, however, is not even the point. Why? Why do these commentators even care whether or not the Marches go to church? What's more, does the fact that it's not mentioned, mean they didn't? Why is it suspect that a happy home would be chosen as the place to take marriage vows? Do any reviewers seriously question the church-going habits of Hans Brinker, Huckleberry Finn, Tom Sawyer, or Heidi? They are of the same era. Why pick on *Little Women?* The knowledge that the Marches were based on the Alcotts may be a clue. Bronson Alcott was a philosopher, a thinker, a promoter of progressive teaching methods—and he and his family, indeed most of their circle of relations and creative and literary friends, were liberals. There were and are those who do not consider liberals religious. Thus they transfer their attitudes about the Alcotts to the alter egos, the Marches. Yet, anyone dispassionately and unprejudicially studying either the lives of the Alcotts or the fictional Marches would find truly religious people who lived their religion every day.

The other theme that emerged in some reviews comes out of modern times. By the 1970s, the women's movement that began in the previous decade was in full swing and feminists began to look at *Little Women* askance. In "Does *Little Women* Belittle Women?" Stephanie Harrington gives examples of episodes in the book that seem to her to depict marriage as woman's only end, and servitude her only virtue:

> ...Louisa May Alcott's story of the four March sisters of Concord, Mass., and how they grew, might understandably strike a contemporary woman with only fellow-traveling ties to the movement as a perfectly disgusting, banal, and craven service to male supremacy.... These (previously described episodes) are, of course, precisely the kinds of sentiments—sentimentality—and conclusions that today's feminists reject, illusions that have served the feminine mystique and kept women in their place....
> *The New York Times,* June 10, 1973, Sec. 2, pp. 19, 37

Patricia Meyer Spacks objected to the kind of man Jo is "resigned" to (yet, oh how many readers adored that warm, lovable Fritz Bhaer—Amy could have Laurie—Jo deserved the dear professor), and attacked the "distribution of virtues" she perceived in the book:

> ...The novel—one hesitates to call it that, since the narrative complexity is on the level of a child's story: all, of course, it purports to be—exhaustively examines the feminine role of "taking care," yet makes clear from the outset that the masculine kind of taking care—providing financial aid and serious moral support—is the kind that counts.... The glorification of altruism as feminine activity in *Little Women* reaches extraordinary heights....
> *The Female Imagination,* New York: Alfred A. Knopf, 1972, 1975

In those early days of the women's movement, when the most ardent burned their bras and tried to breach the bastions of male-only organizations, there were a few who decried *Little Women* as chauvinistically old-fashioned. Even the term "little women" itself was denounced, although it meant nothing more than the father's loving designation for his growing daughters. If ever there was a born feminist, it was Jo March, Louisa's alter ego. Her feistiness and independence were what made her, from 1868 to current times, the character with whom most readers identified. But the feminist movement brought with it many angry, frustrated women, who found reasons and justification for denouncing anything smacking of domesticity.

Reviews and Critical Analysis 161

Jo and the Professor under the umbrella. Illustration by Frank T. Merrill from *Little Women*. Boston, Roberts Brothers, 1880.

The fact that the March sisters entered into marriage does not make the story chauvinistic. Neither marriage nor non-marriage are the ultimate criteria for liberation. Many people, both men and women, have proven that they can be themselves and nevertheless establish loving relationships with other human beings. Even in present times, many women desire to be good wives and mothers, never interpreting this to mean that they cannot be independent thinkers as well. Men, too, want to be good husbands and fathers. One can call such goals old-fashioned or traditional — but they are also fundamental. Basically, the message in *Little Women* is that one should care about and support one's loved ones.

Here's what novelist David Delman had to say about *Little Women* in 1988, inserted into a review about the republication of Alcott's thrillers:

> ...But I'll tell you what to do if you really want to have some fun. Do what I did: Get hold of a copy of *Little Women* and bask in it. Here the writing is at an enviably high level throughout — direct, slightly tart, always controlled and surprisingly Austin-like in places. Sentimental? Yes, but not sick-making. Preachy? Alcott has enough bred-in-the-bone astringency to keep that sort of thing in check. And, truly, the four March sisters are still irresistible....
>
> "A Look at Racier Side of Louisa May Alcott"
> *Philadelphia Inquirer,* July 3, 1988, p. 5-H

Little Women is a strong story about family life. It depicts the joys and trials of learning to live with others in harmony. It also shows the triumph of will over diversity. The story has become a classic because it depicts reality and handles it with universality. Its abiding place in literature is demonstrated by its continuing sales and the collectibility of early editions. The first 2000 copies of *Little Women* were sold out the first month; after six months the number was up to 7,000; after fourteen months, it was up to 30,000; and by 1855, 175,000 copies had been sold. One writer reported that in 1925 *Little Women* was selling better than it had twenty-five years earlier in 1896. The fact that the book went into public domain in 1924/25 might have influenced this. Anyone who wanted to could print the book. Hence, the world was flooded with some beautiful, and some cheap versions.

In 1932, Little, Brown and Company, who since 1898, and up to the time the book went into public domain, had been the "authorized" publishers, reported selling over 1,500,000 copies in the United States alone. By 1950, worldwide estimates were over 5,000,000. With all the editions in existence, all over the world, it would be difficult to even know how many different editions there are, much less estimate a sales figure today. One can only conclude that sales continue, because publishers don't reprint books that don't sell. In the United States, 29 different editions, some reprintings, some new, were being marketed in 1988, the 100th anniversary of Louisa's death.

Sarah Baldwin, writing in *AB Bookman's Weekly*, (March 28, 1988) notes, "...To collectors and booksellers, (Alcott's) work presents various challenges. A fine matched set of *Little Women* is a rarity. Generally her juvenile titles are rubbed, cocked, worn and dog-eared, showing the wear only love can endow...."

The first edition appeared as *Little Women or, Meg, Jo, Beth, and Amy*. By Louisa M. Alcott, Illustrated by May Alcott, Boston, Roberts Brothers, 1868. *Part One,* does not, of course, bear any notation as such, nor does it contain any advertisement for *Part Two*. It should be noted, however, that there were at least three printings dated 1869 which are neither marked *Part One* nor bear any advertisement for *Part Two*. Copies of the 1868 early printings bear the price of the book as $1.25. (Although there are believed to be later 1868 printings marked $1.50, none are extant.)

The 1868, *Part One* is described thus: Pages i–vi; 7–341; p. 342 blank. Six pages of advertisements. Frontispeice and 3 plates inserted. Size: 6½" × 4 7/16". Cloth: green, purple, terra-cotta. Brown-coated end papers. Flyleaves.

Attempts were made to forge both the title-page and the binding of *Little Women, Part One,* 1868. As a matter of record, an example of the forgery is on deposit at the New York Public Library.

The first edition of *Part Two* appeared as *Little Women or Meg, Jo, Beth, and Amy. Part Second.* By Louisa M. Alcott. Boston, Roberts Brothers, 1869.

The 1869, *Part Two* is described thus: Pages i–iv; 5–359; p. 360 blank.

Eight pages of advertisements. Frontispiece and 3 plates inserted. Size: 6 5/8" × 4 5/16". Cloth: green, purple, terra-cotta. Brown-coated end papers. Flyleaves. (Some 1869 copies bear on page iv, a note about *Part One;* others do not.)

Louisa May Alcott has become "collectible." Anyone making the rounds of antiquarian and used-book stores can find a few recycled 20th-century editions of her books. Finding good copies of 19th-century editions is a harder task. But booksellers report they don't have either century's editions on the shelves very long.

There are probably few literate families in which there does not exist someone who has read *Little Women.* Many old, ragged copies have their allocations of shelf space. Many new editions are put into the hands of new readers each day. Whether one reads an old copy or a new one, the same joy is there.

Most librarians say that the book is still being checked out on a frequent enough basis to be called popular. Many girls over the age of 10 can tell you all about their emotional bond-sisters, Meg, Jo, Beth, and Amy. Daughters, mothers, and grandmothers alike respond with affectionate memories to Marmee March's four girls who lived their lives in a setting and culture far different from that of the latter 20th century. Grown women reread the book and still laugh and cry over it. Literate men are beginning to admit they might have missed something by avoiding, in their youth, a book labeled as a "girls' book," and are delving into its pages.

A book that can span the centuries and still evoke the strong responses that *Little Women* does, must be considered an important, contemporary influence. No longer a mere "child's book," it is a designated classic. Unlike many other books with that designation, it is still readable. This is one book that will not be relegated to owned-but-not-read status. And whatever anyone says about it, the millions of people who have loved it, know it is a masterpiece.

Chapter 12

1868–Now: *Little Women* and Alcott in Polls and Lists

Librarians continue to verify that *Little Women* is checked out on a constant enough basis to be considered popular. Publishers, with their numerous editions of *Little Women* in print, continue to sell them, thus validating its popularity in a substantial way. But perhaps nothing underscores a book's status as a classic as much as its occurrence and reoccurrence on polls and lists.

It's interesting to note the books which are fellows on a list; is the book one is tracking (in this case, *Little Women*) in good company? Is the list specific to books for young people or is it a general list? It's enlightening, also, to recognize the transient nature of such lists. Some books, the real classics, continue to appear no matter how long ago they were first published. Others may be known to literature scholars or teachers, but are not familiar to the general reading public; of these, some are read, but others live only as subjects for study. Others yet, made a flash, but are little heard of or even known today. Alcott's *Little Women* has held a steady ground in gaining the estimation of listmakers. Along with *Huckleberry Finn* and *Tom Sawyer*, it rises to the fore time after time.

In her own lifetime, Louisa May Alcott, and Mary Mapes Dodge, her editor at *St. Nicholas*, friend, and author of *Hans Brinker*, were jointly awarded the French Academy's Monthyon Prize. In 1922, both the delegates to the American Library Convention in Detroit and the delegates to the National Educational Association in Boston were given ballots on which were listed the names of 100 books considered to be children's favorites. The delegates were asked to choose the 25 books they thought the best for a one-room country school. When the votes were counted, *Little Women* was at the top of the list, with Lewis Carroll's combined volume of *Alice's Adventures in Wonderland* and *Through the Looking Glass* in second place.

Sometimes even being a "near winner" places a name on a list of recognition. New York University's Hall of Fame for Great Americans started in 1900, with elections every five years until 1970, and every three years since 1973. There is at least one voting-elector from each state. In 1905, Louisa May Alcott

Polls and Lists 165

Louisa May Alcott United States five-cent postage stamp, 1940

and Dorothea Dix tied for second place from making it onto the list (closest loser was vice president John C. Calhoun). In both 1915 and 1920, Louisa May Alcott received the most votes of anyone not elected.

In 1927, *Current Literature* conducted a poll among high school students, asking, "What book has interested you most?" An essay contest, in conjunction, invited submissions for the best-written essays on the subject of the named book. Louisa May Alcott's classic was named first choice, followed by the Bible. Readers of the adventures of the March family, who played at *Pilgrim's Progress,* will note with interest the placement of that book on the list.

1. *Little Women* by Louisa May Alcott
2. The Bible
3. *Pilgrim's Progress* by John Bunyon
4. *Story of My Life* by Helen Keller
5. *Pollyanna* by Eleanor H. Porter
6. *As Gold in the Furnace* by E.J. Copus
7. *Ramona* by Helen Hunt Jackson
8. *Ben-Hur* by Lew Wallace
9. *The Man Nobody Knows* by Bruce Barton
10. *The Bent Twig* by Dorothy Canfield (Fisher)
11. *So Big* by Edna Ferber
12. *Trail Makers of the Middle Border* by Hamlin Garland

The essay contest was won by an essay on *Little Women*.

In 1939, David A. Randall and John T. Winterich included *Little Women* on their list of "One Hundred Good Novels." (*Publisher's Weekly,* June 17, 1939, pp. 2183-2184.)

In 1940, the United States Postal Service undertook one of its largest commemorative stamp sets, "The Famous American Series," honoring 35 prominent Americans. With five individuals included in each category, the 1940 issues were for authors, poets, educators, scientists, and composers, with the 1941 issues for artists and inventors. The five authors and the stamp denominations were:

Washington Irving (1783–1859) one-cent
James Fenimore Cooper (1789–1851) two-cent
Ralph Waldo Emerson (1803–1882) three-cent
Louisa May Alcott (1832–1888) five-cent
Samuel Clemens (1835–1910) ten-cent

The five-cent Louisa May Alcott stamp is ultra-blue (a medium blue) and perforation size 10½ × 11. There were 22,104,950 issued. The first issue was February 5, 1940, at Concord, Masschusetts. Close to 50 years later, an unused stamp could be bought from most stamp dealers for about 35 to 40 cents; a used stamp cost about 20 cents.

In 1947, Frank Luther Mott compiled a list of "Over-All Best Sellers in the United States" in his book, *Golden Multitudes: The Story of Best Sellers in the United States*. With over two million copies sold in America, *Little Women* was accorded a place on the "over-all best seller" list.

Also in 1947, the Committee on College Reading (44 professors, librarians, and editors, with an additional advisory board of 13 writers) published *Good Reading: A Guide to the World's Best Books*. The book contained descriptions of more than 1000 volumes. The section on "Novels, 19th Century American," was a relatively small list of 22, and it is interesting that no distinction was made as to whether works were originally intended for children or adults. Classics, in time, transcend these categories. (Only the descriptive text for *Little Women* is given here.)

Alcott, Louisa May (1832–1888)—*Little Women* (1868). Jo was a tomboy. Amy a fuss-and-feathers. Beth an angel, and Meg a dove! This delightful story of an old-fashioned family achieves the rarity of being tender and not saccharine.
Bellamy, Edward (1850–1898)—*Looking Backward: 2000–1887* (1888).
Cooper, James Fenimore (1789–1851)—*The Last of the Mohicans* (1826); *The Pilot* (1823).
Crane, Stephen (1871–1900)—*The Red Badge of Courage* (1895).
Eggleston, Edward (1837–1902)—*The Hoosier Schoolmaster* (1871).
Hawthorne, Nathaniel (1804–1864)—*The House of the Seven Gables* (1851); *The Scarlet Letter* (1850).
Howells, William Dean (1837–1920)—*The Rise of Silas Lapham* (1885).
Jackson, Helen Hunt (1831–1885)—*Ramona* (1884).
James, Henry (1843–1916)—*The Ambassadors* (1902 [sic]); *The American* (1877); *Daisy Miller* (1878); *Golden Bowl* (1904); *Portrait of a Lady* (1881).
Melville, Herman (1819–1891)—*Moby Dick* (1851); *Omoo* (1847); *Typee* (1846).

Stowe, Harriet Beecher (1811–1896) — *Uncle Tom's Cabin* (1852).
Twain, Mark (1835–1910) — *Huckleberry Finn* (1885); *The Adventures of Tom Sawyer* (1876).
Westcott, Edward Noyes (1847–1898) — *David Harum* (1898).

May Hill Arbuthnot's major work, *Children and Books,* includes recognition of *Little Women,* but none of Louisa's other books, except for a passing reference to *Little Men.* In the 1947 edition, 23 children's books from 1846 to 1908 were noted as significant. *Little Women* was included. In 1964, in the book's third revision, the list of 46 "turning points in children's literature" covered the years 1484 to 1908. The list grew not only in that it went back to 1484, but had increased to 27 within the 1846 to 1908 listings. A few books on the earlier list were dropped, and some were added in that section, as well as the pre-1846 part, to complete the new list of 46. *Little Women* was still there, pointed out for its role as a turning point in children's literature. Arbuthnot said of *Little Women:*

> . . .Here is the first great juvenile novel of family life — a warm, loving family group, struggling with poverty and with individual problems but sustained by an abiding affection for each other and an innocent kind of gaiety that could make its own fun. This is just the kind of home group every child would like to belong to — struggles and all. Not until the Laura Ingalls Wilder series or perhaps Hilda Van Stockum's *The Cottage at Bantry Bay* or Monica Shannon's *Dobry* (Shannon only in 1947 edition) or Margot Benary-Isbert's *The Ark,* or Madeleine L'Engle's *Meet the Austins* (Benary-Isbert and L'Engle only in 1964 edition) do we again encounter such a picture of a family. None of these recent examples is any better, and in no one of them is each member of the group so distinctly drawn as are the unforgettable Beth, Jo, Meg, and Amy. . . *(Little Women* and *Tom Sawyer)* both provide insight into group loyalties and group living, not didactically analyzed and underscored but emerging unobtrusively in absorbing stories.

In 1958 Nancy Larrick warned parents not to expect children to like the same books they liked, but added, that sometimes the children do. She wrote, "*Little Women, The Adventures of Tom Sawyer, Heidi* and *The Wizard of Oz* are high on any list of favorites." (*A Parent's Guide to Children's Reading,* New York: Pocket Books, 1958).

In 1976, as part of the 200th anniversary of the United States, the Children's Literature Association, an international group of librarians, teachers, authors and publishers, named the following the best eleven American children's books of the last 200 years. *Little Women* and Mark Twain's two books were the only ones from the 19th century. (A suggested children's reading age was also included.)

1. *Charlotte's Web* (1952: all ages) by E.B. White
2. *Where the Wild Things Are* (1963: 4–8) by Maurice Sendak
3. *The Adventures of Tom Sawyer* (1876: 10 & up) by Mark Twain

4. *Little Women* (1868: 10 & up) by Louisa May Alcott
5. *Adventures of Huckleberry Finn* (1885: 10 & up) by Mark Twain
6. *Little House in the Big Woods* (1932: 6–10) by Laura I. Wilder
7. *Johnny Tremaine* (1943: 10 & up) by Ester Forbes
8. *The Wonderful Wizard of Oz* (1900: 8 & up) by Frank Baum
9. *Little House on the Prairie* (1935: 6–10) by Laura I. Wilder
10. *Island of the Blue Dolphins* (1960: 12 & up) by Scott O'Dell
11. *Julie of the Wolves* (1972: 12 & up) by Jean Craighead George

When this list was repeated in "For a Grown-up Writer's (Re)Reading?" in *Pen Points*, it was accompanied with several quotes about rereading. These are particularly pertinent in view of the frequent comments from reviewers and readers, that they reread *Little Women* frequently, and even, for surprisingly many, annually.

> "No book is really worth reading at the age of ten which is not equally (and often far more) worth reading at the age of fifty and beyond." — C.S. Lewis
> "There are some books one needs maturity to enjoy just as there are books an adult can come upon too late to savor." — Phyllis McGinley
> "The stories of childhood leave an indelible impression, and their author always has a niche in the temple of memory from which the image is never cast out to be thrown on the rubbish heap of things that are outgrown and outlived." — Howard Pyle
> "When you reread a classic you do not see more in the book than you did before; you see more in *you* than was there before." — Clifton Fadiman
> *Pen Points: The Newsletter of the Philadelphia Writers' Conference*, Spring 1987

The Children's Literature Association issued a special committee's report in 1985 presented in a pamphlet titled, "Touchstones: A List of Distinguished Children's Books." In the committee's judgment, each book on the list "has some particular significance; it is itself an important innovation or breakthrough." *Little Women* is one of some 68-plus books (a few are listed as "series," so the exact number is indistinct.)

In 1986, to coincide with the centennial of the Statue of Liberty, *Ladies' Home Journal* issued a list of "The 25 most important WOMEN in American History." The lead began, "In celebration of the restoration of the Statue of Liberty, the great lady who has held the torch of freedom aloft for one hundred years, LHJ salutes twenty-five American women who have made a difference in our history and who have truly influenced us all. . . ." The lists were chosen in consultation with the Institute for Research in History in New York and the Schlesinger Library at Radcliffe College in Cambridge, Massachusetts. Louisa May Alcott was one of three authors on the list. The honor is significant when assessed alongside the names of the others on the list, and the range of time periods represented. One wonders how the names on the list will be remembered in yet another 100 years.

Alphabetically, the 25 are: (Those marked with an asterisk were living at the time the list was made.)

Jane Addams, first female American winner of the Nobel Prize
Louisa May Alcott, author
Susan B. Anthony, suffragette
Clara Barton, founder of the American Red Cross
Pearl S. Buck, author
Rachel Carson,* environmentalist
Joan Ganz Cooney,* force behind the Children's Television Workshop
Isadora Duncan, dancer
Amelia Earhart, pioneer aviator
Mary Baker Eddy, founder of Church of Christ, Scientist
Geraldine Ferraro,* former vice presidential candidate
Betty Friedan,* feminist
Clare Boothe Luce,* writer-politician
Rosa Parks,* civil rights activist
Frances Perkins, first female Cabinet member
Mary Pickford, actress
Lydia Pinkham, business tycoon
Sally Ride,* astronaut
Eleanor Roosevelt, former first lady
Sacajawea, Lewis-and-Clark expedition guide
Margaret Sanger, leader in birth-control education
Harriet Beecher Stowe, author
Harriet Tubman, former slave
Martha Washington, former first lady

(The above descriptions are not the *Journal*'s.) In the magazine, each name was accompanied with a short subtitle, and a paragraph of description of the woman's accomplishments. Of Louisa May Alcott (Subtitle: "Little women are people, too"), the comments included, "Generations of schoolgirls have curled up with the irresistible novels of Louisa May Alcott, the first popular women's writer who recognized that the intimate details of family life were indeed the stuff of which page-turners are made ... readers absorbed important history lessons as well as the author's passionate views on the reform movements of her day, most notably the fight for women's suffrage and coeducation...." *The Ladies' Home Journal,* July 1986, pp. 83–85, 127–130.

Polls and lists don't *make* a classic; but they underscore the status. They point out a considered judgment. Frequently, readers are led to learn more about an individual or a book by virtue of seeing the name or title on a list of distinction.

Books and people contemporary at the time a list is made may be forgotten or less important in the scheme of things only a decade or so down the road. When new lists are made, perhaps even with the same headings or criteria, some names will have been dropped and some new ones added. That is the difference between ephemeral fame and classic standing.

In literature, the true classic is the book that continues to be read well beyond the author's lifetime. *Little Women* is a classic. The writer deserving of continued note is the author of a classic. Ergo, Louisa May Alcott, 1832–1888, who made her mark in 1868 with the writing of that classic, *Little Women,* deserves the recognition she has been accorded.

Chapter 13

1868–Now: Adaptations

Adaptations or uses of the "little women" image have appeared in several forms. Although script versions predominate, a few maverick uses are curious or interesting additions to the genre of alterations-on-the-original.

Miscellaneous Adaptations

The Little Women Club by Marion Ames Taggart, a children's novel, appeared at the turn of the century (Philadelphia: Henry Altemus Company, 1905). The story line concerns four girls who decide to form a club patterned on their favorite book, *Little Women*. After forming the Mybogjameeth Club (the letters of Meg, Jo, Beth, and Amy scrambled) they go through the trauma of deciding who is to play which fictional March sister. Once this is settled, the story progresses with parallels to the early chapters of *Little Women* with a young woman friend cast as the counterpart to "Laurie." The girls secretly try to live their lives as the March sisters would have, which proves to be somewhat impossible. They do, however, help resolve a mystery in finding the long-lost granddaughter of the "Mr. Laurence" counter-character. They finally decide to keep the club without trying to emulate the March sisters' every action. It is an interesting exercise in paralleling the original with the story-within-the-story concept.

The Louisa May Alcott Cookbook compiled by Gretchen Anderson and illustrated by Karen Milone (Boston: Little, Brown, 1985), contains "recipes based on the dishes mentioned in *Little Women* and *Little Men* and recreated from nineteenth-century cookbooks by the nine-year-old author." Each section is preceded with a short excerpt from either of the two Alcott books mentioned. Although the book is listed as a juvenile, most of the recipes require some degree of general cooking skill.

A Louisa May Alcott Diary was compiled and illustrated by Karen Milone (Boston: Little, Brown, 1987). It is "a 'scrap-bag' of things: quotes from the books and stories of Louisa May Alcott, a calendar for dates and events you wish to remember, quotes from Louisa's own journals, crafts and activities, and topic and journal pages for you to record your thoughts." Intended for juveniles, the crafts can be completed by young girls in the preteen to early teen years. The journal pages are a combination of questions to respond to and blank pages for personal entries.

The Little Women Keepsake Diary by Suzanne Weyn (New York: Scholastic, Inc., 1988) is a paperback designed for young users to answer the questions posed on various pages: "If I could make a fortune, this is how I would like to do it:_____"; "The dumbest new summer fad is_____"; "When I get grouchy it's usually because_____"; "If I could have ten wishes, this is what they would be:_____"; etc.

Louisa May Alcott's Little Women Paper Dolls by Janet Nason (Walnut Creek, CA: Evergreen Press, 1981), with its six 11" × 14" pages, is more of a giant greeting card than a set of paper dolls intended to be cut out. The pages contain a very short summary of *Little Women* and are ornamented with indoor and outdoor background scenes. The "Meg" character looks middle-aged, the "Jo" one, a young adult, and both Beth and Amy preteen. Although there is a young adult "Laurie" cutout, there are no paper clothes for him. Among the girls, there is a dress and a cape for "Meg," only one dress for "Jo," one outfit for "Beth," and two dresses and a bonnet for "Amy."

A modern eight-panel and cartoon-strip parody, "Little Women," by Victoria Roberts, began as a series in *Ms. Magazine* in February 1988, running through December 1988. It begins with Meg unhappy because she has no Anne Klein clothes, Amy upset because she cannot afford a nose job, Jo declaring she cannot possibly write without a computer, and Beth cursing at an inadequate piano. Laurie is the millionaire boy next door who gives his annual Fourth of July costume party, with an American flag in red snapper, whitefish, and caviar. Professor Fritz von Bhore, who has a degree in artificial intelligence and a German accent, can read several languages but has not learned to read women. It is an irreverent lark.

Playscripts

There have been a number of script adaptations of *Little Women*, including, no doubt, a number of unknown ones used in schools and local areas for amateur productions. At Orchard House, the Alcott museum where Louisa wrote the story of the four March sisters, there have been numerous scripts and performances of not only *Little Women*, but of Alcott family life. (See Chapter 16.)

According to Julian Hawthorne, in "The Woman Who Wrote Little Women," it was dramatized even before it was a book:

> ...In its first conception, it was a fanciful, informal drama of New England domestic life, with her sisters and herself and a few friends as *dramatis personae* ... she felt obliged to select me for Laurie—an amiable idealization, of course, she herself being Jo. But of these details we knew nothing until the book was done and Louisa read part of it to us.
>
> *The Ladies' Home Journal,* October 1922, pp. 120–122, 124

Adaptations

Louisa wrote to Anna from Bex, Switzerland, on July 27, 1870: "...Did you know that Higginson and a little girl friend had written out the Operative Tragedy in 'Little Women' and set the songs to music and it was all to be put in 'Our Young Folks.' What are we coming to in our old age?..."

Casual drama adaptations after the appearance of the book *Little Women* had been performed in Boston well before November of 1872, when Louisa received a formal request from William Henry Venable for permission to use scenes from *Little Women* for the purpose of instruction and amusement. She gladly gave permission, and soon after, in 1873, Venable, a teacher at the Chickering Institute in Cincinnati, published *The School Stage: A Collection of Juvenile Acting Plays* which included two short plays adapted from *Little Women*.

The *Chicago Tribune* on March 22, 1874, (p. 13), made mention of a performance that included "Playing Pilgrims," "Jo's Christmas Play," and "The Witch's Curse, an operatic tragedy in five acts," with Florence Hilton playing Jo. It was performed at Standard Hall, on March 1, 1874. Louisa later wrote to Florence Hilton, president of the Philocalian Society of Chicago, which had sponsored the production, to say she was glad to know that her stories were thought worthy of representation. She asked, "Did you have russet boots? I would have lent you the genuine article, for they still adorn my wardrobe, and occasionally my feet."

In 1883, Louisa was made a member of "The Little Women Society" by a Mrs. Leavitt, who also asked for a copy of dramatized scenes. Louisa told her that she had none but said she knew scenes had been acted in many places. She suggested that it was easy to arrange a short play by taking conversation and various scenes.

In 1900, "The 'Little Women' Play," adapted by Elizabeth Lincoln Gould was published by both the Curtis Publishing Company, Philadelphia, and Little, Brown, & Company, Boston. (See also, "The 'Little Men' Play" mentioned near the end of this chapter.) There does not appear to have been Alcott family sanction of the Gould adaptations.

At the time of the first Broadway production of *Little Women*, John A.P. Alcott, the nephew Louisa had legally adopted in order to pass on her copyrights, wrote about the family decision to give permission for the adaptation. The first request had evidently come around 1904.

> ...Because it is all about our own dear relatives,—my brother, "Amy's" daughter and I—hesitated for eight years or more before we would sanction the dramatization of "Little Women." It wasn't that we thought that our Aunt Louisa wouldn't like it—on the contrary, we had every reason to believe that she would, since she was always keenly interested in the stage, even to the extent of wanting to make it her own profession at one time—but because we feared that no dramatists could or would make a play of the book that would preserve its atmosphere of sweet wholesomeness; we feared that the taint of theatricality might

make a sacrilege of our home. To us, "Little Women" was the story of our home and our family, a theme too intimate for the publicity to which the stage might subject it.

But when we grew to appreciate the reverence and the love which Miss Jessie Bonstelle,—one of the first and *the* most persistent applicants for the stage rights of the book—harbored for Jo and for "Little Women," and when she agreed to submit everything to us for approval before making it final, we gave in. And we have not once had cause to regret it—not even when I saw myself brought on the stage as a papiermache baby in swaddling clothes.... We have come to realize, too, that instead of hurting the book, as we had feared it would do, the dramatization is helping it by bringing its story into the lives of people who have never read it, but who would go to see the play. How many men and boys, who scorn to read what they regard as a girls' book, will refuse to escort their wives or sister or friends or sweethearts to the theatre?

"The 'Little Women' of Long Ago," *Good Housekeeping*,
February 1913, pp. 182–189

Little Women: A Comedy in Four Acts

Produced in New York City at the Playhouse, October 1912.
Produced by William A. Brady.
Script adaptation by Marian De Forest.
Staged in New York by Jessie Bonstelle and Bertram Harrison.
Original Cast:

Jo	Marie Pavey
Meg	Alice Brady
Beth	Gladys Hulette
Amy	Beverly West
Marmee	Gertrude Berkeley
Laurie	Howard Estabrook
Mr. Laurence	Carson Davenport
Fritz Bhaer	Carl Sauerman
Aunt March	Mrs. E.A. Eberle
John Brooke	John Cromwell
Mr. March	Lynn Hammond
Hannah	Lillian Dix

Franklin Sanborn, an old family friend, made a few comments about the production when he wrote "Reminiscences of Louisa M. Alcott." "The representation of Miss Alcott's *Little Women* as a drama, in theaters from Buffalo westward, amid applause and appreciation, is a long-deferred tribute to the dramatic element in her gifted nature...."—*Independent*, March 7, 1912, pp. 496–498

Little Women: A Comedy in Four Acts

Produced in London at the New Theatre, November 10, 1919.
Script adaptation by Marian De Forest.
Staged in London by Jessie Bonstelle.
Original Cast:

Jo	Katherine Cornell
Meg	Joyce Cary
Beth	Hattie Hanson
Amy	Eva Rowland
Marmee	Henrietta Watson
Laurie	Antony Holles
Mr. Laurence	Sydney Paxton
Antoine Baret*	Leslie Faber
Aunt March	Kate Phillips
John Brooke	Henry C. Hewitt
Mr. March	Alfred A. Harris
Hannah	Ada Palmer

*For the English production the character of Professor Friedrich (Fritz) Bhaer, which is German, was changed to that of Professor Antoine Baret, and the speeches were rewritten into French. Even theatre patrons watching an American play that took place during the Civil War could not quite transcend the English anti-German feelings still ingrained from World War I. If Jo's Professor was to be regarded as a sympathetic character, it was safer to cast him as a Frenchman.

The famous stage actress, Katherine Cornell, in the role of Jo March, would have added considerable stature to the London production.

Samuel French, publisher of plays for professional and amateur production, in 1921, published the script by Marian De Forest for the 1912 and 1919 stage productions described above.

Another live performance, in 1932, featured stage star, Jessie Royce Landis.

"Little Women, A Play in Three Acts and an Epilogue," listed as "a new dramatization of Louisa M. Alcott's famous book," was dramatized by Roger Wheeler, Boston: W.H. Baker (Baker's professional plays), 1934. Based on the radio adaptation broadcast over Station WEEI in Boston during the spring of 1934, Concord was the setting for the entire action, which included events from both parts of *Little Women*.

In 1940, Samuel French published a musical version, "The Vocal Score and Libretto of Little Women, an Operetta ... Dramatic Treatment by John Ravold, Lyrics by Frederick Howard, Music by Geoffrey O'Hara."

When another production was put on in 1944, the well-known critic George Jean Nathan was favorably impressed with the story:

Little Women, believe it or not, is, in short, still serviceable theatre, and a felicitous journey out of the hard-boiled present into the lace-valentine of

Scene from Broadway production, 1913. Illustration from *Little Women or, Meg, Jo, Beth, and Amy*. Boston: Little, Brown, and Company, 1913.

> yesterday. The argument that it is overly sentimental is true. But it could not well be otherwise, since it happens to deal with overly sentimental people. As soundly argue that *The Depths* is overly cynical. There are some people, critics among them, who insist upon a villain in even something like *Ode to a Nightingale*.
> *Theatre Book of the Year: 1944-45*, New York: Knopf, 1945

A 1990 playscript is *Christmas with the "Little Women": Two Performance Versions; Pantomime and Playscript* by Gloria T. Delamar (Melrose Park, PA: Rabbit Press/O.R. Inc., 1990). The pantomime version is acted out to the reading of the original text from *Little Women*, up through the visit to the Hummels and the giving away of breakfast; the playscript version reverses

Adaptations

some of the original scenes in order to place all the activity on a single morning, but is an accurate reflection of the dialogue in Alcott's book, taking the one-act play through the beginning scenes, the uproarious rehearsal for the Christmas skit by the March sisters, the Hummel visit, and the poignant response to their father's letter. Both versions are preceded with a brief biographical narration about Louisa May Alcott.

Radio

Katharine Hepburn, who played Jo March in the 1933 film classic adapted from *Little Women* (described following), twice appeared in radio scripts of the story:

Little Women: with Katharine Hepburn, Oscar Homolka, John Davis Lodge, Elliot Reid. The Theatre Guild on the Air, ABC, December 23, 1945. (In the 1933 film version, John Davis Lodge played the part of John Brooke.)

Little Women: with Katharine Hepburn and Paul Lukas. Theatre Guild on the Air, ABC, December 21, 1947. (In the 1933 film version, Paul Lukas played Professor Fritz Bhaer.)

One radio play that was printed later in a classroom anthology for children was based on Chapter 3 of the book. "The Laurence Boy," adapted from *Little Women* by Walter Hackett, was presented as a project of writing radio scripts: "... This radio play was written by a professional writer and may give you some hints. You can easily compare it with the chapter in *Little Women* from which he got the story.... Notice particularly the way the author makes you "see" through your ears...."—*Reading Roundup: Book One*, from *Plays, the Drama Magazine for Young People*, (eds. Witty; Peterson; Parker) D.C. Heath & Co., 1954, 1958.

How many local stations may have performed scripts based on *Little Women*, similar to the presentation on *Spider Web's* radio show in 1983, is unknown.

Recordings

Recordings have included some about Louisa: "Invincible Louisa" (juvenile biography by Cornelia Meigs) available on record or cassette, 44:25 minutes, Miller-Brody, 1970. Also "Invincible Louisa," and "Louisa May Alcott," a filmstrip with cassette, both from Listening Library, 1988.

More recordings have been done, though, about the book: "Little Women" read by Julie Harris, record or cassette, Caedmon; "Louisa May Alcott's Little Women" which is chapters 1 and 2, read by Elinor Basescu, on record or cassette, Miller-Brody; "Little Women" read by Flo Gibson, twelve 90-minute cassettes, unabridged, Listening Library, 1988.

Films

Radio, and even Broadway productions, reached some people. But the real focus of adaptations that delighted young and old with the exploits of Meg, Jo, Beth, and Amy were on film. Males who never would have been caught reading a "girls' book," were induced to take in the story at the movies or at home on their television screens.

The films are what most people think of when one mentions adaptations, and with good reason. Films capture the main characters in action. For those who love the book, one version may be better than another, but all of them bring back Meg, Jo, Beth, and Amy for delectation.

The first version of *Little Women* on celluloid was a silent film of 1919, produced by Famous Players, Lasky Corporation, with Dorothy Bernard starring as Jo. But memorable cinema treatment of Louisa's famous story begins with talking films. And it is with these that documentation matters to most viewers.

Movie: *Little Women* — 1933

United States, RKO; Directed by George Cukor.
Script by Sarah Y. Mason and Victor Heerman.
Black and white; 115 minutes.
(MGM/UA Home Video: Great Books on Video Collection; 1985.)
Cast:

Jo	Katharine Hepburn
Meg	Frances Dee
Beth	Jean Parker
Amy	Joan Bennett
Marmee	Spring Byington
Laurie	Douglass Montgomery
Mr. Laurence	Henry Stephenson
Fritz Bhaer	Paul Lukas
Aunt March	Edna May Oliver
John Brooke	John Davis Lodge
Mr. March	Samuel S. Hinds
Hannah	Mabel Colcord

Not credited on screen as producer, but actually responsible for preparing the film as production chief, was the legendary David O. Selznick. Cukor later said he felt as though *Little Women* was one of Selznick's forerunners to *Gone with the Wind*.

Almost immediately called a "screen classic," there were a number of awards. Academy Award nominations came for Best Picture, Best Direction,

The "little women" and Marmee. Illustration by Frank T. Merrill from *Little Women*. Boston, Roberts Brothers, 1880.

and Best Screenplay Adaptation, winning the Oscar in the latter category for the wife and husband team of Sarah Y. Mason and Victor Heerman. Katharine Hepburn won the 1934 Cannes Film Festival best actress award. *Little Women* was Hepburn's fourth film and her second directed by Cukor. She was given sole above-the-title billing for this performance, ranked among the highlights of her screen career. Also released in 1933 was Hepburn's third film, *Morning*

Glory, for which she received the Academy Award as Best Actress; many critics felt that her strong interpretation of "Jo March" weighed heavily in her favor in the Oscar decision on *Morning Glory.*

The critics loved *Little Women* (*Halliwell's Film Guide,* 1977):

> ...One of the most satisfactory pictures I have ever seen....
> E.V. Lucas, *Punch*

> ...That *Little Women* attains so perfectly, without seeming either affected or superior, the courtesy and rueful wisdom of its original is due to expert adaptation by Sarah Y. Mason and Victor Heerman, to Cukor's direction, and to superb acting by Katharine Hepburn. An actress of so much vitality that she can wear balloon skirts and address her mother as "Marmee" without suggesting quaintness, she makes Jo March one of the most memorable heroines of the year, a girl at once eager and puzzled, troubled, changing and secure....
> *Time*

> ...It is, of course, the mood which is the important part of the work, and it is the unashamed straightforwardness of the writing, the unpatronizing shrewdness of George Cukor's direction and, above all, Miss Hepburn's beautiful playing which make *Little Women* an exquisite screen play in which everyone is supposed to be charming all over the place and makes it all seem true....
> Richard Watts, Jr., *New York Herald Tribune*

> ...As an antidote to the febrile dramas of underworld and backstage musical spectacles, *Little Women* comes as a reminder that emotions and vitality and truth can be evoked from lavender and lace as well as from machine guns and precision dances.... It is a tribute to those who shared in bringing it to the screen that there is no betrayal either of the spirit or feeling of the original. The hoydenish Jo is capitally performed by Katharine Hepburn; Joan Bennett is excellent as Amy, as are Frances Dee and Jean Parker as Meg and Beth. Also, George Cukor and the producers deserve praise for a production that has been carried out with taste as well as skill....
> Thornton Delehanty, *New York Post*

When the film began to appear around the country on television, Leonard Maltin rated it among the best films available:

> This film offers endless pleasure no matter how many times you've seen it; a faithful adaptation of Alcott's book, with uniformly superb cast.
> *TV Movies: 1983-84 Edition,* 1982

Writing a retrospective in 1957, Richard Griffith and Arthur Mayer said:

> Under the regime of Decency, Hollywood, with considerable grinding of gears, dragged its cameras away from their fixation on contemporary life and turned them on a sweeter and safer day. Charles Dickens, Louisa May Alcott, and Sir James

Adaptations

Barrie were the spiritual, as they were often the actual, authors of the stories on which the screenplays .. were based. Victorian England and America, reconstructed with all the skill and care of which the makers of talking pictures were now capable, replaced the penthouse, the gangster and the shady lady. The favorable audience response to these nostalgic memorabilia caused the trade to reflect that the public might possibly be glutted with sophistication. More likely is that the gradual return of confidence brought about by the New Deal made it possible for people to believe in goodness again.... The success of this vibrant version of the Alcott classic, *(Little Women)* ... helped the forces of Decency prove that the public really did want "good" films.

The Movies, New York: Simon and Schuster, 1957

One reviewer noted that "a very young Joan Bennett is superb as Amy, ever scheming for the good life." One adaptation of script took place right on the spot, when Bennett told Cukor she was pregnant and reluctant to take a scheduled fall; the scene was altered and the fall was given to Hepburn's Jo. Bennett, speaking of the making of the film, said that Kate and Cukor were wonderful to work with. When Cukor wanted them on the set he would yell, "Come on, you four bitches."

In the mid-forties, David O. Selznick had plans to remake *Little Women* himself, with his protégée Jennifer Jones as Jo, Dorothy McGuire as Meg, Diana Lynn as Beth, and Shirley Temple as Amy. Despite being as far along as casting the main roles, the plans were eventually abandoned.

Movie: *Little Women* — 1949

United States, MGM; Directed by Mervyn Le Roy.
Script by Andrew Solt, Sarah Y. Mason and Victor Heerman.
Technicolor; 122 minutes.
Cast:

Jo	June Allyson
Meg	Janet Leigh
Beth	Margaret O'Brien
Amy	Elizabeth Taylor
Marmee	Mary Astor
Laurie	Peter Lawford
Mr. Laurence	C. Aubrey Smith
Fritz Bhaer	Rossano Brazzi
Aunt March	Lucile Watson
John Brooke	Richard Stapley
Mr. March	Leon Ames
Hannah	Elizabeth Patterson

An Academy Award nomination for Photography was accorded to Franz Planer. Although two of the three scriptwriters had also written the 1933 script, critics generally had little good to say about this version, inevitably compared to the 1933 film.

Alvin H. Marill said of the role of Jo, "...June Allyson attempted the part...."

"...Syrupy Christmas-card remake, notably lacking the light touch...." —Leslie Halliwell, *Halliwell's Film Guide*.

"...It will raise a smile and draw a tear from the sentimental...."— M.F.B., *Halliwell's Film Guide*.

Most of the main characters were played by actors already known for their screen work, raising the question of whether their casting in the classic was "showcase" motivated. The critics notwithstanding, many viewers found June Allyson appropriately tomboyish and perky in the role of Jo; to the new generation, June Allyson was Jo March, and they loved the film as much as they loved the book. When the film was being shown on television, Leonard Maltin included it in his book of comments about contemporary fare: "Glossy remake of Louisa May Alcott's gentle account of teenage girls finding maturity and romance—patly cast."—*TV Movies: 1983-84 Edition*, 1982.

Television Movie: *Little Women*—1978

United States; NBC.
Color; 200 minutes (4 hours with commercials).
Cast:

Jo	Susan Dey
Meg	Meredith Baxter Birney
Beth	Eve Plumb
Amy	Ann Dusenberry
Marmee	Dorothy McGuire
Laurie	Richard Gilliland
Mr. Laurence	Robert Young
Fritz Bhaer	William Shatner
Aunt March	Greer Garson
John Brooke	Cliff Potts
Mr. March	William Schallert
Hannah	Virginia Gregg

This version of the story had as stars young people known for other television roles, most in series, along with a cast of mature movie actors. NBC promoted it with, "An all-star cast brings to life this magnificent classic of love and loss. It's the story of Meg ... Jo ... Beth ... Amy ... the eternal story of four little girls becoming 'Little Women.'"

An anonymous *TV Guide* reviewer said, "This 1978 TV-movie is generally true to the original story, and captures its sentiment and period flavor — thanks to appropriately tuned performances and authentic-looking sets and costumes."

Leonard Maltin reviewed the television adaptation and said, "Sugarplum refining of the classic, sparked by McGuire's Marmee and Garson's Aunt March.... Above average." — *TV Movies: 1983-84 Edition*, 1982.

An interesting note is the 1978 casting of Dorothy McGuire as Marmee; in the mid-forties, she had been chosen by Selznick to play one of the March girls in the version of the film that he never made. As for Academy Award holder Greer Garson, this production marked her television-movie debut.

A short-lived series spun off from this production, with Mildred Natwick replacing Greer Garson, but the production was generally acknowledged to be pallid.

Television Movie: *Little Women* — 1970

England; BBC.
Color; nine one-hour installments.
Angela Down in the lead role of "Jo."

Made in 1970, this BBC production was seen in the United States on Public Television at various times, according to geography, in the 1970s.

When Stephanie Harrington asked, "Does *Little Women* Belittle Women?" her conclusion was, "...No.... Nobody ever called Jo March baby." Reviewing the BBC production, she made several other comments:

> ..the BBC-TV version . is, from a feminist point of view, more palatable than the novel. It is necessarily pared down, and in adapting the novel for television, writers Denis Constanduros and Alistair Bell stripped it of the author's moral kibbitzing, sparing us the homilies with which she rationalizes the eventual domestication of all, including the strong-minded Jo. .. At times, though, the performances are so studied that there is no question that a proscenium arch separates the actors from your living room   filmed in England in 1970, and though the social consciousness of the novel is attuned to the 1860s, this version does include lines in which the March sisters object to being considered men's playthings and insist that they will go on with their work, Jo with her writing and Amy with her painting, even if they do marry....
>
> *New York Times*, June 10, 1973, pp. 19, 37

The BBC production was, in some ways, a new experience for the American viewer. It was strange to hear Meg, Jo, Beth, and Amy March talk in English accents. Although fairly attuned to the accents indigenous to British actors through other imported BBC programs, hearing *the little women* talk that way was a bit of a shock. Louisa May Alcott's book was published in England shortly after its first American publication in 1868, and has been a classic there as well as in the United States. One has to wonder, then, if the March sisters loved by the English sounded strange to them when they first heard the characters speak in American-made films.

Before listing the film versions that go further afield, mention should be made that for parents concerned that children who watch television versions of classics may be deterred from reading, the indications are quite the reverse. When children saw classic films like *Little Women, Heidi,* and *Black Beauty* they searched out the books in order to read the originals. Barbara Lee and Masha Kabakow Rudman, Ed.D., in *Mind over Media* (1982) advised parents that seeing classics in dramatized versions could lead their children to seek out the books on which they were based.

Movie: *Foxes*—1980

United States; Directed by Adrian Lyne.
Color; 106 minutes.

Joe Baltake, in reviewing this picture, titled his review, "Louisa May Alcott Was Never Like This." Excerpts from his review sum it up:

> With "Foxes," producer-writer Gerald Ayres has come up with an inspired idea which makes for a vivid, occasionally messy, but never uninteresting film. Imagine what it would be like if Louisa May Alcott dropped into contemporary San Fernando Valley and updated her "Little Women" to fit this milieu.
>
> Although none of the ads or publicity for the film make mention of it, Ayres "Foxes" is indeed an updated, R-rated variation of the Alcott classic in which the four heroines are still plagued with the problems of growing up. The twist, of course, is that their travails include bouts with drugs, sex, boys and uncompassionate parents and that these problems are played out against the seediness of Hollywood Boulevard and the cacophony of rock music.
>
> Actually, Ayres' script and Adrian Lyne's head-on direction efficiently obscure the source of their film, but if you look closely, you'll find Alcott's four heroines (all renamed, natch) and their vaguely familiar problems. Jodie Foster's Jeanie is clearly the Jo character—stubborn, determined, street smart. Foster's vivid performance clearly makes Jeanie a survivor and hints she'll probably go on to be a great writer, deriving much of her material from the wild times and deep feelings she shared with her three dear friends.
>
> Deirde (Kandice Stroh) is the modern counterpart for Amy, still vain and materialistic, while Madge (Marilyn Kagan) is Meg, whose normal family life, is more or less, the inspiration for her to marry young and settle down. Then there's Annie (Cheri Currie in a commanding debut) who, like Beth, will reach a sad, inevitable conclusion.... Jeanie's mother (Sally Kellerman), meanwile is a gay divorcee.
>
> The plot, however, is less Alcott.... But the bottom line is that beneath its sordid, unsettling atmosphere, "Foxes" is a moral film—often a preachy, sentimental one ...
>
> *Philadelphia Daily News,* April 18, 1980, p. 29

Adaptations

The conscious or subconscious naming of two characters in *Foxes* with initials that match their Alcott counterparts is curious; Jeanie is Jo, and Madge is Meg; even Annie who is Beth, uses the initial of the other character, Amy, who in *Foxes* is called Deirdre. The entire structure would seem to indicate that the makers of the film were perhaps more influenced by the original story than publicly admitted.

Television Situation Comedy: *Facts of Life* — 1979-1988

Another adaptation of *Little Women* is a television series that ran for nine years, from 1979 to 1988, the situation comedy, *Facts of Life*. After the non-focused first year, the focus was on four of the girls at Eastland School, a private girls' school. Jo Polniazek — the character was actually named Jo — (played by Nancy McKeon) was the "topsy-turvy" tomboy character, the independent one, who bristled at propriety, was down-to-earth, tough and self-sufficient. (She was also the obligatory scholarship student.) Blair Warner (Lisa Whelchel) epitomized the Amy character — overly concerned with her looks, boy-crazy, conscious of what money means. Natalie Green (Mindy Cohn) was the nurturing, impressionable Meg, but in this version's twist she took over the writer-aspiration. Tootie Ramsey (Kim Fields) was the Beth character, sweet, a little naïve, and a little different — in *Little Women* Beth was the sickly one; in *Facts of Life* the difference was race — Tootie was a black student. Even the housemother, Edna Garrett (Charlotte Rae), was appropriately "Marmee-ish," and always addressed by the girls as Mrs. Garrett. (In the last years she was replaced by an upbeat modernized version, Mrs. Garrett's sister, whom the girls always first-named, Beverly Ann [Cloris Leachman]. Also added in later years was a sort of foster-boy, Andy [Mackenzie Astin] — "Laurie?")

The interactions of the four girls, played out as boarding school life, with Mrs. Garrett to mother them, was the very picture of the family life of *Little Women* — squabbling, making up, getting into trouble, crying together, laughing together, and in the end, always supporting each other.

Video Cartoon: "Little Women" — 1983

Produced by Children's Video Library; 60 minutes.
Ages 6-9; rated "average" by Harold Schechter.

Harold Schechter, Ph.D., in *A Parents Guide to Children's Videos* (1986) said, "... The drama, excitement, laughter, and pathos — are completely missing from this slick but soulless cartoon.... It's less like an animated version of the original book than a cartoon adaptation of the Cliff Notes." He goes on to say that there is decent artwork, and that the character of Jo is fairly well captured, but that "the other three March sisters are ciphers, and the film as a whole is flat and mechanical. (In this version, Beth does not die; she is ill a few days and then makes a complete recovery.) In conclusion, Schechter advises parents to rent the 1933 George Cukor film of *Little Women* instead.

Television Cartoon: "Tales of Little Women" — 1987–1988

Original animation: Nippon Animation, Ltd.
English version: Saban Productions for HBO Family Series.
Saban Executive Producer: Winston Richard.
48 weekly half-hour episodes.

The "little women" were recreated in an "animated series based on the family classic." Originally produced in Japan by Nippon Animation, Ltd., HBO acquired the rights and arranged to have Saban Productions reedit, add music and effects, and dub each episode into English. Because the Japanese adaptation contains some degree of variance from Louisa May Alcott's original text, the series was retitled, "Tales of Little Women." Overall, the script retained much of the charm and character of the original, but the dialogue delivery in the dubbing of the earliest episodes was for the most part stilted and awkward, though it improved somewhat in later episodes. For some reason, the character of John Brooke was changed to schoolteacher, Mr. Sutton. The Japanese cartoonist had portrayed Hannah Mullet, the housekeeper, as a stereotypical black "Mammy" or "Aunt Jemima," which Saban had to retain, of course. Unfortunately the decision to have her, most of the time, speak in an exaggerated "negro" southern accent creates a negative reaction from those who are concerned about racial stereotypes. The delivery here is uneven, however, as occasionally the voice is deep and clean and the accent radio-announcer clear, which, had it been consistent, would have nicely counterbalanced and atoned for the cartoon-caricature. The tale is told from Amy's viewpoint and the script and delivery come out decidedly self-centered. The music is good and the theme song is delightfully bouncy.

There are many who regard the book as the ultimate experience. There is some contention that radio is not an entirely passive activity, but many feel that movies and television films offer a basically passive pastime. This, of course, may depend on the depths of perception with which any given viewer watches the delineation of character and adventure. Curiously, live theater is generally judged to be active, although the same basic situation exists as with films — the audience sits there and laughs or cries as moved.

Arguments on the merits of watching a performance as opposed to reading the book aside, those who love the March sisters flock to see performances because they enjoy the reinforcement of the warm feeling they had from the book. They are frequently moved to reread the original after seeing an adaptation. Those adaptations are made, and more editions of the original are printed, because *Little Women* is a book that can stand up under reading, rereading, and repetition.

Adaptations of Other Alcott Stories

The lives of the "little women" went beyond the initial book of *Little Women*. Louisa continued the saga of the March family in *Little Men*, though now it was the Marches, Bhaers, Brookes, and Laurences. Because of the popularity of *Little Women*, the sequels were of interest to readers who wanted to know what would happen next in the lives of the beloved Meg, Jo, and Amy (Beth died in Part Two of *Little Women*). After *Little Men: Life at Plumfield with Jo's Boys*, there was *Jo's Boys, and How They Turned Out*. Each of these was dramatized in one or more medias.

Other stories of Louisa's were also made into plays and films. It is easy to see that their popularity did not approach that of *Little Women* adaptations. And there is a dearth of adaptations after the mid-twentieth century. Nevertheless, they deserve documentation.

Books

Little Men: Life at Plumfield with Jo's Boys (1871):
  Dramatization: "The 'Little Men' Play." Two-act. Adapted by Elizabeth Lincoln Gould. Boston: Little, Brown, 1900. Also: Philadelphia: Curtis Publishing Co., 1900.
  Dramatization: (published as) "Daisy's Ball." By Ruth Putnam Kimball. Boston: Baker's Plays, 1970.
  Movie: "Little Men." Feature film; Director, Phil Rosen; Starring Dickie Moore. (80 min., 16mm, sound, b/w.) Mascot, 1934.
  Movie: "Little Men." Feature film; Starring Kay Francis. (75 min., 16mm, sound, b/w.) RKO, 1940.

Jo's Boys and How They Turned Out: A Sequel to "Little Men" (1886)
  Dramatization: "The 'Little Men' Play." Adapted by Alma Johnson. Evanston, Illinois: Row, Peterson & Co., 1940.

Eight Cousins: or, The Aunt-Hill (1875)
  Dramatization: "Eight Cousins a Play in Three Acts Made from Miss Alcott's Story." By Ethel Hale Freeman. New York: Samuel French, 1934.

Rose in Bloom: A Sequel to Eight Cousins (1876)
  Dramatization: "Rose in Bloom a Play in Three Acts from the Book by Louisa May Alcott." By John D. Ravold. New York: Samuel French, 1934, 1935.

An Old-Fashioned Girl (1870)
  Dramatization: "An Old-Fashioned Girl a Play in Three Acts." By John D. Ravold. Samuel French, 1934, 1935.

Movie: "An Old-Fashioned Girl." Director, Arthur Dreifuss. Eagle Lion, 1948.

Movie: "An Old-Fashioned Girl." Feature film. Pathé Industries, 1949.

Story

"A Christmas Dream" (1882)
 Dramatization: (published as) "Effie's Christmas Dream, a Play for Children." By Laure Clair Foucher. Boston: Little, Brown, 1912.

Chapter 14

1868–Now: On Foreign Ground

One might wonder if a young people's story set in 19th-century New England, United States, would have much appeal to young readers in other countries. The fact that *Little Women* was published in England almost immediately after its first appearance in the United States should provide one answer. But in this case the language is the same, at least — more or less — when offered in the form of the printed word. Idioms differ. More importantly, lifestyle differs. It differed in 1868 and it differs now. Even presentation of the story of the four March sisters differs; in England and Canada it appears as two books, *Little Women* and *Good Wives*. In the United States the two parts were combined long ago to make one volume, *Little Women*.

Translating the book into non–English, there is the risk of misinterpretation. And there still remains the matter of differing life-styles.

But writing which speaks to universal issues (or the fantasy of fairy tales or adventures) will be adopted by readers regardless of origin. American children have enjoyed *The Swiss Family Robinson* (1818), and *Heidi* (1884) for almost the same length of time that children of other countries have savored *Huckleberry Finn* (1885), *Tom Sawyer* (1876) and *Little Women* (1868). *Hans Brinker* (1865) should also be added to the foregoing, but it has the unique distinction of being about life in Holland written purely from the research of its American author, Mary Mapes Dodge.

As far back as 1890, Edward Salmon, an English reviewer writing primarily about English books, nevertheless included Louisa May Alcott, saying:

> ... The best defence which can be made of boys' and girls' literature in general is to assert ... that it is peopled chiefly with boys not far removed in their chivalrous rectitude of character from Tom Brown, and with girls as worthy to be loved as the sweet, if somewhat tomboyish central figure of *Little Women*.
> "Should Children Have a Special Literature?"
> *Parents Review*, 1890, p. 334

An anonymous writer in 1897 had some interesting comments:

> There is your regular English purist who boils over with rage because we will go on spelling "honor" and "favor" without the "u." There are others who fume over

what are called "Americanisms" when in ninety-nine cases in a hundred these so-called Americanisms are good, old Elizabethan words or phrases, which it has been our good fortune to retain and, more than that, cherish. But to take Miss Alcott's "Little Women" and to gouge out of it "all expressions distinctly American" is silly. So, all out of its proportion, is "Little Women" to be published in England, and there will be no longer any "Little Women," but awkward gawks, without nationality.
"Books and Authors," *The New York Times—Saturday Review of Books and Art,*
March 20, 1897, p. 8

A delightful essay in the *Little Women* centennial year was by E.M. Almedingen, writing about *"Little Women* in Russia." Though written in 1968, it dealt with events mostly centered on the late 19th century to roughly 1917. The writer's great-aunt, Catherine Almedingen, had translated Alcott's books into Russian some time in the 1870s, brought out, she thought, anonymously by Wolf's, a St. Petersburg publishing house. Catherine Almedingen started a children's monthly *Rodnik* in 1882, and in the mid-'80s published an article about Louisa May Alcott, followed in the 1890s by a serialization of *Little Women*. E.M. Almedingen goes on to report on the many dog-eared copies of *Málenkiye Zhéntchiny* that she saw in various village schools. In her final year at one school, in a "course of most elementary psychology" their professor told them how happy he was to see *Little Women* treasured in so many Russian homes. He then gave them an essay to write on "Why I Like *Little Women*." She reported:

> ...There were twenty-nine of us; and one—a rather grave, beautiful girl, niece of the very last Russian Prime Minister—wrote a paper which Lobov read aloud to us. It was short, incisive and to the point. Its final sentence is graven in my memory, and I translate it into English. *Little Women*, which I have read so many times, has always left me with a desire to do as much good as I can.
> *The Horn Book,* October 1968, pp. 673–674

In 1920, Katherine Fullerton Gerould reported, "I remembered perfectly that French playmates of mine in Paris had loved *Les Quatre Filles du Docteur March* (though the French version was probably somewhat expurgated). If children of a Latin—moreover, of a Royalist and Catholic—tradition could find no flaw in Miss Alcott's presentment of young life, I could not see why any free-born American child should fail to find it sympathetic."

An article titled, "When the Alcott Books Were New," by Dorothea Lawrance Mann, captured comments current to 1929, about several foreign editions:

> ..*Little Women* was translated into French, German and Dutch, and was well known in England and on the continent. In Holland the first book was published under the title, *Under the Mother's Wings,* while the second part was known as

On Foreign Ground 191

Illustration by M.V. Wheelhouse from *Good Wives* (original in pastel colors). London: G. Bell & Sons Ltd., 1911

> *On Their Own Wings.* In 1890, when he was in Athens, Frank Sanborn found a copy of it in modern Greek. Just a few years ago *Little Women* was translated into Chinese by the Misses Sung Tsing-yung and Martha E. Pyle, and appeared in red-linen covers with golden Chinese characters and a fanciful colored-picture in time to be a gift for the Chinese New Year. The fame of the book is world-wide. In the Royal Free Hospital of London not so long ago there was established a *Little Women* bed....
>
> *Publisher's Weekly,* September 28, 1929, pp. 1619, 1623–1624

An English magazine for girls, usually devoted to stories about sports and school-days, decided, in 1934, to serialize *Little Women*. It was not only their first "domestic" story, but also the first Victorian-background one. The editor introduced it warmly in "Whispers from the Den," with:

> ..Set in America, yet a firm favourite with girls all over the world for many years. Just ask your mummy how she liked it. Her enthusiasm will be unbounded ... and so will yours be.
>
> *Schoolgirl*, May 1934, p. 11

Alexander Woollcott (1887-1943), author and critic, recorded an experience he had:

> When I made a speech one day at a girls' school in Tokyo they understood all my little jokes, and when, in comparing their school to the one which Jo March launched in "Little Women," I groped through my memory for the name of it, my rescuing prompter was a round, dusky little Japanese girl who helped me out by supplying "Plumfield" in a stage whisper.
>
> Retold by John T. Winterich in "One Hundred Good Novels,"
> *Publisher's Weekly*, June 17, 1939, pp. 2183-2184

The centennial of *Little Women*'s publication came in 1968. Virginia Haviland, head of the Children's Book Section of the Library of Congress, prepared a list of 30 countries in which *Little Women* had been published. (As reported above, there was an edition in China in the 1920s.)

Argentina	Germany	Netherlands
Belgium	Greece	Norway
Brazil	Hungary	Persia
Czechoslovakia	Iceland	Poland
Denmark	India	Portugal
Egypt	Indonesia	Russia
Eire	Israel	Spain
England	Italy	Sweden
Finland	Japan	Taiwan
France	Korea	Turkey

In that same year, 1968, Elizabeth Janeway wrote "Between Myth and Morning," saying:

> Meg, Jo, Beth and Amy are 100 years old ... and except for Natasha Rostova, who is almost exactly their contemporary (*War and Peace* appeared over the years 1865 to 1869), the Marches must be the most read about and cried over young women of their years. In my time we read *Little Women* of course, but we liked to think it was because our sentimental mothers had loved the book so and urged it on us. For all I know, this is still the cover story today, but just the same, the answer to "Have you read *Little Women*?" is still "Of course." In the last week I've

heard it from three Americans, an Italian and an English girl, all in their twenties—the English girl quoted the whole opening.... Read 'Little Women?' Of course....
The New York Times Book Review, September 29, 1968, pp. 42, 44, 46

Brian Doyle, in an important British publication of 1968, implied that *Little Women,* an American book, was more popular than any then-current British-written one; along with a summary of Louisa's life and work, he made several comments:

...It was an immediate success and to this day is probably the most popular and widely-read book ever written for girls ... the book is full of charm, humour and sentiment ... it is on *Little Women* that her fame rests and it is a sign of its universal appeal that it has been translated into nearly twenty languages....
The Who's Who of Children's Literature, London: Hugh Evelyn, 1968

Reviewing a reissue of *Little Women,* Nora L. Magid, in "Clear the Stage for a Repeat Performance," gave a Canadian point of view.

...Generations of girls, have, of course, loved it, and their impressions of it stay with them all their lives. I must say, having just laughed and cried my way through it, that the standard American edition comes as an astonishment. We Canadians read it as two books, "Little Women" and "Good Wives," and conditioned perhaps by memory I find it more successful that way. Between the original and its sequel there is a distinct break in tone and emphasis, and the parts seem better left physically separated....
The New York Times Book Review, November 1969, p. 65

In 1975, British commentators were still giving the highest accolades to the 1868 tale of Meg, Jo, Beth, and Amy. Margery Fisher, one of England's leading authorities in children's literature, wrote:

...The Katy books [by Susan Coolidge: 1872, 1873, 1886] are vigorous and entertaining and, to British children, full of fascinating and unfamiliar detail. Their heroine, however, is not as strongly alive for readers today as Jo March and her sisters are. Nothing could be more different from the humane, civilized, household of the Marches than the breezy, games-playing, unmistakably middle-class home of the Carrs. The Marches even in childhood are never less than little women; they enjoy childish pleasures and display childish attitudes but emotional experience is always deep for them.... Louisa Alcott's moral philosophy and psychology seem to go deeper than the bracing didacticism of Susan Coolidge ... [Katy's] experiences do not transcend the barriers of time and fashion in the way that those of Jo March undoubtedly do....

Louisa Alcott was a true novelist, with a technique both simple and adroit. She established her characters by physical description, sparing and usually dramatic; she focused on each one in a particular scene.... She managed dialogue in a somewhat formal way. Most often the sisters speak antiphonally, each with one sentence at a time; Jo's first words—"Christmas won't be Christmas without any presents"—start the first of many four-sided conversations in which no single voice

can be mistaken for another .. Marmee's exhortations to the girls, too (so much more naturally maternal than critics are always willing to concede) seem to touch a deeper level when she is talking to Jo. . The wholesome simplicity, the ease and smoothness of the writing, should not be allowed to mask the fact that the stories of the March family are most skillfully written and planned as well as being among the most warmly human, entertaining and absorbing of all family stories.
Who's Who in Children's Books, London: Weidenfeld & Nicolson, 1975

When printed in foreign editions, the characters are usually illustrated with the characteristics of the natives. The Spanish edition, for instance, has Spanish-looking little women in long dresses, with roses behind their ears.

In one Japanese cartoon, however, the characters do not look at all Oriental. The Marches and their friends look typically Aryan, albeit of the Civil War era, but the illustrator's conception of the housekeeper, Hannah Mullet, is that of an "Aunt Jemima" look-alike.

In 1969, the Library of Congress reported that it held sixteen foreign editions of *Little Women*. In 1988 they reported that few translations of United States' classics had been added to its collections. The foreign titlings are not necessarily straight translations of the original. These offer a look at the translators' art. Many used illustrations from American editions (full details are in the Chronological Bibliography of Louisa May Alcott's Works later in this book). Following is a list of the LOC's holdings:

Arabic: Nisā' Saghīrāt. New York: Franklin Publications, 1958. Two-volume set (LOC has only Vol. II). Color plates and line drawings by Louis Jambor from 1947 Illustrated Junior Library edition.

Bengali: Cāra Bona Cāra Mana. New York: Franklin Publications, 1960. Part One. Color plates and line drawings by Louis Jambor from 1947 Illustrated Junior Library edition.

Dutch: Meisjesjaren. [Nederlandsche bewerking van Julia Huys.] Antwerpen: Uitgeverij "De Sleutel," 1946. Part One. A cover illustration shows the four March sisters.

Dutch: Het Levin In. [Nederlandsche bewerking van Julia Huys.] Antwerpen: Uitgeverij "De Sleutel," 1946. Part Two. A cover illustration shows Jo in front of a turreted Plumfield.

Earlier Dutch translations bore the titles *Under Moedervleugels* (Under Mother's Wings), and *Op Eigen Wieken* (With Their Own Wings).

French: Le Dr. March Marie Ses Filles. Texte français de Denise Hamoir. Illustrations de Gilles Valdès. Paris: Hachette, 1955. Part Two. Bright watercolor and black-and-white halftone illustrations.

French: Petites Américaines. Traduit par Mme. Tissier de Mallerais. Paris: Hachette, 1935. ("Les meillieurs romans étrangers.") Abridged version of Part Two. No illustrations.

An earlier French translation was titled, *Les Quatre Filles du Docteur March* (The four girls of Doctor March).

German: Junge Menschen (sic). Ein Buch für dir Jugend, übers. und bearb. von Elisabeth Stark. Fürth/Bay.: K. Bernheim, 1947. One cover illustration. Contents: Bd. *Die Töchter der Frau March* (The daughters of Mrs. March). Volume I of a two-volume set with the following.

German: Paradies Plumfield (Little Men) (not in the LOC collections). Ein Buch für dir Jugend, übers. und bearb. von Elisabeth Stark. Furth/Bay.: K. Bernheim, 1949. One cover illustration.

German: Teenager Wachsen Heran. Bearb. von Inge Lehmann. Rastatt: Favorit-Verlag, 1965. Mit 16 Illustrationen (in modern dress). Part Two of *Little Women.*

Indonesian: Puteri Remadja. Diterdjemahkan oleh Gadis Rasid. Djakarta: Indira, 1962. A two-volume set. Line drawings by Louis Jambor from 1947 Illustrated Junior Library edition.

Irish: Mná Beaga. Nioclás Toibin d'aistrigh. Baile Átha Cliath, Oifig an tSoláthair, 1948. No illustrations.

Japanese: Yonin No Shōjo. Arukotta saku. Matsubara Michitomo yaku. Tokyo: Dai Nihon Yūbenkai Kōdansha, 1950. Four volumes: (1) Wagaya no maki; (2) O tomodachi no maki; (3) Betā hāfu no maki; (4) Jinsei no maki. The LOC has vol. 2 (*Friends*) and vol. 4 (*Life*). Two-color illustrations, with an American setting.

Russian: Malen'kiia Zhenshchiny; Ili Dietstvo Chetyrekh Sester; Poviest Dlia Dietei. Per. s. angliiskago. Izd. 2. S. Petersburg, Izd. Stasovoi i Trubnikovoi, 1895. Part One. No illustrations. Paperback.

Russian: Malen'kiia Zhenshchiny; Ili Meg, Dzho, Betsi i Emi. Izd. 2. Moskva, M.O. Vol'f, 1902. Part One. Frank Merrill's 1880 vignette drawings appear on almost every page.

Reference has also been made to the Russian title, *Málenkiye Zhéntchiny*, translated by Catherine Almedingen. St. Petersburg: ?Wolf, c1870.

Spanish: Mujercitas. Version española de Maria Sepulveda. Buenos Aires: Editorial Juventud Argentina, 1942. (Biblioteca Primor, 64.) Part One. Illustration of four sisters and mother. Paperback.

Swedish: Unga Kvinnor. [Amerikanska originalets titel: Little women. Översättning: Ann Bucht. Omslag och illustrationer; Stig Södersten. Stockholm] Svensk läraretidnings förlag, 1965. (Saga 477. Sagas berömda böcker.) Part One of two-volume set. Black and white illustrations, modern, but with period detail.

Swedish: Vara Vänner Fran Iffol. ([English] originalets titel: Good Wives. Till svenska av Ann Bucht. Omslag och illustrationer: Stig Södersten. Stockholm) Svensk läraretidnings förlag, 1967. (Saga 512. Sagas berömda böcker.) Part Two of two-volume set. Black and white illustrations, modern, but with period detail.

Urdu: Dhup Cha On. Lahore: Dar al-Ishā'at Panjab, 1959. Translation by Wali Ashraf Sabuhi. Part Two. No illustrations.

Mention should be made of editions published in England:

English: Little Women. London: Sampson, Low, 1868. The first English edition. Part One.

Little Women. London: Sampson, Low, 1869. The first English edition. Part Two.

Little Women. London: Sampson, Low, 1870. Parts One and Two. Reissued 1872 and 1874.

At least 23 other English publications of either Part One, Part Two, or Parts One and Two in one volume appeared between 1871 and 1896. The copyright implications of the many publishers involved in English editions raise questions. Roberts Brothers held the American copyright. From other arrangements recorded, it can be inferred that Sampson and Low held the English and European ones. In another English/American dispute, in a letter to Thomas Niles around 1874, Louisa had written, "If the copyright matter annoys publishers it certainly bewilders authors and leaves them in very defenceless positions at times, for there seems to be no law to guide or protect them."

Contemporary English and Canadian readers refer to Part One as *Little Women* and a separate volume of Part Two as *Good Wives*. English publishers, however, used various titles for Part Two: *Little Women Wedded* (1872, 1874), *Little Women Married* (1873, 1874, 1893, 1894) and *Nice Wives* (1875, 1890), before the *Good Wives* title appeared in 1895. Curiously, although the book is almost always seen as two volumes in English publications, the 1895 edition by Nisbet & Company was a single volume with two parts, *Little Women* and *Good Wives*.

As noted, the centennial of Louisa May Alcott's death came in 1988. Centennial dates tend to prompt interest in commentary. It seemed appropriate, therefore, to solicit remarks from a few who first read *Little Women* in foreign editions. (Initials or only first names by request.)

Joan, a Korean-American teenager, newcomer to the United States, first read the book in Korean. She said, "All my friends and I read it. We loved it. It was interesting. I would call it good. Now that I am learning English, I want to read it again. It will be interesting to read the story in its original language."

Nans Case, now a United States citizen living in Harvard, Massachusetts, where the ill-fated Alcott Fruitlands experiment took place, (and where the Fruitlands Museums are now located) first read the book in Dutch. "I liked the family life, which didn't seem any different, really, from what I knew of my own family and friends. In all the Scandinavian countries, books of other countries are widely read—the March sisters were familiar because they were like families everywhere."

Maria F., who grew up in Puerto Rico, read *Little Women* in Spanish. She said, "The March sisters made me want to see the United States. I knew the story was written a long time ago, but the family life was so happy, and even though they were supposed to be poor, they didn't seem very poor to me."

Christina, who read the book as a teenager in Germany, said, "The family was *gemütlich* — good-natured. The sisters fought just like my sister and I did, and there were all kinds of problems, but the book had a happy feeling. I think all of my friends had read the book."

Marie grew up in a little town in the south of France where any American tourist received much attention. She said, "I read the book in French. I suppose the translation was true to the book. I liked the sisters and their family love, but I especially liked Laurie. I never had a brother, and I just wished I had a brother like him, or at least a boy next door. The best would have been a boy like Laurie who liked me as much as he liked Jo. I didn't mind that he married Amy, though. It seemed right."

Maya Kravitzky offered a twist in response to the question. She said, "I grew up in Russia, and earned the equivalent of a Ph.D. I never read *Little Women* in Russian, but it was the first novel I read in English. I liked it very much."

Anne Field, a school librarian in Capetown, South Africa, grew up in Zimbabwe, Africa (then Southern Rhodesia). She says, "*Little Women* and the other L.M. Alcott books certainly were enjoyed and read and reread by myself and my friends, and did not seem irrelevant nor foreign. In South Africa we were between cultures and read many English and American books, though mostly English editions. Working as a school librarian in Capetown, I've found that the books are popular with the girls, especially after the series has been shown on television. The period setting is popular with many girls. As we in South Africa today have many of the same problems dealt with in *Little Women* — war situation — poverty — it's easy to relate to the situations and characters."

Tamar Yaron, now a young mother and psychologist in Philadelphia, Pennsylvania, where Louisa was born, read the book in Israel in her native Hebrew. Even now she recalls, with an edge of sadness in her voice, that she lent her copy of *Little Women* to a friend and never got it back. She recently read it in English, however, and said, "I found that reading it invoked the same feelings I had when I first read it as a teenager. Then, I got a feeling of how adults — of how women — should be. As an adult, I'm more aware of the lovey-dovey aspects, of certain unrealistic scenes, and of some sense of cynicism in Jo. Yet, there were other scenes that brought back memories of the ideal family — how wonderful it would be to talk with each other like that. There were scenes in which I could relate to the handling of my own toddler."

Despite noting flaws, her overall reaction was the same as it had been when she read it in Hebrew 15 years before. "I loved it." Poetically, she worded her memory of *Little Women* and its mystique when she was growing into maturity: "It was the gift to give."

Little Women — The Book

AUNT JO'S SCRAP-BAG.

SHAWL-STRAPS.

THE DOWNWARD ROAD.

Two Yankee maids of simple mien,
   And earnest, high endeavor,
Come sailing to the land of France,
   To escape the winter weather.
When first they reached that vicious shore
   They scorned the native ways,
Refused to eat the native grub,
   Or ride in native shays.
'Oh, for the puddings of our home!
   Oh, for some simple food!
These horrid, greasy, unknown things
   How can you think them good?"
Thus to Amanda did they say,
   An uncomplaining maid,
Who ate in peace and answered not
   Until one day they said, —
"How *can* you eat this garbage vile
   Against all nature's laws?
How *can* you cut your nails in points,
   Until they look like claws?"
Then patiently Amanda said,
   "My loves, just wait a while,
The time will come you will not think
   The nails or victuals vile."
A month has passed, and now we see
   That prophecy fulfilled;
The ardor of those carping maids
   Is most completely chilled.
Matilda was the first to fall,
   Lured by the dark gossoon,
In awful dishes one by one,
   She dipped her timid spoon.
She promised for one little week
   To let her nails grow long,
But added in a saving clause
   She thought it very wrong.
Thus did she take the fatal plunge,
   Did compromise with sin:

Then all was lost, from that day forth
   French ways were sure to win.
Lavinia followed in her train,
   And ran the self-same road,
Ate sweet-bread first, then chopped-up brains,
   Eels, mushrooms, pickled toad.
She cries, "How flat the home *cuisine*,
   After this luscious food!
Puddings and brutal joints of meat,
   That once we fancied good!"
And now in all their leisure hours,
   One resource never fails,
Morning and noon and night they sit
   And polish up their nails.
Then if in one short fatal month,
   A change like this appears,
Oh, what will be the net result
   When they have stayed for years?

Title page illustration and verse from *Aunt Jo's Scrap-Bag II* (Shawl Straps). Boston: Roberts Brothers, 1872

III.
Louisa May Alcott — The Legacy

Chapter 15

1855–Now: The Range, Dimension, and Legacy of Alcott's Works

There is no argument that Louisa May Alcott's historical reputation is built primarily on *Little Women*. That was not true in her own time when her first book, *Flower Fables*, made a nice stir and her second, *Hospital Sketches*, received more than little literary acclaim. Her serious poetry was considered good enough for critics to say she could make a name as a serious poet if she chose. Her name was already known before the publication of her most famous book. Her previous children's short stories and her children's stories and novels after *Little Women* were among the most popular of the day. Her thrillers, whether appearing anonymously, pseudonymously, or credited, were definitely on the wanted list of many editors. Only her adult novels failed to get as much attention as she would have liked.

In looking at *Little Women,* most American readers accept the fat volume as Alcott's format. (A contemporary alternative to a fat volume is a paperback edition that, though not so fat, has very small print which in itself conveys the length.) Few except scholars even know that it was originally two books, the second being the sequel. In Canada and England, it always was, and is, published as two volumes. For the sake of consistency, and as Alcott was an American writer, we accept the premise that *Little Women* is one fat book divided into two parts. The time periods between the original and its sequels were considerable:

Little Women (1868/1869)
Little Men: Life at Plumfield with Jo's Boys (1871)
Jo's Boys and How They Turned Out: A Sequel to "Little Men" (1886)

Although the sequels did well in their own era, they have not had the continued attention that *Little Women* has enjoyed, and indeed, although some readers today know that there was a sequel named *Little Men* many have never heard of *Jo's Boys*.

The other juvenile novels appeared, in summary, as follows:

An Old-Fashioned Girl (1870)
Eight Cousins; or, The Aunt-Hill (1875)

Louisa May Alcott, 1886, from a photograph by A.W. Elson & Co., Boston

Rose in Bloom. A Sequel to "Eight Cousins" (1876)
Under the Lilacs (1877)
Jack and Jill: A Village Story (1880)

In 1988, 100 years after their author died, every one of the juvenile novels was still in print. As they were in public domain, any publisher could publish them and some appeared from more than one publisher.

Naturally, the characters, episodes, and plots differ in each novel, but they all have the stamp of Louisa May Alcott's style and philosophical and ethical inclinations. The main characters are drawn with distinctive and consistent character and personality traits, and the stories are believable depictions of "real life." There is an overtone of moral instruction, there is humor and wit, and the stories have happy endings.

Alcott's short stories for young people have that same stamp. Most, though not all, of the short stories appeared first in juvenile magazines such as *Merry's Museum, The Youth's Companion,* or *St. Nicholas.* Some were published as slim single-story books. (The complete details for the short stories, including a listing of the stories in each anthology, are in the Chronological Bibliography of Louisa May Alcott's Works later in this reference.) In all, there were 16 anthologies that she assembled herself:

Flowers Fables (1855)
On Picket Duty, and Other Tales (1864)
Three Proverb Stories (1868)
Hospital Sketches and Camp and Fireside Stories (1869)
Aunt Jo's Scrap-Bag I (1872)
Aunt Jo's Scrap-Bag II (1872)
Aunt Jo's Scrap-Bag III (1874)
Aunt Jo's Scrap-Bag IV (1877)
Aunt Jo's Scrap-Bag V (1879)
Aunt Jo's Scrap-Bag VI (1882)
Proverb Stories (later titled *Kitty's Class Day*) (1882)
Spinning Wheel Stories (1884)
Lulu's Library I (1886)
Lulu's Library II (1887)
A Garland for Girls (1888)
Lulu's Library III (1889)

Of the short story anthologies compiled in her lifetime, only *A Garland for Girls* was being offered for young readers in 1988. *On Picket Duty, and Other Tales* was available in a scholarly edition. Some of the short stories appeared in anthologies excerpted from various original volumes and one or two were available as slim single-story books for young people.

As can be seen from the poems included in various chapters of the biography section of this book, her poetry extended through literary serious poetry, pious serious poetry, clever and witty verse, and doggerel or ditty-type verse. There are enough examples to give a good picture of her command of the verse-form. Some are better than others. "Thoreau's Flute" and "With a Rose, That Bloomed on the Day of John Brown's Martyrdom" deserve serious attention; "Parody on 'The Graves of a Household'" can hold its own with any light verse currently being written; the poem, "Love," which was found amongst her papers of the 1880s, is poignant; but, the writing of poetry or verse was incidental to Louisa's career-drive, with the exception of some she wrote expressly for publication in juvenile magazines. She wrote serious poetry when moved by circumstances: periods of despondency, the deaths of Henry David Thoreau, John Brown, her parents, her sisters, etc.; she wrote some of the light-hearted verses for inclusion in the short stories or novels intended for young readers. For the most part, the poetry she left behind is serviceable, and though noteworthy from the point of view of seeing Louisa May Alcott's dimensions in verse form, it is not of the literary tradition or volume that would make her name a household word as a poet.

Hospital Sketches, her Civil War–time letters home while she was serving as a Union Army nurse, bridge the juvenile/adult line. Some were excerpted as juvenile stories, though the original publications were aimed at adult readers. Their cohesiveness as stories indicates a certain amount of fictionalization, but this does not detract from the basic nonfiction base of their origin. The writing is lucid and witty, yet filled with compassion. They still serve as a remarkably vivid picture of the historical era they describe. In 1863, published first in magazine serialization and then in book form, they established her credibility as a writer.

Louisa's adult novels never got the kind of praise or literary acclaim she hoped for. Though there have been some contemporary reprints, they seem to be of interest primarily to those with a professional interest in literature. Older libraries, with holdings that were acquired during Louisa May Alcott's lifetime visibility, are the ones that have copies of the adult works in their original editions. If one counts the revision of *Moods* as another book—and it really is—she wrote four adult novels in all:

Moods (1864)
Work: A Story of Experience (1873)
A Modern Mephistopheles (1877)
Moods. A Novel (revised edition) (1882)

The adult novels show a writer with the passion of purpose. Her heroines are advocates for women's rights, and her portrayals of them are socially and psychologically sound. In treatment and style, these books take her skills as a juvenile writer and use them in an adult format, creating characters that are believable, and plots and themes with a firm base in real life.

It is in her "blood and thunder" thrillers that we see Louisa May Alcott—

the writer—the personality behind the writer—in quite another fashion than that associated with her image as the writer of *Little Women*. Here are stories of high adventure, intrigue, suspense, and passion.

Lest the term *passion* be misinterpreted, it should, perhaps, be clarified. There were stories of explicit sex in the 19th century, but they were "underground" publications. Open distribution of stories with the intimacy of sex detailed for the reader is a phenomenon of the mid-to-late 20th century. The passions of Louisa's characters ran the full gamut from jealousy and hate to sexuality, but in the case of the latter, readers could expect hinted at or implicit scenes or comments evoked with a traditional delicate exposition. The *femme fatale* mystique was evident in many of the tales.

The stories dealt with sensational themes that came in the forms of insanity, murder, mesmerism, satanism, mind control, Hindu Thuggee, addiction to hashish or opium, magic potions, and poison, as well as the intrigue and manipulation instigated by jealousy, hate, revenge, deceit, despair, the drive for control or power, and deep, dark secrets. Romance—love—and man vs. woman was a constant thread.

Woman vs. man was the thrust upon which Louisa May Alcott's thrillers thrived. The ink of purple passion drove her heroines to resist the efforts of men, whose desire to dominate had to be thwarted. The power struggle was a firm stand for feminism, and her heroines always won. Some did so with hard lessons or concessions, but many also triumphed in the traditional romantic happily-ever-after ending.

There is a strong element of melodrama, as opposed to drama, in many of the stories, though some hold up quite well as stories of adventure that do not show their 19th-century origins except in the details of dress and customs. The characters are real. They are, for the most part, believable.

Louisa May Alcott brought to her thrillers the same sense of character and story that she brought to her juveniles. But these are stories that delve into the darker side of human nature. The thrillers were sold to magazines like *The Flag of Our Union, Frank Leslie's Illustrated Newspaper,* and *Frank Leslie's Chimney Corner.* For a long time, the "blood and thunder" stories were a staple in Louisa's writing repertoire, as well as a much-needed source of income. At one time, she recorded negotiating for the publication of a story, with a higher payment offered if she would allow the use of her name—an offer she declined. This was in line with her identity as a writer before the 1868 success of *Little Women*.

She wrote no thrillers that are known of after the 1868 success. Some scholars contend that her heart was really with the thrillers. Given that she could have continued to earn money by using her pseudonym to keep her name as a juvenile writer untarnished, it would seem that she could have continued to write them if she had wanted to. Of course, there would have been the risk that the secret of A.M. Barnard would be found out. That was the reason for the anonymous tales and the pseudonyms to begin with. The writers and other intellects who were part of the Alcott circle would hardly have applauded the thrillers as literary works. (The thrillers, too, are listed in the Chronological Bibliography of Louisa May Alcott's Works. They are also mentioned in the discussion of contemporary reprints in Chapter 17.)

Louisa wrote in her journal in the summer of 1862, "...Wrote two tales for L(eslie). I enjoy romancing to suit myself; and though my tales are silly, they are not bad; and my sinners always have a good spot somewhere. I hope it is a good drill for fancy and language, for I can do it fast; and Mr. L. says my tales are so 'dramatic, vivid, and full of plot,' they are just what he wants."

In January 1865, Louisa had written, "...fell back on rubbishy tales, for they pay best, and I can't afford to starve on praise, when sensation stories are written in half the time and keep the family cosey."

With *Little Women,* Louisa May Alcott catapulted into a successful career. She felt she had found her true style, and her numerous juvenile writings after 1868 would indicate that was her preference.

The number of works in each genre—particularly on one hand the thrillers and on the other the juveniles—reveals a writer who was certainly most prolific. Today, having a successful career in two widely disparate genres would be acknowledged as the feat of a rare talent. Delving into Alcott's poetry, into her adult novels, into the lurid thrillers, and into the family-oriented juveniles gives the reader a rare look at the diverse accomplishments of Louisa May Alcott.

Chapter 16

1845–1887: Louisa's Lyrics to Songs

Alcott scholars will be interested to know that Louisa submitted one of her verses as a lyric for a hymn and wrote two especially meant to be sung as hymns. Several versions of musical settings are included here. The Alcotts, along with many others of their circle, were Unitarians. Louisa May Alcott's maternal uncle, Samuel May, was a Unitarian minister, as was his son, Joseph May. Other Unitarian ministers in the Alcott circle included Ralph Waldo Emerson and Theodore Parker. Louisa wrote a number of poems in her lifetime, many of them religious, so it is quite understandable that she would have been responsive to the requests for lyrics for hymns.

Also included here are the words Louisa wrote to be sung at three school festivals at Concord; they are sung to then-contemporary or old folk tunes. Her interest in the school festivals was strengthened by the fact that her father, Bronson Alcott, was superintendent of Concord schools. The festival itself was an all-village event, with participation of its literati regardless of whether or not they had children in the schools at the time.

The last two songs have newer musical settings; that is, one has been newly arranged to music known in Louisa's time, and the other has a completely new musical setting. (The term *arranged* is customarily used when someone matches words from one existing source and music from another. In this sense it differs from its usage as a term to reflect a *musical arrangement* of notes, key, tempo, and in the case of orchestral music, variations for several instruments.)

"My Kingdom"

In 1875, Louisa responded to a request for a verse that might be used as a lyric for a hymn by sending the words to "My Kingdom," which she had actually written in 1845. It was published, with untitled music by A.P. Howard, in *The Sunny Side: A Book of Religious Songs for the Sunday School and the Home*, edited by Charles W. Wendte and H.S. Perkins. Among other "original poetical contributions," the book included work by "Miss Louisa Alcott" and coincidentally, "Mrs. Ednah Cheney," the Alcott family friend

The Marches at the piano. Illustration by Frank T. Merrill from *Little Women*. Boston, Roberts Brothers, 1880.

who would, after Louisa's death, edit *Louisa May Alcott: Her Life, Letters, and Journals* (1889). Along with "My Kingdom" appeared Louisa's words:

> I send you a little piece which I found in an old journal, kept when I was about thirteen years old.... Coming from a child's heart, when conscious of its wants and weaknesses, it may go to the hearts of other children in like mood.

This was marked "Extract from a private letter." The poem had four verses.

As an example of "a child's heart," it shows the precociousness of young Louy's, not only in its seriousness, but also in its style and vocabulary. Though the tone is somewhat pious, the words indicate that the writer was a thoughtful child.

When she wrote *Under the Lilacs* in 1878, Louisa incorporated "My Kingdom" into the story. As the children are talking with each other they decide to learn a hymn because "it is a good thing to do Sundays." As they look for one, the knowledgeable reader can see the autobiographical aspect of at least this part of the story:

> ..."Look at the end, and see if there isn't a piece of poetry pasted in. You learn that and see how funny Celia will look when you say it to her. She wrote it when she was a girl, and somebody had it printed for other children. *I* like it best, myself." Pleased by the prospect of a little fun to cheer his virtuous task, Ben whisked over the leaves, and read with interest the lines Miss Celia has written in her girlhood:— ... ("My Kingdom," etc.) ... "I like that!" said Ben, emphatically, when he had read the little hymn. "I understand it, and I'll learn it right away. Don't see how she could make it all come out so nice and pretty...."

My Kingdom (1875)

8.6.8.6.8.6.8.6.

Words by Miss LOUISA ALCOTT ("Little Women") 1845   A.P. Howard

[Sheet music for "MY KINGDOM," No. 45. Words by Miss LOUISA ALCOTT ("Little Women"). A. P. HOWARD. By per. of OLIVER DITSON & CO. Note: "I send you a little piece which I found in an old journal, kept when I was about thirteen years old.... Coming from a child's heart, when conscious of its wants and weaknesses, it may go to the hearts of other children in like mood."—Extract from a private letter.]

1. A little kingdom I possess, Where thoughts and feelings dwell; And very hard I find the task Of governing it well. For passion tempts and troubles me, A wayward will misleads, And selfishness its shadow casts On all my will and deeds.

2. How can I learn to rule myself, To be the child I should, Honest and brave, nor ever tire Of trying to be good? How can I keep a sunny soul To shine along life's way? How can I tune my little heart To sweetly sing all day?

3. Dear Father, help me with the love That casteth out my fear! Teach me to lean on thee, and feel That thou art very near; That no temptation is unseen, No childish grief too small, Since thou, with patience infinite, Dost soothe and comfort all.

4. I do not ask for any crown
But that which all may win;
Nor try to conquer any world
Except the one within.
Be thou my guide until I find,
Led by a tender hand,
Thy happy kingdom in *myself*,
And dare to take command.

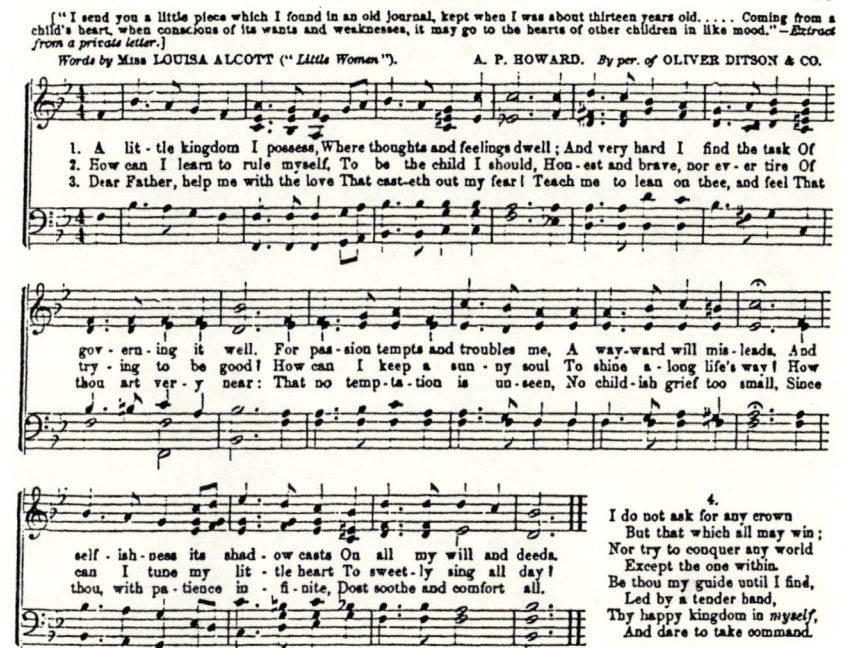

"My Kingdom," like most of Louisa's poetry, is little known outside the field of Alcott scholars. *Under the Lilacs* is little-read today. It's strange to suddenly hear the first four lines quoted at the end of a lighthearted television film with secret agents, deadly gadgets, and mad scientists, as it was in *Once Upon a Spy* (1980), though the writer obviously knew it would not be recognized and had another character ask who the quotation was from.

In 1908, Charles W. Wendte, who had edited *The Sunny Side,* included the song in another hymnal, *Heart and Voice,* where it appeared with a tune called "June Days."

In 1910, the lyrics appeared as "A Little Kingdom" in *The Life Hymnal: A Book of Song and Service for the Sunday School,* this time from a Universalist publisher. The lyrics were set to the music of Von Weber, and the verses were cut to three. Curiously, the last verse was created from the first half of the original third verse and the second half of the original fourth verse. Also, Louisa's name was spelled as Louise.

In 1975, the Unitarian-Universalist Association published *Singing Our History: Tales, Texts and Tunes from Two Centuries of Unitarian and*

A Little Kingdom (1910)

8.6.8.6.8.6.8.6.

Louise M. Alcott 1845

Von Weber
Arranged by E.T. Mitchell

1. A lit-tle king-dom I pos-sess Where tho'ts and feel-ings dwell, And ver-y hard I find the task Of gov-ern-ing it well. For pas-sion tempts and trou-bles me, A way-ward will mis-leads; And sel-fish-ness its shad-ow casts On all my will and deeds.

2. How can I learn to rule my-self To be the child I should, Hon-est and brave, nor ev-er tire Of try-ing to be good? How can I keep a sun-ny soul To shine a-long life's way? How can I tune my lit-tle heart To sweet-ly sing all day?

3. Dear Fa-ther, help me with the love That cast-eth out my fear! Teach me to lean on thee, and feel That thou art ver-y near. Be thou my guide un-til I find, Led by a ten-der hand, Thy hap-py king-dom in my-self, And dare to take com-mand.

Louisa's Lyrics to Songs

A Little Kingdom I Possess (1975)

Forest Green 8.6.8.6.8.6.8.6.

Louisa May Alcott 1845

English Folk Melody ("The Ploughboy's Dream")
Mus. arr. Ralph Vaughan Williams 1906 (retitled)
Arranged by Eugene B. Navias 1975

1. A little kingdom I possess,
   Where thoughts and feelings dwell;
   And very hard I find the task
   Of governing it well;
   For passion tempts, and troubles me,
   A wayward will misleads;
   And selfishness its shadow casts
   On all my will and deeds.

2. How can I learn to rule myself
   To be the child I should—
   Honest and brave, nor ever tire
   Of trying to be good?
   How can I keep a sunny soul
   To shine along life's way?
   How can I tune my happy heart
   To sweetly sing all day?

3. Dear Father, help me with the love
   That casteth out all fear;
   Teach me to lean on Thee and feel
   That Thou art very near;
   That no temptation is unseen,
   No childish grief too small,
   Since Thou with patience infinite,
   Dost soothe and comfort all.

4. I do not ask for any crown,
   But that which all may win,
   Nor try to conquer any world
   Except the one within;
   Be Thou my guide until I find,
   Led by a tender hand,
   Thy happy kingdom in myself,
   And dare to take command.

Universalist Hymns, collected and edited by Eugene B. Navias. This time Louisa's work was in the company of several others who had been part of her life, including Ralph Waldo Emerson, the lifelong family friend and benefactor; James T. Fields, the publisher who had played a pivotal role in her career; Mary Livermore, the early feminist; Theodore Parker, who had encouraged her when she was a young woman; and Julia Ward Howe, literary friend who wrote "The Battle Hymn of the Republic."

Navias played over the tunes for "My Kingdom" in the early collections and found them awkward and somber; he feels his choice of setting is far livelier and lighter, but in deference, states, "but such is a matter of taste." His choice of tune for "A Little Kingdom I Possess," was "Forest Green," an English folk melody which had appeared in *Hymns for the Celebration of Life* (1964), though it was extant in Louisa's time. (Actually, "Forest Green" acquired that title in 1906 from folk-hymnodist Ralph Vaughan Williams, who had prepared a musical arrangement from an English folk song, "The Plowboy's Dream.") Navias also suggested that if "Forest Green" did not appear somber enough for "A Little Kingdom I Possess," singers might try "Old 137th," "St. Matthew," "Salvation," (all of which appear elsewhere in *Singing Our History*), or "Ellacombe" (which appears in *Hymns for the Celebration of Life*).

Navias explains that, traditionally, hymn tunes are named in order to make them identifiable regardless of the text being used with them. Thus, beneath the title of a hymn, one frequently sees a second title, this being the melody's. Some composers favor Biblical names, some choose great personages of the church such as saints, some choose other people they admire, and others may name the tune after a place. The numbers which appear with most hymn titles are a meter count of the syllables per line, thus making it easy to mix and match lyrics and music.

"Oh, the Beautiful Old Story"

Another lyric of Louisa's used as a hymn, "Oh, the Beautiful Old Story," was set to the music known as "Beecher," composed by John Zundel in 1870. Zundel used the music with a text by Charles Wesley, "Love Divine, All Loves Excelling." Zundel named the hymn himself, but authorities disagree as to whether it was named after Lyman Beecher, a Protestant clergyman, or for one of Lyman's children: Henry Ward Beecher, a Congregational minister, for whose magazine, *The Christian Union,* Louisa wrote a number of articles; Charles Beecher; or Harriet Beecher Stowe, coeditor of *The Christian Union,* and author of *Uncle Tom's Cabin.* In all four of the previously-known publications of "Oh, the Beautiful Old Story," the musical setting was "Beecher," a coincidental matching of Louisa's lyrics with a tune carrying the family name of her colleagues.

Louisa's Lyrics to Songs

Oh, the Beautiful Old Story

Beecher 8.7.8.7.8.7.8.7.

Louisa May Alcott 1886 — John Zundel 1870

1. Oh, the beau-ti-ful old sto-ry! Of the lit-tle child that lay
2. Oh, the pleas-ant, peace-ful sto-ry! Of the youth who grew so fair,
3. Oh, the won-der-ful, true sto-ry! Of the mes-sen-ger from God,
4. Oh, the sad and sol-emn sto-ry! Of the cross, the crown, the spear,

In a man-ger on that morn-ing, When the stars sang in the day;
In his fath-er's hum-ble dwell-ing, Pov-er-ty and toil to share,
Who a-mong the poor and low-ly, Brave-ly and de-vout-ly trod,
Of the par-don, pain, and glo-ry That have made this name so dear.

When the hap-py shep-herds kneel-ing, As be-fore a ho-ly shrine,
Till a-round him, in the tem-ple, Mar-vel-ling, the old men stood,
Work-ing mir-a-cles of mer-cy, Preach-ing peace, re-buk-ing strife,
This ex-am-ple let us fol-low, Fear-less, faith-ful to the end,

Bless'd God and the ten-der moth-er For a life that was di-vine.
As through his wise in-no-cen-cy Shone the meek boy's an-gel-hood.
Bless-ing all the lit-tle chil-dren, Lift-ing up the dead to life.
Walk-ing in the sa-cred foot-steps Of our broth-er, mas-ter, friend

Louisa evidently wrote this nativity verse in 1886, specifically for inclusion in *The Carol: A Book of Religious Songs for the Sunday School and the Home*, edited by the same Charles W. Wendte who had edited *The Sunny Side*. Although somewhat sanctimonious in tone, the general gist is in keeping with the moral values that pervaded most of Louisa's work, but lacks the lightness of her stories for children. It is, however, in the same righteous tone that appears in "A Free Bed," the "charity" story she wrote in 1888. "Oh, the Beautiful Old Story" was published again in 1895 in *A Book of Song and Service for Sunday School and Home*, in 1914 in *The New Hymn and Tune Book*, and in 1975 in *Singing Our History*.

"What Shall Little Children Bring"

In 1884, the words to "What Shall Little Children Bring" were published in "The Thirty-Fifth Annual Report of the Executive Committee of the Children's Mission to the Children of the Destitute, in the City of Boston; with an Account of the Proceedings at the Annual Meeting, May 28, 1884." Indications are that the Children's Mission was an outreach program of Unitarian churches in and outside of Boston. In the midst of the reports, on pages 22–23, comes the statement, "The children from the Female Orphan Asylum . . . then sang a hymn; and afterward the children of the Mission sang the following original hymn written by Miss Louisa M. Alcott, to a tune arranged for them by their teacher. . . ."

What Shall Little Children Bring (1884)

Lyrics. — Louisa May Alcott

Tune. — Pleyel 7.7.7.7
Ignaz Pleyel 1791, adapted
Arranged by Gloria T. Delamar 1988

Louisa's Lyrics to Songs 215

What Shall Little Children Bring (1884)

Lyrics. — Louisa May Alcott   Tune(s). — Vienna or Pleyel
Arranged by Gloria T. Delamar 1988

> What shall little children bring
> As a grateful offering,
> For the ever watchful care
> That surrounds us everywhere?
>
> Gathered in this happy fold,
> Safe from wintry want and cold,
> Fed by hands that never tire;
> Warmed at love's unfailing fire.
>
> Sheltered by protecting arms
> From the great world's sins and harms,
> While a patience, wise and sweet,
> Guides our little wandering feet, —
>
> Thou who hear'st the ravens call,
> Thou who seest the sparrows fall,
> Thou who holdest safe and warm
> Lost lambs in thy tender arm, —
>
> Father! dearest name of all,
> Bless thy children great and small;
> Rich and poor alike are thine,
> Knit by charity divine.
>
> Willing hearts and open hands,
> Love that every ill withstands,
> Faith and hope in Thee our King, —
> These shall be our offering.

These are the six verses to "What Shall Little Children Bring." Its republication here appears to be the first since its publication in the 1884 report.

The words to "What Shall Little Children Bring" are simple, and true to basic Judeo-Christian tenets. The phraseology and feeling are remarkably contemporary.

The exact hymn-tune chosen by the Mission children's teacher is not known. However, two arrangements are suggested here, "Vienna" and "Pleyel," which are sufficiently different from each other to offer a choice. Each was extant in Louisa's time. Other hymn-tunes which would also be appropriate are "Brasted," "Culbach," "Innocents," and "Orientus Partibus," all of which appear in *Hymns of the Spirit*. "Savannah," which is also suitable, is in *Hymns for the Celebration of Life*. They no doubt appear in other hymnals as well.

Louisa May Alcott—The Legacy

What Shall Little Children Bring (1884)

Lyrics.—Louisa May Alcott

Tune.—Vienna 7 7.7.7
Justin Heinrich Knecht 1799
Arranged by Gloria T. Delamar 1988

"The Children's Song"

In March 1860, Louisa recorded in her journal:

> Wrote a song for the school festival, (March 30) and heard it sung by four hundred happy children. Father got up the affair, and such a pretty affair was never seen in Concord before. He said, "We spend much on our cattle and flower shows; let us each spring have a show of our children, and begrudge nothing for their culture." All liked it but the old fogies who want things as they were in the ark.

"The Children's Song" was evidently not published outside of Concord until 1889, when Ednah Cheney included it in *Louisa May Alcott: Her Life, Letters, and Journals,* indicating that it was intended to be sung to the tune of "Wait for the Wagon," a familiar melody of the time. The verses are an ode to the village of Concord. Verse three alludes to three prominent Concord men: the first line refers to Ralph Waldo Emerson, the second to Henry David Thoreau, and the third and fourth to Amos Bronson Alcott.

Louisa's Lyrics to Songs

The Children's Song (1860)

Lyrics. — Louisa May Alcott Tune. — "Wait for the Wagon."
R.B. Buckley 1851

The Children's Song (1860)

Lyrics. — Louisa May Alcott Tune. — "Wait for the Wagon."
By R.B. Buckley 1851

    The world lies fair about us, and friendly sky above;
    Our lives are full of sunshine, our homes are full of love;
    Few cares or sorrows sadden the beauty of our day;
    We gather simple pleasures like daisies by the way.
        Chorus. — Oh! sing with cheery voices,
            Like robins on the tree;
           For little lads and lasses
            As blithe of heart should be.

The village is our fairyland: its good men are our kings;
And wandering through its by-ways our busy minds find wings.
The school-room is our garden, and we the flowers there,
And kind hands tend and water us that we may blossom fair.
    Chorus. — Oh! dance in airy circles,
        Like fairies on the lee;
        For little lads and lasses
        As light of foot should be.

There's the Shepherd of the sheepfold; the Father of the vines;
The Hermit of blue Walden; the Poet of the pines;
And a Friend who comes among us, with counsels wise and mild,
With snow upon his forehead, yet at heart a very child.
    Chorus. — Oh! smile as smiles the river,
        Slow rippling to the sea;
        For little lads and lasses
        As full of peace should be.

There's not a cloud in heaven but drops its silent dew;
No violet in the meadow but blesses with its blue;
No happy child in Concord who may not do its part
To make the great world better by innocence of heart.
    Chorus. — Oh! blossom in the sunshine
        Beneath the village tree;
        For little lads and lasses
        Are the fairest flowers we see.

"Wait for the Wagon" is generally credited to having been composed by R. Bishop Buckley (1810–1867), an Englishman who came to the United States and organized Buckley's Minstrels in 1843. The earliest printing of the melody was 1851, where it was identified as an "Ethiopian Song"; it has also been suggested that it was of minstrel origin.

"Young America"

In March 1861, Louisa wrote a song for another Concord School Exhibition at the Town Hall, recording the circumstances in her journal.

> Father had his usual school festival, and Emerson asked me to write a song, which I did. On the 16th, the schools all met in the hall (four hundred), — a pretty posy bed, with a border of parents and friends. Some of the fogies objected to the names Phillips and John Brown. But Emerson said: "Give it up? No, no; *I* will read it." Which he did, to my great contentment; for when the great man of the town says "Do it," the thing is done. So the choir warbled, and the Alcotts were uplifted in their vain minds.

The School Committee's report indicates that Henry David Thoreau also made a few remarks at the festival.

Louisa's Lyrics to Songs 219

"Young America" (untitled in its publication in the Concord School Exhibition brochure of 1861) is a patriotic song to be sung to the tune of "All the Blue Bonnets Are Over the Border." The melody is an ancient Scottish "Border Ballad" which was widely popular in the United States in the early 19th century; it appeared with the "blue bonnet" lyrics (c1820) by Sir Walter Scott in his *Monastery*.

Louisa's lyrics are full of names that were already history in 1861. It has not, to the best of records, been published before, except as part of the original local school festival.

Young America (1861)

Lyrics. — Louisa May Alcott　　　Tune. — Ancient Scottish Border Ballad; "All the Blue Bonnets Are Over the Border," c1820

I

March, march, mothers and grand-mammas!
Come from each home that stands in our border!
March, march, fathers and grand-papas!
Now young America waits in good order!
　Here is a flower show,
　Grown under winter snow,
Ready for spring with her sunshine and flowers;
　Here every blossom grows
　Shamrock, thistle and rose,
And fresh from our hillsides the Pilgrim's May flowers.

II

Here is the New World that yet shall be founded;
Here are our Websters, our Sumners, and Hales,
And here, with ambition by boat-racing bounded,
Perhaps there may be a new Splitter of rails.
　Here are our future men,
　Here are John Browns again;
Here are young Phillips's eyeing our blunders,
　Yet may the river see
　Hunt, Hosmer, Flint and Lee
Stand to make Concord hills echo their thunders.

III

Here are the women who make no complaining,
Dumb-bells and clubs chasing vapors away,
Queens of good health and good humor all reigning,
Fairer and freer than we of today;
　Fullers with gifted eyes,
　Friendly Eliza Frys,
Nightingales born to give war a new glory;
　Britomarts brave to ride
　Thro' the world far and wide,
Righting all wrongs, as in Spenser's sweet story.

Young America (1861)

Lyrics. — Louisa May Alcott

Tune. — Ancient Scottish Border Ballad; "All the Blue Bonnets Are Over the Border" c1820

IV

Come now from Barrett's mill, Bateman's blue water,
Nine Acre Corner, the Centre and all;
Come from the Factory, the North and East Quarter,
For here is a Union that never need fall;
  Lads in your blithest moods,
  Maids in your pretty snoods,
Come from all homes that stand in our border;
  Concord shall many a day
  Tell of the fair array
When young America met in good order.

"The John Brown Song"

The brochure of the Concord School Exhibition for March 15, 1862, included "The John Brown Song." Several Alcott scholars believe that Louisa wrote these verses, as it is in her style and related brochures are among her papers. Though actual documentation of her authorship has been lost, it seems reasonable to assume that she did indeed write "The John Brown Song." There is also the circumstantial evidence that she had written the songs for the 1860 and 1861 festivals, thus probably also wrote the one for the 1862 event.

As to the words themselves, either Louisa wrote an anachronistic song (given that John Brown died in 1859), or she had written it when Captain John Brown was brought to the Concord Town Hall in May of 1859 by Franklin Sanborn, or she wrote it as a symbolic narrative. The song details the coming of John Brown; verses 4, 5, and 6 are set in quotation marks to indicate, presumably, that John Brown is saying them.

The lyrics were intended to be sung to the melody of "John Brown's Body," which became popular after Brown's execution on December 2, 1859. (The original verse, "John Brown," by H.H. Brownell, began with "Old John Brown lies a-mouldering in the grave, etc.," stated only once, with other statements following. But the lines were quickly corrupted; the now-traditional lines are "John Brown's body lies a-mouldering in the grave,"—sung three times. Another of Brownell's lines was adopted for the familar triple-repetition of the traditional version, but the two other verses of the traditional version start with lines not seen in Brownell's verse. As the indication with Louisa's words are that they are to be sung to "John Brown's Body," it may be fair to assume that the corruption of Brownell's words had taken place by 1862, when Louisa wrote the words to "The John Brown Song.")

The John Brown Song (1862)

Lyrics.—?Louisa May Alcott   Tune.—Hymn c1857–58; "John Brown's Body" 1860; "The Battle Hymn of the Republic" 1862

  Welcome Fathers! here's welcome to you all!
  Welcome Mothers! right welcome to the Hall!

222   Louisa May Alcott—The Legacy

The John Brown Song (1862)

Lyrics. — ?Louisa May Alcott   Tune — Hymn c1857–58; "John Brown's Body" 1860; "The Battle Hymn of the Republic" 1862

Sisters, Brothers! we welcome one and all!
  The children's day has come.
Chorus: Glory, Glory Hallelujah, Glory, Glory Hallelujah,
      Glory, Glory Hallelujah, The children's day has come.

Slow goes the Winter in icy armor forth,
Spring comes slowly to thaw the frosty North,—
Sing till birds come, ye children of the North!
  Until the blue birds come.
Chorus: Glory, Glory Hallelujah, Glory, Glory Hallelujah,
      Glory, Glory Hallelujah, The blue birds soon shall come.

Northward flying a little bird I hear,
Blue birds singing not half so loud and clear,—
All ye children his sounding voice may hear,
  When to the North he's come.
Chorus: Glory, Glory Hallelujah, Glory, Glory Hallelujah,
      Glory, Glory Hallelujah, To counsel us he's come.

Raise loud anthems to Him who reigns above,
Sing His praises, His mighty power and love, —
Oft your fathers have known his power and love,
 And seen his judgments come.
Chorus: Glory, Glory Hallelujah, Glory, Glory Hallelujah,
 Glory, Glory Hallelujah, His jubilee has come!

"Drums shall echo the Lord's high decree,
Cannons thunder, and then declareth He,
Bugles blowing, His heavenly decree —
TO ALL SHALL FREEDOM COME!
Chorus: Glory, Glory Hallelujah, Glory, Glory Hallelujah,
 Glory, Glory Hallelujah, To all shall Freedom come!

Sing ye children, ye children of the North!
Freedom's banner shall lead your army forth,
Victory's coming to meet the marching North,
 And Liberty shall come!
Chorus: Glory, Glory Hallelujah, Glory, Glory Hallelujah,
 Glory, Glory Hallelujah, Fair Liberty has come!

This melody was also heard with "The Battle Hymn of the Republic" in 1862. Earlier, in 1857-58, the song had appeared as a Sunday school hymn, published as both, "My Brother, Will You Meet Me," and "Say Brothers, Will You Meet Me." Though persistent claims have arisen, variously attributing the song to William Steffe of Philadelphia, Thomas Brigham Bishop of New York City, or Frank E. Jerome of Russell, Kansas, no documentation exists for any, though William Steffe has been credited in several community songbooks as composer of the melody accompanying "The Battle Hymn of the Republic."

"The Fairy Spring"

Louisa wrote a short story for children, "The Fairy Spring," that was first published in *Lulu's Library. Volume II,* in 1887; it was one of her stories that did not first appear in a magazine. Many of the "Lulu's Library" tales were originally written for the amusement of her niece, Lulu Nieriker. The poem, "The Fairy Spring," is from the story of the same name.

The story is a delightful fantasy wherein "little wood-people" decide that the song of the brook should be revealed to the sweet child, May, who comes regularly to the babbling brook, but "never throws pebbles in the water to disturb the minnows, nor breaks the ferns only to let them die . . . (she) sings to herself as if she were half a bird." The song of the brook leads upward through the woods to the happy secret of the spring: "whoever climbs up and drinks this water will leave all pain and weariness behind, and grow healthy in body, happy in heart. . . ."

The lilting "sweet voice" of "the song of the brook," is a natural for arrangement with the short piece of music by Frédéric Chopin (1810–1849) — music that was extant in Louisa's time. (First appearance in print.)

The Fairy Spring (1887)

Louisa May Alcott 1887   Frédéric Chopin (1810–1848)
Arranged by Gloria T. Delamar 1988

    I am calling, I am calling,
        As I ripple, run and sing.

The Fairy Spring (1887)

Louisa May Alcott 1887   Frédéric Chopin (1810–1848)
Arranged by Gloria T. Delamar 1988

    Come up higher, come up higher,
        Come and find the fairy spring.

Who will listen, who will listen
    To the wonders I can tell
Of a palace built of sunshine
    Where the sweetest spirits dwell?

Singing winds and magic waters,
    Golden shadows, silver rain,
Spells that make the sad heart happy,
    Sleep that cures the deepest pain.

Cheeks that bloom like summer roses,
    Smiling lips and hours that shine,
Come to those who climb the mountain,
    Find and taste the fairy wine.

I am calling, I am calling,
    As I ripple, run and sing;
Who will listen, who will listen,
    To the story of the spring?

Louisa's Lyrics to Songs 225

"Come, Butter, Come"

"Come, Butter, Come," is a verse that Louisa incorporated into the short story, "Morning Glories," in 1867. The lyrics were set to music by Gloria T. Delamar in 1982 to accompany a classroom lesson in the principle of butter-making; as they sang the song, the children passed around a jar containing heavy cream, taking turns shaking/churning the jar until the liquid turned into butter. This is the first printing of Louisa's "Come, Butter, Come" in its musical setting.

From "Morning Glories" by Louisa May Alcott:

> ...All round on white shelves stood the shining pans, full of milk; the stone floor was wet; and a stream of water ran along a narrow bed through the room, and in it stood jars of butter, pots of cream, and cans of milk. The window was open, and hopvines shook their green bells before it. The birds sang outside, and maids sang inside, as the churn and the wood spatters kept time....

Come, Butter, Come (1867)

Louisa May Alcott 1867   Gloria T. Delamar 1982

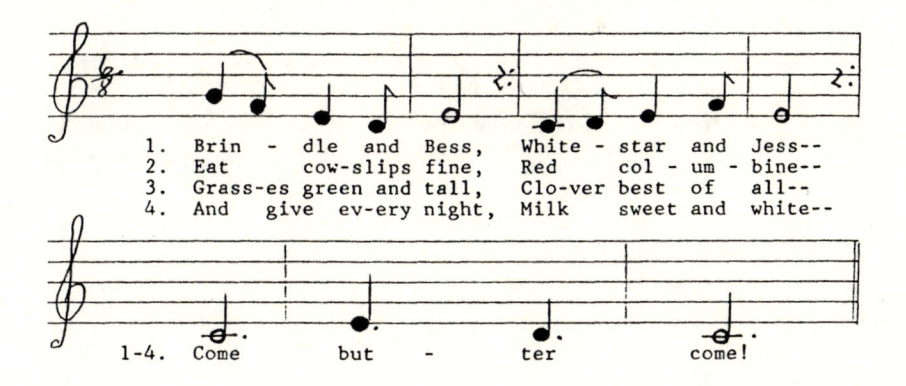

1. Brin - dle and Bess,   White - star and Jess--
2. Eat   cow-slips fine,   Red   col - um - bine--
3. Grass-es green and tall,   Clo-ver best of all--
4. And   give ev-ery night,   Milk   sweet and white--

1-4. Come   but   -   ter   come!

Chapter 17

1888–Now: Alcott as the Subject of Literary Studies

When an author's work grows into the designation of "classic," it is inevitable that the author becomes the subject of study. After the publication of *Little Women,* Louisa had contemporary literary recognition, and even though her other books and stories never attained the same heights of popularity, her reputation had been made.

Although published as a girls' story, *Little Women* got adult attention right from the start. The phenomenon of "Little Women Clubs"—groups of four females who divided among themselves the new names of Meg, Jo, Beth, and Amy—ranged from the younger female readers for whom the book had been intended, to college-aged girls, including the group at Vassar who adopted the personae of all the major characters of the book.

Louisa's involvement in, and writing about, adult concerns (abolition, suffrage, women's rights) and her novels, albeit they were not highly successful in their time, contributed to her being perceived as more than a writer for children. But her status as writer of a book that was already a classic in the writer's lifetime assured her a place in literary discussions. *Little Women* does not appear only on lists of children's books; it can be found just as regularly on general lists of "good books."

The studies about her, from her death in 1888 to the present, fall into roughly six categories: letters and journals; recollections; biographies; contemporary republications of her works, with introductory notes; critical analyses; and bibliographies.

There will be no attempt here to mention all the studies, as all the major and most of the minor ones that had any bearing on Louisa's life or works are included in the Reference Bibliography, with the pertinent details. Some, however, form such a basis for further study, that they should be pointed out.

Contemporary republications of Louisa's stories and books indicate the interest that has taken study of her beyond the fact of *Little Women* to a new assessment of her other work. *Little Women* has remained in print well into its second 100 years. A few of her other children's novels are available, some anthologies of short stories, and some reprints of the adult novels. All are listed in, and the details for those discussed here are in, the Chronological Bibliography of Louisa May Alcott's Works.

The first biographical memorial to Louisa came from Ednah Cheney, old family friend, in *Louisa May Alcott: The Children's Friend*. The emphasis was on the influence Louisa's tales had had on child readers. Coming in 1888, the year Louisa died, it was far more memorial than critical treatment.

That Louisa May Alcott is worthy of study is evident in the number of institutions that have Alcott holdings. Among these institutions are Barnard College, Boston Public Library, Boston University, Bowling Green State University, Brigham Young University, Brown University, Cincinnati Historical Society, Columbia University, Concord Free Public Library, Cornell University, Fruitlands Museums, Harvard University, Historical Society of Pennsylvania, Huntington Library, Indiana University, Iowa State Historical Library, Library of Congress, Maine Historical Society, Massachusetts Historical Society, Minnesota Historical Society, Morristown National Historic Park, New York Historical Society, New York Public Library, New York University, Newberry Library, Orchard House/Louisa May Alcott Memorial Association, Pierpont Morgan Library, Princeton University, Radcliffe College, Smith College, Swarthmore College, University of Florida, University of Michigan, University of Texas, University of Virginia, Vanderbilt University and Yale University.

Letters and Journals

The first real indepth look into Louisa's life came in 1889, after Cheney had been given access to those letters and journals that Louisa had not destroyed in her effort to keep the world's prying eyes out of her affairs. Cheney edited these and wove the documentation along with other biographical material into *Louisa May Alcott: Her Life, Letters, and Journals*. This still stands as primary material. Of course, Cheney had to edit the letters and journal entries into a manageable size; later criticism was that her basic theme of "Duty's Faithful Child" may have kept her from including more relevant entries. More important is the fact that much of what might have been truly insightful records had been destroyed by their originator.

Louisa wanted her privacy. Privacy is lost, however, to those who gain the public eye. Unfortunately, Louisa did not have the historian's attitude, so that she took measures that would, even after her death, prohibit the many facets of her character to be put on open view.

The letters and journals that do remain, however, are invaluable source material. Many more than appeared in Cheney's book exist, most on deposit in the Houghton Library at Harvard, though there are other sundry holdings at various universities, historical societies, and libraries.

LOUISA MAY ALCOTT

Louisa May Alcott. Engraving from a photograph. Illustration in "Louisa May Alcott" (juvenile booklet). Boston: Educational Publishing Company, Vol. III, No. 63. October 15, 1896.

Cheney, in her introduction to *Life, Letters, and Journals,* said, "She (Louisa) was not a voluminous correspondent; she did not encourage many intimacies, and she seldom wrote letters except to her family, unless in reference to some purpose she had strongly at heart. Writing was her constant occupation, and she was not tempted to indulge in it as a recreation. Her letters are brief, and strictly to the point, but always characteristic in feeling and expression. . . ."

Other letters and journals were examined and parts recorded, in such books as *A. Bronson Alcott: His Life and Philosophy,* cowritten by longtime friends, Frank(lin) Sanborn and William T. Harris, who had bought Orchard House from the Alcotts and continued a friendship with them. Ralph Waldo Emerson's journals included entries that revealed his relationship with the Alcotts.

A few letters that Louisa wrote were eventually published, although she had wanted all of her letters destroyed. It is possible that the Lukens sisters were unaware of this wish, but the letters, when printed, were done so "by special permission of Miss Alcott's heirs." Edited by Edward W. Bok, "Louisa May Alcott's Letters to Five Girls," published in 1896, 24 years after they were written, show the side of Louisa that responded to her fans in order to encourage those like the Lukens sisters in their activity of putting out a little newsletter, just as the Alcott-March sisters had done.

In 1901, Alfred Whitman published parts of 12 letters Louisa had written to him between October 1858 and January 1869. Presented as "Miss Alcott's Letters to Her 'Laurie,'" he included an introduction about his times with the Alcotts. Many of the letters are addressed to "Dear Dolphus" and signed "Sophy," a habit derived from when they acted together as Dolphus and Sophy Tetterby in Dickens's "The Haunted Man." As prelude to the letters, Whitman wrote, "Deference to the wishes of the surviving members of the Pratt family compels me to omit several of the letters and part of others. Enough remains, however, in the letters which follow to prove to all lovers of Louisa M. Alcott that justice has never been done to the sweetest and most attractive side of her nature...." The concluding letter in the two-part article documents the real-life inspirations for the character of Laurie of *Little Women,* as resulting in a composite of Alf and the Polish boy, Ladislas Wisniewski.

It becomes evident that the heirs and friends of the author began to recognize the historical seriousness of preserving and documenting Louisa's papers. John S.P. Alcott (Anna's son, John Pratt), whom Louisa had adopted in order to have a legal heir to administer her affairs after her death, gained copyright in 1914 for *Little Women Letters from the House of Alcott.* The papers themselves were edited by Jessie Bonstelle and Marian De Forest.

Cheney's *Louisa May Alcott: Her Life, Letters, and Journals* was reprinted in 1928, and again in 1981—and was still in print at the 100th anniversary of Louisa's death in 1988.

It was not until 1957 that another group of letters was published. In "The Alcott's through Thirty Years: Letters to Alfred Whitman," Elizabeth Bancroft Schlesinger edited letters written from March 1858 to May 1891 between Louisa, Anna, and their mother, Abby (Abba) May Alcott and Alfred Whitman from March 1858 to May 1891.

In 1979, a few excerpts of Louisa's letters to Mary Mapes Dodge were included in a biography of that editor of *St. Nicholas* for whom Louisa had written a number of her stories and serializations of the children's novels. As Dodge was the author of the book usually referred to as *Hans Brinker* the biography of her by Cath'arine Morris Wright was called *Lady of the Silver Skates: The Life and Correspondence of Mary Mapes Dodge, 1830–1905*.

It would be 1987 before another edition of Alcott's letters would appear. As the centennial of her death approached, scholarly interest increased. Joel Myerson, Daniel Shealy, and Madeleine Stern edited *The Selected Letters of Louisa May Alcott*, including many not previously published. This would be followed in 1989 with Myerson, Shealy, and Stern's *The Journals of Louisa May Alcott*. Both are invaluable additions to Alcott scholarship.

Recollections

The first recollection that should be noted is one written by Louisa herself. Before her death (March 6, 1888), she had written a recollection of her own life. With her usual wit, she told about childhood escapades, her education, her religious feelings, her family, and her career. She concluded with, "So the omen proved to be a true one, and the wheel of fortune turned slowly, till the girl of fifteen found herself a woman of fifty with her prophetic dream beautifully realized, her duty done, her reward far greater than she deserved. November 2 (1888)." It appeared in *The Youth's Companion*, May 24, 1888; *The Woman's Journal*, May 26, 1888; was reprinted in part in *Our Dumb Animals*, July 1888; and was the preface to *Lulu's Library III* which was published in 1889.

Particularly interesting are the recollections of Louisa's peers. For the most part they are casually written, having been published more for their content of reminiscences than for literary merit. But, they have life in them. They are warm memories of little events in the shared life of the writer and Louisa May Alcott. It is in these that one can see Louisa as her friends saw her.

Maria S. Porter was a friend in Louisa's adulthood. Her little book, *Recollections of Louisa May Alcott, John Greenleaf Whittier, and Robert Browning, together with several memorial poems*, was published in 1893. Along with events she shared with Louisa, she also includes experiences of Louisa's childhood as told to her by Louisa.

The major part of Annie L(awrence) Clarke's 1902 book, *The Alcotts in Harvard*, is a straight nonfiction treatment of the Fruitlands experiment. When the Alcotts left Fruitlands in Harvard, they went to Still River. Just at the end of the book, appear reminiscences about the days in Still River and the school there, with Clarke and the Alcott girls as playmates.

In Clara Gowing's *The Alcotts As I Knew Them*, of 1909, she combined a general biography of the family with personal experiences she had with the various members of the family.

Another recollection of interest was written by John Pratt Alcott in 1913.

Literary Studies

In "Little Women of Long Ago," he discussed his famous aunt, his mother, their sisters, and his own upbringing.

Also in 1913 Lydia Hosmer Wood wrote "Beth Alcott's Playmate," in which she gave some insight into the lives of the Alcott sisters as young girls.

Alcott Memoirs: Posthumously Compiled from Papers, Journals, and Memoranda of the Late Dr. Frederick L.H. Willis by Edith Willis Linn and Henry Bazin, though posthumous, as the title indicates, was written in the format of a reminiscence; Edith Willis Linn wrote in the prelude, "...I offer its pages as a tribute to my father and not as a contribution to the already extensive literature concerning the early literary period of New England.... I have eliminated all references that might be deemed critical or over-laudatory, that might create controversy, or that touched upon the more sacred human relationships, believing this would have been my father's wish." It is, nevertheless a warmly told history, almost three-fourths of the small book being devoted to the Alcotts, in particular Bronson and Louisa, and the balance being chapters about Emerson, Thoreau, Fuller, and Hawthorne.

Julian Hawthorne, son of Nathaniel Hawthorne, and younger friend to the mature Alcott girls, waited until 1922 to write "The Woman Who Wrote *Little Women*." He would have been well into his 70s at that time, and parts of his reminiscence do not correlate with the dates generally accepted, but are interesting nevertheless.

Insights into Louisa and Concord life appeared in Mary Hosmer Brown's 1926 *Memories of Concord*, and Caroline Ticknor's *Classic Concord* of the same year. Caroline Ticknor also wrote a biography of May Alcott (Nieriker) in 1929, *May Alcott: A Memoir*, a book frequently misfiled, or mislabeled, even in *Books in Print*, as being about Louisa May.

In 1967, the Americanist Press reprinted *Alcott Memoirs: Posthumously Compiled from Papers, Journals, and Memoranda of the Late Dr. Frederick L.H. Willis;* the facsimile edition was limited to 200 copies. In 1978, Folcroft Library Editions reprinted both Clara Gowing's *The Alcotts As I Knew Them* and Maria S. Porter's *Recollections of Louisa May Alcott (etc.)*. The reprintings of these recollections are an indication of the interest that study of Louisa May Alcott had reached in literature.

Biographies

Several biographies of Louisa should be noted either for their historical or academic value. What may be the first (and certainly, an early) treatment of Louisa's life for juvenile readers is a 5½" × 7½", 29-page booklet, *Young Folks Library of Choice Literature: Louisa May Alcott*. (Boston: Educational Publishing Co., Vol. III, No. 63, October 15, 1896.) Intended for third-graders, each simple sentence set as a paragraph, it begins with:

Illustration by Lizbeth B. Comins. Frontispiece from *The Children's Friend*, by Ednah D. Cheney. Boston: L. Prang & Co., 1888.

"Girls may become famous as well as boys.

"A little girl came into a happy home in Germantown, near Philadelphia, in 1832.

"They called her Louisa, and her father was Mr. Alcott.

"Louisa Alcott was always the children's friend."

The booklet has two illustrations, pen and ink sketches of Louisa and of Orchard House. No writer's byline is given.

In Seth Curtis Beach's *Daughters of the Puritans* of 1905, the section on Louisa is obviously based on *Life, Letters, and Journals*, but it is noteworthy in that it contains the first real acknowledgment of Louisa's activities in women's suffrage.

The first major biography, *Louisa May Alcott, Dreamer and Worker: A Study of Achievement*, was written by Belle Moses in 1909. It drew upon Cheney's *Life, Letters, and Journals*, as all subsequent biographies would, but included greater details of the works and their publications, as well as some comments by a few who had known Louisa. As with many early books, however, it lacks an index.

In 1927, Honore Willsie Morrow came out with a viewpoint biography that did not treat Amos Bronson Alcott as much as himself — as educator and philosopher — as by the designation he had been given in the years after his daughter became famous. The book was called *The Father of Little Women*.

Invincible Louisa by Cornelia Meigs, although a juvenile book, is significant in Alcott history because it won the Newbery Medal for 1933 as best American juvenile book. Its emphasis is on family life and Louisa's determination to succeed. Well-written though it is, it has limited value to the serious researcher, for it makes short shrift of any but Alcott's juvenile writings, and in fact, concludes the story of her life with the successful publication of *Little Women* in 1868, completely ignoring the works and experiences of the last 20 years of Louisa's life.

The first psychoanalytical biography of Louisa made its appearance in 1938. As written by Katharine S. Anthony, *Louisa May Alcott,* although acknowledged as the "first mature biography" of Alcott, was also controversial for its undocumentable interpretations.

If any Alcott researcher can be called the definitive Alcott scholar, it must be Madeleine B. Stern. After a succession of critical articles about Louisa, she wrote her 1950 biography, *Louisa May Alcott.* With unimpeachable and abundant documentation, she produced a biography that is a valuable resource for those to follow her. Its bibliography is discussed later in this book.

The year 1950 also brought another viewpoint biography, Sandford Salyer's *Marmee: The Mother of Little Women.*

A similar biography was published in the *Little Women's* centennial year of 1968. *We Alcotts: The Story of Louisa May Alcott's Family As Seen Through the Eyes of "Marmee," Mother of Little Women,* by Aileen Fisher and Olive Rabe, was a juvenile book and highly fictionalized, but interesting in that it was told from Marmee's viewpoint. Obviously, the text had to end with Marmee's death in 1877; the rest of the family life story is summarized in two and a half pages.

A few more biographies, laden with psychoanalytical interpretations, came in the last third of the 20th century as the entire field of literature began to be inundated with psycho-sociological critiques.

There have also been, over the years, a number of biographies aimed at young readers. The quality of writing ranges from pretty good to awful. The dedication to accurate research runs the same gamut.

Critical Analyses

Only three books in recent years (one my own) have presented other aspects of Alcott study. In 1983, Joy A. Marsella published *The Promise of Destiny: Children and Women in the Stories of Louisa May Alcott.* The 60 stories of *Aunt Jo's Scrap-Bag* were studied and a comparison drawn to modern times in their concern about public versus private roles for women.

The anthology, *Critical Essays on Louisa May Alcott,* edited by Madeleine B. Stern, brings together many of the articles, essays, and reviews written about Louisa's work up to the year of the anthology's publication in 1984.

The present work is the only reference which takes a triple approach to Alcott study. The biography section is a documentable telling of Alcott's life, incorporating numerous Alcott poems; a section on *Little Women* is a history and critical analysis of that book; and a third section discusses the Alcott legacy and contemporary relevance.

Reprints

Republications of *Little Women* have been numerous, and some of Louisa's other novels have also stayed in print. The collections of short stories, *Aunt Jo's Scrap-Bag* (six volumes), *Lulu's Library* (three volumes), *Proverb Stories* which is also known as *Kitty's Class Day,* and *Spinning Wheel Stories,* however, appeared primarily in scholarly reissues of sets of Alcott's works. *A Garland for Girls,* reprinted in 1971, has remained available, and the single story *An Old-Fashioned Thanksgiving* has been consistently in print since 1972. Several of her adult works were reprinted individually and several publishers issued complete sets of Louisa May Alcott's works. Some of the individual stories have been included in anthologies of Alcott's works and some in general anthologies. (See the Chronological Bibliography of Louisa May Alcott's Works.)

In 1929, one of Louisa's little-known stories was reprinted. "M.L." was ahead of its time when first published in 1863, as it dealt with the love and marriage of a white girl and mulatto. It was published in the *Journal of Black History* with the statement that the story was "definite in its stand against prejudice." Although still largely unknown, the reprinting of the story is a hallmark in that it was the first acknowledgment of the fact that she had incorporated some of her personal philosophy about the issue of race into her literary works.

The 1960s, '70s, and '80s brought the interest of feminists to Louisa's work. (Some of the articles are discussed in Chapter 11.) Concomitant to the women's movement was a renewed interest in Louisa's work in the field of stories for adults, with their evidence of an early feminist at work, as well as a general scholarly renewal of interest in lost Alcott works.

Madeleine Stern is responsible for unearthing a book published without Louisa's knowledge. Published in 1975 as *Louisa's Wonder Book—An Unknown Alcott Juvenile,* Stern writes in the introduction, "...Leafing through the pages of *The American Catalogue* for the imprints of an altogether different publisher, I found the listing of an anonymous book entitled *Will's Wonder Book,* published in 1870 by Horace B. Fuller of Boston. "Will's Wonder-Book" was familiar to me as an Alcott serial, thanks to my research on Alcott biography and bibliography. Could the two be the same? With palpitations known only to the literary sleuth I examined the one recorded copy of the book—that in the Library of Congress—and, with trembling fingers, compared it with the serial that had run in *Merry's (Museum)*...."

Later, three other copies of that anonymous edition were found; they are currently held by the Harvard University Library, the University of Virginia Library, and the Clarke Historical Library at Central Michigan University, the latter being the publisher of the important reprint. Stern's finding of *Will's Wonder Book* is a most fortuitous case of serendipity.

Also published in 1975, was *Transcendental Wild Oats and Excerpts from the Fruitlands Diary*. Here was Louisa's 1873 satire of that communal-living experiment of six months in 1843 at Fruitlands, along with some of her diary entries written at the age of 11. This edition provided a backward look at the Fruitlands experiment, the Transcendental movement, and Louisa May Alcott as a child who expressed herself in words worthy of many adult thinkers.

Suddenly, there was an interest in Louisa's adult novel of 1873. *Work: A Story of Experience* was republished by one publisher in 1976, and two others in 1977. Though not a book to make the modern best-seller list, *Work* is remarkably modern in its philosophy of self-reliance. Louisa's feminist attitude is evident, though set against the time period and social background that she knew. Her heroine, Christie Devon, she describes as "... one of that large class of women who, moderately endowed with talents, earnest and true-hearted, are driven by necessity, temperament, or principle out into the world to find support, happiness, and homes for themselves ... the strongest struggle on, and after danger and defeat, earn at last the best success this world can give us, the possession of a brave and cheerful spirit, rich in self-knowledge, self-control, self-help. This was the real desire in Christie's heart...."

In the 1960s, one of Louisa's manuscripts was found in an old trunk in the attic of a home formerly owned by the daughter of a Boston minister who had also been a publisher of religious material. "A Free Bed" was handwritten, initialed L.M.A., which was crossed out, and replaced with "by Louisa May Alcott" written in different handwriting. The manuscript passed through several hands before becoming the property of Brigham Young University. The story itself, very short, about two elderly women in a hospital, is what one might call a "charity" tale. Madeleine Stern wrote an informative introduction for its publication in 1978 as a memorial pamphlet on the 90th anniversary of Louisa's death. Only 350 copies were printed.

The publication of "Diana and Persis," a previously unpublished manuscript, is fraught with academic interpretation or misinterpretation. The manuscript was not truly lost, but it did lie for years among Louisa's papers at the Houghton Library of Harvard University. Eighty sheets of pale blue stationery held the untitled manuscript. Given the title "Diana and Persis," the tale combines letters and experiences of a painter, Persis, and Diana, a sculptor, as they try to attain their goals, simultaneously confronting the concerns of career versus marriage. It has a strong element of feminism. On January 28th, 1879, May Alcott, Louisa's artist sister, had written in her diary, "Louisa is at the Bellevue writing her Art story in which some of my adventures will appear." Persis is deemed to be based on May, and Diana on the persona of Louisa.

An important point—Louisa's work habits—would indicate that "Diana and Persis" was not really finished, a possibility that the first editor of the story does not mention in that edition. One clue to its being unfinished is that it was untitled—not yet ready for submission. It is highly unlikely that Louisa would have held onto a completed manuscript. There are no records of it having been submitted anywhere, so the logical assumption is that it was not given to any editor for consideration. Indeed, if finished, the likelihood is that Louisa would have submitted it. Her attitude was always that of the professional writer—she wrote for the money—and even when financially secure, was always driven to keep the money flowing in. Another factor to consider would be that a manuscript of four chapters indicates the intention of a longer book, rather than a short story. It is much longer than Louisa's usual short stories, and what is more, divided as chapters. Yet four chapters, in themselves, do no comprise a book, nor does the manuscript's length, as found. This, in itself, offers no conclusion, though it ought to be considered. In analyzing the story, and placing it alongside Alcott's other works, one sees that the story is not in the vein of her thrillers, some of which she did format in a few chapters; the short stories for young people were "of a piece," that is, not chaptered. "Diana and Persis," in tone and style, is far removed from her thrillers; it is akin to her young adult romances (with the "lovering" involved). The strongest conclusion that the story is unfinished is in its ending. Louisa's endings, in either genre, were always straightforward. Her heroes and heroines did not "think to themselves." Everything was spoken out and spelled out—dangling ambiguities were eschewed.

When Sarah Elbert edited the first printing in 1978, she edited the four chapters exactly as they were in manuscript. (*Diana and Persis*, Arno, 1978.) Then, in 1988, Elaine Showalter included the story in an anthology (*Alternative Alcott*, Rutgers University Press, 1988). Showalter changed the order of the last two chapters, concluding on "internal evidence" and "correction of mistranscriptions" that that was Alcott's intention. The evidence of the manuscript itself, however, would indicate that Louisa numbered the pages as they were written and intended; otherwise, surely, the chapters would have been numbered as individual chapters, with each chapter beginning with page one, rather than on a sequential numbering of the manuscript. Showalter does, however, call the manuscript unfinished.

Finished, finished but not written in the intended order, or unfinished— no one will ever really know unless additional manuscript pages are found or a published version emerges from the past. But it is important, in any case, that the story, as we have it, be added to the ranks of Alcott's published works. Unfortunately, those reading only the Elbert-edited version will think the story is complete, and those reading the Showalter-edited one, if they do not read

Literary Studies 237

the section of the introduction that explains her editing, will assume the ordering of the chapters is Louisa's. Even those reading the introduction will not have the benefit of the "internal evidence" and "correction of mistranscriptions" unless they perhaps have Elbert's version with which to compare Showalter's word for word. For the true scholar, the manuscript in the Houghton Library is the truest resource.

Among the important finds are the largely unheard of, unknown thrillers—"blood and thunder" stories—that Louisa wrote early in her career. The two people responsible for bringing these to the attention of scholars and the general reading public are Leona Rostenberg and Madeleine Stern, partners in the bookselling firm of Leona Rostenberg and Madeleine Stern—Rare Books. Rostenberg wrote about these stories in 1943, in "Some Anonymous and Pseudonymous Thrillers of Louisa May Alcott." It was in the journals and letters of Louisa and her family, deposited at the Houghton Library at Harvard University that Leona Rostenberg discovered Louisa's use of the A.M. Barnard pseudonym and references to a number of stories. Publisher's letters or records of payments provided additional clues. Although it is not likely, it is entirely possible that there are yet more anonymous or pseudonymous Alcott thrillers buried in old gazettes.

Stern eventually edited or coedited three volumes of the tales. *Behind a Mask: The Unknown Thrillers of Louisa May Alcott* (1975) and *Plots and Counterplots: More Unknown Thrillers of Louisa May Alcott* (1978) were unfortunately, out of print only ten years later. *A Double Life: Newly Discovered Thrillers of Louisa May Alcott* (1988) appeared in the centennial of Louisa's death. David Delman, in reviewing the latter, wrote, "...I found the stories somewhat overblown but occasionally redeemed by sheer energy and flashes of decent writing.... Reviewing the first batch of 'thrillers' the Christian Science Monitor made the point that never again would we be able to consider Alcott solely in the light of *Little Women*. That's true, I suppose. And rather too bad." (*Philadelphia Inquirer,* July 3, 1988.)

An important reprint in 1984, was that of *Hospital Sketches,* Louisa's second book. It appeared in combination with another work on nursing, coming out as *Hospital Sketches; Memoir of Emily Elizabeth Parsons* by Louisa May Alcott and Emily E. Parsons.

Two editions of Louisa's brooding 1877 novel, *A Modern Mephistopheles* appeared simultaneously in 1987. This is a book based on Goethe's *Faust,* modernized to Alcott's era. Madeleine Stern combined it with another Alcott story which is based (with role-reversals) on Shakespeare's *Taming of the Shrew.* The edition edited by Stern is *A Modern Mephistopheles and Taming a Tartar;* the one edited by Octavia Cowan is simply *A Modern Mephistopheles.* The very fact of these reprintings is important to Alcott scholarship.

It remains, now, only for Louisa's *Moods* to be reprinted. Here is a dilemma, however, for her first version (1865) was considerably revised for the second *Moods: A Novel* (1882). The heroine, Sylvia, had desired death in 1865, but in 1882, had learned to conquer her moods. Perhaps an edition that gives both versions would present a provocative study of Louisa's changing perceptions and evolving skills as a writer.

Bibliographies

Among the categories of scholarly treatment of an author's work is that of bibliography. Marking the 1932 centennial of Louisa's birth was the important publication of *Louisa May Alcott: A Bibliography*, compiled by Lucile Gulliver, with an "Appreciation" by Cornelia Meigs. This was the first documentation of all the known editions of Louisa's work.

When Madeleine Stern published *Louisa May Alcott* in 1950, she appended to the biography a chronological bibliography of Louisa's works. This was enlarged in 1971, incorporating additional works found to a total number of 274 entries. By the time she edited *Louisa's Wonder Book* in 1975 the included bibliography was up to 291 records.

In the meantime, in 1955, Jacob N. Blanck included Louisa May Alcott in *Bibliography of American Literature*, taking up pages 27 to 45 of Volume One, with entries 141 to 244 plus errata. (A few of these were notations of one-sentence comments by Alcott on various issues; the quotes were not included.) He included a chronological listing of all first editions, briefly described those books that included first appearances of given prose or poetry, and indicated the states of first editions and variant issues.

In celebration of the *Little Women* centennial, the Rare Book Division of the Library of Congress prepared a bibliography, compiled by Judith C. Ullom. This was an annotated, selected bibliography called *Louisa May Alcott: A Centennial for "Little Women." Louisa May Alcott: A Reference Guide* by Alma J. Payne was published in 1980.

The "Chronological Bibliography of Louisa May Alcott's Works" included in *Louisa May Alcott and "Little Women"* builds on what has gone before, as all must. A few new entries will be found, bringing the total to 400. Also included in this treatment, as a helpful resource, are internal listings of the short stories contained in the major anthologies, both those by Alcott and those by later anthologists; this offers the researcher the titles of Alcott stories which had not been previously published, either in magazines or as single volumes, and would not otherwise be reflected in the bibliography at all.

The treatments and reissues noted above are only a portion of the publications that bear on Louisa's life and work. From these, however, one can see the ever-growing scholarly interest in Alcott's contributions—interest that goes beyond her identification as the "classic author of *Little Women*."

Chapter 18

Now: Alcott Sites as Literary Mecca

Though she was born in Germantown, Philadelphia, Louisa May Alcott spent most of her life either in Boston or Concord, Massachusetts, as the family made the 15-mile move a number of times.

Germantown/Philadelphia, Pennsylvania

Germantown, Louisa's birthplace, is now a part of the city of Philadelphia. The house in which she was born, which her mother called "The Little Paradise of Pine Place," is no longer standing. It had at one time been called "The Pines," and when the Alcott's moved into it, "The Rookery Cottage." Situated on what was then a dirt road, the current address is 5427 Germantown Avenue. Since the demolition of that house in 1874, the site has held a Masonic Hall, and currently is a piano sales and service company. Interestingly, in the back area of the premises is a small garden, reminiscent of how Abba Alcott described the property; it adjoins a church Sunday school, where children play—somehow a fitting setting for what remains of the juvenile author's birthplace.

A mile up the road, at 6026 Germantown Avenue, is Wyck, the home of the Quaker, Reuben Haines, who was instrumental in bringing Bronson Alcott to Germantown. Louisa played in the rose gardens of Wyck as a child, and went back to visit the historic 1690 house when she visited Philadelphia in 1876. Wyck is currently open to visitors.

A New Jersey Rumor Correction

There is a persistent rumor, happily passed on to anyone researching Louisa May Alcott, that she visited the Cape May, New Jersey, area and set up a charitable fund there. Researchers are always faced with decisions about whether or not to include such undocumented claims. It seems pertinent to at least acknowledge such.

It is said that Louisa May Alcott once stayed at Huntington House, which today maintains an "Alcott Room." Huntington House was founded in 1878 as the Arlington Hotel, so Louisa would have had to visit there sometime between 1878 and 1888, or more likely 1887, as she died after a lingering illness in March of 1888. To add to the Alcott mystique, from about 1900 to some time in the 1930s, the Arlington Hotel/Huntington House was called the Alcott House. Indeed, perhaps the rumor comes only from some perceived connection between the name and the persona.

Furthermore, the tale adds that Louisa set up a fund for female writers which was administered out of the Cape May courthouse. Another version avers that the fund was for working women. (Certainly, either is plausible, given Louisa's known interests, as well as her known generosities to charitable causes.) Another source speculates that the working-women's fund was perhaps set up by the Ladies Garment Workers Union.

Historians at the Cape May County Historical Museum have been researching the Alcott connection for years, but have found nothing substantive to support the claim.

It is particularly pertinent to note that neither the Director of Orchard House nor Louisa's heirs, all of whom have ready access to Louisa's journals, financial records, and other papers, know anything about any visit she might have made to Cape May or any fund set up by her in that area.

Boston, Massachusetts

When her family was settled in Concord, Louisa still "got away" to Boston periodically, to live either in apartments or hotel rooms. Her earlier Boston homes were many, some with relatives. Later, she rented homes on prestigious Beacon Hill. Of particular note, are just a few addresses. All can be seen from the street; none are open to visitors.

The row house at 20 Pinckney Street, on the north edge of Beacon Hill, has a plaque identifying it with Louisa May Alcott. It is equally of note in connection with Elizabeth Palmer Peabody, "the Grandmother of Boston," who introduced kindergartens to America. Elizabeth Peabody had worked previously with Bronson Alcott at his experimental school in Boston. The Alcotts lived in the house from fall of 1852 to the summer of 1855. It was here, in the third floor garret, where Louisa retreated with apples to finish work on her first published book, *Flower Fables*. Curiously, she returned to the house in January of 1862 to learn the new kindergarten techniques from Miss Peabody. She opened a kindergarten in the Warren Street Chapel, but taught only from January to May, journeying in from Concord most of the time.

One of Louisa's favorite retreats was the Bellevue Hotel Apartments at 21 Beacon Street; she frequently took a room there when she wanted to escape the domesticity of Concord life. Only the site exists today, but the view of Boston's famous city park, the Common, remains essentially the same. The Common, with its Frog Pond, is where Louisa often played as a child, when the family lived in nearby rented houses.

Alcott Sites

20 Pinckney Street, Beacon Hill, Boston, Massachusetts. This is typical of the many Boston rowhouses with garrets ("sky-parlors") Louisa and her family lived in. Photograph by Gloria T. Delamar.

The last home (not counting her last days at Dunreath Place, the Roxbury nursing home) in which Louisa and her remaining family lived, was on Beacon Hill, facing the little park of Louisburg Square. It was here where she raised May's daughter, Lulu, and where Louisa, with Anna and her sons, tended to the ailing Bronson Alcott. The gracious, brick, furnished house at No. 10 Vernon Street was her home from 1885 to 1888. No longer living in poverty, at this time Louisa was comfortable financially and well-recognized as a successful writer and public figure.

The Old Corner Bookstore, at the corner of School and Washington streets, is associated with many writers of the day. It has been restored to its 19th-century appearance. (It now houses the in-town offices of the *Boston Globe*.) It was here that Louisa first met James T. Fields and Thomas Niles, when she took her manuscript about her domestic experience (eventually to appear as "How I Went Out to Service") to Fields. On that day in 1854, he uttered the words that at first sent her into a tailspin of depression, "Stick to your teaching, Miss Alcott. You can't write." She turned them into a challenge. After Fields began publishing *The Atlantic* in a small back room, Louisa was happily vindicated to have him begin publishing her work. Of particular interest at The Old Corner Bookstore is a diorama of the store showing many of the literary visitors who used to visit there. Among others, are Harriet Beecher Stowe, who is shown outside a window looking at Bibles, as Henry Wadsworth Longfellow stands nearby. At the counter near the door Ralph Waldo Emerson is shown talking with Louisa May Alcott. (Officially, The Old Corner Bookstore was known as William D. Ticknor and Co., or Ticknor and Fields; the successor to the Ticknor bookstore is several blocks south at 50 Bromfield. It, too, is known as The Old Corner Bookstore.)

Fruitlands Museums, Harvard, Massachusetts

Sitting on sloping acreage at 102 Prospect Hill Road (two miles west off State Route #110) is the complex known as the Fruitlands Museums, site of Amos Bronson Alcott's ill-fated communal-living experiment for the "Consociate Family." On the grounds are a Reception Center, Shaker House, American Indian Museum, and Fruitlands Farmhouse. The farmhouse is dated back to the 18th century. It was in 1914 that Miss Clara Endicott Sears, a prominent Boston novelist and poet, founded the Fruitlands Museums, which are now designated as both state and national historic landmarks. It was her goal to preserve not only objects and artifacts, but also to foster an appreciation of the diverse spiritual forces that helped shape the country.

It is the Fruitlands Farmhouse which draws Alcott fans. Few of the original pieces are left in the house from the Alcott occupancy, which was from June 1843 to January 1844. Bronson Alcott, however, had drawn a detailed plan of the house, which the curators used to recreate the Alcott era. The girls were assigned the little garret room, where the beds caught the warmth of the chimney stones. Louisa, who turned 11 while at Fruitlands, loved the red farmhouse and the woods in which she could run. The peculiarities of the others who shared the house, along with the strict rules and hard work imposed on all, were another matter. In her diary she noted that poetry began to flow at this time in a thin but copious stream. (The Alcott sojourn at Fruitlands is described in Chapter 2.)

The house contains many books and memorabilia of the Transcendentalist leaders—Bronson Alcott, Ralph Waldo Emerson, Henry David Thoreau, Margaret Fuller, Charles Lane, and others. Especially interesting is Louisa's account of those months at Fruitlands which is her short story, "Transcendental Wild Oats"; pages from her Fruitlands diary are also on display.

On the wall of her parents' bedroom is a framed lock of Louisa's hair. From the hillside, Mts. Monadnock, Wachusett, and Escutney form a magnificent vista, just as they did when Louisa looked at them over 15 decades ago.

Concord, Massachusetts

Concord can only be described as a typical New England village. Several roads lead into town, including the Lexington Road on which the Alcotts lived and walked. In the center of town is a village green. Here also, is the site of the milldam, where Louisa contemplated her fate. The spire of the First Parish in Concord—Unitarian Universalist, which gathered in 1636, marks the church where the Alcotts worshipped.

The Thoreau-Alcott-Pratt house, at 255 Main Street heading west from the town square, was once the home of Henry David Thoreau. Louisa helped buy it for her widowed sister, Anna Alcott Pratt, although the entire family lived there for a while after leaving Orchard House. The room to the left of the front entrance was Louisa's study. Franklin Benjamin Sanborn, family friend and editor of Louisa's work in *The Commonwealth,* later had a school in the back of the house, and even later occupied it as a home. It is now a private residence, only visible from the street.

Concord, in addition to its connection with the Revolutionary War, has several other homes of famous literary personages, making it a popular tourist attraction.

Outside of town and south, at 915 Walden Street, is Thoreau's Walden Pond, where Louisa and her sisters communed with the hermit poet and with nature.

To visit the "final resting place" of the famous and revered, is a common pilgrimage. Northeast of the town square, on Bedford Street, State Route 62, is Sleepy Hollow Cemetery, with its "Author's Ridge." Here are buried the Alcotts (with the exception of May Alcott Nieriker), Ralph Waldo Emerson, Nathaniel Hawthorne, Henry David Thoreau, and William Ellery Channing,

II (the Younger). In death, as in life, Louisa is surrounded by the same circle of family and friends. As a veteran of the Civil War, her grave is permanently adorned with an American flag.

The Hillside/The Wayside, Concord, Massachusetts

When the Alcotts bought their first home in 1846, it was a dilapidated four-room structure that had been built about 1700. Two skills Bronson Alcott possessed were carpentry and imagination. He cut in half the wheelwright's shop that sat on one side and attached a half to each side of the house. He named it The Hillside, for the uphill slope that rose behind the house.

The house is situated right on the Lexington Road just over a mile from the center of Concord, Massachusetts, a third of a mile from the home of Ralph Waldo Emerson, who helped the Alcotts finance the purchase. It was in this house that the Alcott sisters played "Pilgrim's Progress" on the stairs, based on their father's favorite book.

The activity appears in *Little Women*, where the March sisters play just as the Alcotts did. In the barn their father moved from across the street, Louisa and her sisters wrote and acted in melodramatic plays. Many of the real-life events while living at The Hillside were accorded to the fictional March family of *Little Women*.

In The Hillside's barn, Louisa started her first school—with her playmates and the Emerson children as her pupils. It was then that she first wrote the stories for *Flower Fables*.

The Alcotts lived in The Wayside when Louisa was 13 years old, growing out of childhood and into a young woman of 20 years.

In 1852, finances dictated that the family move to Boston where Abba Alcott had been offered employment. The Alcotts retained title to the house, which by now had several more of Mr. Alcott's building additions. They sold The Hillside to Nathaniel Hawthorne later in 1852; he renamed it The Wayside, and added a tower and several second floor rooms. Hawthorne died in 1864, but his wife stayed there until 1868. It was sold in 1870.

In 1879, Hawthorne's daughter Rose and her husband, George Lathrop, bought the house, which they sold in 1883 to Boston publisher, Daniel Lothrop and his wife Harriet; she was better known as Margaret Sidney, author of the *Five Little Pepper* books (which grew to a series of 12) and other books. First opened to the public in 1927 by their daughter, Margaret Mulford Lothrop, in 1965, The Wayside was acquired from her by the National Park Service.

In all, The Hillside/The Wayside was home at some time to 12 authors (of at least one book), all of whom, by birth or marriage, were connected with three families. Three other names might be added as well.

The Alcotts: Amos Bronson Alcott, Louisa May Alcott, and Abba May Alcott (Mrs. Ernest Nieriker). As coauthor, with Louisa, of *Comic Tragedies*

Written by "Jo" and "Meg" and Acted by the "Little Women," perhaps the name of Anna Sewell Alcott (Mrs. John Pratt) should also be added.

The Hawthornes: Nathaniel Hawthorne, Sophia Peabody Hawthorne (Mrs. Nathaniel Hawthorne), Julian Hawthorne (son of Nathaniel and Sophia), Rose Hawthorne Lathrop (daughter of Nathaniel and Sophia—Mrs. George Parsons Lathrop), George Parsons Lathrop (husband of Rose Hawthorne), Mary Peabody Mann (sister of Sophia—Mrs. Horace Mann), and Hildegard Hawthorne (daughter of Julian Hawthorne—Mrs. Oskison). Perhaps Elizabeth Palmer Peabody might also be added, as she frequently stayed at the house of her sisters, Sophia and Mary, although she never officially lived there.

The Lothrops: "Margaret Sidney"—Harriet Mulford Stone Lothrop (Mrs. Daniel Lothrop), and Margaret Mulford Lothrop (daughter of Daniel and Harriet). Perhaps Daniel Lothrop, who was a publisher, should be added, as he too, made his contribution to the literary scene.

The house certainly has a literary history; not the least of which is the fictional one created in *Little Women* by the author who had lived there in her maturing years.

Orchard House, Concord, Massachusetts

Though the Alcotts were nomads during Louisa's early days, and Louisa herself basically remained one, home base from July 1858 to November 1877 was Orchard House. On the Lexington Road, next door to their old home, The Hillside (now known as Hawthorne's The Wayside), it was just a little closer to the town square and to Mr. Emerson's home. The house was dilapidated, but Bronson Alcott got out his carpenter's tools and virtually reconstructed it. Situated on 12 acres of mostly hilly land, it possessed a small orchard. Although the family called it Orchard House, Louisa immediately dubbed it "Apple Slump."

Marmee and Father created a home there; Louisa alternated between living alone in apartments or hotels in Boston and with the family in Concord. Beth died shortly before the family moved into Orchard House, but Anna and May lived there, except when teaching or studying elsewhere, until their marriages.

Orchard House is the home in which the Alcotts resided for the greatest length of time.

In the summer of 1878, a School of Philosophy was set up in the vacant Orchard House, so that Bronson Alcott could have a place for his philosophical discussions. In 1879 they decided to rent the house to William Torrey Harris; to the back of the left side yard, they built a wooden chapel-like structure to house a new School of Philosophy. In June 1884 they sold the house to Harris. (William Torrey Harris and Frank Sanborn later wrote the first biography of Amos Bronson Alcott.)

The living room at Orchard House. Louisa's "mood pillow" on couch; when pointed up she was letting the family know she was in a good mood—when pointed down, the reverse. Bronson Alcott's picture is on the wall. Photograph by Gloria T. Delamar.

Harriet Lothrop ("Margaret Sidney," next door at The Wayside) bought the house from Harris in 1900, hoping that one day it could be opened to Louisa May Alcott's young readers. On April 15, 1911, Harriet Lothrop, with Abby F. Rolfe, President of the Concord Woman's Club, formed the Louisa May Alcott Memorial Association, determined to fulfill their dream of creating an Alcott museum. The house was then in terrible condition. Their fund-drive spurred donations, many in small amounts—pennies from school children from all over the country—but they raised $5000, officially purchased the house from Lothrop, and set about repairing, painting, and furnishing it in simple fashion. Orchard House was opened to the public in 1912.

In the first year there were over 7000 visitors, who left over $1000 in the free contribution box at the door. Although the restoration work was still going on, visitors told the guides that they could fairly see the March girls reveling in its cosy corners, its commodious closets and its comfortable little nooks.

Preserved just as they had existed when the Alcotts lived in the house, are the paintings done by May Alcott—the figures with which she decorated her own bedroom, the flowers on the wall above Louisa's half-moon desk, the owl on the front of Louisa's bedroom mantel, and others. The chimneypiece in Bronson's downstairs study still bears May's execution of William Ellery Channing's words, "The hills are reared, the valleys scooped in vain, if Learning's altars vanish from the plain."

Over time, some Alcott-owned furnishings made their way back to Orchard House. Though Beth had never lived there, her melodeon is there. There is a piano, a writing desk, and a mirror. The Colport china handed down to Abba Alcott by her father, Colonel Joseph May, is on display. Also donated have been furnishings of the period—furniture, antique kitchen utensils, books, historical costumes, and such—and paintings by May Alcott. The busts of Plato and Socrates, that accompanied the Alcotts wherever they moved, are prominently displayed. On a settee is Louisa's "mood pillow," which when pointed up signaled that she was in a good mood; if pointed down, she was letting the household know that she was in a bad mood.

Little Women was written at the half-moon desk between the two front windows of Louisa's bedroom. Her sister Anna's marriage (and Meg March's in *Little Women*) took place in the living room of Orchard House.

The mission of the Louisa May Alcott Memorial Association is to preserve Orchard House as a museum and educational center. To this end, they conduct tours, put on special programs and exhibits and foster curatorial work.

A gift shop offers books by and about the Alcotts, Alcott recipes, postcards, and facsimiles of various Alcott items such as poems, articles, order of indoor duties, maxims, and letters.

An ambitious program for young people includes age-designed programs such as "A Visit with the Alcotts," "A Morning in Mr. Alcott's School," "The Alcotts and Antislavery," "Louisa Alcott, Civil War Nurse," "The Alcott Women: Paddling Their Own Canoes," and "Creative Arts with the Alcotts." Special entertainments offer children's games that were popular over one hundred years ago—"Family Coach," "General Post," "Ruth and Jacob," and "Charades," as well as Bronson Alcott's original board game, "The Mansion of Happiness."

For all ages, there are narrated tours, slide programs, "Little Women: Fact and Fiction," and "Story of the Alcotts," and a living-history program, "The Alcotts Are Here." "Parlor Entertainments" for adults feature songs, parlor games, dramatics, and storytelling—based on documents, letters, and reminiscences of Alcott peers. There have been special programs for Valentine's Day, Easter, and Christmas. There are also faculty workshops for teachers, librarians, and curriculum specialists.

Additional activities take place in the School of Philosophy, including lectures such as "Bronson Alcott's Concord," "The Fruitlands Experiment," "Alcott and Emerson," "Alcott and Nathaniel Hawthorne," "The Alcotts and Thoreau," "Women of the School of Philosophy," and one-woman shows like "Letters from Louisa," by actress Carol Anderson and "To Heaven in a Swing," (the setting is Dr. Rhoda Lawrence's clinic in Roxbury where Louisa spent her last days, with the text dealing with Louisa's reminiscences about her life, family, and friends) written and performed by actress Katharine Houghton, niece of actress Katharine (Houghton) Hepburn, who played "Jo" in the 1933 film of *Little Women*.

In 1981, the Association embarked on a long-range fund drive, with Katharine Hepburn as honorary chairman. Phase I of the campaign ended in 1986 with a total contribution of $182,000. In the next few years, special grants from the Massachusetts Historical Commission and private foundations totaled $45,000 and donations from individual donors ran to over $11,000. The campaign continued into the next phase.

In 1988, Orchard House joined with several other Concord organizations, the Concord Museum, Emerson House, Old Manse (Emerson's ancestors), Minute Man National Park, and Walden Pond State Reservation, to form the Concord Historical Collaborative. The Concord Free Public Library (which has an extensive collection of Louisa May Alcott's books), the Historical Commission, and the Historic Districts Commission are included as non-voting members. By sharing resources, their goal is to preserve the heritage of Concord while maintaining the unique characteristics of each organization.

Writers, actors, and royalty have joined the pilgrimage of young and old who visit Orchard House. For special occasions, the staff and volunteers may be seen in period costumes, portraying the Alcott family—presenting the chance to chat with "Louisa" and the others. Though the School of Philosophy programs feature Louisa's accomplishments along with those of Amos Bronson Alcott and other Concord luminaries, the house is a bouquet to Louisa May Alcott, author of *Little Women* and prototype of her own fictional "Jo March." (There are, however, those readers and visitors who name one or more of Louisa's other books as their favorite.)

Louisa and her work are clearly the attraction to the more than 30,000 annual visitors. More than 100 years after her death, the popularity of Orchard House offers concrete testimony to the continuing popularity of Louisa May Alcott.

Chapter 19

Now: The "Little Women" of Today

When Louisa May Alcott wrote her best-known book, *Little Women,* she created a unique legacy. The book transcends its time. It offers the wonderful mystique of reader-identification with the fictional characters.

The "little women" of yesterday and today who have laughed and cried over the adventures and misadventures of Meg, Jo, Beth, and Amy March, relate to them because the characters seem real. With a skill matched by very few writers, Louisa wove together real life Alcott experiences and fictional episodes that made the story fuller and livelier. Together, fact and fiction evolved into a texture that suited the characters exactly. But the ultimate touch that makes *Little Women* a masterpiece is its universality. The March sisters fit into their mid-19th century culture, but with a few changes of clothes, ambience, and adjustment to historical changes, they would fit just as well in the society of the late-20th century.

Perhaps in a way no male can truly empathize with, most female readers of *Little Women* have reactions to memories and current readings that go far beyond the usual reaction of merely liking the story. The response is emotional. Whether one asks young teens, young adults, their mothers, or their grandmothers, most who have read it respond to it with warmth. They rhapsodize. They mention their favorite funny episodes. They mention crying about Beth's death. A large percentage say they idolized Jo. Jo was the heroine they wanted to be—independent, a bit brash but nevertheless caring, brave and creative.

A number of women writers discussed what the "little women" would be like if they existed in today's society. All agreed that their counterparts do indeed exist. It was clear that the sisters' four distinct personalities would determine what they would be like in the modern world. Whether one feels that the characters are broadly sketched or finely drawn (and the attributes of characterization are open to debate), the end result is the same. There was a clear consensus with the hypotheses sketched below.

There are clues throughout the story that show what Meg, Jo, Beth, and Amy would be like if they were to be lifted out of the book and set down in this decade amidst our own young girls.

Situation—suppose the March sisters were faced with the possibility of military draft registration for women:

Bust of Louisa May Alcott (living room at Orchard House). Photograph by Gloria T. Delamar.

The oldest sister, Meg, would feel that as nurturer of family togetherness and supporter and servant of God and country, she, no less than young men, should be expected to register. If called to serve she would go willingly, for one does what one's country asks of one. But Meg would have one reservation — she couldn't help but hope that the uniform would be becoming.

The third sister, Beth, the gentle, frail one who dies in the book, had she lived, and were she in this century, would be in a quandary. At heart she would be a conscientious objector, but would nevertheless feel that young women would be shirking their responsibilities if they did not stand beside their brothers. Her caring heart would make her turn to nursing, which would allow her to soothe the physical and emotional wounds of her sisters and brothers. She wouldn't volunteer, but if drafted would go, and probably would come out of the experience with long-term scars on her own sensitive spirit.

The fourth sister, self-centered, charming, artistic Amy, would not only oppose a woman's draft, but if in line to be drafted herself, would take off for Rome with portfolio under arm to study art and survive in her own winsome way. Her motives wouldn't be that of a conscientious objector, though, for Amy was/is a me-first person, with her own unexpected moments of grace.

Now—the second sister, the Jo that most readers identify with—Jo, the staunch independent whose passions run deep, who always referred to herself as a gentleman, who knew herself to be as self-sufficient as any male, would not only favor the opportunity to be drafted, but would be the first in line to prove it by signing up and thus joining the 150,000 women who have already voluntarily gone into military service. (Jo, the book's main protagonist, is the alter ego of author Alcott, who did indeed sign up as a nurse in the Civil War, only to be stricken with a terrible diphtheria that ended her war career after only six weeks. The calomel treatments caused mercury poisoning, which left her with lifelong ill-effects.) In the event of another unpopular "unjust war," however, Jo, her manner as fervent as of old, her speech as brusque and articulate as ever, but with her language updated and somewhat more earthy, would be out there with the rest of the guys, carrying placards and shouting, "Hell, no, we won't go."

Situation—careers:

Meg would have a turn at a low-rung job, possibly as an entry-level secretary. She would have no ambitions to reach the top of the ladder. Basically, she would be biding time while earning the wherewithal to survive. Ultimately, she would marry and have children. Unless forced to it by financial circumstances, she wouldn't return to the work force. Having matured beyond her former overconcern about fine appearances, she would be a caring wife, and loving mother, happy to live with fewer material things in order to stay home to raise her family.

Beth would no doubt go into one of the helping professions, such as nursing or social work. Whatever she became involved in, her approach would be effective, but low-key. Always, her concern would be for the other person. She might marry or not, and have children or not, but regardless, would continue working, at least part-time.

Amy would pursue a career in art, fashion perhaps. With considerable talent, along with her determination to be noticed, she would have a chance to make a name for herself in her chosen field. In today's culture, she might or might not marry—but any man in her life would have to be very understanding of her nature. Her charm would cover other flaws. In any case, Amy would never do anything that might interfere with having her own way.

Jo, who in fiction established and ran a progressive school, might do the same thing in today's society. Outside of the field of education, she might well be a journalist, but one can be sure she would be in some exciting area, perhaps as a foreign-correspondent, traveling into war zones, taking chances, recording the events of the day with a perceptive eye. She would have written some short stories, but her major focus would be on history-making events. Jo might be married. She might have children. Her career would always have some priority. She would be able to blend it all, for she is a person of consummate energy, with the kind of personality that bonds firm, loving, and vital relationships.

Do you recognize them? In 1868, author Alcott gave certain personalities to those girls—growing into women. But we know them in reality—we see them in homes throughout the country—for they are our daughters and granddaughters, our nieces and aunts, our friends and neighbors. They are the young women who discuss and contemplate military drafts, careers, and family life-styles—by whatever name, we all know a Meg, Jo, Beth, or Amy.

Manners change, customs change, life-styles change; but people are basically the same. They are still shy, vain, kind, courageous, angry, helpful, orderly, artistic, and loving. They are all the things people have always been, having more or less of certain qualities according to their own personalities.

They're called "little women" in the book. But their characteristics are nonsexist. Honesty, kindness, and loyalty are characteristics we want to instill in all our children, whether girls or boys.

The family life depicted in *Little Women* is still true to interrelationships today. It is a strong story of family life. It depicts the joys and trials of learning to live with others in harmony. It also shows the triumph of will over diversity. The story became a classic because succeeding generations could still relate to it. Only the accoutrements are changed today—the "little women" had no televisions or computers, and they never dreamed that spaceships could actually go to the moon.

But they had loving relationships. Just as today, they might squabble with siblings, but would be the first to be there in time of need. Within the family, they were and are responsible for certain chores, and they were and are taught the moral values of their parents.

Those who remember it—and those who have reveled in rereading it—know why the book is still with us today. It is still with us because the "little women"—the real ones, the maturing young females—are with us. Meg, Jo, Beth, and Amy March may have taken form in Louisa May Alcott's mind, but they show us what we are today, and what we can be. They are real.

Little Women will continue to hold its place, in yet another hundred years, as a book of emotion, liberation, and basic human worth.

Chapter 20

Now: The Relevance Today of *Little Women*

Relevance is always a concern in the evaluation of literature. Whether one means literary and academic judgment, or how current readers feel about a book, the question is raised about new books, and most certainly, about those that have been around as long as *Little Women*. To all, naturally, their opinions are valid for themselves, but a broader yardstick must be invoked when it comes to judging whether or not *Little Women* is relevant in a general way for the society of the very late 20th century. And there's a difference in what backgrounds are brought to such contemplation from professionals who work with books and/or children, and from mature and young people who read the book in current times.

Professionals such as educators, librarians, and writers have their own perspectives in looking at the issue. Just-plain-folks, readers at the grassroots, bring another dimension.

Following are some thoughtful comments representative of both categories. All were asked the same question: Is *Little Women* relevant today? They were told that it did not matter if their response was positive or negative, and that they could approach the question from any angle they chose.

Is *Little Women* Relevant Today?

To synthesize and analyze is the reader's task. To gain understanding and insight is the reader's reward. In Alcott's superbly crafted and timeless portrayal of the March family, the young reader is drawn into the constantly evolving nuances of family life. The reader perceives the subtle and not-so-subtle impact that individual personality exerts upon family culture. Certainly, the unique personalities of Meg, Jo, Beth, and Amy make the March family different from all others in that time and our own.

Yet, it is the similarity of the March family to all other families that serves the reader so well. The reader understands the pitting of growing ego against family tradition. One recognizes the trivial kitchen arguments and the constant adjustments to each other's individual needs and desires. But especially, one remembers the love and the promise of enduring family support that enables an

Taking the breakfast. Illustration by Frank T. Merrill from *Little Women*. Boston, Roberts Brothers, 1880.

> individual to move beyond the family. Reading *Little Women* is to experience a powerful recognition of that which keeps us as a culture civilized, loyal, gentle, and — good.
>
> Georgia S. McWhinney, reading specialist, Abington (PA) Schools; instructor, pre-freshman English, Philadelphia Community College

The domestic scene for young girls is so different now. Just think about how their time is spent. School attendance with lengthy homework assignments is required for all through the age of sixteen. Shopping for stylish bargains has replaced sewing at home. Eating in restaurants or opening packages for the microwave has replaced the presence of Hannah. Dancing or "vegging out" while listening to rock groups has replaced hours of piano playing. Commercial art has replaced hours of sketching or modeling clay. Only those girls living in familial islands of cultural antiquity could find *Little Women* relevant as anything but an allegory.

A small child's natural tendency to explore his neighborhood is enhanced today by a vicarious television neighborhood that extends throughout the world. Appropriate agencies employ skilled professionals to help people like the Hummels. Illness requires hospitalization or professionals. A wife or sister would each have specialized training and time commitments. At the end of the twentieth century our lives revolve around our chosen centers in society. The world has become our home; yet, we still need the love of home and family.

Our constantly growing knowledge of emotional needs, learning styles, and behavior has influenced every aspect of our lives. Modern authors weave stories for young people using their knowledge of psychology as the warp. These stories prepare the young reader for coping effectively with the emotional stages of growth and development and for adapting to difficult situations. Yet, seemingly, the chapter entitled, "Laurie Makes Mischief and Jo Makes Peace" could be restyled so that one would think it first appeared in print last year. In fact, a special reverence for human dignity shines from the nineteenth century, through the pages of *Little Women* into our fragmented lives. Maybe we need to create more relevancy.

>Rae Pease, teacher, Catherine M. McGee Middle School, Berlin, Connecticut

Little Women has been a staple of every well-read girl's book list since its initial publication in 1868 and 1869. To the contemporary adult reader, however, the fact that this book has endured is puzzling. The style, at times, is flat and unctuous, the sentimentality grating, and the snobbery of class distinctions disturbing. There are no unique twists of plot, attitudes are dated, and morality dispensed with a heavy hand. Yet, this novel persists. One cannot dismiss its popularity as a result of purchases by librarians or elderly females reliving pleasant childhood memories. Nor can it be explained as the result of reluctant reading of the M.T.V. generation urged by teachers and relatives to try "their favorite childhood book." *Little Women* is truly enjoyed by young girls.

Elements of this book create a bond between reader and story that does not age. One virtue is the carefully recorded detailing of objects and events. The reader becomes intertwined with the March family's daily existence. The lively discourse of Mrs. March's parrot; the clearly layed out plans for the girls' dramatic presentation; the rationale for the choice of the contents of Meg's trunk for her visit to the Moffats; all of these draw the reader into the various scenes.

The characterization also helps create a classic quality. The characters are interesting, if not endearing, but it is clearly Jo who dominates the story line. Through Jo, L.M. Alcott creates a female model of unconventionality, strength, and independence. For all her unconventionality, however, Jo is not a contemporary rebel; she is neither overtly masculine nor anti-social. *Little Women*'s characters are good people. They are charitable and caring. Their altruism is not rendered ineffective by didactic strictures of the author. The four major characters remain true to themselves. They establish individual goals which they achieve. Whether it be Beth's getting past the stone lions to play Laurence's piano or Jo getting published, the girls triumph.

Little Women shows the reader that one can accomplish goals without sacrificing a sense of humanity. This is a message that transcends time.

>Bette P. Goldstone, professor of children's literature, Beaver College; 1988 candidate for the Arbuthnot Award

Anyone doubting the relevance of *Little Women* today should have been watching television in the 1988 election year. Louisa May Alcott's moral values were embraced by both candidates: George Bush stressed the importance of the family; Michael Dukakis emphasized shared social responsibilities. Both men were appealing to an idealized vision of the past — the time of *Little Women* — when individual and social values were clearly understood, and what was "good" was easily differentiated from what was "bad." Today's readers, too, find comfort in the moral world of *Little Women;* there they find the world as it should be, not as it is. And the best of these readers will try to make the values of *Little Women* come alive again and not merely regard them in a nostalgic vein. It is the moral challenge with which *Little Women* presents us that makes it relevant today.

>Joel Myerson, coeditor of *The Selected Letters of Louisa May Alcott* and *The Journals of Louisa May Alcott;* Professor of English, University of South Carolina

Little Women is relevant to children and young people of today in that much that is a part of the book — the absent father, the poverty, the emotions and ambitions of the characters, the romances, etc. — belongs to today as well as yesterday. However, today's children like books with a somewhat faster pace, a little more excitement, a little less moralizing by the author, and a modern setting. Historical novels, which this is for today's young people, have been out of vogue for some time. Also, many children and young people seem reluctant to even consider a book of this length. Which is not to say that *Little Women* is not read today. I am sure it is by the few who like long books and who are not daunted by Miss Alcott's 19th century style, or its, to them, period setting.

        Jean E. Karl, author of *From Childhood to Childhood: Children's Books and Their Creators;* retired juvenile book editor (Atheneum Publishers)

The young adult girl of today would probably read the title, *Little Women*, and say, "How can that be? How can a woman be little in the sense that Alcott portrayed? Certainly, by the mere fact that she is a woman, she is no longer *little*."

But Alcott's little women of yesterday are important for the young adult woman of today, just as it is important that we study any type of historic consciousness, to see how far we have come. And we have come a long way.

The four personalities of Alcott's women, the Beth of hearth and home, Jo the activist, Amy who cared about opinions of others and fought her own demons of selfishness, and Meg with her preoccupation with appearance, all were separated and put in the bodies of four women. Rereading *Little Women* is similar to digging up the bones of some prehistoric animal. Only Jo encompasses more. Only Jo is on her way to becoming today's woman.

What is the value of looking back? To see if we like where we are. To see if we like where we're going. Jo and Beth, Meg and Amy, live in all of us, but the difference is, they have no need to be split into fours. Today's young girl knows she can be Jo and dare to be whatever she chooses, or Amy and be selfish and think of what she needs to survive. She can care about her hair, her clothes, her weight, her grand appearance as did Meg, and she can cherish Beth's home and build the nest. She can do it all, and the four parts can live in one body to create the modern woman.

Little women? "What is that?" the young adult girl would probably ask today. It is important that Alcott be reread so that we remember just how far we've come.

        Harriet Savitz, author of over a half dozen young adult novels, including *The Lionhearted; Come Back, Mr. Magic;* and *Run, Don't Walk* which became an ABC-TV afterschool special

Early on in *Little Women* there is a particularly vivid sequence of scenes: (1) Amy, striking back for not being allowed to go to the theater, burns up a story of Jo's. (2) Jo's rage on discovering the loss is towering, even for her. (3) Jo almost ... almost ... lets Amy drown because the primal part of her is as yet unappeased. These scenes are so brilliantly done, so true, so pointed and compelling, that I read them recently with something close to breathlessness. "Is *Little Women* relevant today?" About as relevant, I should say, as sibling rivalry.

        David Delman, author of eleven novels (two mainstream; nine crime fiction), the latest being *The Liar's League;* book reviewer

When *Little Women* was published, it was relevant because its portrait of family life in New England was familiar to most readers. As Cyrus Bartol wrote: "She (Alcott) unlatches the door to one house, and ... all find it is their own house which they enter."

Today, *Little Women* is relevant because its portrait of family life against the New England background is unfamiliar to many readers. What was, during the nineteenth century, "their own house" has become historic ground for exploration. *Little Women* is still engrossing domestic fiction, but now it has also become invested with documentary importance. Perhaps, therefore, it is more relevant today than when it first appeared.

> Madeleine B. Stern, author of *Louisa May Alcott* (biography); editor of three volumes of Alcott's short "thrillers"; etc.

After rereading *Little Women*, there is no question in my mind that the book is as relevant today as it was when published in 1868. The characterizations are the key to the universality of the story, with its joys, sorrows, and responsibilities. Despite the moral tone there is no sermonizing. For example, whenever Jo starts to moralize, Laurie is quick to make fun of her remarks and threatens to leave. Jo stops immediately. The development of character is shown in the conversations and in the actions of the members of the family and their friends.

The character of Jo would appeal to any young woman of today with her determination to be herself, whether whistling (which was not ladylike in that period) or in keeping Laurie as a friend and not as a lover. Beth is the only one who remains the same and serves as a foil for the character development of the others.

Few children today have the attention span, due to television, to concentrate on a book over 500 pages long. It would be wiser for the publisher to produce the story in two volumes as it was done originally. Part One has the perfect ending to lead to the sequel, "So grouped, the curtain falls upon Meg, Jo, Beth, and Amy. Whether it rises again, depends on the reception given to the first act of the domestic drama called *Little Women*."

> Carolyn W. Field, former Coordinator of the Office of Work with Children, Free Library of Philadelphia; president of U.S. Section of International Board on Books for Young People

Little Women embodies two archetypes which are relevant for today's youth. First, the Father's Daughter, she who must fulfill the father's legend. Jo does this by becoming a writer. Second, the stable, supportive Family.

The actualization of the Father's Daughter archetype was rare when Louisa May Alcott lived and wrote. Today it is the norm. The stable family archetype is now more nostalgia than reality.

While librarians argue among themselves which is the "better" dictionary, Webster's 2nd which defines static language or Webster's 3rd which defines evolving language, users choose Webster's 3rd. While the video version of *Little Women* circulates freely, the book leaves the shelf primarily at the recommendation of mothers, teachers, or reading lists. It is the "older generation" who desires to validate their own experiences by sharing yesterday's archetypal embodiments with today's young.

The TV generation wants its books faster paced, with spicier relationships, occupying fewer inches on the shelf and fewer hours of young reader's lives. Just as few adults choose to read Shakespeare for pleasure, few children freely choose *Little Women*.

> Regardless of the dictates of *Art* or *Literature,* each generation will choose contemporary embodiments of eternal archetypes as relevant to their lives.
> Nancy Stewart Smith, Reference and Audiovisual Librarian, Athens (GA) Regional Library

The following two comments come not from professionals in the fields of communication or literature, but from two individuals who have a special connection to *Little Women.*

The Director of Orchard House, the Louisa May Alcott Museum that was the Alcott home for roughly 20 years, has an admittedly biased point of view, but has, also a particular vantage point from which to assess contemporary interest in Louisa May Alcott:

> Each year at Orchard House, staff members portraying "the Alcotts" welcome hundreds of young visitors who have come to experience a recreation of life in Louisa's home.
>
> Although we are all conscious of surface changes in dress and home decoration as we travel back in time through these living history programs, the children realize very quickly that the interests of the Alcotts transcend any time period. That rich world which they created, a world which depended not on material possessions, but flourished on imagination, a love of nature, and encouragement of individual talents and differences, and dreams, is as alive today as it was when Louisa captured it in the pages of *Little Women.* Whether writing, sketching, singing, or acting out Louisa's favorite melodrama, our twentieth century guests are caught up in that world, as are the thousands and thousands of readers who have come to know the Alcott sisters as Meg, Jo, Beth, and Amy March.
>
> Beyond the activities, however, it is the attitudes and personalities of the Alcott/Marches which have made such an impact on our visitors: the relationships within the family—sister to sister and parent to child—the way the family members solved their problems, supported one another through trials and triumphs, acted on their beliefs, and lived out their convictions, the courage and determination of Louisa, the sweetness of Anna, and the spirit of May, Marmee's strength, and Bronson Alcott's vision. These are the things that have touched so many people who have come to know these characters as fact and fiction.
>
> Yes, *Little Women* is relevant today. Its continuing influence and vitality have made the passage of time irrelevant.
> Jayne Gordon, Director of Orchard House, Concord, Massachusetts (the Louisa May Alcott Memorial Association)

Film actress Joan Bennett played the role of Amy March in *Little Women* when she was a young star in 1933. She had the following to say when asked her thoughts about the relevance of *Little Women* today:

> "Relevance" strikes me as an awkward word in relating *Little Women* to the modern world. It is a story firmly couched in an era of manners, morality, and taste which I am sorry to say are not in great evidence in today's world—at least as I view it. The picture does, of course, elicit fond memories of a bygone era in much the same way "It's a Wonderful Life" does. Touching the heartstrings and evoking

Jo in a vortex. Illustration, probably by Hammatt Billings, from *Little Women or Meg, Jo, Beth and Amy. Part Second* Boston: Roberts Brothers, 1869.

tears of both fond recall and nostalgia for simple values which have gone out of fashion. Both of these films seem to be trotted out every holiday season and apparently have not yet faded into desuetude. I suppose some parents are still eager to share the emotions of their own childhood with their offspring and — hopefully —

pass along, if possible, the gentler values of their forbears. I wish them success.

Joan Bennett (Wilde), Broadway, film, and television actress; listed in *The Great Movie Stars: The Golden Years* by David Shipman, New York: Hill and Wang, 1979

In an informal survey of girls of an age to be reading *Little Women* 120 years after its first publication, it was found that about two in three had read the book. Broken down even further: one third did not read it; one sixth read it and had a neutral reaction; one sixth read it and thought it dull; and one third were absolutely enamored with it, almost always glowing as they said they had read it over and over and loved it. This contrasts sharply with today's middle-aged women, who would have read the book about 75 to 100 years after its debut. Of this group, it is the rare woman who had not read it as a girl, and the even rarer one who had read it and not had an impassioned positive response. Granting the statistic narrowness of the evaluation, it is nevertheless probably safe to say that of this group, 99% read it and 98% loved it. It is from this group that one hears of daughters named specifically for one of the characters from the book, though the most loved character, Jo(sephine), had a name that for these women seemed too old-fashioned to use.

Discussions with college girls revealed that frequently, *Little Women, Huckleberry Finn, Uncle Tom's Cabin,* and *Moby Dick* were assigned readings in American literature courses. The resulting reactions were that for the most part, the girls loved *Little Women* and the boys hated it, but the boys loved *Moby Dick* which the girls hated. At Amherst College, "*Little Women* as Social History," comes in the history department's program.

Among individual comments, from all ages, some were typical:

> I loved that book as a teenager. But, recently I tried to read it again and couldn't get past the third chapter. I don't know why. I suppose it's relevant in a historical way, but I couldn't get into it, and, you know, I feel rather sorry about that. I remember Jo as meaning so much to me at one time.
> J. Maureen Vowell, college student, North Carolina

> The "little women" were so good—are any girls that perfect? But, I confess, I read it several times, and still love it.
> Stacy Klein, college student, New York

> *Little Women* is important to today's feminist because it provides a look at women's roots; it is relevant today in that sense.
> Barbara Ostrum, social psychologist, mother, Massachusetts

> Some of the happiest moments of my girlhood were spent with *Little Women*. I read it. My daughter read it. And now my granddaughters are reading it.
> H.C., mother, grandmother, California

Little Women? I read it as a boy of twelve when I was reading everything and nobody told me I shouldn't read it because it was a girls' book. I loved it, and I attribute at least some of my sensitivity to women today to the feelings I saw in the four March girls.
Robert Gray, chemical engineer; Director, optical aids foundation, New York

Three people representing the grassroots of readers were moved to write considered responses:

Little Women was a different life-style than the one I grew up in, which provided me with an insight of different levels of income at an early age. The various lessons learned from a life-style of hardship were thought-provoking. I was particularly fond of Jo, as she was independent and not afraid to tackle any challenge. The same lessons would be valuable to young girls in today's world, with the addition of some of the more current issues facing today's population.
G. Lichtenstein, young finance officer, Virginia

When I read *Little Women,* I think I was a little envious of the closeness of the sisters to one another, but also aware of how lucky I was to not be living with the strife and hardship that may have woven the fabric of the cohesiveness. I must acknowledge that living in hard times, while not desirable, does tend to give life an "edge of intensity," and can lead to inner growth that many folk who live a softer existence may never achieve. It certainly should enhance the binding together of a family.

Although I was probably fifteen or so at the time, the girls seemed so much *older* than me, except for Amy, I suppose. It was no doubt more the maturity written into their characters that gave me that notion. In Jo, especially, I saw a confidence, self-knowledge, and strength of character that I much admired. Now *there* was a woman who knew her mind and wouldn't hesitate to speak it!

And why shouldn't *Little Women* be relevant today? Relationships, changing events, and life's tough decisions are all timeless issues. We all must struggle with the sacrifices we make to achieve our goals, feelings of loss for a loved one (whether to death or to another alliance), and perceptions of how we fit, or don't fit, with the rest of our world. Even the basics, like selfishness and jealousy, have their place, and Alcott resolves them all with high moral standards and a positive slant, as any good role-model should.

I do hope today's little women have the fine fortune of a strong support system, like the March girls, to guide them toward their goals and inspirations.
K.D. Shields, young social worker, Virginia

Without question, the values expressed in *Little Women* are relevant in today's society. It is a beautiful piece of work depicting familial love which is as old as humanity, and hopefully, will exist as long as there are people on earth. The style of writing is not as current, but the same can be said for Shakespeare and any other work of a previous century. The moralizing might be disturbing to some adults, but probably not to children.

Alcott's writing has strong peaks of emotion that would strengthen any writer today. Occasionally, there's a poor transition. Her characterization is good. Her characters grow as the book progresses. The reader comes to know them well and care for them. The story rambles a bit. The plot is simple and based somewhat on the Christian ethic in that if you do good things, ultimately good things will happen to you.

The book ends in a fit of idealism, with them all living happily ever after in a utopian paradise. Even Beth's dying was romanticized, but after all, the book was written in the romantic era and we accept that in fairy tales. All that is required is the usual willing suspension of disbelief, which we apply with every novel. Alcott still works, and so does *Little Women*.

Douglas Carpenter, mature businessman; writer (who recently read the book for the first time), North Carolina

Relevance is only one factor in determining whether or not a book has validity for contemporary readers. From the scholar's point of view, contemporary pertinence is an important question to raise. From the casual reader's point of view, the only thing that really matters is personal reaction to a book. Head and heart—the majority consensus seems to be that *Little Women* has a place on contemporary bookshelves—and that it's an important one.

Little Women, for most female readers, was more than a book to read. Alcott created an emotional kinship between Meg, Jo, Beth, Amy, and the reader. The reader, too, was one of the little women—sister in thought to the Marches. The bond to the book, for many, was so strong that it transcended readership.

The cultural life-style of the book, however, began to be "period" about the time that women abandoned long skirts. As such, it was read as a historical novel early in the 20th century. But its popularity continued. Always, in those years, there was the identification with the realities of family life and love. The fact that most female readers identified with and idolized the independent Jo surely underscores their basic feminist attitudes.

Curiously, the book only came to be called "old-fashioned" when the women's movement was in full swing, when the perceived lesser independence of Meg and Beth was seen as the standard of male dominance. Amy, with her strong will and selfishness, like Jo, transcended the designation that the era saw as anathema. To be called "domestic" was to be less than a woman, less than a man.

While the book obviously has relevance as a domestic historical novel, readership has dwindled among young girls, partly because of the deep impact of the visual media on literature in general, partly because it is a long book, and partly because of the style of the language. The words may be the same spoken today, but the style has more formality. That the book is basically episodic has little bearing—the "coming of age" theme will always have a certain appeal.

Is there *any* classic that doesn't also have detractors? Some people don't like Shakespeare; some won't read Dickens today because "his books are wordy."

Though fewer young readers reach for *Little Women* today, there are still a significant number who do. For them, as for their mothers and grandmothers, the book is an emotional experience. Can any book that evokes that kind of response be considered irrelevant simply because there are also readers who don't care for it, or those who eschew it entirely?

When nobody reads *Little Women*—when nobody knows who Louisa May Alcott is—then the book will cease being relevant.

A book that has been treasured is a piece of one's past.

That's true for individuals and its true for the annals of literature. Because of its past—and because it has relevance today—there's a place on contemporary bookshelves for *Little Women*.

Appendix A

Biographical Sketches of People in the Alcott Circle

Many of the people who were friends of the Alcotts earned their own places in history books and encyclopedias. The Alcotts lived in a period which has often been referred to as "the flowering of New England." It is interesting to note how many of them wrote about each other.

Rather than digress from Louisa's story in the main text to fill in backgrounds, the short listings below give a few highlights about the particular achievements of the famous people mentioned in this book.

Alcott, Amos Bronson

Born Wolcott, Connecticut, November 29, 1799; died March 4, 1888. Educator, author, philosopher, Transcendentalist, abolitionist. Believed in teaching largely through "conversations" and was an educational pioneer of progressive schools. He was an early organizer of Parent-Teacher-Clubs. Considered a romantic dreamer with little practical sense. Was called a "tedious archangel." Wrote "Orphic Sayings" for *Dial* magazine. Wrote *Conversations with Children* (1836–37), *Tablets* (1868), *Concord Days* (1872), *Table Talk* (1877), *Ralph Waldo Emerson* (1882) and a number of other books. Alcott said, "That is a good book which is opened with expectation and closed in profit."

Beecher, Henry Ward

Born Litchfield, Connecticut, June 24, 1813; died March 8, 1887. Congregational minister, abolitionist. Advocated overthrowing slavery by constitutional mass. He was a powerful and passionate speaker who gained national fame for his emotional and florid sermons. He was an outspoken advocate of reform. In his time, he was called "the greatest preacher the world has seen since St. Paul preached on Mars Hill." Coedited *The Christian Union* magazine with his sister, Harriet Beecher Stowe, and wrote two volumes of the *Life of Jesus Christ* (1871 and 1891) and other books and printed sermons in pamphlet form. Beecher said, "He is rich or poor according to what he *is*, not according to what he *has*."

School of Philosophy at left of Orchard House, Concord, Massachusetts. Photograph by Gloria T. Delamar.

Brown, John

Born Torrington, Connecticut, May 9, 1800; died December 2, 1859. Ardent abolitionist. Favored violence. Kept station of Underground Railroad for escaping slaves in Richmond, Virginia. He claimed to be "an instrument of God," and was an intensely religious fanatic. After capturing the arsenal and freeing slaves at Harper's Ferry, Virginia (later became West Virginia) he was convicted of treason and executed. He was regarded as a martyr by most abolitionists. He was frequently referred to as "Old Brown of Osawatomie." His daughters later went to school in Concord.

Burnett, Frances Eliza (Hodgson)

Born Cheetham Hill, Manchester, England, November 24, 1849; died Plandome, New York, October 29, 1924. Author of novels and plays. She was brought to America as a child, and at age 17 began selling to *Godey's Lady's Book, Peterson's,* and in 1872, *Scribner's Monthly.* Despite her rearing in America, everything she wrote was essentially English in tone, language, and setting. In 1873 she married physician Dr. Swan Moses Burnett. Two of her

Appendix A

books for young people are considered classics, *Little Lord Fauntleroy* (1886), loosely based on her son who it was said had his life ruined by the book, and *The Secret Garden* (1909).

Channing II, William Ellery

Born Newport, Rhode Island, November 29, 1818; died December 23, 1901. Poet and essayist. His poetry was written by "inspiration," and he could not bring himself to revise or amend his work. Among other works, he wrote *Thoreau: The Poet Naturalist* (1873) and *John Brown and the Heroes of Harper's Ferry* (1886). He is frequently referred to as William Ellery Channing II, or as Channing, the Younger, to distinguish him from his famous uncle, the Unitarian divine, the Reverend William Ellery Channing. His wife, Ellen Fuller, was the sister of the famous Transcendentalist, Margaret Fuller. His sister, Mary, was married to Thomas Wentworth Higginson.

Child, Lydia Maria (Francis)

Born Medford, Massachusetts, February 11, 1802; died October 20, 1880. Author, abolitionist. Spoke out that Negroes were emotionally and anthropologically the same as whites. She and her husband, David Lee Child, became extreme and ardent abolitionists to the point where it affected her popularity as a writer. After the Civil War they worked on behalf of freedom and Indian rights. She was the author of *The First Settlers of New England* (1829), *The Frugal Housewife* (1829), *The Mother's Book* (1831), *An Appeal in Favor of the Class of Americans Called Africans* (1833) and other books. She founded *The Juvenile Miscellany*, the first monthly for children in America.

Dix, Dorothea Lynde

Born Hampden, Maine, April 4, 1802; died July 17, 1887. Social reformer. She put primary emphasis on development of moral character. Demanded intelligent and humane treatment of the insane, and was responsible for reorganizing and enlarging state mental hospitals in Massachusetts. During the Civil War she was Superintendent of Women Nurses for the Union Hospitals. She wrote some books of devotion and stories for children, including a popular book, *Conversations on Common Things* (1824).

Dodge, Mary Elizabeth (Mapes)

Born in New York, January 26, 1831; died August 21, 1905. Juvenile writer, editor. She was one of the first to write stories for children that were not moralizing, overbearing and dreary, which made her books immediately popular. Her best-known book is *Hans Brinker; or The Silver Skates* (1865) for which she did so much research about Holland that not even the Dutch knew that she had never visited there. She also wrote *Donald and Dorothy* (1883), as well as other books. From the day of its founding in 1873 until her death 32 years later, she edited *St. Nicholas* magazine for children.

Emerson, Ralph Waldo

Born Boston, Massachusetts, May 25, 1803; died April 27, 1882. Lecturer, writer, philosopher, Transcendentalist. Educated as a Unitarian minister but resigned after three years to write and lecture. Considered one of America's great philosophers. A true genius and original poet. Said, "Every poem must be made up of lines that are poems." Known for his lofty ideals and unfailing courage. He was an eloquent speaker whose oration was called "the intellectual declaration of independence for America." Known everywhere as "The Sage of Concord." He wrote *Nature* (1836), *Essays* (1841–44), *Poems* (1846, 1867, 1876), *Conduct of Life* (1860), *Memories of Margaret Fuller* (1852), and a number of other books, essays, orations, and poems. Emerson said, "Some books leave us free and some books make us free."

Fields, James Thomas

Born Portsmouth, New Hampshire, December 31, 1817; died April 24, 1881. Publisher, author, editor. Fields knew most of the distinguished writers of his day. As a publisher, he published their books. As editor of *The Atlantic Monthly* he printed their articles, stories, and poems. He was the author of *Yesterdays with Authors* (1872), *Hawthorne* (1876), *In and Out of Doors with Charles Dickens* (1876), and others. His second wife, Annie Adams Fields, was also a prominent literary figure as the author of novels and verse. Annie Fields was a second cousin to Louisa May Alcott; she was the daughter of Zabdiel Boylston Adams and Sarah May Holland Adams, her grandmother being the sister of Louisa May Alcott's maternal grandfather, Colonel Joseph May.

Fuller, Sarah Margaret
(Marchioness Margaret Fuller Ossoli)

Born Cambridge, Massachusetts, May 23, 1810; died July 19, 1850. Journalist, feminist, social reformer, Transcendentalist. Main interest lay in developing and advocating the potential of women in modern society. Outspoken on behalf of women's rights. She emphasized "building up the life of thought upon the life of action." Was brilliant and slightly eccentric. Known as the "High-Priestess of Transcendentalism." She was the author of *Conversations with Goethe* (1839), *Summer on the Lakes* (1843), and *Women in the Nineteenth Century* (1845). Her sister, Ellen, was married to William Ellery Channing II. Fuller always went by her middle name, Margaret. She said, "A house is not a home unless it contains food and fire for the mind as well as the body."

Garrison, William Lloyd

Born Newburyport, Massachusetts, December 10, 1805; died May 24, 1879. Abolitionist, reformer, editor. President of the Anti-Slavery Society. One of the first abolitionists to demand complete and immediate emancipation. He was a pacifist who sought abolition of slavery by moral means. Publicly burned Constitution, saying, "No Union with slaveholders," and worked for peaceful disunion. He founded and edited *The Liberator,* an antislavery gazette. Later, he worked for women's suffrage and the fair treatment of Indians. He is the author of *Thoughts of African Colonization* (1832) and *Sonnets and Other Poems* (1843). He said, "Our country is the world — our countrymen are mankind."

Hawthorne, Nathaniel

Born Salem, Massachusetts, July 4, 1804; died May 19, 1864. Writer, diplomat. United States Consul to Liverpool 1853–57. Many of his books dealt with ethics and the grim Puritan past. Some of his adult novels were *The Scarlet Letter* (1850), *The House of the Seven Gables* (1851), *The Marble Faun* (1860), and a biography of his good friend, President of the United States, *Life of Franklin Pierce* (1852). Books for children include *Twice-Told Tales* (1837), *The Wonder Book for Boys and Girls* (1851), and *Tanglewood Tales* (1853). Hawthorne said, "Children possess an unestimated sensibility to whatever is deep or high, in imagination or feeling, so long as it is simple." His wife, Sophia Peabody Hawthorne, was the sister of Elizabeth Palmer Peabody and Mary Peabody Mann (Mrs. Horace Mann). She was an amateur artist and author of *Notes on Italy.* Their son, Julian Hawthorne was a minor writer of romantic novels, as well as of *Life of Hawthorne and His Wife* (1885), *Hawthorne and His Circle* (1903), and *Memoirs* (1938).

Higginson, Thomas Wentworth

Born Cambridge, Massachusetts, December 22, 1823; died May 9, 1911. Reformer, soldier, author. Trained as a Unitarian minister, Higginson early on began his devotion to two favorite causes, women's suffrage and opposition to slavery. From November 1862 to May 1864, he served as a colonel of first Negro regiment in the Union Army. He wrote for *The Atlantic Monthly,* and among many other books was author of a novel, *Malbone* (1869), collected sketches *Oldport Days* (1873), two volumes *Harvard Memorial Biographies* (1866), and biographies, *Henry Wadsworth Longfellow* (1902), and *John Greenleaf Whittier* (1902). His first wife, Mary Elizabeth Channing, was the sister of William Ellery Channing II.

Howe, Julia (Ward)

Born New York, New York, May 27, 1819; died October 17, 1910. Abolitionist, feminist. She and her husband, Samuel Gridley Howe, were considered "champions of the underdog." They coedited *The Commonwealth,* an abolitionist paper, and made their home an antislavery stronghold. She preached frequently in Unitarian churches, and lectured on German philosophy, prison reform, abolition, suffrage, peace, and social reforms in general. She wrote "The Battle Hymn of the Republic" (1862), for which she received the honor of being the first woman to be elected to the American Academy of Arts and Letters. In 1870, she founded the weekly, *The Woman's Journal,* which she edited for 20 years. She also wrote *Margaret Fuller* (1883) and many other books of poetry and prose. The Howes were the parents of writers Laura E. Richards and Maud Howe Elliott.

Leslie, Frank

Born Ipswich, England, March 24, 1821; died January 10, 1880. Publisher, engraver. Introduced new speed in engraving by a process of mass production in which as many as 48 engravers worked on one large picture. Born Henry Carter, but legally changed name to Frank Leslie in 1857. He first used the pseudonym with sketches and engravings to various publications. Founded several gazettes for adults and children, all preceded with his name, of which his *Frank Leslie's Illustrated Newspaper* became influential during the Civil War. It was his desire to provide "mental pabulum for all classes of society."

Livermore, Mary Ashton (Rice)

Born Boston, December 19, 1820; died May 23, 1905. Reformer and suffragist. From 1872 on, she attained distinction as a public speaker on social issues, politics, history, biography, and education. She worked as an abolitionist and later as a women's suffragist and believer in temperance reform. Was organizer of many aid societies. With husband, Unitarian minister the Reverend

Daniel Parker Livermore, coedited *New Covenant*. Wrote two autobiographical works, *My Story of the War: A Woman's Narrative of Four Years Personal Experience* (1888), and *The Story of My Life* (1897). Edited *Biographical Sketches of Leading American Women* (1893). *The Boston Transcript* hailed her as "America's foremost woman."

Mann, Horace

Born Franklin, Massachusetts, May 4, 1796; died August 2, 1859. Lawyer, congressman, reformer. Responsible for establishing the minimum school year in 1839, for improving school houses and equipment, and for increasing teachers' salaries. He fought for the establishment of state hospitals for the insane and for the restriction of slavery, lotteries, and liquor traffic. Was president of Antioch College (1852-59), a nonsectarian school which was open on an equal basis to both sexes. He said, "Be ashamed to die until you have won some victory for humanity." After his death, his widow, Mary Peabody Mann, followed her sister, Elizabeth Peabody, in helping to create kindergartens based on German methods. Her other sister, Sophia, was married to Nathaniel Hawthorne.

May, Samuel Joseph

Born Boston, Massachusetts, September 12, 1797; died July 1, 1871. Unitarian minister, abolitionist. Was one of first to form a Peace Society. He was an advocate of women's rights, temperance, and abolition, sometimes risking his position in his pulpit with his outspokenness. He made his home a link in the Underground Railroad. He was Louisa May Alcott's maternal uncle.

Parker, Theodore

Born Lexington, Massachusetts, August 24, 1810; died May 10, 1860. Unitarian minister, social reformer, Transcendentalist. He caused a great controversy in Boston religious circles with his sermon "The Transient and Permanent in Christianity" (1841). He became convinced that he had a mission to spread the word of enlightened liberalism. Was an active link in helping fugitive slaves to escape, and a member of the secret society that helped John Brown plan the raid on Harper's Ferry. Primarily, he was said to have a "religion of love and good works." After his death, a 14-volume collection of his writings was published. He said, "The books that help you the most are those which make you think the most."

Peabody, Elizabeth Palmer

Born Billerica, Massachusetts, May 16, 1804; died January 3, 1894. Educator, Transcendentalist. After studying the methods of the German, Friedrich Froebel, in 1860 she opened the first American kindergarten, in Boston. She wrote several books on kindergarten methods and the training of kindergarten teachers. She was also interested in Indian education. As one of the leading feminine figures of the Transcendentalist movement, her West Street Bookstore was a meeting place much like a club. She had two nicknames, "The Mother of American Kindergartens," and "The Grandmother of Boston," receiving the matriarchal designations even though she never married or had children of her own. Her sister, Sophia Peabody, became Mrs. Nathaniel Hawthorne and her sister, Mary Peabody, became Mrs. Horace Mann.

Phillips, Wendell

Born Boston, Massachusetts, November 29, 1811; died February 2, 1884. Lawyer, orator, social reformer. An ardent abolitionist, he succeeded William Lloyd Garrison as president of the Anti-Slavery Society. He also advocated prohibition, abolition of capital punishment, currency reform, equal rights for women, and rights for labor. He considered slavery a crime, and would not go to the polls to vote; at first, because the national constitution supported slavery, and afterwards because the government maintained an army and encouraged war. Born in wealth, he lived self-sacrificially and economically in order to save money for the cause of freedom, and for private charities. He was rightly called "Knight Errant of Unfriendly Truth."

Sanborn, Franklin Benjamin

Born Hampton Falls, New Hampshire, December 15, 1831; died February 24, 1917. Teacher, writer, editor, and social reformer. Active in political life working for social legislation. An effective reformer of Massachusetts charities and prison systems. Was arrested because of his close relationship with John Brown, but later released. Among other writings, he edited *Genius of Emerson* (1885), *Life and Genius of Goethe* (1886), and A.B. Alcott's *Sonnets and Canzonets* (1887) and *Memoirs* (1893). He wrote *Henry David Thoreau* (1882), *Life and Letters of John Brown* (1885), *Dr. S.G. Howe: The Philanthropist* (1891), *A. Bronson Alcott: His Life and Philosophy* (cowritten with William T. Harris) (1893), *Ralph Waldo Emerson* (1901), and *Hawthorne and His Friends* (1908).

Stone, Lucy

Born West Brookfield, Massachusetts, August 13, 1818; died October 18, 1893. Lecturer, suffragist, feminist. Headed first National Woman's Rights Convention. Founder and active member of many suffrage associations. She concentrated on trying to gain suffrage by states. She was a coeditor of many journals with her husband, Henry Brown Blackwell. As she led a movement for married women to retain their maiden names, those who followed the practice were called "Lucy Stoners," or "Lucy Stone Leaguers."

Stowe, Harriet Beecher

Born Litchfield, Connecticut, June 14, 1811; died July 1, 1896. Author, humanitarian, abolitionist. She felt that her ardent abolitionist activity was a religious message that she must deliver. Was the first American author to take the Negro seriously as the hero of a novel. Her book *Uncle Tom's Cabin or Life Among the Lowly* (1852) gained immediate popularity and attention. She also wrote *Dred, a Tale of the Great Dismal Swamp* (1856), *The True Story of Lady Byron's Life* (1869), *Principles of Domestic Science* (1870), *Religious Poems* (1867), and *Sam Lawton's Oldtown Fireside Stories* (1872), as well as other books. She coedited *The Christian Union* with her brother, Henry Ward Beecher.

Sumner, Charles

Born Boston, Massachusetts, January 6, 1811; died March 11, 1874. Politician, orator. Sumner was a notable advocate of abolition and the outlawry of war. When he left the United States Senate, he declared that nothing he had seen had made him look upon politics "with any feelings other than loathing." Was primary editor of *The Works of Charles Sumner,* 15 volumes published between 1870–1873. He was a popular and eloquent speaker on behalf of the emancipation of the slave. His opposition to war as a solution to differences was summed up in his statement, "Can there be in our age any peace that is not honorable, any war that is not dishonorable?"

Thaxter, Celia (Laighton)

Born Portsmouth, New Hampshire, June 29, 1835; died Appledore Island, Isles of Shoals, Maine, August 26, 1894. Poet, naturalist. She had a lifelong attachment to the nine Isles of Shoals, ten miles out in the Atlantic Ocean from the mainland, having been reared on White Island (New Hampshire), spent a period at Star Island (New Hampshire) and settled at Appledore

Island (Maine), with a mainland home in Kittery, Maine. She wrote *Stories and Poems for Children* (1883), praised for its realism; many of the pieces had first appeared in *St. Nicholas*. Most of her poetry is about nature, birds, and the ocean; her best-known poem is "The Sandpiper" (1872). Collections include *Among the Isles of Shoals* (1873) and *An Island Garden* (1894). She is known as "the poetess of the Isles of Shoals."

Thoreau, Henry David

Born Concord, Massachusetts, July 12, 1817; died May 6, 1862. Poet, naturalist, philosopher. In 1845, he moved into a hut at Walden Pond which was his home for two years. He was a rare observer of nature. His familiarity with the creatures of the woods was so remarkable that animals came right up to him, birds came at his call, and fish swam directly into his hands. Author of many poems and several books, the best known being *Walden or Life in the Woods* (1854). Many were published after his death, based on his lifelong journals, among them *Excursions* (1863). Thoreau said, "If a man does not keep pace with his companions, perhaps it is because he hears a different drummer. Let him step to the music which he hears, however measured or far away."

Appendix B

Chronology

Only milestone publications and novels are included here. Louisa always wrote stories and poems; their publication dates are listed in the Chronological Bibliography of Louisa May Alcott's Works.

1799
November 29 — Amos Bronson Alcott (Bronson) born to Joseph and Anna Alcox (*Alcox* later refined by Bronson to *Alcott*), Spindle Hill (now part of Wolcott), Connecticut

1800
October 8 — Abigail (Abba/Abby) May born to (Colonel) Joseph and Dorothy Sewall May, Boston, Massachusetts

1827
August 8 — Bronson Alcott and Abba May are introduced by her brother (Rev.) Samuel May, Brooklyn, Connecticut

1830
May 23 — Bronson Alcott and Abba May married, Boston, Massachusetts

1831
March 16 — Anna (Anna/Nan) Bronson Alcott born, Germantown (now part of Philadelphia), Pennsylvania

1832
November 29 — Louisa (Louy/Lu/Wee-Wee/Weedy) May Alcott born, Germantown (now part of Philadelphia), Pennsylvania

1834
September — The Alcotts move to Boston, Massachusetts; Bronson opens the Temple School

1835
June 24 — Elizabeth (Beth/Lizzie) Peabody (later changed to Sewall) Alcott born, Boston

1839
March 23 — The Temple School closes

A GIFT BOOK FOR THE FAMILY.

LITTLE WOMEN.

ILLUSTRATED.

This, the most famous of all the famous books by Miss ALCOTT, is now presented in an illustrated edition, with

Nearly Two Hundred Characteristic Designs,

drawn and engraved expressly for this work. It is safe to say that there are not many homes which have not been made happier through the healthy influence of this celebrated book, which can now be had in a fit dress for the centre table of the domestic fireside.

One handsome small quarto volume, bound in cloth, with emblematic cover designs. Price $2.50.

ROBERTS BROTHERS,
Publishers, Boston.

"Do you remember how you used to play 'Pilgrim's Progress' when you were little things? Nothing delighted you more than to have me tie my piece-bags on your backs for burdens, give you hats and sticks, and rolls of paper, and let you travel through the house from the cellar to the house-top." — *Vide* "LITTLE WOMEN."

Playing "Pilgrim's Progress." Advertisement for *Little Women*, from *Louisa May Alcott: Her Life, Letters, and Journals*, by Ednah D. Cheney. Boston: Little, Brown & Co., 1889.

Appendix B

1840
March 31 — The Alcotts move to Concord, Massachusetts; Ralph Waldo Emerson and Henry David Thoreau are family friends
July 26 — Abigail (Abby/May) May Alcott born, Concord

1841
May 8 — Bronson goes to England to visit Alcott House (named in his honor)

1842
October 20 — Bronson returns to Concord; with him to join the household are Charles Lane, his son, William, and Henry Wright

1843
May 20 — Lane purchases the Wyman Farm (renamed Fruitlands) on Prospect Hill, Harvard, Massachusetts
June 1 — The Alcotts, Lanes, and Wright move to Fruitlands; others join them there

1844
January 14 — All but one man leave Fruitlands; the Alcotts move to Still River, Massachusetts
November 12 — The Alcotts move to Concord

1845
January — The Alcotts buy the Cogswell House (renamed Hillside) on Lexington Road in Concord
April 1 — The Alcotts move into Hillside

1846
March — Louisa gets her longed-for first own room

1848
Summer — Louisa holds a school in the barn for her young friends; she writes "Flower Fables" for Ellen Emerson
Fall — Louisa writes her first adult short story, "The Rival Painters. A Tale of Rome"
November 17 — The Alcotts move to Dedham Street, in Boston; Abba takes a job as missionary to the poor, sets up the Relief Room; Abba, Anna and Louisa teach adult Negros how to read and write; Bronson rents rooms on West Street to give "Conversations"

1849
Summer — Cholera breaks out in Boston; the Alcotts move to (Rev.) Samuel Joseph May's (Abba's brother) house on Atkinson Street, Boston

July 19	Louisa puts together a family newspaper, "The Olive Leaf"
1850	
January	The Alcotts move to Groton Street, Boston; Anna opens a school on Canton Street
Summer	The Alcotts catch smallpox (girls lightly, parents very ill)
July	Anna leaves her school; Louisa takes over the 20 pupils
1851	
September	Louisa's first published work appears in *Peterson's Magazine,* a poem "Sunlight" (under pseudonym, "Flora Fairfield")
Winter	The Alcotts move to 50 High Street, Boston; Abba opens an Intelligence Office; Louisa goes out to service in Dedham, earns four dollars for seven weeks work, her family angrily returns the money
1852	
May 8	"The Rival Painters" is published in the *Olive Branch*
Fall	Nathaniel Hawthorne buys Hillside (renames it Wayside); the Alcotts move to 20 Pinckney Street; Louisa and Anna open a school in the parlor
1853	
January–May	Louisa has a school
Fall	Anna moves to Syracuse to teach
October	Bronson goes on his first mid-western lecture tour
1854	
February	Bronson returns to Boston having earned one dollar
Spring	Louisa prepares *Flower Fables* for publication, working in the garret at 20 Pinckney Street, Boston; Louisa writes a story about how she went out to service, takes it to James T. Fields at The Old Corner Bookstore. He tells her, "Stick to your teaching, Miss Alcott. You can't write."
Summer	Louisa has a school
November 11	"The Rival Prima Donnas" is published in the *Saturday Evening Gazette*
December 19	Louisa's first book, *Flower Fables,* is published
1855	
June	Louisa goes to Walpole, New Hampshire; she joins the Walpole Amateur Dramatic Company
July	The entire Alcott family goes to Walpole

Appendix B

Nov.–Dec.	Louisa has a school in Boston, living with relatives; the family stays in Walpole; Louisa frequents (Rev.) Theodore Parker's lectures and Sunday evening at-homes
1856	
Summer	Louisa goes to Walpole; Beth and May come down with scarlet fever
Fall	Louisa moves to Boston, tutors; frequents Parker's at-homes
1857	
Summer	Louisa goes to Walpole
September	The Alcotts buy the dilapidated John Moore house (naming it Orchard House) on Lexington Road in Concord; Louisa calls it "Apple Slump"
October	The Alcotts move to a rented house in Concord while repairs are made on Orchard House; Beth is still ill, Louisa stays home to help nurse her
Fall	Louisa and Anna act with Frank Sanborn's Concord Dramatic Union; Anna meets John Bridge Pratt; Louisa and Sanborn's young student Alfred Whitman become friends
1858	
March 14	Elizabeth (Beth) Alcott dies
April 7	Anna Alcott and John Pratt get engaged
July	The Alcotts move into Orchard House
October	Louisa returns to Boston to tutor, lives with a relative
1859	
May	Bronson is elected superintendent of Concord Schools, with a salary of $100 a year
1860	
May 10	(Rev.) Theodore Parker dies in Florence
May 23	Anna Alcott and John Pratt are married in Concord
August	Louisa writes *Moods* in four weeks
1861	
January	Louisa starts on "Success" (later named *Work*)
February	Louisa revises *Moods*
July	Louisa goes to Gorham, New Hampshire
August	May takes a job teaching in Frank Sanborn's school
1862	
January	Louisa has a kindergarten at the Warren Street Chapel in Boston; she boards with James T. and Annie Fields

April	Louisa returns to Concord and commutes to Boston for a while; later, she gives up the school
May 6	Henry David Thoreau dies
June	Louisa writes "Pauline's Passion and Punishment"
November	Louisa applies for service as a Union Army nurse in Washington
December 11	Louisa is summoned to the Georgetown Union Hotel Hospital in Georgetown, Washington, D.C.
December 13	Louisa arrives at the hospital
Late December	Louisa hears that "Pauline's Passion and Punishment" won the $100 first prize from *Frank Leslie's Illustrated Newspaper*
1863	
January 3	"Pauline's Passion and Punishment" begins serialization in *Frank Leslie's Illustrated Newspaper* (by an anonymous "lady of Massachusetts")
January 7	Louisa is ill with typhoid pneumonia
January 16	Bronson arrives in Georgetown to take Louisa home
January 24	Louisa and Bronson arrive in Concord; Louisa is delirious and very ill
March 22	Louisa is finally well enough to leave her room
March 28	Frederick Alcott Pratt is born to Anna and John Pratt
May 22	Frank Sanborn serializes "Hospital Sketches" in the *Boston Commonwealth*
August	Louisa's second book, *Hospital Sketches*, is published; its author is praised
1864	
January	*The Rose Family* and *On Picket Duty, and Other Tales* are published
February	Louisa finishes *Moods*
December	*Moods* is published
1865	
Spring	Bronson Alcott leaves superintendency of Concord Schools
June 24	John Sewall Pratt is born to Anna and John Pratt
July 19	Louisa leaves for Europe as companion to Anna Weld
November	Louisa meets and becomes friends with a young Polish man, Ladislas Wisniewski
1866	
July 19	Louisa returns to Boston
1867	
August	Louisa goes to Clarks Island, Massachusetts

Appendix B

September	Thomas Niles of Roberts Brothers suggests that Louisa write a girls' book, she demurs; Horace Fuller asks Louisa to edit *Merry's Museum*
October	Louisa agrees to edit *Merry's Museum* for $500 a year
October 28	Louisa moves to a room she calls Gamp's Garret at 6 Heyward Place, Boston

1868

January	The first issue of *Merry's Museum* edited by Louisa appears; Louisa acts in several plays for charity
February 28	Louisa is needed at home, so moves to Concord; she continues the editorial work and also continues to write stories
May	Mr. Niles again asks Louisa to write a girls' book, she begins *Little Women*
July 15	Louisa finishes *Little Women*
October 1	*Little Women or, Meg, Jo, Beth, and Amy* is published (Part One)
October 26	Louisa moves to Brookline Street, Boston
November 1	Louisa begins to write *Little Women, Part Second*
December	Louisa and May move to rooms at the Bellevue Hotel on Beacon Street, Boston

1869

January 1	Louisa finishes *Little Women, Part Second*
March	Louisa moves to Concord
April 14	*Little Women or Meg, Jo, Beth, and Amy, Part Second* is published
July	Louisa visits at Riviere du Loup, Quebec on the St. Lawrence River
August	Louisa and May visit Mount Desert, Maine
October	Louisa moves to 14 Pinckney Street, Boston

1870

April	*An Old-Fashioned Girl* is published
April 2	Louisa goes to Europe with Alice Bartlett and May
November 17	John Bridge Pratt dies

1871

January	Louisa, still in Europe, begins *Little Men*
June	*Little Men: Life at Plumfield with Jo's Boys* is published
June 6	Louisa returns to Boston; May stays abroad
July 1	Uncle (Rev.) Samuel May dies
October	Louisa moves to a boardinghouse at 23 Beacon Street

November 19	May returns from Europe

1872
October	Louisa moves to a boardinghouse at 7 Allston Street, Boston
November	Louisa revises "Success" as *Work*

1873
April 26	May returns to Europe
June 10	*Work* is published
August	Louisa returns to Concord
November	Louisa moves to a boardinghouse at 26 East Brookline Street, Boston

1874
March	May returns from Europe
May	Louisa moves to Joy Street, Boston
Summer	Louisa, Anna, and Anna's two sons visit Conway, New Hampshire
October	Louisa and May move to the Bellevue Hotel, Boston

1875
February	Louisa accepts invitation to attend Vassar College's tenth anniversary; goes on to New York for a short visit
March	Louisa goes to Concord
September 25	*Eight Cousins* published
October	Louisa goes to Dr. Eli Peck Miller's Bath Hotel, 39 West 26th Street, New York, New York, for an extended stay
December 25	Louisa spends Christmas visiting the Tombs, Newsboys' Home, and Randall's Island

1875
Early January	Louisa leaves New York; she visits Philadelphia, Pennsylvania
February	Louisa goes to Boston
April 19	The Alcotts participate as Concord celebrates the centennial
September 4	May returns to Europe
November	*Rose in Bloom* is published

1876
January	Louisa moves to the Bellevue Hotel, Boston; she writes *A Modern Mephistopheles*
April 28	*A Modern Mephistopheles* is published
May	Louisa and Anna jointly purchase the Thoreau House

Appendix B   283

Frontispiece: Illustration re "Tessa's Surprises" in *Aunt Jo's Scrap-Bag I*. Boston: Roberts Brothers, 1872.

July	Anna and her sons move into the Thoreau House
September 7	Abba very ill, doctor warns that the end is near
October	Louisa fatigued and ill
November 14	Louisa, Abba, and Bronson close Orchard House; they join Anna and her sons at the Thoreau-Alcott-Pratt House; Louisa and Abba are both ill
November 25	Abigail May Alcott dies
1878	
February	May Alcott announces her engagement to Ernest Nieriker

March 22	Abigail May Alcott and Ernest Nieriker married in London; none of the Alcotts can be there
October 15	*Under the Lilacs* is published

1879

January	Louisa moves to the Bellevue Hotel, Boston
Spring	Louisa moves back to the Thoreau-Alcott-Pratt House, Concord
July 15	The Concord School of Philosophy opens in Orchard House
July	Louisa is first woman to register her name as voter in Concord
August	Louisa visits Magnolia, Massachusetts
September	Louisa returns to Concord
November 8	Louisa May Nieriker is born to May and Ernest Nieriker in Paris
December 29	Abigail May Alcott Nieriker dies in Paris; her last wish is that Louisa raise her daughter, Lulu

1880

April	Louisa moves to the Bellevue Hotel, Boston
June	Louisa visits Concord
July-August	Louisa, Fred Pratt, and John Pratt go to New York
August	Louisa moves to Concord
September 19	Lulu Nieriker arrives in America
October 9	*Jack and Jill* is published
Winter	Louisa and Lulu move to Elizabeth Sewall Willis Well's house at 81 Pinckney Street, Boston, facing Louisburg Square

1881

Spring	Louisa moves to Concord
July	Louisa and Lulu visit seashore at Nonquit, Massachusetts

1882

April 27	Ralph Waldo Emerson dies
July 17	New School of Philosophy opens in wooden chapel built beside Orchard House; Orchard House rented out
Summer	Louisa goes to Nonquit, Massachusetts
Fall	Louisa moves to the Bellevue Hotel, Boston, with John; Lulu stays with Anna
October 24	Bronson suffers a paralytic stroke
November	Louisa and John return to Concord

1883

March	Louisa and Lulu (and maid) move to Bellevue Hotel, Boston
April	Louisa and Lulu move to Concord; only seven women vote at town meeting, including Louisa and Anna
July	Louisa and Lulu (and maid) go to Nonquit, Massachusetts
August	Louisa returns to Concord; Anna takes her turn at Nonquit, Massachusetts
November 27	Louisa and Lulu move to Boylston Street, Boston

1884

June	Orchard House is sold to William T. Harris; Louisa buys a furnished cottage at Nonquit, Massachusetts
June 24	Louisa, Lulu, and John go to Nonquit, Massachusetts
August 7	Louisa goes back to Concord; Anna takes her turn at Nonquit, Massachusetts
October	Louisa and John move to Bellevue Hotel, Boston
November	Louisa, Fred, and John move to 31 Chestnut Street, Boston; Anna, Bronson and Lulu are in Concord
December	Louisa exhausted and told not to write for six months

1885

February	Louisa tries mind-cure treatments
Summer	Louisa goes to Nonquit, Massachusetts
August 8	Louisa goes back to Concord; Anna takes her turn at Nonquit, Massachusetts
October 1	Louisa, Lulu, Anna, Fred, John, and Bronson move to a rented furnished house at 10 Louisburg Square, Beacon Hill, Boston

1886

January	Louisa starts treatments with Dr. Rhoda Lawrence
May–June	The household goes to Thoreau-Alcott-Pratt House in Concord for the summer
June	Louisa visits Princeton, Massachusetts
July	Anna and Lulu go to Nonquit, Massachusetts
September	The household moves back into 10 Louisburg Square, Boston
October 9	*Jo's Boys, and How They Turned Out* is published
December	Louisa enters Dr. Lawrence's Dunreath Place, Roxbury for a much needed rest

1887

Summer	The family goes to Melrose, Massachusetts; Louisa visits, but lives at Dunreath Place; Louisa takes a room

	in Concord for a week; completes plans to adopt John so he will be a legal heir; John's name becomes John Sewall Pratt Alcott
July–August	Louisa and Dr. Lawrence go to Princeton, Massachusetts
July 10	At Princeton, Louisa signs the will she had ordered drawn up

1888

February 8	Frederick Alcott Pratt marries Jessica L. Cate; Louisa too ill to attend
March 1	Louisa visits Bronson who is near death, at 10 Louisburg Square; returns to Dunreath Place and becomes ill, she sinks into unconsciousness and the doctor diagnoses either cerebrospinal meningitis or apoplexy
March 4	Amos Bronson Alcott dies
March 6	Louisa May Alcott dies

1889

June	Anna Pratt takes Lulu Nieriker to her father, Ernest Nieriker, in Zurich, Switzerland
(?)	Bronson Alcott Pratt born to Frederick and Jessica Pratt
1891	Elizabeth Sewall Pratt born to Frederick and Jessica Pratt

1893

July 17	Anna Alcott Pratt dies
October	*Comic Tragedies* is published
1900	Louisa May Pratt born to Frederick and Jessica Pratt

1901

(?)	John Sewall Pratt Alcott marries Eunice May Plummer Hunting; John adopts her son, Elverton Hunting
1902	Frederick Woolsey Pratt born to Frederick and Jessica Pratt
19___	Louisa May Nieriker (Lulu) marries Ernst Rasim in Switzerland
19___	Ernestine (Erni) Rasim born to Ernst and Lulu Nieriker Rasim in Switzerland
1910	Frederick Alcott Pratt dies (?Concord, Massachusetts)
1923	John Sewall Pratt Alcott dies (?Newton, Massachusetts)
1975	Louisa May Nieriker Rasim (Lulu) dies in Oberwill, Switzerland

Appendix C

Time-line Chronology

The arbitrary insertion of historical data can be disrupting in the context of a general overview of an author's life and works. The march of time does, however, chronicle what else was going on in the world during the subject's lifetime, often presenting fascinating or surprising juxtapositions. Accordingly, here is a time-line that parallels the significant personal stepping-stones in Louisa May Alcott's life.

1832

Indians defeated in Black Hawk War in Illinois. First railroad in Europe is completed. The first book jacket appears on *The Keepsake,* published by Longman in London. Charles Lutwidge Dodgson (Lewis Carroll) born.
LMA born November 29.

1833

Slavery abolished in British Empire. Early version of baseball is played for first time in United States. First private detective agency, Paris. Alfred Nobel born. First college to admit full-time women students (co-ed) is Oberlin Collegiate Institute, Oberlin, Ohio.

1834

Cyrus H. McCormick patents reaper. Charles Babbage invents an "analytical engine" (precursor to computer). Horatio Alger born. Jacob Abbott publishes first of 36 *Rollo* books.

1835

Halley's Comet makes an appearance. First colored illustration in a children's book, London. Hans Christian Andersen publishes *Fairy Tales,* Denmark. Samuel Clemens (Mark Twain) born.

1836

Battle of the Alamo, entire garrison including Davy Crockett and Jim Bowie are killed. *McGuffey's Reader* becomes standard textbook in United States. Charles Dickens publishes *Pickwick Papers*. First author to receive royalties is Charles Knight for *The British Almanac*.

1837

First kindergarten developed by Friedrich Froebel and opened in Germany. First college exclusively for women (non-degree) is Mount Holyoke Female Seminary, South Hadley, Massachusetts.

1838

Beginning of Underground Railroad in United States. Morse code developed by Alfred Vail and transmitted by Morse telegraph, Morristown, New Jersey.

1839

First form of photography invented by Louis Daguerre in France. First bicycle invented by Kirkpatrick Macmillan, Courthill, Dumfries. Vulcanized rubber developed by Charles Goodyear, Philadelphia, Pennsylvania.

1840

Lower and Upper Canada united. First correspondence course offered in Bath, England. Type-composing machine, "Pianotyp," patented by James Young and Adrien Delcambre, England. Thomas Hardy born.

1841

United States President William Henry Harrison dies after one month in office; John Tyler becomes first vice president to succeed to presidency. First college to grant degrees to women is Oberlin Collegiate Institute, Oberlin, Ohio. First paperback book series published in Leipzig (Bernhard Tauchnitz obtained rights to publish English words in all non–English speaking countries; his contracts were first precursor of modern international copyright). Ralph Waldo Emerson publishes *Essays* (first series). James Fenimore Cooper publishes *The Deerslayer*.

Advertisements for Alcott's works, from *Louisa May Alcott: Her Life, Letters, and Journals,* by Ednah D. Cheney. Boston: Little, Brown & Co., 1889

1842

First anesthetic used by Dr. Crawford Long in Jefferson, Georgia. First book set by type-composing machine is Edward Binn's *The Anatomy of Sleep,* London. First book illustrated with photographs is N.P. Lerebours's *Excursions Daguerriennes,* Paris.

1843

First paid telegrams dispatched over 20-mile-long wire from Paddington to Slough. Henry James born. First Christmas card designed at suggestion of Henry Cole by John Calcott Horsley, London. Charles Dickens publishes *A Christmas Carol.*

The Alcotts are part of a communal-living experiment at Fruitlands; it fails within six months.

1844

Samuel F.B. Morse patents telegraph; first message is "What hath God wrought." Ralph Waldo Emerson publishes *Essays* (second series).

1845

Edgar Allan Poe publishes "The Raven."
The Alcotts buy Hillside.

1846

United States declares war on Mexico. Sewing machine patented by Elias Howe. W.T. Morton first uses ether as anesthetic. Sponge rubber patented by Charles Hancock, London. *Grimm's Popular Stories* translated into English. Edward Lear publishes *Book of Nonsense*. Hans Christian Andersen's *Fairy Tales* translated into English.

1847

First building acquired for preservation is Shakespeare's birthplace, Stratford-on-Avon. First ring-doughnuts introduced by Captain Hanson Gregory, Camden, Maine. Thomas Alva Edison born. Alexander Graham Bell born. Charlotte Brontë publishes *Jane Eyre*. Emily Bronte publishes *Wuthering Heights*.

1848

United States–Mexico War ends. First chewing gum commercially produced by John Curtis, Bangor, Maine. First accurate, scientific state-of-the-weather records published daily for readers to analyze, by Charles Dickens's newspaper the *Daily News*. First Christmas supplement to a magazine, *Illustrated London*.
The Alcotts leave Hillside.

1849

California gold rush begins. Friedrich Froebel establishes first Kindergarten Training School in Germany. Safety pin patented by Charles Rowley, Great Britain.

Appendix C

1850

First photographic slides patented by Frederick Langenheim, Philadelphia, Pennsylvania. First jeans introduced by Levi Strauss (a Bavarian immigrant) in United States. Robert Louis Stevenson born. First magazine prize competitions, *The Family Friend,* London. First National Women's Rights Convention, Worcester, Massachusetts.

1851

First Parent-Teacher Association, Ronges Kindergarten, London. Herman Melville publishes *Moby Dick.* Harriet Beecher Stowe publishes *Uncle Tom's Cabin* (serially 1851-52). International copyright agreement between Great Britain and France.
LMA publishes her first work, poem, "Sunlight."

1852

First public lavatory with water-closets (separate facilities for "gents" and ladies), London. First free public lending library (for working class as well as educated classes), Manchester Free Library, Campfield, England. Nathaniel Hawthorne publishes *A Wonder Book for Girls and Boys.*

1853

First potato crisps prepared at Moon Lake House Hotel, Saratoga Springs, New York, by Red Indian chef George Crum. Specimen of braille included in Edmund Johnson's *Tangible Typography,* Great Britain. Nathaniel Hawthorne publishes *Tanglewood Tales.*

1854

Republican Party formed. Paraffin lamp invented by John H. and George W. Austen, New York. Alfred Lord Tennyson publishes *Charge of the Light Brigade.* Henry David Thoreau publishes *Walden.* Oliver Optic (real name William Taylor Adams) publishes *In Doors and Out; or, Views from the Chimney Corner.*

1855

Florence Nightingale nurses wounded in Crimea. First Christmas tree in United States. First practical programmed computer built by George Scheutz,

Stockholm, Sweden. Walt Whitman publishes *Leaves of Grass*. Henry Wadsworth Longfellow publishes *The Song of Hiawatha*.
LMA publishes her first book, Flower Fables.

1856

George Bernard Shaw born. Oscar Wilde born. First fiction detective novel is *Recollections of a Detective Police Officer* by "Waters" (William Russell), published by J. & C. Brown, England (also first detective novel translated into a foreign language, appearing in German 1857, and French 1868). Horatio Alger, Jr. publishes his first book, *Bertha's Christmas Vacation*.

1857

Dred Scott Decision by Supreme Court rules that a slave is not a citizen. First street parade with decorated floats, Mardi Gras, New Orleans, Louisiana. *The Atlantic Monthly* founded. Thomas Hughes publishes *Tom Brown's Schooldays*.
The Alcotts buy Orchard House.

1858

Lincoln-Douglas debates. First electric burglar alarm, Boston, Massachusetts. Condensed milk advertised by Gail Borden, Burrville, Connecticut. First trans–Atlantic telegraph cable completed by Cyrus W. Field. First pencil with attached eraser patented by Hyman Lipman, Philadelphia.
The Alcotts move into Orchard House.

1859

John Brown's raid on Harper's Ferry; he is caught and hanged. Suez Canal is begun. Arthur Conan Doyle born. Charles Darwin publishes *Origin of the Species*.

1860

Abraham Lincoln is elected president of United States. South Carolina secedes from the Union.

Appendix C 293

1861

Civil War begins. Congress adopts income tax. First postcard copyrighted by John P. Charlton, Philadelphia. James T. Fields becomes editor of *The Atlantic Monthly*.

1862

Civil War battles of Shiloh, Second Battle of Bull Run, Antietam, Fredericksburg, etc. are fought. Commercial Christmas cards produced by Charles Goodall & Sons, London.

LMA goes to Union Hotel Hospital in Georgetown as Union Army nurse. LMA learns that a story, "Pauline's Passion and Punishment," won $100 prize.

1863

President Lincoln issues Emancipation Proclamation. Battle of Gettysburg is fought. First power-driven merry-go-round operated by Thomas Bradshaw, Pot Market, Bolton, England. Henry Ford born. Henry Wadsworth Longfellow publishes *Tales of a Wayside Inn* (inc. "Paul Revere's Ride").

LMA comes down with serious illness and returns home after only six weeks as Army nurse. LMA writes serialized "Hospital Sketches" for publication. LMA publishes her second book, Hospital Sketches.

1864

"Yosemite (Valley) Grant" establishes first U.S. lands put aside for national public protection and recreation. General William Tecumseh Sherman "marches to sea"; Atlanta is burned. Rubber stamp developed by John Leighton, London. Horatio Alger, Jr. publishes first of hundreds of boys' books, *Frank's Campaign*.

LMA publishes The Rose Family. A Fairy Tale *and* On Picket Duty, and Other Tales.

1865

Civil War ends. Rudyard Kipling born. Lewis Carroll (Charles Lutwidge Dodgson) publishes *Alice's Adventures in Wonderland*. Mary Mapes Dodge publishes *Hans Brinker, or the Silver Skates*.

LMA publishes Moods. *LMA goes to Europe.*

1866

Alfred Nobel of Sweden invents dynamite. Indelible pencil patented by Edson P. Clark, Northampton, Massachusetts. Newspaper, *Eastern Morning*

News, is set by type-composing machine. Beatrix Potter born. John Greenleaf Whittier publishes *Snowbound.*
LMA returns home from Europe.

1867

United States buys Alaska from Russia. Barbed wire patented by Lucien B. Smith, Kent, Ohio. Oliver Optic (real name William Taylor Adams) establishes *Oliver Optic's Magazine for Boys and Girls* (it folds 18 months later). Martha Finley publishes *Elsie Dinsmore,* first of 29 books in Dinsmore series. Horace Fuller establishes magazine for children, *Merry's Museum.*
LMA begins to edit Merry's Museum.

1868

Andrew Johnson is first United States president to be impeached by House; Senate acquits him. First traffic lights go into operation, London. Stapler patented by C.H. Gould, Birmingham, England.
LMA publishes Morning Glories, and Other Stories. *LMA publishes* Three Proverb Stories. *LMA writes* Little Women *in six weeks.* Little Women, Part One *is published.*

1869

First United States transcontinental rail route completed. Suez Canal opened. Margarine patented by Hippolyte Mege-Mouries, Paris. First novel in raised type for blind, Charles Dickens's *The Old Curiosity Shop,* Perkins Institute, Boston. First novel with dust jacket, *Tom Brown's School Days,* Macmillan, London.
LMA publishes Little Women, Part Two. *LMA publishes* Hospital Sketches and Camp and Fireside Stories.

1870

Keyboard typewriter (first version, 1808) has commercial production (typist cannot see text), Copenhagen (Milwaukee, 1872; New York, 1873). Books in braille, *Advent Hymns* and *John Gilpin,* Britain. Thomas Bailey Aldrich publishes *Story of a Bad Boy.* Lucy Stone and husband Henry Blackwell found *The Woman's Journal.* Henry Ward Beecher founds and edits *The Christian Union.*
LMA publishes An Old-Fashioned Girl. *LMA leaves for Europe.*

Appendix C

1871

William Marcy (Boss) Tweed indicted for fraud in New York City. Stanley meets Livingston in Africa. Fourteenth Amendment giving civil rights to blacks is ratified. Fighting with Apaches begins in West. Toilet roll created by Seth Wheeler, New York.

LMA publishes Little Men. *LMA returns from Europe.*

1872

Congress grants amnesty to most Confederates. Yellowstone National Park designated, Wyoming. Jules Verne publishes *Around the World in 80 Days*. Christina Rossetti publishes *Sing-Song*. Lewis Carrol publishes *Through the Looking Glass*. Susan Coolidge publishes first of English "Katy" series, *What Katy Did*.

LMA publishes Aunt Jo's Scrap-Bag I *and* Aunt Jo's Scrap-Bag II.

1873

United States establishes gold standard. Charles Kingsley publishes *The Water Babies*. Mary Mapes Dodge begins editing (until her death in 1905) new juvenile magazine for Scribners, *St. Nicholas*.

LMA publishes Work. *LMA publishes* Aunt Jo's Scrap-Bag III.

1874

National Woman's Christian Temperance Union formed, Cleveland, Ohio. Dewey Decimal System developed by Melvil Dewey, student of Amherst College, Massachusetts, and adopted by college library. Ladies' sidesaddle bicycle produced by James Starley and William Hillman (awkward mechanism; a fall could cause serious injury).

1875

First Kentucky Derby. Electric (battery-powered) dental drill patented by George F. Green, Kalamazoo, Michigan. First literary agency founded by A.P. Watt, London.

LMA publishes Eight Cousins. *LMA goes to New York.*

1876

Battle of Little Big Horn; Sioux Indians kill General George A. Custer and 264 troopers. First carpet sweeper of practical design patented by Melville R. Bissell, Grand Rapids, Michigan. Alexander Graham Bell patents first telephone capable of sustained articulate speech; first message was, "Come

here, Watson, I want you," Boston. Mark Twain (Samuel Clemens) publishes *The Adventures of Tom Sawyer.*
    LMA visits Philadelphia. LMA publishes Silver Pitchers. *LMA publishes* Rose in Bloom.

1877

Reconstruction ends in the South. Thomas Alva Edison designs phonograph; first recording is verse, "Mary had a little lamb...." Anna Sewell publishes *Black Beauty.*
    LMA publishes A Modern Mephistopheles. *LMA publishes* Aunt Jo's Scrap-Bag IV.

1878

Speed of light measured accurately by Albert A. Michelson, United States (he won a 1907 Nobel Prize). Esperanto developed by 19-year-old Ludovic Zamenhof, Poland.
    LMA publishes Under the Lilacs.

1879

Thomas Alva Edison invents first practical electric light (first form 1879; revised technically 1880). First cash register patented by James J. Ritty, Dayton, Ohio. First commercial milk bottles introduced by Echo Farms Dairy, New York. Albert Einstein born. Magazine *Harper's Young People* founded.
    LMA publishes Aunt Jo's Scrap-Bag V.

1880

First newspaper photography (New York's Shantytown), *New York Daily Graphic,* halftone illustration executed from photograph. First universal compulsory school attendance, school-leaving age 10, England and Wales. Joel Chandler Harris publishes *Uncle Remus: His Songs and Sayings.* Lucretia P. Hale publishes *The Peterkin Papers.* Johanna Spyri publishes *Heidi,* Switzerland.
    LMA publishes Jack and Jill.

1881

First magazine in braille, *Progress,* London. Blueprints introduced by Marion & Co., London.

Appendix C

1882

Tuberculosis germ discovered by Robert Koch, Berlin. First Christmas tree lit by electricity, New York. First commercial electric fan produced by Dr. Schuyler Skaats Wheeler, New York. Judo developed by Dr. Jogoro Kano, Tokyo.

LMA publishes (revised) Moods. A Novel. *LMA publishes* Proverb Stories *(later known as* Kitty's Class Day*). LMA publishes* Aunt Jo's Scrap-Bag VI.

1883

First typewriter manufactured with text visible to typist, the Horton, Toronto, Canada. Congress creates Civil Service Commission. Carlo Collodi publishes *The Adventures of Pinocchio,* Italy (translated into English 1891). Robert Lewis Stevenson publishes *Treasure Island.* Joel Chandler Harris publishes *Nights with Uncle Remus.* Howard Pyle publishes *The Merry Adventures of Robin Hood.*

1884

First ladies' bicycle with dropped frame patented by H.J. Lawson. Linotype machine patented by Ottmar Mergenthaler, a German-American. Johanna Spyri's *Heidi* translated into English. Mark Twain publishes *The Adventures of Huckleberry Finn.*

The Alcotts sell Orchard House. *LMA publishes* Spinning Wheel Stories.

1885

Louisa Pasteur develops rabies vaccine, France. First motorcycle built by Gottlieb Daimler, Germany. First sunglasses manufactured from tinted window glass, Philadelphia. Robert Louis Stevenson publishes *A Child's Garden of Verses.*

LMA publishes Lulu's Library I.

1886

Statue of Liberty dedicated. Apache Chief Geronimo surrenders. First book set by linotype machine, *The Tribune Book of Open Air Sport,* New York. Frances Hodgson Burnett publishes *Little Lord Fauntleroy.*

LMA publishes Jo's Boys.

1887

United States obtains right to build naval base at Pearl Harbor, Hawaii. First Esperanto textbook, *Lingvo Internacia* by Dr. Ludovic Zamenhof (Polish oculist) published in Russian, Warsaw. Sir Arthur Conan Doyle publishes first Sherlock Holmes story, "A Study in Scarlet."

LMA publishes Lulu's Library II. *LMA publishes* A Garland for Girls.

1888

First motion picture film patented by Louis Aime Augustin Le Prince, United States. George Eastman introduces the Kodak box camera.

LMA dies March 6.

1889

LMA's Lulu's Library III *is published.*

1893

LMA's Comic Tragedies Written by "Jo" and "Meg" and Acted by the "Little Women" (cowritten with Anna Alcott Pratt circa 1848) *is published.*

Chronological Bibliography of Louisa May Alcott's Works

Unpublished:

"The Mysterious Page or Woman's Love." Manuscript at Houghton Library, Harvard.

"The Prince and the Peasant or Love's Trials." Manuscript at Houghton Library, Harvard.

"Providence. A Drama." Manuscript at Houghton Library, Harvard.

"The Rival Prima Donnas." Dramatized version of 1854 story. Manuscript at Orchard House.

"The Bandit's Bride." Dramatized adaptation by Orchard House staff. The original manuscript is missing.

"The Fairie Dell." Manuscript at Concord Public Library.

Publications:

Short stories contained in the major anthologies, both those by Louisa May Alcott and those by many later anthologists, are listed by title internally, as some had not been published previously and their publication, therefore, would not be reflected otherwise in the bibliography. The numerous 20th-century reprints of the juvenile novels, unless significantly illustrated, are not included, being redundant reprints. This is a bibliography of Louisa May Alcott's publications in the United States.

"Sunlight" (poem). *Peterson's Magazine,* Vol. XX, No. 3 (September 1851). Published under pseudonym of Flora Fairfield.

"The Rival Painters. A Tale of Rome." *Olive Branch,* Vol. XVII, No. 19 (May 8, 1852). Published with only Alcott's initials.

"The Masked Marriage." *Dodge's Literary Museum,* Vol. VI, No. 2 (December 18, 1852).

"The Rival Prima Donnas." *Saturday Evening Gazette,* Series for 1854, No. 45 (November 11, 1854). Published under pseudonym of Flora Fairfield. There is a dramatized version manuscript at Orchard House.

"The Flower's Lesson" (poem). In *Margaret Lyon, or, A Work for All* (Boston: Crosby, Nichols, 1854). Reprinted with slight changes in *Flower Fables.*

"The Little Seed." In *Margaret Lyon, or, A Work for All* (Boston: Crosby, Nichols, 1854).

Flower Fables. Boston: George W. Briggs, 1855. LMA's first book. ("The Frost King; or, the Power of Love"; "Eva's Visit to Fairyland"; "The Flower's Lesson"; "Lily-Bell and Thistledown"; "Little Bud"; "Clover-Blossom"; "Little Annie's Dream; or, the Fairy Flower"; "Ripple, the Water-Spirit"; "Fairy Song" [poem].) Portion reprinted in *Lulu's Library, II; Lulu's Library* (selections from the series, 1930).

"A New Year's Blessing." *Saturday Evening Gazette*, Quarto Series, No. 1 (January 5, 1856).
"The Sisters' Trial." *Saturday Evening Gazette*, Quarto Series, No. 4 (January 26, 1856).
"Little Genevieve." *Saturday Evening Gazette*, Quarto Series, No. 13 (March 29, 1856).
"Little Paul" (poem). *Saturday Evening Gazette*, Quarto Series, No. 16 (April 19, 1856).
"Bertha." *Saturday Evening Gazette*, Quarto Series, Nos. 16 and 17 (April 19 and 26, 1856).
"Mabel's May Day." *Saturday Evening Gazette*, Quarto Series, No. 21 (May 24, 1856).
"Beach Bubbles" (poems). *Saturday Evening Gazette*, Quarto Series, Nos. 25, 26, 28, 30, 31, 33, 34 (June 21, 28; July 12, 26; August 2, 16, 23, 1856).
"The Mother-Moon" (poem, one of "Beach Bubbles"). *Saturday Evening Gazette*, Quarto Series, No. 34 (August 23, 1856). Reprinted in *The Little Pilgrim*, Vol. V, No. I (January 1858).
"The Lady and the Woman." *Saturday Evening Gazette*, Quarto Series, No. 40 (October 4, 1856).
'Ruth's Secret." *Saturday Evening Gazette*, Quarto Series, No. 49 (December 6, 1856).
"Songs from a Sea-Shell—The Patient Drop" (poem). *The Little Pilgrim*, Vol. V, No. 4 (April 1858).
"The Rock and the Bubble" (poem). *The Little Pilgrim*, Vol. V, No. 9 (September 1858). Reprinted with slight changes in "Fancy's Friend" in *Morning-Glories, and Other Stories*.
"Mark Field's Mistake." *Saturday Evening Gazette*, Vol. XLV, No. 11 (March 12, 1859).
"Mark Field's Success" (sequel to "Mark Field's Mistake"). *Saturday Evening Gazette*, Vol. XLV, No. 16 (April 16, 1859).
"With a Rose, That Bloomed on the Day of John Brown's Martyrdom" (poem). *The Liberator*, Vol. XXX, No. 3 (January 20, 1860). Reprinted in *Echoes of Harper's Ferry* (By James Redpath. Boston: Thayer and Eldridge, 1860).
"Love and Self-Love." *The Atlantic Monthly*, Vol. V, No. 29 (March 1860).
"The Children's Song" (poem: written as lyric to song). "Exhibition of the Schools of Concord at the Town Hall. March 30, 1860" (brochure). Concord: 1860. Reprinted in *Louisa May Alcott: Her Life, Letters, and Journals*. (By Ednah D. Cheney. Boston: Roberts Brothers, 1890.) Reprinted as song in the present work.
"A Modern Cinderella: or, The Little Old Shoe." *The Atlantic Monthly*, Vol. VI, No. 36 (October 1860). Reprinted in *Hospital Sketches and Camp and Fireside Stories; A Modern Cinderella or the Little Old Shoe and Other Stories*.
"March, march, mothers and grand-mammas!. ." (untitled poem: written as lyric to song). "Exhibition of the Schools of Concord, at the Town Hall, on Saturday, March 16, 1861" (brochure). Also printed in *Reports of the School Committee . . of Concord, Mass. . . . Saturday, March 16, 1861* (Concord: Benjamin Tolman, 1861). Reprinted as song, "Young America," in the present work.
"The John Brown Song" (poem: written as lyric to song). *Reports of the School Committee and Superintendent of the Schools of the Town of Concord, Mass., with A Notice of an Exhibition of the Schools in the Town Hall on Saturday, March 15th, 1862* (Concord: Printed by Benjamin Tolman, 1862). Specific documentation lost, but to all appearances, written by Louisa May Alcott. Reprinted as song in the present work.
"The King of Clubs and the Queen of Hearts." *The Monitor*, Vol. I, Nos. 1, 2, 3, 4, 5, 6, 7 (April 19, 26; May 3, 10, 17, 24; June 7, 1862). Reprinted in *On Picket Duty, and Other Tales; Hospital Sketches and Camp and Fireside Stories*.
"Pauline's Passion and Punishment." *Frank Leslie's Illustrated Newspaper*, Vol. XV,

Louisa May Alcott, crayon drawing by Stacy Tolman

Nos. 379 and 380 (January 3, 10, 1863). Published anonymously. Reprinted in *Behind a Mask: The Unknown Thrillers of Louisa May Alcott* (Editor, Madeleine Stern. Morrow, 1975).

"M.L." *The Commonwealth*, Vol. I, Nos. 21, 22, 23, 24, 25 (January 24, 31; February 7, 14, 22, 1863). Reprinted in *The Journal of Negro History*, Vol. XIV, No. 4 (October 1929).

"Hospital Sketches." *The Commonwealth*, Vol. I, Nos. 38, 39, 41, 43 (May 22, 29; June 12, 26, 1863). Portion reprinted as "Night Scene in a Hospital," *The Daily Morning Drum-Beat*, Extra No. (March 11, 1864.) Portion reprinted as "John," *Merry's Museum*, Vol. II, No. 8 (August 1869). Reprinted (revised and enlarged) as *Hospital Sketches; Hospital Sketches and Camp and Fireside Stories.*

Hospital Sketches. Boston: James Redpath, 1863. LMA's second book. Reprint issued as *No. 6 of Redpath's Books for the Camp Fire Series* (Boston: James Redpath, 1864). Reprinted in *Hospital Sketches and Camp and Fireside Stories.*

"A Whisper in the Dark." *Frank Leslie's Illustrated Newspaper*, Vol. XVI, Nos. 401, 402 (June 6, 13, 1863). Published anonymously. Reprinted in *A Modern Mephistopheles and A Whisper in the Dark; Plots and Counterplots: More Unknown Thrillers of Louisa May Alcott* (Editor, Madeleine Stern. Morrow, 1976).

"Letters from the Mountains." *The Commonwealth*, Vol. I, Nos. 47, 48, 49, 51 (July 24, 31; August 7, 21, 1863).

"Debby's Debut." *The Atlantic Monthly*, Vol. XII, No. 70 (August 1863). Reprinted in *A Modern Cinderella or the Little Old Shoe and Other Stories.*

"Thoreau's Flute" (poem). *The Atlantic Monthly*, Vol. XII, No. 71 (September 1863). Reprinted in *Poems of Places. America. New England. I.* (Editor, Henry W. Longfellow. Boston: Houghton, Osgood, and Co., 1879); *Louisa May Alcott; Her Life, Letters, and Journals.* (By Ednah D. Cheney. Boston: Roberts Brothers,

1890); *Library of the World's Best Literature* (Editor, E.B. Hill. Detroit: Stylus Press, 1899).

"A Pair of Eyes; or, Modern Magic." *Frank Leslie's Illustrated Newspaper,* October 24, 31, 1863. Published anonymously. Reprinted in *A Double Life: Newly Discovered Thrillers of Louisa May Alcott* (Editors, Stern, Myerson, Shealy. Boston: Little, Brown, 1988).

"My Contraband; or, The Brothers" (first called "The Brothers"). *The Atlantic Monthly,* Vol. XII, No. 73 (November 1863). Reprinted in *Hospital Sketches and Camp and Fireside Stories; A Modern Cinderella or the Little Old Shoe and Other Stories.*

The Rose Family. A Fairy Tale. Boston: James Redpath, 1864 LMA's third book.

"A Hospital Christmas." *The Commonwealth,* Vol. II, Nos. 19, 20 (January 8, 15, 1864). Reprinted in *Hospital Sketches and Camp and Fireside Stories.*

On Picket Duty, and Other Tales. Boston: James Redpath, 1864. LMA's fourth book. ("On Picket Duty"; "The King of Clubs and the Queen of Hearts"; "The Cross on the Old Church Tower"; "The Death of John.") Portions reprinted in *Hospital Sketches and Camp and Fireside Stories.*

"The Hospital Lamp." *The Daily Morning Drum-Beat,* Nos. III and IV (February 24, 25, 1864). Reprinted in *The Youth's Companion,* Vol. XLI, No. 27 (July 2, 1868).

"Night Scene in a Hospital" (from *Hospital Sketches*). *The Daily Morning Drum-Beat,* Extra No. (March 11, 1864.)

"A Golden Wedding: and What Came of It." *The Commonwealth,* Vol. II, Nos. 35, 36 (April 29; May 6, 1864). Reprinted with changes in *Moods;* reprinted in *Good Times. By Favorite Authors* (Boston: Lothrop, 1877).

"Enigmas." *Frank Leslie's Illustrated Newspaper,* Vol. XVIII, Nos. 450, 451 (May 14, 21, 1864). Reprinted in *Frank Leslie's Popular Monthly,* Vol. I, No. 4 (April 1876).

"Colored Soldiers' Letters." *The Commonwealth,* Vol. II, No. 44 (July 1, 1864).

"Love and Loyalty." *The United States Service Magazine,* Vol. II, Nos. 1, 2, 3, 5, 6 (July, August, September, November, December 1864). Reprinted in *Hospital Sketches and Camp and Fireside Stories.*

"An Hour." *The Commonwealth,* Vol. III, Nos. 13, 14 (November 26; December 3, 1864). Reprinted in *Hospital Sketches and Camp and Fireside Stories.*

"Mrs. Podgers' Teapot, A Christmas Story." *Saturday Evening Gazette,* Vol. L, No. 52 (December 24, 1864). Reprinted in *Hospital Sketches and Camp and Fireside Stories.*

Moods. Boston: Loring, 1865. LMA's fifth book. (Later revised; 1882.)

"V.V.: or, Plots and Counterplots." *The Flag of Our Union,* Vol. XX, Nos. 5, 6, 7, 8 (February 4, 11, 18, 25, 1865). Bylined as "By a Well Known Author." Reprinted as ten-cent novelette under pseudonym of A.M. Barnard (Boston: Thomas and Talbot, c1870). Reprinted in *Plots and Counterplots: More Unknown Thrillers of Louisa May Alcott* (Editor, Madeleine Stern. Morrow, 1976).

"The Fate of the Forrests." *Frank Leslie's Illustrated Newspaper,* February 11, 18, 25, 1865. Published anonymously. Reprinted in *A Double Life: Newly Discovered Thrillers of Louisa May Alcott* (Editors, Stern, Myerson, Shealy. Boston: Little, Brown, 1988).

"In the Garret" (poem). *The Flag of Our Union,* Vol. XX, No. 11 (March 18, 1865). Reprinted in *Little Women. Part Second.*

"The Sanitary Fair" (poem). *The Flag of Our Union,* Vol. XX, No. 16 (April 22, 1865).

"Nelly's Hospital" (pamphlet—from *Our Young Folks,* Vol. I, No. 4 (April 1865). No page, no date: ?Boston: U.S. Sanitary Commission, 1865 (mentioned in a report filed Boston, July 12, 1865 by the Supply Department of the New England Women's

Auxiliary Association of the U.S. Sanitary Commission). Reprinted in *Aunt Jo's Scrap-Bag III; A Modern Cinderella or the Little Old Shoe and Other Stories.*

"A Marble Woman: or, The Mysterious Model, a Novel of Absorbing Interest." *The Flag of Our Union,* Vol. XX, Nos. 20, 21, 22, 23 (May 20, 27; June 3, 10, 1865). Published under pseudonym of A.M. Barnard. Reprinted in *Plots and Counterplots: More Unknown Thrillers of Louisa May Alcott* (Editor, Madeleine Stern. Morrow, 1976).

"A Double Tragedy. An Actor's Story." *Frank Leslie's Chimney Corner* (June 3, 1865). Published anonymously. Reprinted in *A Double Life: Newly Discovered Thrillers of Louisa May Alcott* (Editors, Stern, Myerson, Shealy. Boston: Little, Brown, 1988).

"Ariel. A Legend of the Lighthouse." *Frank Leslie's Chimney Corner,* (July 8, 15, 1865). Published anonymously. Reprinted in *A Double Life: Newly Discovered Thrillers of Louisa May Alcott* (Editors, Stern, Myerson, Shealy. Boston: Little, Brown, 1988).

"Our Little Ghost" (poem). *The Flag of Our Union.* Vol. XXI, No. 37 (September 15, 1866). Reprinted in *Merry's Museum,* Vol. I, No. 11 (November 1868); *The Horn of Plenty of Home Poems and Home Pictures with New Poems by Miss Louisa M. Alcott . and Others.* (Boston: William F. Gill, 1876); *Sparkles for Bright Eyes* (New York: Crowell, 1879).

"Behind a Mask: or, A Woman's Power." *The Flag of Our Union,* Vol. XXI, Nos. 41, 42, 43, 44 (October 13, 20, 27; November 3, 1866). Published under pseudonymn of A.M. Barnard. Reprinted in *Behind a Mask: The Unknown Thrillers of Lousia May Alcott* (Editor, Madeleine Stern. Morrow, 1975).

"An Autumn Song" (poem). *The Flag of Our Union,* Vol. XXI, No. 45 (November 10, 1866).

"The Abbot's Ghost: or, Maurice Treherne's Temptation." *The Flag of Our Union,* Vol. XXII, Nos. 1, 2, 3, 4 (January 5, 12, 19, 26, 1867). Published under pseudonym of A.M. Barnard. Reprinted in *Behind a Mask: The Unknown Thrillers of Louisa May Alcott* (Editor, Madeleine Stern. Morrow, 1975).

"Up the Rhine." *The Independent,* Vol. XIX, No. 972 (July 18, 1867).

"Note on Dickens" (untitled). *The Commonwealth,* Vol. VI, No. 3 (Sept. 21, 1867).

"Living in an Omnibus. A True Story." *Merry's Museum,* Vol. LIV, No. 4 (October 1867). Reprinted in *Merry Times for Boys and Girls* (Philadelphia: Porter and Coates, 1878). Reprinted with changes as part of "The Autobiogrpahy of an Omnibus." *St. Nicholas,* Vol. I, No. 12 (October 1874); *Aunt Jo's Scrap-Bag, IV.*

"Life in a Pension." *The Independent,* Vol. XIX, No. 988 (November 7, 1867).

"The Skeleton in the Closet." In *The Foundling* (By Perley Parker. Boston: Elliot, Thomes and Talbot, 1867 (No. 49 in series *Ten-Cent Novelettes. Standard American Authors*). Bylined as L.M. Alcott. Reprinted in *Plots and Counterplots: More Unknown Thrillers of Louisa May Alcott* (Editor, Madeleine Stern. Morrow, 1976).

"Letter to Mr. Prang. Chromo-Lithography" (advertisement). *Boston Daily Advertiser,* Supplement, Vol. CX, No. 126 (November 23, 1867).

"Taming a Tartar." *Frank Leslie's Illustrated Newspaper,* November 30; December 7, 14, 21, 1867. Published anonymously. Reprinted in *A Modern Mephistopheles and Taming a Tartar* (Editor, Madeleine Stern. New York: Praeger, 1987); *A Double Life: Newly Discovered Thrillers of Louisa May Alcott* (Editors, Stern, Myerson, Shealy. Boston: Little, Brown, 1988).

"A Song for a Christmas Tree" (poem). *Merry's Museum,* Vol. LIV, No. 6 (December 1867). Reprinted in *Morning-Glories, and Other Stories; Merry Times for Boys and Girls* (Philadelphia: Porter and Coates, 1878).

"What the Bells Saw and Said." *Saturday Evening Gazette*, Vol. LIII, No. 51 (December 21, 1867). Reprinted in *Proverb Stories* (later retitled *Kitty's Class Day*).
The Mysterious Key, and What It Opened. Boston: Elliot, Thomes and Talbot, 1867 (No. 50 in series *Ten-Cent Novelettes. Standard American Authors*). Bylined as L.M. Alcott. Reprinted in *Behind a Mask: The Unknown Thrillers of Louisa May Alcott* (Editor, Madeleine Stern. Morrow, 1975).
"A Dickens Day." *The Independent*, Vol. XIX, No. 995 (December 26, 1867). Reprinted with small changes in *Aunt Jo's Scrap-Bag II*.
Morning-Glories, and Other Stories. Boston: Horace B. Fuller, 1868 (copyrighted December 1867). ("A Christmas Song"; "Morning-Glories"; "The Rose Family"; "Shadow-Children"; "Poppy's Pranks"; "What the Swallows Did"; "Little Gulliver"; "The Whale's Story"; "Godfin and Silvertail"; "A Strange Island"; "Peep! peep! peep!"; "Fancy's Friend"; "The Nautilus"; "Fairy Fire-Fly.") Identical to *Morning-Glories, and Other Stories*. (New York: Carleton, 1871.) There is also said to be an edition with the imprint, New York: Carleton, 1867 for which there is no extant copy; it has been reported to have the full text of the Fuller edition and also noted as having half the text of the Fuller edition. Portions reprinted in *Aunt Jo's Scrap-Bag VI*.
"Tilly's Christmas." *Merry's Museum*, Vol. I (n.s.), No. I (January 1868). Reprinted in *Aunt Jo's Scrap-Bag I*. Reprinted as "The Fairy Bird" in *Merry's Museum*, Vol. LXII, No. 4 (October 1872); *Happy Days for Boys and Girls* (Philadelphia: Porter and Coates, 1877).
"Wishes" (poem). *Merry's Museum*, Vol. I, No. I (January 1868).
"What Polly Found in Her Stocking" (poem). *Merry's Museum*, Vol. I, No. I (January 1868).
"Grandmother's Specs." *Merry's Museum*, Vol. I, No. 1 (January 1868). Reprinted in *Sparkles for Bright Eyes* (New York: Crowell, 1879); *Meadow Blossoms*. (New York: Crowell, 1879.)
"Merry's Monthly Chat with His Friends." *Merry's Museum*, Vols. I, II (January 1868; December 1869). The "Chat" for January 1868, includes the "taking the breakfast" incident reprinted in *Little Women*. The "Chat" for September 1868, is similar to "Baa! Baa!" (1869) and "A Beautiful Picture Which Louisa M. Alcott Saw on a Hot and Dusty Journey" (1887).
"My Little Friend." *Merry's Museum*, Vol. I, No. 2 (February 1868). Reprinted as "Buzz" in *Aunt Jo's Scrap-Bag I* (1872); *Sparkles for Bright Eyes* (New York: Crowell, 1879).
"Where Is Bennie?" (poem). *Merry's Museum*, Vol. I, No. 2 (February 1868).
"My May Day Among Curious Birds and Beasts." *Merry's Museum*, Vol. I, No. 3 (March 1868). Reprinted as "Curious Birds and Beasts" in *Will's Wonder Book*. (1870). Reprinted in *Aunt Jo's Scrap-Bag I; Sparkles for Bright Eyes* (New York: Crowell, 1879); *Santa Claus Annual* (Chicago: Morrill, Higgins & Co., no date/?c1875).
"My Doves" (poem). *Merry's Museum*, Vol. I, No. 3 (March 1868).
"Our Little Newsboy." *Merry's Museum*, Vol. I, No. 4 (April 1868). Reprinted in *The Youth's Companion*, Vol. XLI, No. 25 (June 18, 1868); *The Christian Register*, Vol. LI, No. 47 (November 23, 1872); *Aunt Jo's Scrap-Bag I; Sparkles for Bright Eyes* (New York: Crowell, 1879). Reprinted as *Our Little Newsboy, 1880*.
"Happy Women." *The New York Ledger*, Vol. XXIV, No. 7 (April 11, 1868).
"Will's Wonder-Book." *Merry's Museum*, Vol. I, Nos. 4, 5, 6, 7, 8, 9, 10, 11 (April, May, June, July, August, September, October, November 1868). Reprinted in *Will's Wonder Book* as Vol. II of *The Dirigo Series* (Boston: Horace B. Fuller, 1870); and in *Mink Curtiss; or Life in the Backwoods* (New York: James Miller,

1877); *Mink Curtiss; or Life in the Backwoods* (New York: Thomas R. Knox & Co., ?1885). Reprinted in *Louisa's Wonder Book*.

Kitty's Class Day. Boston: Loring, 1868. Reprinted in *Louisa M. Alcott's Proverb Stories; Three Proverb Stories; Kitty's Class Day at Harvard; Proverb Stories* (later retitled *Kitty's Class Day*).

Aunt Kipp. Boston: Loring, 1868. Reprinted in *Louisa M. Alcott's Proverb Stories; Three Proverb Stories; Kitty's Class Day at Harvard; Proverb Stories* (later retitled *Kitty's Class Day*).

Psyche's Art. Boston: Loring, 1868. Reprinted in *Louisa M. Alcott's Proverb Stories; Three Proverb Stories; Kitty's Class Day at Harvard; Proverb Stories* (later retitled *Kitty's Class Day*).

Louisa M. Alcott's Proverb Stories. Boston: Loring, 1868 (paperback, each story paged separately, printed from previous three plates) ("Kitty's Class Day"; "Aunt Kipp"; "Psyche's Art"). Reprinted as *Three Proverb Stories; Kitty's Class Day at Harvard* (c1876). Reprinted in *Proverb Stories* (later retitled *Kitty's Class Day*).

Three Proverb Stories. Boston: Loring, 1868, 1870 (clothbound, new plates) ("Kitty's Class Day"; "Aunt Kipp"; "Psyche's Art"). Reprinted as *Kitty's Class Day at Harvard* (c1876). Reprinted in *Proverb Stories* (retitled *Kitty's Class Day*).

"The Blue and the Gray, A Hospital Sketch." *Putnam's Magazine*, Vol. I, No. 6 (June 1868). Reprinted in *Camp and Fireside Stories*.

"The Baron's Gloves." *Frank Leslie's Chimney Corner*, Vol. VII, Nos. 160, 161, 162, 163 (June 20, 27; July 4, 11, 1868). Reprinted in *Proverb Stories* (later retitled *Kitty's Class Day*).

"A Royal Governess," *The Independent*, Vol. XX, No. 1023 (July 9, 1868).

Little Women or, Meg, Jo, Beth, and Amy. Boston: Roberts Brothers, 1868. Reprinted in *Little Women or, Meg, Jo, Beth, and Amy. Parts I and II*. Portions reprinted in *Louisa Alcott's People* (Arranger, May Lamberton Becker. New York: Scribner's, 1936). Chapters 1 and 2 reprinted in *The Home Book of Christmas* (Editor, May Lamberton Becker. New York: Dodd, Mead & Co., 1941). Portion of Chapter 2 reprinted in *The Children's Anthology* (Editor, William Lyon Phelps. Garden City, New York: Doubleday, Doran & Co., 1941).

"Mr. Emerson's Third Lecture." *National Anti-Slavery Standard*, Vol. XXIX, No. 26 (October 31, 1868).

"My Polish Boy." *The Youth's Companion*, Vol. XLI, Nos. 48, 49 (November 26; December 3, 1868). Reprinted as part of "My Boys" in *Aunt Jo's Scrap-Bag I*.

"Tessa's Surprises." *Merry's Museum*, Vol. I, No. 12 (December 1868). Reprinted in *Aunt Jo's Scrap-Bag I*.

"Sunshiny Sam." *Merry's Museum*, Vol. I, No. 12 (December 1868). Reprinted in *Sparkles for Bright Eyes* (New York: Crowell, 1879); *Water-Cresses*. (New York: Crowell, 1879).

"Back Windows." *Merry's Museum*, Vol. II, No. I (January 1869). Reprinted in *Aunt Jo's Scrap-Bag I*.

"Lost in a Pyramid; or The Mummy's Curse." *The New World*, Vol. I, No. I (January 16, 1869).

"Dan's Dinner." *Merry's Museum*, Vol. II, No. 2 (February 1869).

"A Curious Call." *Merry's Museum*, Vol. II, No. 2 (February 1869). Reprinted in *Aunt Jo's Scrap-Bag I*.

"Perilous Play." *Frank Leslie's Chimney Corner*, Vol. VIII, No. 194 (February 13, 1869). Bylined as L.M.A. Reprinted in *Frank Leslie's Popular Monthly*, Vol. II, No. 5 (November 1876); *Plots and Counterplots: More Unknown Thrillers of Louisa May Alcott*.

"A Visit to the School-Ship." *Merry's Museum*, Vol. II, No. 3 (March 1869).
"The Little Boats." *Merry's Museum*, Vol. II, No. 4 (April 1869). Reprinted as "Dandelion" in *Aunt Jo's Scrap-Bag I* (1872).
Little Women or Meg, Jo, Beth, and Amy. Part Second. Boston: Roberts Brothers, 1869. Reprinted in *Little Women or, Meg, Jo, Beth, and Amy. Parts I and II.* Portions reprinted in *Louisa Alcott's People* (Arranger, May Lamberton Becker. New York: Scribner's, 1936).
"Milly's Messenger." *Merry's Museum*, Vol. II, No. 5 (May 1869).
"What Fanny Heard." *The Youth's Companion*, Vol. XLII, No. 19 (May 13, 1869). Reprinted in *Aunt Jo's Scrap-Bag III.*
"A Little Gentleman." *Merry's Museum*, Vol. II, No. 6 (June 1869). Reprinted as "My Little Gentleman" in *Aunt Jo's Scrap-Bag I* (1872).
"My Fourth of July." *Merry's Museum*, Vol. II, No. 7 (July 1869).
"Scarlet Stockings." *Putnam's Magazine*, Vol. IV, No. 19 (July 1869). Reprinted in *Silver Pitchers.*
"An Old-Fashioned Girl." *Merry's Museum*, Vol. II, Nos. 7, 8, 9, 10, 11, 12 (July, August, September, October, November, December 1869). Enlarged and reprinted as *An Old-Fashioned Girl.* Portions reprinted in *Happy Days for Boys and Girls* (Philadelphia: Porter and Coates, 1877); *Louisa Alcott's People* (Arranger, May Lamberton Becker. New York: Scribner's, 1936).
"Madam Cluck, and Her Family." *Merry's Museum*, Vol. II, No. 8 (August 1869). Reprinted in *Aunt Jo's Scrap-Bag I.*
"John" (from "Hospital Sketches"; *Hospital Sketches*). *Merry's Museum*, Vol. II, No. 8 (August 1869).
Hospital Sketches and Camp and Fireside Stories. Boston: Roberts Brothers, 1869. (*Hospital Sketches*; "The King of Clubs and the Queen of Hearts"; "Mrs. Podger's Teapot"; "My Contraband"; "Love and Loyalty"; "A Modern Cinderella"; "The Blue and the Gray"; "A Hospital Christmas"; "An Hour.")
"A Marine Merry-Making." *Merry's Museum*, Vol. II, No. 10 (October 1869). Reprinted in *Aunt Jo's Scrap-Bag III.*
"Preface to *Concord Sketches Consisting of Twelve Photographs from Original Drawings by May Alcott*" (By May Alcott. Preface and editing, Louisa May Alcott. Boston: Fields, Osgood, & Co., 1869).
Little Women or, Meg, Jo, Beth, and Amy. Parts I and II. Boston: Roberts Brothers, ?c1869/c1870. An English edition is noted as being "two volumes in one" (London: Sampson Low, 1870). Portions reprinted in *Louisa Alcott's People* (Arranger, May Lamberton Becker. New York: Scribner's, 1936). Chapters 1 and 2 reprinted in *The Home Book of Christmas* (Editor, May Lamberton Becker. New York: Dodd, Mead & Co., 1941). Portion of Chapter 2 reprinted in *The Children's Anthology* (Editor, William Lyon Phelps. Garden City, New York: Doubleday, Doran & Co., 1941).
"Becky's Christmas Dream." *Merry's Museum*, Vol. III, No. 1 (January 1870). Reprinted in *Sparkles for Bright Eyes* (New York: Crowell, 1879); *Water-Cresses* (New York: Crowell, 1879). Reprinted as *Becky's Christmas Dream* (1880).
"Little Things." *The Youth's Companion*, Vol. XLIII, No. 3 (January 20, 1870). Reprinted as "A Genuine Little Lady" in *The Christian Register*, Vol. XLIX, No. 48 (November 26, 1870). Reprinted in *Spinning Wheel Stories.*
"Uncle Smiley's Boys." *The Youth's Companion*, Vol. XLIII, Nos. 5, 6 (February 3, 10, 1870).
"Ripple" (from *Flower Fables*). *Merry's Museum*, Vol. III, No. 5 (May 1870).
"Mother's Trial." *The Youth's Companion*, Vol. XLIII, No. 21 (May 26, 1870).

An Old-Fashioned Girl (enlarged from "An Old-Fashioned Girl"). Boston: Roberts Brothers, 1870. Portions reprinted in *Happy Days for Boys and Girls* (Philadelphia: Porter and Coates, 1877); *Louisa Alcott's People* (Arranger, May Lamberton Becker. New York: Scribner's, 1936).

"A Sermon in the Kitchen" (from *An Old-Fashioned Girl*). *The Christian Register,* Vol. XLIX, No. 29 (July 16, 1870)

"The Nautilus" (poem from *Morning-Glories, and Other Stories*). *Merry's Museum,* Vol. III, No. 8 (August 1870).

"V.V.: or, Plots and Counterplots" (Ten-Cent Novelette—from *The Flag of Our Union:* bylined as "By a Well Known Author"). Boston: Thomas and Talbot, c1870. Published under pseudonym of A.M. Barnard. Reprinted in *Plots and Counterplots: More Unknown Thrillers of Louisa May Alcott* (Editor, Madeleine Stern. Morrow, 1976).

Will's Wonder Book. Boston: Horace B. Fuller, 1870. Published anonymously. Evidence indicates Alcott did not know about this publication. (Eight chapters from Alcott's serial "Will's Wonder-Book"; one chapter from her retitled "My May Day Among Curious Birds and Beasts," here called "Curious Birds and Beasts"; one chapter by an unknown "Cousin Alice"; one chapter by Martha G. Sleeper. All had appeared in *Merry's Museum.*

"Recent Exciting Scenes in Rome." *Boston Daily Evening Transcript,* Vol. 44, No. 12523 (February 3, 1871).

Little Men: Life at Plumfield with Jo's Boys. Boston: Roberts Brothers, 1871. (An English edition preceded by one month [May vs. June], London: Sampson Low, Son, & Marston, 1871.) Portions reprinted in *Louisa Alcott's People* (Arranger, May Lamberton Becker. New York: Scribner's, 1936).

Aunt Jo's Scrap-Bag. My Boys. [I]. Boston: Roberts Brothers, 1872. ("My Boys"; "Tessa's Surprises"; "Buzz"; "The Children's Joke"; "Dandelion"; "Madam Cluck, and Her Family"; "A Curious Call"; "Tilly's Christmas"; "My Little Gentleman"; "Back Windows"; "Little Marie of Lehon"; "My May-Day Among Curious Birds and Beasts"; "Our Little Newsboy"; "Patty's Patchwork.") Portion reprinted in *Aunt Jo's Scrap-Bag* (selections from the series, 1929).

"Women in Brittany." *The Christian Register,* Vol. LI, No. I (January 6, 1872). Reprinted as part of "Brittany" in *Aunt Jo's Scrap-Bag II.*

"Kate's Choice." *Hearth and Home,* Vol. IV, Nos. 2, 3 (January 13, 20, 1872). Reprinted in *Aunt Jo's Scrap-Bag III.*

"Shawl Straps." *The Christian Union,* Vol. V, Nos. 12, 13, 14, 15 (March 13, 20, 27; April 3, 1872). Reprinted in *Aunt Jo's Scrap-Bag II.*

"Lines to a Good Physician, from a Grateful Patient." *The Pellet. A Record of the Massachusetts Homoeopathic Hospital Fair,* No. 9 (April 15–27, 1872).

"Cupid and Chow-Chow." *Hearth and Home,* Vol. IV, Nos. 20, 21 (May 18, 25, 1872). Reprinted in *Aunt Jo's Scrap-Bag III.*

"Pelagie's Wedding." *The Independent,* Vol. XXIV, No. 1227 (June 6, 1872). Reprinted as part of "Brittany" in *Aunt Jo's Scrap-Bag II.*

"The Romance of a Summer Day." *The Independent,* Vol. XXIV, No. 1239 (August 29, 1872). Reprinted in *Silver Pitchers.*

"Address of the Republican Women of Massachusetts. To the Women of America." Boston: September 25, 1872. Single leaf. Signed at the end by Lousia May Alcott and others.

"The Fairy Bird." (Formerly "Tilly's Christmas.") *Merry's Museum,* Vol. LXII, No. 4 (October 1872).

"Grandma's Team." *The Youth's Companion,* Vol. XLV, No. 48 (November 28, 1872).

Reprinted in *The Christian Register*, Vol. LI, No. 52 (December 28, 1872); *Aunt Jo's Scrap-Bag III*.

Aunt Jo's Scrap-Bag. Shawl-Straps. [II]. Boston: Roberts Brothers, 1872. ("Off"; "Brittany"; "France"; "Switzerland"; "Italy"; "London.")

"Work; or Christie's Experiment." *The Christian Union*, Vol. VI, Nos. 26, 27; Vol. VII, Nos. 1–25 (December 18, 25, 1872; January 1, 8, 15, 22, 29; February 5, 12, 19, 26; March 5, 12, 19, 26; April 2, 9, 16, 23, 30; May 7, 14, 21, 28; June 4, 11, 18, 1873). First chapter reprinted as advertisement in *The Independent*, Vol. XXV, No. 1257 (January 2, 1873); *Hearth and Home*, Vol. V, No. 3 (January 18, 1873). Reprinted as *Work: A Story of Experience* (1873).

"The Mystery of Morlaix." *The Youth's Companion*, Vol. XLV, No. 51 (December 19, 1872).

"Bonfires." *The Youth's Companion*, Vol. XLVI, No. 2 (January 9, 1873).

"Huckleberry." *The Youth's Companion*, Vol. XLVI, No. 3 (January 16, 1873). Reprinted in *The Christian Register*, Vol. LII, No. 4 (January 25, 1873); *Aunt Jo's Scrap-Bag III*.

"Mamma's Plot." *The Youth's Companion*, Vol. XLVI, No. 6 (February 6, 1873). Reprinted in *Aunt Jo's Scrap-Bag III*.

"Little Boston." *The Youth's Companion*, Vol. XLVI, No. 24 (June 12, 1873). Reprinted in *The Christian Register*, Vol. LII, No. 25, (June 21, 1873).

"Seven Black Cats." *The Youth's Companion*, Vol. XLVI, No. 31 (July 31, 1873). Reprinted in *Aunt Jo's Scrap-Bag V*.

"How We Saw the Shah." *The Youth's Companion*, Vol. XLVI, No. 33 (August 14, 1873). Reprinted in *The Christian Register*, Vol. LII, No. 35 (August 30, 1873). The reprint is bylined as "May Alcott."

"Anna's Whim." *The Independent*, Vol. XXV, No. 1291 (August 28, 1873). Reprinted in *Silver Pitchers*.

"Hope for Housekeepers." *Boston Transcript*, Vol. XLVI, No. 14 (November 13, 1873). Reprinted as "The Servant-Girl Problem" in *The Christian Register*, Vol. LII, No. 49 (December 6, 1873).

"Transcendental Wild Oats." *The Independent*, Vol. XXV, No. 1307 (December 18, 1873). Reprinted in *The Woman's Journal*, Vol. V, No. 8 (February 21, 1874); *Silver Pitchers; Laurel Leaves. Original Poems, Stories and Essays* (Boston: William Gill, 1876); *Bronson Alcott's Fruitlands* (By Clara Endicott Sears. Boston: Houghton Mifflin, 1915); *Golden Book Magazine*, Vol. XIX, No. 112 (April 1934); "Transcendental Wild Oats" (pamphlet). (Concord, MA: Thoreau Lyceum, 1970, 1974); *Transcendental Wild Oats and Excerpts from the Fruitlands Diary* (Boston: Harvard Common Press, 1975).

Work: A Story of Experience. Boston: Roberts Brothers, 1873.

Aunt Jo's Scrap-Bag. Cupid and Chow-Chow. [III]. Boston: Roberts Brothers, 1874. ("Cupid and Chow-Chow"; "Huckleberry"; "Nelly's Hospital"; "Grandma's Team"; "Fairy Pinafores"; "Mamma's Plot"; "Kate's Choice"; "The Moss People"; "What Fanny Heard"; "A Marine Merry-Making.") Portion reprinted in *Aunt Jo's Scrap-Bag* (selections from the series, 1929).

"Patty's Place." *Young Folks' Journal* (private enterprise), Vol. III, Nos. 11, 12 (January, February 1874). Reprinted in *Aunt Jo's Scrapbag IV*.

"A Happy Birthday." *The Youth's Companion*, Vol. XLVII, No. 6 (February 5, 1874). Reprinted in *The Christian Register*, Vol. LIII, No. 10 (March 7, 1874); *Aunt Jo's Scrap-Bag IV*.

"Roses and Forget-Me-Nots." *St. Nicholas*, Vol. I, No. 5 (March 1874). Reprinted in *Aunt Jo's Scrap-Bag IV*.

Frontispiece: Illustration re "My Boys" in *Aunt Jo's Scrap-Bag I*. Boston: Roberts Brothers, 1872.

"Lost in a London Fog." *The Youth's Companion,* Vol. XLVII, No. 15 (April 9, 1874). Reprinted in *The Christian Register,* Vol. LIII, No. 23 (June 6, 1874); *Aunt Jo's Scrap-Bag IV.*
"Little Neighbors." *Hearth and Home,* Vol. VI, Nos. 15, 16 (April 11, 18, 1874). Reprinted in *Aunt Jo's Scrap-Bag IV.*
"Dolly's Bedstead." *The Youth's Companion,* Vol. XLVII, No. 18 (April 30, 1874). Reprinted in *Lulu's Library III.*
"What the Girls Did." *The Youth's Companion,* Vol. XLVII, No. 20 (May 14, 1874). Reprinted in *The Christian Register,* Vol. LIII, No. 29 (July 18, 1874); *Aunt Jo's Scrap-Bag IV.*
"How I Went Out to Service. A Story." *The Independent,* Vol. XXVI, No. 1331 (June 4, 1874).
"A Little Cinderella." *The Youth's Companion,* Vol. XLVII, No. 26 (June 25, 1874).

"London Bridges." *The Youth's Companion*, Vol. XLVII, No. 30 (July 23, 1874).
"The Autobiography of an Omnibus." *St. Nicholas*, Vol. I, No. 12 (October 1874). Reprinted in *Aunt Jo's Scrap-Bag IV*.
"Letter of Miss Louisa Alcott." *The Woman's Journal*, Vol. V, No. 46 (November 14, 1874).
"My Rococo Watch." *The National Elgin Watch Company Illustrated Almanac for 1875* (New York: Elgin Watch Company, 1874). Reprinted with slight changes in *Silver Pitchers*.
"Eight Cousins." *Good Things: A Picturesque Magazine for the Young of All Ages*, Vol. I, Nos. 1, 2, 5, 7, 9, 11, 14, 17, 19, 21, 22, 26, 28, 30, 32, 34, 36, 38, 40, 42, 44, 47, 49, 52 (December 5, 12, 1874; January 2, 16, 30; February 13; March 6, 27; April 10, 24; May 1, 15, 29; June 12, 26; July 10, 24; August 7, 21; September 4, 18; October 2, 23; November 6, 27, 1875); *St. Nicholas*, Vol. II, Nos. 3–12 (January–October 1875). Reprinted as *Eight Cousins; or, The Aunt Hill* (1875). Portion reprinted in *Louisa Alcott's People* (Arranger, May Lamberton Becker. New York: Scribner's, 1936).
"Tribulation's Travels." *The Youth's Companion*, Vol. XLVIII, No. 3 (January 21, 1875).
"An Advertisement" (poem). *The Woman's Journal*, Vol. VI, No. 4 (January 23, 1875).
"Red Tulips." *The Youth's Companion*, Vol. XLVIII, No. 8 (February 25, 1875). Reprinted in *The Christian Register*, Vol. LIV, No. 40 (October 2, 1875); *Aunt Jo's Scrap-Bag IV*; *Frank Leslie's Chimney Corner*, Vol. XXXIX, No. 1003 (August 16, 1884).
"What a Shovel Did." *The Youth's Companion*, Vol. XLVIII, No. 15 (April 15, 1875). Reprinted in *Aunt Jo's Scrap-Bag V*; *Frank Leslie's Chimney Corner*, Vol. XXXIX, No. 1006 (September 6, 1884).
"Woman's Part in the Concord Celebration." *The Woman's Journal*, Vol. VI, No. 18 (May 1, 1875). Reprinted in *Saturday Evening Gazette*, Vol. LXIII, No. 19 (May 8, 1875). Reprinted as "The Concord Centennial: The Town Delegation" (pamphlet; Concord, MA: Louisa May Alcott Memorial Association, no date).
"Silver Pitchers. A Temperance Tale." *The Youth's Companion*, Vol. XLVIII, Nos. 18–23 (May 6, 13, 20, 27; June 3, 10, 1875). Reprinted in *Silver Pitchers*.
"By the River." *The Independent*, Vol. XXVII, No. 1384 (June 10, 1875). Reprinted in *The Woman's Journal*, Vol. VI, Nos. 25, 26, 27 (June 19, 26; July 3, 1875); *Silver Pitchers*.
"Old Major." *The Youth's Companion*, Vol. XLVIII, No. 31 (August 5, 1875). Reprinted in *The Christian Register*, Vol. LIV, No. 34 (August 21, 1875); *Aunt Jo's Scrap-Bag IV*.
"My Little School-Girl." *The Youth's Companion*, Vol. XLVIII, No. 44 (November 4, 1875). Reprinted in *The Christian Register*, Vol. LV, No. 6 (February 5, 1876); *Aunt Jo's Scrap-Bag V*.
"Letty's Tramp." *The Independent*, Vol. XXVII, No. 1412 (December 23, 1875). Reprinted in *The Woman's Journal*, Vol. VII, No. 5 (January 29, 1876); *Silver Pitchers*.
Eight Cousins; or The Aunt-Hill. Boston: Roberts Brothers, 1875. Portion reprinted in *Louisa Alcott's People* (Arranger, May Lamberton Becker. New York: Scribner's, 1936).
"My Kingdom" (poem: words used as lyric for song). In *The Sunny Side* (Editors, Charles W. Wendte and H.S. Perkins. New York: William A. Pond, 1875). Reprinted in *Heart and Voice* (Editor, Charles W. Wendte Boston: Ellis Co., 1908); *The Life Hymnal a Book of Song and Service for the Sunday School*

(Boston: Universalist Publishing House, 1910); *Singing Our History: Tales, Texts and Tunes from Two Centuries of Unitarian and Universalist Hymns* (Editor, Eugene Navias. Boston: Unitarian Universalist Association, 1975); also reprinted in the present work.

"Marjorie's Birthday Gifts." *St. Nicholas*, Vol. III, No. 3 (January 1876). Reprinted as "Marjorie's Three Gifts," in *Aunt Jo's Scrap-Bag IV* (1878).

"Helping Along." *St. Nicholas*, Vol. III, No. 5 (March 1876). Reprinted in part as "How One Sister Helped Her Brother" in *The Christian Register*, Vol. LV, No. 24 (June 10, 1876).

"A New Way to Spend Christmas." *The Youth's Companion*, Vol. XLIX, No. 10 (March 9, 1876).

"Only an Actress." *Demorest's Monthly Magazine*, Vol. XII, No. 4 (April 1876).

"An Evening Call." *The Youth's Companion*, Vol. XLIX, No. 15 (April 13, 1876).

"A Visit to the Tombs." *The Youth's Companion*, Vol. XLIX, No. 21 (May 25, 1876).

"Letter from Louisa M. Alcott." *The Woman's Journal*, Vol. VII, No. 29 (July 15, 1876).

Silver Pitchers: and Independence, A Centennial Love Story. Boston: Roberts Brothers, 1876.

Rose in Bloom. A Sequel to "Eight Cousins." Boston: Roberts Brothers, 1876.

"Merry Christmas" (poem). In *The Horn of Plenty of Home Poems and Home Pictures with New Poems by Miss Louisa M. Alcott ... and Others* (Boston: William Gill, 1876).

Kitty's Class Day at Harvard (reprint of *Louisa May Alcott's Proverb Stories; Three Proverb Stories*) Boston: Loring, c1876. ("Kitty's Class Day"; "Aunt Kipp"; "Psyche's Art.") Reprinted in *Proverb Stories* (later retitled *Kitty's Class Day*).

A Modern Mephistopheles. Boston: Roberts Brothers, 1877. (No Name Series.) LMA's name did not appear. Reprinted with Alcott's name as author in *A Modern Mephistopheles and A Whisper in the Dark; A Modern Mephistopheles and Taming a Tartar* (Editor, Madeleine Stern. New York: Praeger, 1987).

"Clams, a Ghost Story." *The Youth's Companion*, Vol. L, No. 18 (May 3, 1877). Reprinted in *Aunt Jo's Scrap-Bag V*.

"Clara's Idea." *The Youth's Companion*, Vol. L, No. 37 (September 13, 1877). Reprinted as "A Bright Idea" in *Aunt Jo's Scrap-Bag V* (1879).

"Letter to N.W.C.T.U." *Our Union*, Vol. III, No. 6 (November 1877).

Selections from *An Old-Fashioned Girl* for anthology. In *Happy Days for Boys and Girls* (Philadelphia: Porter and Coates, 1877). ("The Accident"; "Polly Arrives"; "Sweet One for Polly.")

Selections for anthology. In *Merry Times for Boys and Girls* (Philadelphia: Porter and Coates, 1878). ("Living in an Omnibus. A True Story"; "A Song for a Christmas Tree" [poem].)

Aunt Jo's Scrap-Bag. My Girls. [IV]. Boston: Roberts Brothers, 1878. ("My Girls"; "Lost in a London Fog"; "The Boys' Joke, and Who Got the Best of It"; "Roses and Forget-Me-Nots"; "Old Major"; "What the Girls Did"; "Little Neighbors"; "Marjorie's Three Gifts"; "Patty's Place"; "The Autobiography of an Omnibus"; "Red Tulips"; "A Happy Birthday.") Portion reprinted in *Aunt Jo's Scrap-Bag* (selections from the series, 1929).

"Under the Lilacs." *St. Nicholas*, Vol. V, Nos. 2–12 (December 1877; January–October 1878). Reprinted as *Under the Lilacs*.

"Mrs. Gay's Prescription." *The Woman's Journal*. Vol. IX, No. 34 (August 24, 1878).

"Transfiguration" (poem). In *A Masque of Poets* (Editor, George Parsons Lathrop. Boston: Roberts Brothers, 1878). (No Name Series.) Reprinted in *The Woman's Journal*, Vol. XIX, No. 10 (March 10, 1888; "Transfiguration. In Memoriam. .").

Under the Lilacs. Boston: Roberts Brothers, 1878.
"John Marlow's Victory." *The Independent,* Vol. XXX, No. 1568 (December 19, 1878).
"Two Little Travellers." *St. Nicholas,* Vol. VI, No. 8 (June 1879). Reprinted in *Aunt Jo's Scrap-Bag V.*
"Jimmy's Cruise in the 'Pinafore'." *St. Nicholas,* Vol. VI, No. 12 (October 1879). Reprinted in *Aunt Jo's Scrap-Bag V.*
"Letter from Louisa M. Alcott." *The Woman's Journal,* Vol. X, No. 41 (October 11, 1879).
Aunt Jo's Scrap-Bag. Jimmy's Cruise in the Pinafore. [V]. Boston: Roberts Brothers, 1879. ("Jimmy's Cruise in the Pinafore"; "Two Little Travellers"; "A Jolly Fourth"; "Seven Black Cats"; "Rosa's Tale"; "Lunch"; "A Bright Idea"; "How They Camped Out"; "My Little Schoolgirl"; "What a Shovel Did"; "Clams"; "Kitty's Cattle Show"; "What Becomes of the Pins.") Portion reprinted in *Aunt Jo's Scrap-Bag* (selections from the series, 1929).
Selections for anthology. *Sparkles for Bright Eyes. With Contributions by Louisa May Alcott.* (New York: Crowell, 1879). ("Our Little Ghost" [poem]; "Buzz"; "My May Day Among Curious Birds and Beasts"; "Our Little Newsboy"; "Grandmother's Specs"; "Sunshiny Sam"; "Becky's Christmas Dream.")
Selected stories for anthology. *Water-Cresses. By L.M. Alcott ... and Others.* New York: Crowell, 1879. ("Sunshiny Sam"; "Becky's Christmas Dream.")
Selected story for anthology. *Meadow Blossoms. By L.M. Alcott .. and Others.* New York: Crowell, 1879. ("Grandmother's Specs.")
"Jack and Jill." *St. Nicholas,* Vol. VII, Nos. 2–12 (December 1879; January–October 1880). Reprinted as *Jack and Jill: A Village Story.* Portions reprinted in *Louisa Alcott's People* (Arranger, May Lamberton Becker. New York: Scribner's, 1936).
"Letter from Louisa M. Alcott." *The Woman's Journal,* Vol. XI, No. 14 (April 3, 1880). Reprinted in *Concord Freeman,* Vol. IV, No. 20 (April 8, 1880).
Jack and Jill. A Village Story. Boston: Roberts Brothers, 1880. Portions reprinted in *Louisa Alcott's People* (Arranger, May Lamberton Becker. New York: Scribner's, 1936).
Little Women. Boston: Roberts Brothers, 1880. Illustrated by Frank Thayer Merrill.
"How It All Happened." *Harper's Young People,* Vol. II, No. 60 (December 21, 1880). Reprinted in *Aunt Jo's Scrap-Bag VI.*
Becky's Christmas Dream. New York: Crowell, 1880. [No known extant copies.]
Our Little Newsboy. New York: Crowell, 1880. [No known extant copies.]
Selected stories for anthology. In *Chatterbox Junior.* "A volume of original stories by Miss Alcott ... and others" (New York: R. Worthington, 1881). [No known extant copies.]
"Victoria. A Woman's Statue." *Demorest's Monthly Magazine,* Vol. XVII, Nos. 3, 4, 5 (March, April, May 1881).
"An Old-Fashioned Thanksgiving." *St. Nicholas,* Vol. IX, No. I (November 1881). Reprinted in *Aunt Jo's Scrap-Bag VI; The St. Nicholas Anthology* (Editor, Henry Steele Commager. New York: Random House, 1948).
"My Red Cap." *The Sword and Pen,* Vol. I, Nos. 1, 2, 3, 4 (December 7, 8, 9, 10, 1881). Reprinted in *Proverb Stories* (later retitled *Kitty's Class Day*).
"A Country Christmas." *The Independent,* Vol. XXXIII, Nos. 1724, 1725 (December 15, 22, 1881). Reprinted in *Proverb Stories* (later retitled *Kitty's Class Day*).
"Preface to *Prayers by Theodore Parker*" Boston: Roberts Brothers, 1882.
Moods. A Novel (revised edition of 1865 book: "...several chapters have been omitted, several of the original ones are restored; and those that remain have been pruned..."). Boston: Roberts Brothers, 1882.

"Letter from Louisa M. Alcott." *The Woman's Journal*, Vol. XIII, No. 6 (February 11, 1882).

"Reminiscences of Ralph Waldo Emerson." *The Youth's Companion*, Vol. LV, No. 21 (May 25, 1882). Reprinted in *Emerson at Home and Abroad* (Boston: James R. Osgood and Co., 1882); *Some Noted Princes, Authors, and Statesmen of Our Time* (Editor, James Parton. New York: Crowell, 1885).

"W.C.T.U., of Concord." *Concord Freeman*, Vol. X, No. 26 (June 30, 1882).

"R.W. Emerson." *Demorest's Monthly Magazine*, Vol. XVIII, No. 9 (July 1882).

"An Interview with Jean Ingelow." In *Pen Pictures of Modern Authors* (New York: G.P. Putnam's Sons, 1882).

"Number Eleven." *The Youth's Companion*, Vol. LV, No. 33 (August 17, 1882).

Proverb Stories. Boston: Roberts Brothers, 1882. Later retitled *Kitty's Class Day*. ("Kitty's Class Day"; "Aunt Kipp"; "Psyche's Art"; "A Country Christmas"; "On Picket Duty"; "The Baron's Gloves"; "My Red Cap"; "What the Bells Saw and Said.")

Aunt Jo's Scrap-Bag. An Old-Fashioned Thanksgiving [VI]. Boston: Roberts Brothers, 1882. ("An Old-Fashioned Thanksgiving"; "How It All Happened"; "The Dolls' Journey from Minnesota to Maine"; "Morning-Glories"; "Shadow-Children"; "Poppy's Pranks"; "What the Swallows Did"; "Little Gulliver"; "The Whale's Story"; "Fancy's Friend.") Portion reprinted in *Aunt Jo's Scrap-Bag* (selections from the series, 1929).

"Grandmamma's Pearls." *St. Nicholas*, Vol. X, No. 2 (December 1882).

"A Christmas Dream." *Harper's Young People*, Vol. IV, Nos. 162, 163 (December 5, 12, 1882). Reprinted in *Lulu's Library I*.

Selections for anthology. In *Christmas Plum Pudding Stories by Louisa M. Alcott . . . and Others* (New York: Crowell, 1882).

"Mr. Alcott's True Condition."*The Woman's Journal*, Vol. XIV, No. 1 (January 6, 1883).

"Letter from Miss Alcott." *The Woman's Journal*, Vol. XIV, No. 10 (March 10, 1883).

"Mrs. Gay's Hint, and How It Was Taken" ("from *The Press*"). *The Union Signal*, Vol. IX, No. 33 (August 30, 1883).

"Little Pyramus and Thisbe." *St. Nicholas*, Vol. X, Nos. 11, 12 (September, October 1883). Reprinted as "A Hole in the Wall," in *Lulu's Library I* (1886). Reprinted as *A Hole in the Wall*.

"Sophie's Secret." *St. Nicholas*, Vol. XI, Nos. 1, 2 (November, December 1883). Reprinted in *Lulu's Library III*.

"Bertie's Box. A Christmas Story." *Harper's Young People*, Vol. V, No. 218 (January 1, 1884).

"Grandma's Story." *St. Nicholas*, Vol. XI, No. 3 (January 1884). Reprinted in *Spinning-Wheel Stories*.

"Address to a Robin"; Extract from a letter, Dec. 28, 1869, addressed to Roberts Brothers. In *Our Famous Women. An Authorized Record of the Lives and Deeds of Distinguished American Women of Our Times* (Hartford, CT: A.D. Worthington & Co., 1884).

"Tabby's Table-Cloth." *St. Nicholas*, Vol. XI, No. 4 (February 1884). Reprinted in *Spinning-Wheel Stories*.

"Eli's Education." *St. Nicholas*, Vol. XI, No. 5 (March 1884). Reprinted in *Spinning-Wheel Stories*.

"Onawandah." *St. Nicholas*, Vol. XI, No. 6 (April 1884). Reprinted in *Spinning-Wheel Stories; The Second St. Nicholas Anthology* (Editor, Henry Steele Commager. New York: Random House, 1950).

"Little Things." *St. Nicholas*, Vol. XI, No. 7 (May 1884). Reprinted in *Spinning-Wheel Stories*.

"Letter from Miss Louisa M. Alcott." *The Woman's Journal,* Vol. XV, No. 20 (May 17, 1884).
"What Shall Little Children Bring..." ("original hymn," untitled). In *The Thirty-Fifth Annual Report of the Executive Committee of the Children's Mission to the Children of the Destitute, in the City of Boston; with an Account of the Proceedings at the Annual Meeting, May 28, 1884* (Boston: Rooms of the Children's Mission, 1884, pp. 22-23). Reprinted in *The Thirty-Seventh Annual Report ... Children's Mission to the Children of the Destitute, in the City of Boston* (Boston: Rooms of the Children's Mission, 1886, p. 11). Reprinted as hymn, "What Shall Little Children Bring," in the present work.
"The Banner of Beaumanoir." *St. Nicholas,* Vol. XI, No. 8 (June 8, 1884). Reprinted in *Spinning-Wheel Stories.*
"Jerseys, or, The Girl's Ghost." *St. Nicholas,* Vol. XI, No. 9 (July 1884). Reprinted in *Spinning-Wheel Stories.*
"The Little House in the Garden." *St. Nicholas,* Vol. XI, No. 10 (August 1884). Reprinted in *Spinning-Wheel Stories.*
"Daisy's Jewel-Box, and How She Filled It." *St. Nicholas,* Vol. XI, No. 11 (September 1884). Reprinted in *Spinning-Wheel Stories.*
"Corny's Catamount." *St. Nicholas,* Vol. XI, No. 12 (October 1884). Reprinted in *Spinning-Wheel Stories.*
"The Cooking-Class." *St. Nicholas,* Vol. XII, No. I (November 1884). Reprinted in *Spinning-Wheel Stories.*
Spinning-Wheel Stories. Boston: Roberts Brothers, 1884. ("Grandma's Story"; "Tabby's Table-Cloth"; "Eli's Education"; "Onawandah"; "Little Things"; "The Banner of Beaumanoir"; "Jerseys"; or, "The Girls' Ghost"; "The Little House in the Garden"; "Daisy's Jewel-Box, and How She Filled It"; "Corny's Catamount"; "The Cooking-Class"; "The Hare and the Tortoise.")
Little Men; Life at Plumfield with Jo's Boys. Boston: Roberts Bros., 1885. Four wood engravings by Frank Thayer Merrill.
"The Hare and the Tortoise." *St. Nicholas,* Vol. XII, Nos. 2, 3 (December 1884; January 1885). Reprinted in *Spinning-Wheel Stories.*
"In Memoriam Sophia Foord." *The Woman's Journal,* Vol. XVI, No. 15 (April 11, 1885).
"Miss Alcott on Mind-Cure." *The Woman's Journal,* Vol. XVI, No. 16 (April 18, 1885).
"Old Times at Old Concord." *The Woman's Journal,* Vol. XVI, No. 16 (April 18, 1885).
"Kind Words from Miss Alcott." *The Woman's Journal,* Vol. XVI, No. 20 (May 16, 1885).
"Baa! Baa!" *Harper's Young People,* Vol. VI, Nos. 307, 308 (September 15, 22, 1885). Reprinted in *Lulu's Library I.* Similar to "Merry's Monthly Chat," September 1868 and "A Beautiful Picture Which Louisa M. Alcott Saw on a Hot and Dusty Journey," (1887). Reprinted in *Lulu's Library I.*
"The Candy Country." *St. Nicholas,* Vol. XIII, No. 1 (November 1885). Reprinted in *Lulu's Library I.*
"To My Father on His 86th Birthday" (poem). *The Woman's Journal,* Vol. XVI, No. 50 (December 12, 1885).
"A Christmas Turkey, and How It Came." *Harper's Young People,* Vol. VII, No. 321 (December 22, 1885). Reprinted in *Lulu's Library III.*
The Alcott Calendar for 1886. (By F. Alcott Pratt. Boston: Roberts Brothers, 1885.) ("...a selection for every day in the year, culled from the writings of the author of *Little Women,* mounted on a card illustrated with a portrait of Miss Alcott, and a view of her present residence in Concord.") [No known extant copy.]

Lulu's Library. Vol. I. A Christmas Dream. Boston: Roberts Brothers, 1886. ("A Christmas Dream"; "The Candy Country"; "Naughty Jocko"; "The Skipping Shoes"; "Cockyloo"; "Rosy's Journey"; "How They Ran Away"; "The Fairy Box"; "A Hole in the Wall"; "The Piggy Girl"; "The Three Frogs"; "Baa! Baa!") Portion reprinted in *Lulu's Library* (selections from the series, 1930).

"Oh, the Beautiful Old Story" (lyric to hymn). In *The Carol: A Book of Religious Songs for the Sunday School and the Home.* (Editor, Charles W. Wendte. Cincinnati: The John Church Company, 1886.) Reprinted in *A Book of Song and Service for Sunday School and Home.* (Boston: Unitarian Sunday-School Society, 1896); *The New Hymn and Tune Book.* (Boston: American Unitarian Association, 1914); *Singing Our History: Tales, Texts and Tunes from Two Centuries of Unitarian and Universalist Hymns* (Editor, Eugene Navias. Boston: Unitarian Universalist Association, 1975). Also reprinted in the present work.

"When Shall Our Young Women Marry?" *The Brooklyn Magazine,* Vol. IV, No. 1 (April 1886).

"Letter on Amos Bronson Alcott." *The Brooklyn Magazine,* Vol. IV, No. 1 (April 1886).

"The Lay of a Golden Goose" (poem). *The Woman's Journal,* Vol. XVII, No. 19 (May 8, 1886).

Jo's Boys and How They Turned Out. A Sequel to "Little Men." Boston: Roberts Brothers, 1886. Portion reprinted in *Louisa Alcott's People* (Arranger, May Lamberton Becker. New York: Scribner's, 1936).

"The Blind Lark." *St. Nicholas,* Vol. XIV, No. 1 (November 1886). Reprinted in *Lulu's Library III.*

"Little Lord Fauntleroy" (review). *The Book Buyer,* Vol. III, No. 11 (December 1886).

"Little Robin." *Harper's Young People,* Vol. VIII, No. 371 (December 7, 1886).

"Jimmy's Lecture: No. 2 The Press Leaflets." *The Press: A Monthly Journal Devoted to the Temperance Reform.* (Boston: no date c1887).

"A Glorious Fourth: No. 4 The Press Leaflets." *The Press: A Monthly Journal Devoted to the Temperance Reform* (Boston: no date c1887).

"What It Cost." *The Young Crusader,* Vol. I, No. 6 (February 11, 1887). Also printed as "What It Cost: No. 5 The Press Leaflets" for *The Press: A Monthly Journal Devoted to the Temperance Reform* (Boston: no date c1887).

"A Flower Fable" (from *Woman Suffrage Bazaar Journal*). *The Woman's Journal,* Vol. XVIII, No. 9 (February 26, 1887). Reprinted in *The Union Signal,* Vol. XIII, No. 10 (March 10, 1887). Reprinted as "Queen Aster" in *Lulu's Library II* (1887); *Morning Glories and Queen Aster.*

"A Beautiful Picture Which Louisa M. Alcott Saw on a Hot and Dusty Journey." *The Voice,* Vol. IV, No. 20 (May 19, 1887). Similar to "Merry's Monthly Chat," September 1868 and "Baa! Baa!," September 1885.

"Early Marriages." *The Ladies' Home Journal,* Vol. IV, No. 10 (September 1887).

"An Ivy Spray." *St. Nicholas,* Vol. XIV, No. 12 (October 1887). Reprinted as "An Ivy Spray and Ladies' Slippers" in *A Garland for Girls.*

Lulu's Library. Vol. II. The Frost King. Boston: Roberts Brothers, 1887. (From *Flower Fables:* "Lilybell and Thistledown, or the Fairy Sleeping Beauty"; "Ripple, the Water Spirit"; "Eva's Visit to Fairyland"; "Little Bud." Also: "Sunshine, and Her Brothers and Sisters"; "The Fairy Spring"; "Queen Aster"; "The Brownie and the Princess"; "Mermaids"; "The Flower's Story"; "The Frost King and How the Fairies Conquered Him." Portion reprinted in *Lulu's Library* (selections from the series, 1930).

"Pansies." *St. Nicholas,* Vol. XV, No. 1 (November 1887). Reprinted in *A Garland for Girls.*

"The Silver Party." *Harper's Young People*, Vol. IX, No. 421 (November 22, 1887). Reprinted in *Lulu's Library III*.

"The Little Red Purse." *Harper's Young People*, Vol. IX, No. 423 (December 6, 1887). Reprinted in *Lulu's Library III*.

Three story selections. In *The White Ribbon Birthday Book* (Editor, Anna A. Gordon. Chicago: Woman's Temperance Publication Association, 1887).

Three Sketches. In *Our Girls* ([By L.M. Alcott and Others.] New York: Belford, Clarke, 1887).

A Garland for Girls. Boston: Roberts Brothers, 1888. ("May Flowers"; An Ivy Spray and Ladies' Slippers"; "Pansies"; "Water-Lilies"; "Poppies and Wheat"; "Little Button-Rose"; "Mountain-Laurel and Maidenhair.")

"Trudel's Siege." *St. Nicholas*, Vol. XV, No. 6 (April 1888). Reprinted in *Lulu's Library III*.

"Recollections of My Childhood." *The Youth's Companion*, Vol. LXI, No. 21 (May 24, 1888). Reprinted in *The Woman's Journal*, Vol. XIX, No. 21 (May 26, 1888). Reprinted in part in *Our Dumb Animals*, Vol. XXI, No. 2 (July 1888); *Lulu's Library III*.

A Modern Mephistopheles and a Whisper in the Dark. Boston: Roberts Brothers, 1889.

Lulu's Library. Vol. III. Recollections. Boston: Roberts Brothers, 1889. ("Recollections of My Childhood"; "A Christmas Turkey, and How It Came"; "The Silver Party"; "The Blind Lark"; "Music and Macaroni"; "The Little Red Purse"; "Sophie's Secret"; "Dolly's Bedstead"; "Trudel's Siege.") Portion reprinted in *Lulu's Library* (selections from the series, 1930).

Louisa May Alcott: Her Life, Letters, and Journals (Editor, Ednah D. Cheney). Boston: Roberts Brothers, 1889. Also included 19 poems by Louisa May Alcott.

Material by Louisa May Alcott. In *The Woman's Story As Told by Twenty American Women* (Editor, Laura C. Holloway. New York: John B. Alden, 1889).

"Transfiguration. In Memoriam" . . . Written by Louise (sic) M. Alcott on the Death of Her Mother . . . "To My Father on His 86th Birthday." By Miss Louise (sic) M. Alcott" (poems). *The News*, Orange, California, December 3, 1890.

Comic Tragedies Written by "Jo" and "Meg" and Acted by the "Little Women" (Editor, Anna Alcott Pratt). Boston: Roberts Brothers, 1893. Melodramas written circa 1848 by Louisa May Alcott and Anna Alcott (Pratt). ("A Foreword by Meg"; "Norna; or, The Witch's Curse"; "The Captive of Castile; or, The Moorish Maiden's Vow"; "The Greek Slave"; "Ion"; "Bianca: An Operatic Tragedy"; "The Unloved Wife; or, Woman's Faith."

Selections for anthology. In *The Boys' Best Book Stories, Poems and Sketches, by . . Louisa M. Alcott* (New York: W.B. Conkey, 1894).

Selected stories for anthology. In *Becky's Christmas Dream and Other Stories* (New York: W.B. Conkey, 1895.) ("Becky's Christmas Dream"; "Our Little Newsboy"; "Sunshiny Sam"; "My May-Day Among Curious Birds and Beasts"; "Our Little Ghost"; "My Little Friend"; "Grandmother's Specs"; "On the Keel.") Compare to *My Little Friend and Other Stories* (1896) and *Becky's Christmas Dream and Other Stories* (1902).

Selected stories for anthology. In *My Little Friend and Other Stories* (By Louisa M. Alcott [and others]. New York: W.B. Conkey, 1896). ("Becky's Christmas Dream"; "Grandmother's Specs"; "My Little Friend"; "My May-Day Among Curious Birds and Beasts"; "On the Keel"; "Our Little Ghost"; "Our Little Newsboy.") Compare to *Becky's Christmas Dream and Other Stories* (1895; 1902).

The Spinning-Wheel Series (four volumes). Boston: Roberts Brothers, 1897. *(Spinning-Wheel Stories; Silver Pitchers; Proverb Stories; A Garland for Girls.)*

Frontispiece: Illustration re "The Autobiography of an Omnibus" in *Aunt Jo's Scrap-Bag IV*. Boston: Roberts Brothers, 1878.

An Old-Fashioned Girl. Boston: Roberts Bros., 1897. Three wood engravings by Frank Thayer Merrill.
Flower Fables. Philadelphia: Henry Altemus, 1898.
A Hole in the Wall (from *Lulu's Library I*). Boston: Little, Brown, 1899.
Marjorie's Three Gifts (from *Aunt Jo's Scrap-Bag IV*). Boston: Little, Brown, 1899. (Also includes "Roses and Forget-Me-Nots" from *Aunt Jo's Scrap-Bag IV*.)
May Flowers (from *A Garland for Girls*). Boston: Little, Brown, 1899.
The Candy Country (from *Lulu's Library I*). Boston: Little, Brown, 1900.
Poppies and Wheat (from *A Garland for Girls*). Boston: Little, Brown, 1900.
The Mysterious Key: The Leisure Hour Library, No. 382. (Reprint of "The Mysterious Key.") New York: F.M. Lupton, no date c1900.
Flower Fables. Chicago: W.B. Conkey, 1900.
Flower Fables. New York: H.M. Caldwell, no date ?c1900.
A Christmas Dream (from *Lulu's Library I*). Boston: Little, Brown, 1901. (Also includes "Baa! Baa!" from *Lulu's Library I*).
Little Button Rose (from *A Garland for Girls*). Boston: Little, Brown, 1901.
Little Men. Boston: Little, Brown, 1901. Illustrated by Reginald Birch.
An Old-Fashioned Girl. Boston: Little, Brown, 1902. Illustrated by Jessie Wilcox Smith.
Selected stories for anthology. In *Becky's Christmas Dream and Other Stories* (By Louisa M. Alcott [and others]. Chicago: Homewood Pub. Co., c1902). (From *My Little Friend and Other Stories*: "Becky's Christmas Dream"; "Grandmother's Specs"; "My Little Friend"; "My May-Day Among Curious Birds and Beasts"; "On the Keel"; "Our Little Ghost"; "Our Little Newsboy." Also: "The Accident"; "The Fairy Bird.") Compare to *My Little Friend and Other Stories* (1896) and *Becky's Christmas Dream and Other Stories* (1895).
The Doll's Journey (from *Aunt Jo's Scrap-Bag VI*). Boston: Little, Brown, 1902. (Also

includes "Shadow-Children" from *Aunt Jo's Scrap-Bag VI;* "The Moss People" from *Aunt Jo's Scrap-Bag III.*)
Pansies and Water-Lilies. Boston: Little, Brown, 1902.
"Lu Sing." *St. Nicholas,* Vol. XXX, No. 2 (December 1902). Story written for Louisa May Alcott's niece, Louisa May Nieriker, circa 1886 and held by her until this publication.
"The Eaglet in the Dove's Nest." *St. Nicholas,* Vol. XXX, No. 3 (January 1903).
Mountain-Laurel and Maidenhair (from *A Garland for Girls*). Boston: Little, Brown, 1903.
Morning Glories and Queen Aster. Boston: Little, Brown, 1904. (Includes "Morning Glories" from *Morning Glories, and Other Stories; Aunt Jo's Scrap-Bag VI* and "Queen Aster" from *Lulu's Library II.*)
"May" (poem from "The Fairy Spring" in *Lulu's Library II*). In *Woman's Home Companion,* Vol. XXXII, No. 5 (May 1905).
The Louisa Alcott Reader; a Supplementary Reader for the Fourth Year of School (from Lulu's Library I). Boston: Little, Brown, 1908. ("A Christmas Dream"; "The Candy Country"; "Naughty Jocko"; "The Skipping Shoes"; "Cockyloo"; "Rosy's Journey"; "How They Ran Away"; "The Fairy Box"; "A Hole in the Wall"; "The Piggy Girl.")
A Modern Cinderella or the Little Old Shoe and Other Stories. New York: Hurst & Company, 1908. ("A Modern Cinderella"; "Debby's Debut"; "The Brothers"; "Nelly's Hospital.")
Material by Louisa May Alcott. In *Bronson Alcott at Alcott House, England, and Fruitlands, New England (1842-1844) by F.B. Sanborn* (Cedar Rapids, Iowa: The Torch Press, 1908).
The Louisa Alcott Story Book Edited for Schools by Fanny E. Coe. Boston: Little, Brown, 1910. ([Biographical sketch: "Little Louisa Alcott" by Fanny E. Coe] "Tessa's Surprises"; "Grandma's Team"; "Patty's Place"; "Lunch"; "The Red Purse"; "Cory's Catamount"; "Patty Pans"; "Nelly's Hospital"; "My Little Gentleman"; "Kate's Choice.")
Little Women; or Meg, Jo, Beth, and Amy. Boston: Little, Brown, 1913. Illustrated with photographs from the stage play.
Little Women Letters from the House of Alcott (Selected by Jessie Bonstelle and Marian DeForest). Boston: Little, Brown, 1914.
A Garland for Girls. Boston: Little, Brown, 1914.
Little Women. Boston: Little, Brown, 1915. Illustrated by Jessie Wilcox Smith. Reprinted 1924, 1934, and as Centennial Edition, 1968.
Three Unpublished Poems by Louisa May Alcott. Editor, Clara Endicott Sears. Fruitlands Collection, 1919. ("A.B.A."; "A Little Grey Curl"; "To Papa.")
The Frost King (from *Flower Fables*). No pagination, no date, Racine, Wisconsin: Whitman, c1925.
Little Women. Philadelphia: John C. Winston Co., 1926. Illustrated by Clara M. Burd.
An Old-Fashioned Girl. Boston: Little Brown, 1926. Illustrated by Elenore Abbott.
Aunt Jo's Scrap-Bag I; II; III; IV; V; VI (six volumes). Boston: Little, Brown, 1927.
Little Women; or Meg, Jo, Beth, and Amy (Editor, Francis Lester Warner). Boston: Ginn; Standard English classics, 1928. With study notes, a school edition.
An Old-Fashioned Girl. Philadelphia: J.C. Winston Co., 1928. Illustrated by Clara M. Burd.
Little Men; Life at Plumfield with Jo's Boys. Philadelphia: J.C. Winston, 1928. Illustrated by Clara M. Burd.
Louisa May Alcott: Her Life, Letters, and Journals (ed. Ednah D. Cheney). R. West, 1928.

"M.L." (reprinted from *The Commonwealth*, Vol. I, Nos. 21, 22, 23, 24, 25 [January 24, 31; February 7, 14, 22, 1863]). *The Journal of Negro History*, Vol. XIV, No. 4 (October 1929).

Aunt Jo's Scrap-Bag. Edited by Helen Martin. New York: Grosset and Dunlap, 1929; Boston: Little, Brown, 1929. Selections from the *Aunt Jo's Scrap-Bag* series. ("Jimmy's Cruise in the Pinafore"; "The Doll's Journey from Minnesota to Maine"; "Morning Glories"; "Clams"; "Little Marie of Lehon"; "Rosa's Tale"; "Dandelion"; "How They Camped Out"; "What Becomes of the Pins"; "Nelly's Hospital"; "An Old-Fashioned Thanksgiving"; "Kate's Choice"; "Autobiography of an Omnibus"; "Roses and Forget-Me-Nots"; "Tessa's Surprises"; "My Boys"; "A Happy Birthday.")

Lulu's Library. Edited by Eva G. Leslie. New York: Grosset and Dunlap, 1930; Boston: Little, Brown, 1930. Selections from the *Lulu's Library* series. ("The Silver Party"; "The Skipping Stones"; "Eva's Visit to Fairyland"; "The Frost King and How the Fairies Conquered Him"; "Lilybell and Thistledown, or The Fairy Sleeping Beauty"; "The Candy Country"; "Sophie's Secret"; "Trudel's Siege"; "Music and Macaroni.")

Little Women; or Meg, Jo, Beth, and Amy. New York: Garden City, NY: Garden City Publishing Co., 1932. Illustrated by Hervé Stein.

Little Men; Life at Plumfield wth Jo's Boys. Garden City, New York: Garden City Publishing Co., 1933. Illustrated by Hervé Stein.

Louisa Alcott's People (Arranger, May Lamberton Becker). New York: Charles Scribner's Sons, 1936. Illustrated by Thomas Fogarty. Selected chapter excerpts from *Little Women, Little Men, Jo's Boys, An Old-Fashioned Girl, Eight Cousins, Jack and Jill*).

Little Women; or Meg, Jo, Beth, and Amy. Boston: Little, Brown, 1946. Illustrated by Elinore Blaisdell.

Little Women; or Meg, Jo, Beth, and Amy. (Introduction, May Lamberton Becker.) Cleveland: World Publishing Co., 1946. Illustrated by Hilda van Stockum.

Little Women; or Meg, Jo, Beth, and Amy. New York: Grosset & Dunlap, 1947. Illustrated by Louis Jambor.

Little Men; Life at Plumfield with Jo's Boys. (New York: Grosset & Dunlap, 1947). Illustrated by Douglas W. Gorsline.

Little Women; or Meg, Jo, Beth, and Amy. (New York: Crowell, 1955). Illustrated by Barbara Cooney.

An Old-Fashioned Girl. (Introduction, May Lamberton Becker.) Cleveland: World Publishing Co., 1947. Illustrated by Nettie Weber.

Little Men; Life at Plumfield with Jo's Boys. (Introduction, May Lamberton Becker.) Cleveland: World Publishing Co., 1950. Illustrated by Hilda van Stockum.

Little Women. (Especially edited and abridged by Emma Gelders Sterne.) New York: Golden Press, 1956. Illustrated by Julian Paul.

Hospital Sketches. (Introduction, Earl Schenck Miers.) New York: Sagamore Press Inc., 1957.

Hospital Sketches. (Editor, Bessie Z. Jones.) Boston: Belknap Press of Harvard University Press, 1960.

Little Women; or Meg, Jo, Beth, and Amy. (Afterword by Clifton Fadiman.) New York: MacMillan, 1962. Illustrated by Betty Fraser. One of 95 titles chosen by the American Institute of Graphic Arts for its 1961–1962 Children's Book Show as having typographic and artistic merit.

"A Sprig of Andromeda: A Letter from Louisa May Alcott on the Death of Henry David Thoreau." (With an introductory note by John L. Cooley.) New York: Pierpont Morgan Library, 1962. 10 pages. 1250 copies printed.

Little Men; Life at Plumfield with Jo's Boys. (Afterword by Clifton Fadiman.) New York: MacMillan, 1963. Illustrated by Paul Hogarth.

A Round Dozen: Stories by Louisa May Alcott. (Editor, Anne Thaxter Eaton.) New York: Viking, 1963. ("A Hole in the Wall"; "Baa! Baa!"; "The Silver Party"; "The Brownie and the Princess"; "Tabby's Tablecloth"; "Lunch"; "How They Camped Out"; "The Hare and the Tortoise"; "Jersey's, or the Girls' Ghost"; "The Cooking Class"; "Music and Macaroni"; "The Banner of Beaumanoir.")

Little Women; or Meg, Jo, Beth, and Amy. (Introduction, Edward Weeks.) New York: Limited Editions Club, 1967. Illustrated by Henry Pitz. Collector's edition. Illustrations are hand-colored.

Glimpses of Louisa: A Centennial Sampling of the Best Short Stories by Louisa May Alcott. (Editor, Cornelia Meigs.) Boston: Little, Brown, 1968. ("Onawandah"; "An Ivy Spray and Ladies' Slipper"; "My Red Cap"; "Poppies and Wheat"; "Kate's Choice"; "Tessa's Surprises"; "Mountain Laurel and Maidenhair"; "Corny's Catamount"; "Water Lilies"; "My Boys.")

"Transcendental Wild Oats" (pamphlet). Concord, MA: Thoreau Lyceum, 1970, 1974.

Transcendental Wild Oats and Excerpts from the Fruitlands Diary. Boston: Harvard Common Press, 1975.

Two hymns. In *Singing Our History: Tales, Texts and Tunes from Two Centuries of Unitarian and Universalist Hymns.* (Editor, Eugene Navias. Boston: Unitarian Universalist Association, 1975.) ("A Little Kingdom I Possess" [poem: lyric to hymn]; "Oh, the Beautiful Old Story" [lyric to hymn].)

Louisa's Wonder Book. An Unknown Alcott Juvenile. (Editor, Madeleine Stern), Mount Pleasant, Michigan: Clarke Historical Library and Central Michigan University, 1975. (Formerly called *Will's Wonder Book.* Published anonymously, Boston: Horace B. Fuller, 1870.) Eight chapters from Alcott's serial "Will's Wonder-Book"; one chapter from her re-titled "My May Day among Curious Birds and Beasts," here called "Curious Birds and Beasts"; one chapter by an unknown "Cousin Alice"; one chapter by Martha G. Sleeper. All had appeared in *Merry's Museum.* (Evidence indicated Alcott did not know about the 1870 publication.)

Behind a Mask: The Unknown Thrillers of Louisa May Alcott. (Editor, Madeleine Stern.) New York: Morrow, 1975. Stories originally written about 1860 to 1870 under Alcott's pseudonym A.M. Barnard or anonymously, except for "The Mysterious Key..." which bore the byline of L.M. Alcott. ("Behind a Mask, or A Woman's Power"; "Pauline's Passion and Punishment"; "The Mysterious Key and What It Opened"; "The Abbot's Ghost, or Maurice Treherne's Temptation.")

Plots and Counterplots: More Unknown Thrillers of Louisa May Alcott. (Editor, Madeleine Stern.) New York: Morrow, 1976. Stories originally written about 1860 to 1870 under Alcott's pseudonym of A.M. Barnard, initials L.M.A., or anonymously. ("V.V.: or, Plots and Counterplots"; "A Marble Woman: or, The Mysterious Model"; "The Skeleton in the Closet"; "A Whisper in the Dark"; "Perilous Play.")

Work: A Story of Experience. St. Clair Shores, MI: Regency, 1976.

Work. (Studies in the Life of Women.) New York: Schocken, 1977.

Work. A Story of Experience. (Rediscovered Fiction by American Women.) Salem, New Hampshire: Ayer, 1977.

Little Women. New York: Playmore, Inc. (under I. Waldman), 1977. Adapted by Lucia Monfried. Illustrated by Pablo Marcus Studio. Parts I & II highly condensed for young readers.

"A Free Bed." Provo, Utah: Friends of the Brigham Young University, 1978. Written 1887 or early 1888, the previously unpublished handwritten pages were discovered in an old trunk in the 1960s, in the attic of the Boston minister to whom Alcott evidently sent the manuscript; 350 copies were published as a memorial pamphlet on the 90th anniversary of her death.

Diana and Persis. (Editor, Sarah Elbert.) New York: Arno, 1978. Previously unpublished, untitled manuscript. For variation, see "Diana and Persis" in *Alternative Alcott* (1988).

Works of Louisa May Alcott. (Editor, Claire Booss.) New York: Avenel Books, 1982. Single volume, containing *Little Women; Little Men;* 24 Short Stories. Illustrated by Frank T. Merrill, Reginald Birch, Addie Lenyard, and others.

Poems by Louisa May Alcott. (Editor, Brenda K. Bhavnani.) Concord, Massachusetts: Louisa May Alcott Memorial Association, 1984. Pamphlet: 20 poems, most undated.

Little Women. New York: MacMillan, 1986.

Little Women. New York: Scholastic, 1986.

Little Women. New York: Dell, 1987. Afterword by Lois Duncan.

A Modern Mephistopheles. (Editor, Octavia Cowan.) New York: Bantam, 1987.

A Modern Mephistopheles and Taming a Tartar. (Editor, Madeleine Stern.) New York: Praeger, 1987.

The Selected Letters of Louisa May Alcott. (Editors, Joel Myerson, Daniel Shealy, Madeleine B. Stern.) Boston: Little, Brown, 1987.

The Works of Louisa May Alcott, 1832–1888. Tustin, California: American Biographical Service, 1987. Reprint of an 1886 edition.

Hospital Sketches. Cambridge, Massachusetts: Applewood, 1988.

Little Women. New York: Knopf, 1988.

On Picket Duty and Other Tales. Tustin, California: American Biographical Services, 1988.

Works of Louisa May Alcott. Mattituck, New York: Aconian Press/Amereon Ltd., 1988. For grades 5–6.

Alternative Alcott. (Editor, Elaine Showalter.) New Brunswick, New Jersey: Rutgers University Press, 1988. Selected stories, including "Diana and Persis" with last two chapters editorially reversed. See *Diana and Persis* (1978).

A Double Life: Newly Discovered Thrillers of Louisa May Alcott. (Editor, Madeleine Stern.) Boston: Little, Brown: 1988. Stories originally written about 1860 to 1870 under Alcott's pseudonym of A.M. Barnard, initials L.M.A., or anonymously. ("Taming a Tartar"; "A Pair of Eyes"; "The Fate of the Forrests"; "An Actor's Story"; "Ariel.")

The Journals of Louisa May Alcott. (Editors, Joel Myerson, Daniel Shealy, Madeleine B. Stern.) Boston: Little, Brown, 1989.

An Old-Fashioned Thanksgiving. New York: Holiday House, 1989.

Reader's Digest Best Loved Books for Young Readers: Little Women. Great Neck, New York: Choice Publishing New York, 1989.

Little Women. New York: Penguin, 1989.

The Works of Louisa May Alcott. Irvine, California: Reprint Services, 1989. Reproductions of first editions of most volumes, including juvenile and adult.

Thirty-six poems by Louisa May Alcott. Included in the present work.

Eight songs with lyrics by Louisa May Alcott. Included in the present work. ("My Kingdom" [poem: lyric to hymn; three different melodies]; "Oh, the Beautiful Old Story" [lyric to hymn]; "What Shall Little Children Bring" [lyric to hymn; two melodies]; "The Children's Song" [poem: lyric to song]; "Young America" [poem: lyric to song]; "The John Brown Song" [poem: lyric to song]; "Come, Butter Come" [poem: lyric to song]; "The Fairy Spring" [poem: lyric to song].)

A Modern Mephistopheles. Mattituck, New York: Amereon, 1990.

Reference Bibliography

Alcott, Amos Bronson. *Concord Days.* Boston: Roberts Brothers, 1872.
Alcott, John Pratt. "The 'Little Women' of Long Ago." *Good Housekeeping,* February 1913, pp. 182–189.
Alcott, Louisa May (For this reference, all her books were consulted, as well as all available published short stories and articles; data for these may be found in the Chronological Bibliography of Louisa May Alcott's Works.)
"Alcott Campaign Newsnotes." Concord, Massachusetts: The Louisa May Alcott Memorial Association, (various issues).
"Alcott Newsnotes." Concord, Massachusetts: The Louisa May Alcott Memorial Association, (various issues).
Allen, Francis H. *Men of Concord.* New York: Bonanza Books, 1936.
American Authors 1600–1900: A Biographical Dictionary of American Literature. New York: H.W. Wilson, 1936.
Anderson, Gretchen (compiler). *The Louisa May Alcott Cookbook* (juvenile). Boston: Little, Brown, 1985.
Anthony, Katherine. *Louisa May Alcott.* New York: Alfred A. Knopf, 1938.
Arbuthnot, May Hill. *Children and Books.* Chicago: Scott, Foresman, 1947; Glenview, Illinois: Scott, Foresman, 1964.
Baldwin, Sarah. "New England Women Writers 1870–1910." *A B Bookman's Weekly,* March 28, 1988, pp. 1261–1268.
Baltake, Joe. "Louisa May Alcott Was Never Like This." *Philadelphia Daily News,* April 18, 1980, p. 29.
Beach, Seth Curtis. *Daughters of the Puritans.* Boston: American Unitarian Association, 1905.
Bedell, Madelon. *The Alcotts, Biography of a Family.* New York: Clarkson N. Potter, 1980.
―――. "Louisa's Centennial Fury (1875)." *The New York Times,* March 31, 1975, p. 31.
Blanck, Jacob (compiler). *Bibliography of American Literature.* Volume I, pp. 27–45. New Haven: Yale University Press, 1955.
Bok, Edward W. "Louisa May Alcott's Letters to Five Girls." *The Ladies' Home Journal,* April 1896, pp. 1–2.
Bolton, Sarah K. (Revised by William A. Fohey.) *Famous American Authors.* New York: Thomas Y. Crowell, 1954, 1965.
Bonstelle, Jessie, and De Forest, Marian (selected by). *Little Women Letters from the House of Alcott.* Boston: Little, Brown, 1914.
"Books and Authors." *The New York Times Saturday Review of Books and Art,* March 20, 1897, p. 8.
"Books That Separate Parents from Their Children." *The New York Times Saturday Review of Books and Art,* January 8, 1898, p. 1–2.

Bridgwater, William. *The Columbia-Viking Desk Encyclopedia*. Two Volumes. New York: Viking Press, 1960.
Brooks, Van Wyck. *The Flowering of New England: 1815–1865*. New York: E.P. Dutton, 1936.
———. *New England: Indian Summer, 1865–1915*. New York: E.P. Dutton, 1940.
———. *A New England Reader*. New York: Atheneum, 1962.
Brophy, Brigid. "A Masterpiece, and Dreadful." *The New York Times Book Review*, January 17, 1965, Sec. 7, pp. 1, 44.
Brown, Mary Hosmer. *Memories of Concord*. Boston: Four Seas, 1926.
Brown, Pamela. *Louisa Alcott: Biography of Louisa May Alcott* (juvenile). New York: Thomas Y. Crowell, 1955.
Burke, Kathleen. *Louisa May Alcott, Author* (juvenile). New York: Chelsea House, 1988.
Carlsen, G. Robert. "Teaching Literature for the Adolescent: A Historical Perspective." *English Journal*, November 1984, pp. 28–30.
Chandler, Anna C. *Famous Mothers and Their Children* (Abba May Alcott). New York: Frederick A. Stokes, 1938.
Cheney, Ednah D. *Louisa May Alcott — Her Life, Letters & Journals*. Boston: Little, Brown, 1889, 1928.
———. *Louisa May Alcott, The Children's Friend*. Boston: L. Prang, 1888.
———. *The Story of The Alcotts*. Concord: Louisa May Alcott Memorial Association, no date.
Chesterton, G.K. "Louisa Alcott." *A Handful of Authors: Essays on Books*. Editor, Dorothy Collins. New York: Sheed & Ward, 1953. Originally from *The Nation*, 1907.
Children's Literature Association Committee. *Touchstones: A List of Distinguished Children's Books* (pamphlet). West Lafayette, Indiana: ChLA Publications, 1986–87.
Clark, Annie M.L. *The Alcotts in Harvard*. Lancaster, Massachusetts: J.C.L. Clark, 1902.
Cobblestone: The History Magazine for Young People. "The Transcendentalists and Their Message" (theme issue). June 1987. Editor, Carolyn P. Yoder. (Articles by D.H. DeFord and H.S. Stout; Jill H. Lawler; others.)
Comic Tragedies, Review of. *The New York Times*, November 5, 1893, p. 19.
Commire, Anne (editor). *Yesterday's Authors of Books for Children* (three volumes). Detroit: Gale, 1979.
Committee on College Reading. *Good Reading: A Guide to the World's Best Books*. (Sponsored by The National Council of Teachers of English.) New York: Penguin Books, 1947.
Condon, Dierdre. "The Best Kiddie-O Video." *Parents Magazine*, November 1985, p. 240.
Connoly, Francis. *The Types of Literature*. New York: Harcourt, Brace, 1955.
Dapper, Julie (written and compiled by). "The Concord School of Philosophy" (pamphlet). Concord, Massachusetts: The Louisa May Alcott Memorial Association, no date.
"Death of Miss Alcott." *The Ladies' Home Journal*, May 1888, p. 3.
De Forest, Marian. *Little Women: A Comedy in Four Acts* (playscript). New York: Samuel French, 1911, 1949.
Delamar, Gloria T. *Christmas with the "Little Women": Two Performance Versions; Pantomime and Playscript*. Melrose Park, Pennsylvania: Rabbit Press/O.R.I., 1990.

Orchard House in Concord, Massachusetts, today. Two windows at right on second floor are to Louisa's bedroom and writing desk. Photograph by Gloria T. Delamar.

_____. "Germantown Home to 'Little Women' Author." *Chestnut Hill Local*, Part One: November 25, 1982, p. 29; Part Two: December 2, 1982, p. 42.

_____. "Louisa May Alcott, Poet." *Cobblestone: The History Magazine for Young People*. (Louisa May Alcott theme issue.) December 1988.

_____. "Louisa May Alcott's Turning Point: The Civil War Service of the Author of 'Little Women.'" *North South Trader*. May–June 1983, pp. 29-32, 34.

_____. "One of the 'Little Women.'" *Cobblestone: The History Magazine for Young People*. (Louisa May Alcott theme issue.) December 1988.

_____. "Putting One's Philosophy into One's Work." (Louisa May Alcott, Ralph Waldo Emerson, etc.) (Sermon) Unitarian Society of Germantown, Philadelphia, Pennsylvania, November 24, 1985. (Alcott and Emerson portions also used for religious education curriculum development.)

_____. (editor). "For a Grown-up Writer's (Re)Reading?" *Pen Points: The Newsletter of the Philadelphia Writers' Conference*, Spring 1987, p. 3.

Delman, David. "A Look at the Racier Side of Louisa May Alcott." *The Philadelphia Inquirer*, July 3, 1988, p. 5-H.

Dickens, Homer. *The Films of Katharine Hepburn*. Secaucus, New Jersey: The Citadel Press, 1973.

Dictionary of American Biography. New York: Charles Scribner's Sons, 1927, 1957.

Doyle, Brian. *The Who's Who of Children's Literature*. London: Hugh Evelyn, 1968.

Elbert, Sarah. *A Hunger for Home: Louisa May Alcott's Place in the American Culture*. New Brunswick, New Jersey: Rutgers University Press, 1987. (A revision of *A Hunger for Home: Louisa May Alcott and Little Women*. Philadelphia: Temple University Press, 1984.)

Faris, John T. *Old Roads Out of Philadelphia*. Philadelphia: J.B. Lippincott, 1917.

Fenn, Mary R. *Old Houses of Concord.* Concord, Massachusetts: Daughters of the American Revolution, Old Concord Chapter, 1974.
Fetterley, Judith. "*Little Women:* Alcott's Civil War." *Feminist Studies,* Summer 1979, pp. 369-370.
Fisher, Aileen, and Rabe, Olive. *We Alcotts: The Story of Louisa May Alcott's Family As Seen Through the Eyes of "Marmee," Mother of Little Women* (juvenile). New York: Atheneum, 1968.
Fisher, Margery. *Who's Who in Children's Books.* London: Weidenfeld & Nicolson, 1975.
"Forty Years of a Classic." *The New York Times Saturday Review of Books and Art,* August 8, 1908, p. 442.
French, Allen. *The Drama of Concord: A Pageant of Three Centuries.* Concord, Massachusetts: Tercentenary Celebration Production Committee, 1935.
Gerould, Katharine Fullerton. *Modes and Morals.* New York: Charles Scribner's Sons, 1920.
Gilmore, Edith. "Louisa May Alcott: Views and Reviews." *School Library Journal,* March 1988, pp. 130-131.
The Golden Book Encyclopedia. New York: Golden Press, 1959.
Gordon, Jayne. "The Alcott Experience." *The Concord Patriot,* May 1979.
Gordon, Patricia. *The Story of Louisa May Alcott* (juvenile). New York: Grosset and Dunlop, 1955.
Gowing, Clara. *The Alcotts As I Knew Them.* Boston: C.M. Clark, 1909.
Graff, Polly Anne (Colver). *Louisa May Alcott* (juvenile). Champaign, Illinois: Garrard, 1969.
Greene, Carol. *Louisa May Alcott: Author, Nurse, Suffragette* (juvenile). Chicago: Children's Press, 1984.
Griffith, Richard, and Mayer, Arthur. *The Movies.* New York: Simon and Schuster, 1957.
Gulliver, Lucile. *Louisa May Alcott, A Bibliography.* Boston: Little, Brown, 1932.
Hackett, Walter. "The Laurence Boy" (radio script). *Reading Roundup: Book One* (editors: Witty, Peterson, Parker). Boston: D.C. Heath, 1954, 1958. (From *Plays, the Drama Magazine for Young People.*)
Halleck, Reuben Post. *The Romance of American Literature.* New York: American Book Co., 1934.
Halliwell, Leslie. *Halliwell's Film Guide.* New York: Charles Scribner's Sons, 1977.
Harrington, Stephanie. "Does *Little Women* Belittle Women?" *The New York Times,* June 10, 1973, Sec. 2, pp. 19, 37.
Hawthorne, Edith Garrigues. Editor. *The Memoirs of Julian Hawthorne.* New York: MacMillan, 1938.
Hawthorne, Julian. "The Woman Who Wrote *Little Women.*" *The Ladies' Home Journal,* October 1922, pp. 25, 120-124.
Hawthorne, Nathaniel. *A Wonder Book* (1851). New York: Lancer Books, 1968.
Holbrook, Stewart H. *Dreamers of the American Dream.* New York: Doubleday, 1957.
The Horn Book Magazine. "Louisa May Alcott Centennial Issue." October 1968, Editor, Paul Heins. (Articles by E.M. Almedingen; Aileen Fisher and Olive Rabe; Paul Heins; Heddie Kent; John Keller; Cornelia Meigs; Lavinia Russ.) Boston: The Horn Book, 1968.
Howard, Alice B *Mary Mapes Dodge of St. Nicholas* (juvenile). New York: Junior Literary Guild and Julian Messner, 1943.
Howard, Joan. *The Story of Louisa May Alcott* (juvenile). New York: Grosset & Dunlap, 1955.

Reference Bibliography

Howe, M.A. DeWolfe. *Memories of a Hostess: A Chronicle of Eminent Friendships — Drawn Chiefly from the Diaries of Mrs. James T. Fields.* Boston: The Atlantic Monthly Press, 1922.

James, Henry. "Review of *Eight Cousins* (reference to *Little Women*)." *The Nation*, 1875.

_____. "Review of *Moods.*" *North American*, 1865.

Janeway, Elizabeth. "Between Myth and Morning." *The New York Times Book Review*, September 29, 1968, pp. 42, 44, 46; Reprinted as "Those Four Little Women." *Famous Writers Annual: Famous Writers and Writing.* Westport, Connecticut. Famous Writers School Inc., 1970.

Jenkins, Charles F. *Guidebook to Historic Germantown.* Philadelphia: Site & Relic Society of Germantown, 1926.

Jones, Bessie Z. Editor. "Introduction" to *Hospital Sketches* by Louisa May Alcott. Cambridge, Massachusetts: The Belknap Press of Harvard University Press, 1960.

Kent, Louise Andrews. *Village Greens of New England.* New York: M. Barrows, 1948.

Keyser, Namann. et al. *History of Old Germantown.* Germantown, Pennsylvania: Horace F. McCann, 1907.

Kolba, Ellen D. "Out on a Limb." *English Journal*, November 1984, pp. 38–41.

Krutch, Joseph Wood (editor). *Thoreau: Walden and Other Writings.* New York: Bantam Books (1854), 1971.

The Ladies' Home Journal. Premium supplement (volumes of Alcott books in return for subscribers). May 1888, p. 14.

Large, Laura Antoinette. *Little People Who Became Great.* New York: Platt & Munk, 1935.

Larrick, Nancy. *A Parent's Guide to Children's Reading.* New York: Pocket Books, 1958.

Lee, Barbara, and Rudman, Masha Kabakow. *Mind over Media: New Ways to Improve Your Child's Reading and Writing Skills.* New York: Seaview Books, 1982.

Lerman, Leo. "*Little Women:* Who's in Love with Miss Louisa May Alcott? I Am." *Mademoiselle*, December 1973, p. 40.

"Letter to the Editor: A Word for Miss Alcott" by M.L.S. *The New York Times Saturday Review of Books and Art*, February 26, 1898, p. 142.

"Letters to the Editor: Little Women." (Responses to an article.) *The New York Times Book Review*, February 7, 1965, p. 34.

Linscott, Robert N. *The Journals of Ralph Waldo Emerson.* New York: The Modern Library, Random House, 1909, 1960.

"Literary Landmarks to Be Saved." By N.H.D. *The New York Times Book Review*, September 24, 1911, p. 574.

Little Women, Review of. *Arthur's Home Magazine*, December 1868.

_____. *The Commonwealth*, April 24, 1969.

_____. *Golden Hours*, 1868.

_____. *Golden Hours*, 1869.

_____. *Harper's New Monthly Magazine*, August 1869.

_____. *The Nation*, October 22, 1868.

_____. *National Anti-Slavery Standard*, May 1, 1869.

_____. *The Youth's Companion.* October 22, 1868.

Lothrop, Margaret M. *The Wayside: Home of Authors.* Boston: American Book, 1940, 1968.

"Louisa May Alcott Memorial Association: Statement of Mission, Goals, and Objectives." Concord, Massachusetts: Louisa May Alcott Memorial Association, no date.

Mabie, Hamilton Wright (editor) & Hale, Edward Everett (asst. editor). *Men and Women of Achievement; Self-Help*. Philadelphia: The After School Club, 1909.

MacDonald, Ruth K. *Louisa May Alcott*. Twayne United States Authors Series, No. 457. Boston: Twayne, 1983.

Magid, Nora L. "Clear the Stage for a Repeat Performance" (Part II). *The New York Times Book Review*, November 9, 1969, p. 65.

Magill, Frank N. (editor). *Magill's Cinema Annual 1983*. Englewood Cliffs, New Jersey: Salem, 1983.

Maltin, Leonard (editor). *TV Movies: 1983–84 Edition*. New York: Signet/New American Library, 1982.

Mann, Dorothea Lawrance. "When the Alcott Books Were New." *Publisher's Weekly*, September 28, 1929, pp. 1619, 1623–1624.

Marill, Alvin H. "Katharine Hepburn." *Pyramid Illustrated History of the Movies*. New York: Pyramid, 1973.

Marsella, Joy. *The Promise of Destiny: Children and Women in the Short Stories of Louisa May Alcott*. Contributions to the Study of Childhood and Youth, No. 2. Westport, Connecticut: Greenwood, 1983.

McGill, Frederick T., Jr. *Channing of Concord: A Life of William Ellery Channing II*. New Brunswick, New Jersey: Rutgers University Press, 1967.

McGill, Marci Ridlon. *The Story of Louisa May Alcott, Determined Writer* (juvenile). New York: Yearling/Dell, 1988.

McGuire, Edna. *They Made America Great*. New York: Macmillan, 1950, 1967.

Meigs, Cornelia. *Invincible Louisa* (juvenile). Boston: Little, Brown, 1933, 1951.

_____ (editor). "Editor's Notes" to *Glimpses of Louisa: A Centennial Sampling of the Best Short Stories of Louisa May Alcott* (juvenile). Boston: Little, Brown, 1968.

Miller, Perry. *The American Transcendentalists, Their Prose and Poetry*. New York: Anchor Books, 1957.

_____. *The Transcendentalists*. Cambridge, Massachusetts: Harvard University Press, 1950.

_____ (general editor). *Major Writers of America* (Volume I). New York: Harcourt, Brace & World, 1962.

Milone, Karen (compiler). *A Louisa May Alcott Diary* (juvenile). Boston: Little, Brown, 1987.

Moers, Ellen. *Literary Women, The Great Writers*. New York: Doubleday, 1976.

Morrow, Honore Willsie. *Father of Little Women*. Boston: Little, Brown, 1927.

Moses, Belle. *Louisa May Alcott, Dreamer and Worker, A Story of Achievement*. New York: D. Appleton-Century, 1938.

Mott, Frank Luther. *Golden Multitudes: The Story of Best Sellers in the United States*. New York: Macmillan, 1947.

Moulton, Louisa Chandler. *Our Famous Women*. Hartford, Connecticut: Worthington, 1884.

Myerson, Joel, and Shealy, Daniel (editors); Stern, Madeleine (associate editor). *The Selected Letters of Louisa May Alcott*. Boston: Little, Brown, 1987.

Navias, Eugene B. (editor). *Singing Our History (Tales, Text and Tunes from Two Centuries of Unitarian and Universalist Hymns.)* Boston: Published by UUA, 1975.

O'Faolain, Sean. "This Is Your Life ... Louisa May Alcott." *Holiday*, December 1973, p. 40.

Oliver, Edith. "The Theatre—Off Broadway." *The New Yorker*, April 2, 1984, p. 116.

"Orchard House, Home of the Alcotts and *Little Women*" (pamphlet). Concord, Massachusetts: The Louisa May Alcott Memorial Association, no date.

"Orchard House, Home of the Alcotts: 75 Years of Support" (pamphlet). Concord, Massachusetts: The Louisa May Alcott Memorial Association, no date.

"Orchard House: The Campaign for Orchard House" (pamphlet). Concord, Massachusetts: The Louisa May Alcott Memorial Association, no date.

Osmont, Noel. "The Darker Side of Author Alcott." *The San Diego Union*, November 18, 1987, p. D.-3.

Pancoast, Henry S. *An Introduction to American Literature*. New York: Henry Holt, 1898, 1928.

Papashvily, Helen. *Louisa May Alcott* (juvenile). Boston: Houghton Mifflin, 1965.

Payne, Alma J. *Louisa May Alcott: A Reference Guide*. Boston: G.K. Hall, 1980.

Peare, Catherine Owens. *Louisa May Alcott, Her Life* (juvenile). New York: Holt, Rinehart & Winston, 1954.

Pennell, Elizabeth Robins. *Our Philadelphia*. Philadelphia: J.B. Lippincott, 1914.

Perenyi, Eleanor. "Dear Louisa." *Harper's Magazine*, October 1955, pp. 69-72.

Perry, Bliss (editor). *The Heart of Emerson's Journals*. Boston: Houghton Mifflin, 1926.

Plays based on *Little Women*, Review of Three. *Chicago Tribune*, March 22, 1874, p. 13.

Porter, Maria S. *Recollections of Louisa May Alcott, John Greenleaf Whittier, and Robert Browning, together with several memorial poems*. Published for the author by The New England Magazine Corporation, Boston: 1893; reprint—Folcroft, Pennsylvania: Folcroft Library Editions, 1976.

Porter, Mary J. (sic) "Louisa May Alcott." *Zion's Advocate* with credit to *Christian Intelligencer*, January 21, 1891.

Randall, David A., and Winterich, John T. "One Hundred Good Novels." *Publisher's Weekly*, June 17, 1939, pp. 2183-2184.

Reinfeld, Fred. *Stamp Collectors Handbook*. Garden City, New York: Doubleday, 1970, 1980.

Reynolds, Moira Davison. *Nine American Women of the Nineteenth Century*. Jefferson, North Carolina: McFarland, 1988.

Roberts, Victoria. "Little Women" (cartoon strip). *Ms Magazine*, 1988: February, p. 96; March, p. 96; April, p. 96; May, p. 96; June, p. 96; July, p. 96; August, p. 96; September, p. 96; October, p. 96; November, p. 96; December, p. 96.

Robinson, Martha. *The Young Louisa M. Alcott* (juvenile). New York: Roy, 1963.

Rostenberg, Leona. "Some Anonymous and Pseudonymous Thrillers of Louisa May Alcott." *Bibliographical Society of America Papers*, #37, 2nd Quarter 1943, pp. 131-140.

Russell, Phillips. *Emerson, The Wisest American*. New York: Blue Ribbon Books, 1929.

Salmon, Edward. "Should Children Have a Special Literature?" *Parent's Review*, 1890.

Salyer, Sandford. *Marmee, The Mother of Little Women*. Norman, Oklahoma: University of Oklahoma Press, 1949.

Sanborn, Franklin B. *Recollections of Seventy Years of Concord*. Boston: Richard Badger, 1909.

_____. "Reminisscences of Louisa M. Alcott." *Independent*, March 7, 1912, pp. 496-498.

_____. and Harris, William T. *A. Bronson Alcott: His Life and Philosophy*. (Two volumes) Boston: Roberts Brothers, 1893.

Saxton, Martha. *Louisa May, A Modern Biography of Louisa May Alcott*. Boston: Houghton Mifflin, 1977.

Schechter, Harold. *A Parent's Guide to Children's Videos*. New York: Pocket Books, 1986.

Schlesinger, Elizabeth Bancroft. "The Alcott's Through Thirty Years: Letters to Alfred Whitman." *Harvard Library Bulletin,* August 11, 1957, pp. 363-385.
Scudder, Townsend. *Concord: American Town.* Boston: Little, Brown, 1947.
Sears, Clara Endicott. *Bronson Alcott's Fruitlands.* (With "Transcendental Wild Oats" by Louisa Alcott.) Boston: Houghton Mifflin, 1915.
Shepard, Odell. *The Journals of Bronson Alcott.* Boston: Little, Brown, 1938.
_____. *Pedlar's Progress: The Life of Bronson Alcott.* Boston: Little, Brown, 1937.
Showalter, Elaine (editor). *Alternative Alcott.* The American Women Writers Series. New Brunswick, New Jersey: Rutgers University Press, 1988.
Simons, Sarah E. *American Literature Through Illustrative Readings.* New York, Charles Scribner's Sons, 1915, 1922.
Spacks, Patricia Meyer. *The Female Imagination.* New York: Alfred A. Knopf, 1972, 1975.
Spiller, Robert. Thorp, Willard. Johnson, Thomas H. Canby, Henry Seidel. Ludwig, Richard M. *Literary History of the United States.* New York: Macmillan, 1963.
Stearns, Frank Preston. *Sketches from Concord and Appledore.* New York: Portnames, 1895.
Sterling, Adaline Wheelock. Halbrook, Florence. Hale, Edward Everett. *Nature and Life: (A Fourth Reader).* New York: Globe School Book, 1901.
Stern, Madeleine B. *Critical Essays on Louisa May Alcott.* Boston: G.K. Hall, 1984.
_____. *Louisa May Alcott.* Norman, Oklahoma: University of Oklahoma, 1950, 1971.
_____. "A Writers' Progress: Louisa May Alcott at 150." *AB Bookman's Weekly,* November 22, 1982, pp. 3579, 3582, 3584, 3586, 3590, 3592, 3594-3597.
Swayne, Josephine Latham (editor). *The Story of Concord: Told by Concord Writers.* Boston: E.F. Worchester, 1905, 1906.
Tharp, Louise Hall. *The Peabody Sisters of Salem.* Boston: Little, Brown, 1950.
Thomas, Henry, and Thomas, Dana Lee. *Living Biographies of Famous Novelists.* Philadelphia: Blakiston, 1943.
_____. *Living Biographies of Great Philosophers.* New York: Garden City Publishing, 1941.
Thorndike, Joseph J., Jr. "Fruitlands." *American Heritage,* February/March 1986, pp. 72-75.
Ticknor, Caroline. *Classic Concord: As Portrayed by Emerson, Hawthorne, Thoreau and the Alcotts.* Boston: Houghton Mifflin, 1926.
_____. *May Alcott: A Memoir.* Boston: Little, Brown, 1927, 1928.
Torgerson, Ellen. "Little Women." *TV Guide,* September 30, 1978, pp. A-3-4. Film and cast, p. A-74.
Tracy, Henry Chester. *American Naturalists.* New York: E.P. Dutton, 1936.
Trent, William P. Erskine, John. Sherman, Stuart P. Van Doren, Carl. *The Cambridge History of American Literature. Volume I: Colonial & Revolutionary Literature.* New York: Macmillan, 1961.
Turner, Lorenzo Dow. "Louisa May Alcott's 'M.L.'" *Journal of Negro History,* October 14, 1929, pp. 495-522.
"The 25 Most Important Women in American History." *Ladies' Home Journal,* July 1986, pp. 83-85, 127-130.
Ullom, Judith C. *Louisa May Alcott—A Centennial for Little Women: An Annotated Selected Bibliography.* Washington: Library of Congress, 1969.
United States Department of the Interior. "The Wayside: (A History of the House)" (leaflet). United States Department of the Interior National Park Service, Minute Man National Historical Park, no date.

_____. "The Wayside: (A Room by Room Layout)" (leaflet). United States Department of the Interior, National Park Service. Minute Man National Historical Park, no date.
Wade, Mason. *Margaret Fuller.* New York: Viking, 1940.
Wagenknecht, Edward. *Nathaniel Hawthorne: Man and Writer.* New York: Oxford University Press, 1961.
Wagoner, Jean Brown. *Louisa Alcott: Girl of Old Boston* (juvenile). New York: Bobbs-Merrill, 1943.
Wendell, Barrett. *A Literary History of America.* New York: Charles Scribner's Sons, 1900.
Weyn, Suzanne. *The Little Women Keepsake Diary* ("Based on the beloved book by Louisa May Alcott" [juvenile]). New York: Scholastic, 1988.
"Whispers from the Den." *Schoolgirl,* May 1934, p. 11.
Whiting, Lilian. *Boston Days: The City of Beautiful Ideals, Concord and Its Authors, etc.* Boston: Little, Brown, 1902.
Whitman, Alfred. "Miss Alcott's Letters to Her 'Laurie.'" *The Ladies' Home Journal,* Part One: September 1901, pp. 5-6; Part Two: October 1901, p. 6.
Who Was Who in America: Historical Volume 1607-1896. Chicago: Marquis Who's Who, 1963, 1967.
"Why Miss Alcott Still Lives." *The New York Times Saturday Review of Books and Art,* January 18, 1902, p. 40.
Willis, Frederick L.H. (Posthumously compiled by Edith Willis Linn & Henri Bazin.) *Alcott Memoirs.* Boston: Richard G. Badger, (1915); Pottstown, Pennsylvania: Americanist, 1967.
Wood, Lydia Hosmer. "Beth Alcott's Playmate." *Harper's Bazar* (sic). May 1913, pp. 213, 246.
Worthington, Marjorie. *Miss Alcott of Concord: A Biography.* New York: Doubleday, 1958.
Wright, Catharine Morris. *Lady of the Silver Skates: The Life and Correspondence of Mary Mapes Dodge.* Jamestown, Rhode Island: Clingstone, 1979.
Young Folk's Library of Choice Literature: Louisa May Alcott (juvenile booklet). Boston: Educational Publishing Company, Vol. III, No. 63, October 15, 1896.

Index

A • indicates a work by LMA; a † indicates a general anthology that includes LMA's works

Page numbers starting from 299 indicate listings in the Chronological Bibliography of LMA's Works. Many of Alcott's titles were published with variations of punctuation and with words added or deleted; in the chronological bibliography they are given as they appeared in the specific publications, but one variation has been chosen for the index. Many of the stories had more than one title; alternatives are shown parenthetically "Titles" are of short stories unless otherwise specified

A , L M (pseudonym of LMA) 36, 299, 305, 320, 321
"A.B A."• (poem) 318
AB Bookman's Weekly 158, 162
A. Bronson Alcott: His Life and Philosophy† 229
Abott, Elenore 318
Abott, Jacob 287
"Abbot's Ghost; or, Maurice Treherne's The Temptation"• 303, 320
"The Accident"• 311, 317
"An Actor's Story"• 321
Adams, Sarah May Holland 268
Adams, Zabdiel Boylston 268
Addams, Jane 169
"Address of the Republican Women of Massachusetts "• 307
"Address to a Robin"• (extract from letter) 313
"An Advertisement"• (poem) 310
Alcott, Abigail "Abba" (May): re antislavery 7, 8, 15, 34; biography of 233; birth 275; as character in *Little Men* 100, 229, 239, 244, 247; as character in *Little Women* 3, 85; as city missionary 33, 36, 277; courtship 5, 275; death 117, 283; illness 10, 35, 49, 79, 107, 115, 117, 283; as intelligence agency manager 36; life *1830–1840* 5–14; *1840–1847* 14–30; *1848–1855* 31–42; *1856–1860* 43–54; *1861–1862* 55–63; *1863–1867* 63–80; *1868–1869* 80–94; *1870–1874* 95–110; *1875–1879* 110–117; marriage 5, 275; as seamstress 14; stillbirth 10; as teacher 277; re women's rights 37
Alcott, Abigail May "May" *see* Nieriker, May Alcott

Alcott, Amos Bronson: re antislavery 15, 34; as author 9, 83, 117, 244; biographical sketch 265; biography of 232; birth 275; as character in *Little Men* 100, 159, 216, 218, 231, 239, 242, 245, 247; as character in *Little Women* 3, 85; courtship 5, 275; death 139, 286; Europe 15; as farmer 14, 19, 20; as fictional character 97, 106, 229; illness 24, 35, 127, 131, 139, 242, 284; lectures 12, 21, 33, 36, 37, 43, 46, 47, 49, 75, 80, 89, 108, 110, 120, 277, 278; life *1830–1840* 3–14; *1840–1847* 14–30; *1848–1855*; 31–42; *1856–1860* 43–54; *1861–1862* 55–63; *1863–1867* 63–80; *1868–1869* 80–94; *1870–1874* 95–110; *1875–1879* 110–122; *1880–1885* 123–131; *1886–1888* 132–139; marriage 5, 275; as superintendent of Concord schools 52, 207, 279; as teacher 5, 6, 8, 9, 10, 11, 36, 93, 240; withdrawal 24, 30, 33; re women's rights 35, 79; works of 9, 83, 117, 265
Alcott, Anna Bronson *see* Pratt, Anna Bronson Alcott
Alcott, Elizabeth [Peabody] Sewall "Beth" 247; as actress 31; birth 8, 76, 275; as character in *Little Women* 3, 85, 86, 87, 91; death 48, 49, 73, 245, 279; as fictional character 43, 83; as housekeeper 35; illness 43, 46, 47, 279; life *1835–1840* 8–14; *1840–1847* 14–30; *1848–1855* 31–42; *1856–1858* 43–49; and music 28, 35
Alcott, Grandma 46; *see also* Alcox, Anna
Alcott, John Sewall Pratt *see* Pratt, John Sewall
Alcott, Junius 15, 28

333

Alcott, Louisa May: as actress 3, 25, 27, 29, 31, 35, 42, 43, 73, 75, 80, 119, 120, 140, 281; anonymous publications 302, 303, 311, 320, 321; re antislavery 3, 8, 15, 35, 37, 44, 49, 51, 56, 67, 69, 75, 126, 140, 226, 234; as army nurse 3, 58–64, 68, 71, 140, 280, 293; biographies of 227, 230–233, 234; birth 6, 275, 287; as character in *Little Men* 100; as character in *Little Women* 3, 85, 86, 87, 91; re Civil War 55, 57, 58; as companion 36; copyrights 135, 149, 152, 229; critical analyses of works of 145–163, 201–206, 233–234, 253–263; death 139, 286, 298; in Europe 76–78, 96–102, 280, 293, 294; as fictional character 43, 53, 68, 81, 82, 83, 97, 105, 133, 135, 236; glory cloak 32, 55, 79, 83; as housemaid 36, 37; illness 63, 64, 65, 70, 71, 79, 93, 94, 95, 97, 103, 109, 113, 117, 120, 128, 129, 132, 133, 135, 136, 139, 280, 283, 286; letters and journals of 227–230; life chronology 275–286; life *1832–1840* 3–14; *1840–1847* 14–30; *1848–1855* 31–42; *1856–1860* 43–54; *1861–1862* 55–63; *1863–1867* 63–80; *1868–1869* 80–94; *1870–1874* 95–110; *1875–1879* 110–122; *1880–1885* 123–131; *1886–1888* 132–142; literary studies of 226–238; lyrics to songs 207–225; re marriage 24, 34, 47, 52, 54, 73, 75, 81, 82; "mind-cure" 129, 285; mood pillow 31, 246, 247; in New York City 113–114, 282, 295; re "Pathetic Family" 46, 54, 83; in Philadelphia, Pennsylvania 5–7, 114–115, 239, 282, 296; on postage stamp 166; pseudonym 36, 65, 71, 72, 73, 82, 95, 116, 205, 237, 278, 299, 302, 303, 305, 307, 320, 321; rewriting 10, 14, 22, 23, 24, 26, 31, 32, 38, 50, 51, 53, 56, 70, 71, 72, 73, 75, 80, 81, 82, 86, 88, 94, 95, 96, 104, 105, 117, 120, 121, 135, 136, 137, 206; Roderigo's russet boots 32, 87, 173; as seamstress 3, 31, 37, 43, 45, 140; sites connected with 239–248; as teacher 3, 31, 35, 43, 45, 46, 56, 140, 244, 277, 278, 279; re temperance movement 126; vegetarian diet 14, 19, 20, 26, 28, 54, 60, 130; will 135, 286; re women's rights 3, 37, 79, 89, 103, 104, 107, 108, 109, 111, 112, 113, 114, 115, 121, 125, 126, 128, 140, 226, 235, 284, 285; works, bibliographies of 238
The Alcott Calendar for 1886 • 314
Alcott House (Cape May, N.J) 240
Alcott House School (Ham Common, Surrey, England) 15, 277
Alcott Memoirs: Posthumously Compiled from Papers, Journals, and Memoranda of the Late Dr. Frederick L.H. Willis 231
The Alcotts as I Knew Them 230, 231

The Alcotts in Harvard 230
"The Alcotts through Thirty Years: Letters to Alfred Whitman"† 229
Alcox, Anna 275; *see also* Alcott, Grandma
Alcox, Joseph 275
Aldrich, Thomas Bailey 294
Alger, Horatio 287, 292, 293
Alice's Adventures in Wonderland 164
Allegheny County, Pa 104
"All the Blue Bonnets Are Over the Border" 219
Allyson, June 181, 182
Almedingen, Catherine 190, 195
Almedingen, E M 159, 190
Alternative Alcott • (anthology) 236, 321
The Ambassadors 166
The American 166
The American Catalogue 234
American Library Convention 164
Ames, Leon 181
Amherst College 260
Andersen, Hans Christian 287, 290
Anderson, Gretchen 171
"Anna's Whim" • 308
Anonymous publications of LMA 302, 303, 311, 320, 321
Anthony, Katherine S 153, 233
Anthony, Susan B. 169
Anti-Slavery Convention 35
Antioch College 37
Appeal for Woman's Right to Suffrage 79
Appomattox, Virginia 75
Arbuthnot, May Hill 167
"Ariel. A Legend of the Lighthouse" • 303, 321
The Ark 167
Arlington Hotel (Cape May, N.J) 239, 240
Arthur's Home Magazine 147
An Artist's Holiday 122
As Gold in the Furnace 165
Association for the Advancement of Women 114
Astin, Mackenzie 185
Astor, Mary 181
The Atlantic Monthly 51, 54, 66, 242, 268, 292, 293
Aunt Jo's Scrap-Bag • (anthology: selections from series) 319
Aunt Jo's Scrap-Bag • (series of six volumes) 136, 234; analysis of stories 233
Aunt Jo's Scrap-Bag I. My Boys • 203, 295, 307
Aunt Jo's Scrap-Bag II. Shawl-Straps • 203, 295, 308
Aunt Jo's Scrap-Bag III. Cupid and Chow-Chow • 203, 295, 308
Aunt Jo's Scrap-Bag IV. My Girls • 203, 296, 311
Aunt Jo's Scrap-Bag V. Jimmy's Cruise in the Pinafore • 203, 296, 312

Index 335

Aunt Jo's Scrap-Bag VI. An Old-Fashioned Thanksgiving • 203, 297, 313
Aunt Jo's Scrap-Bag, I; II; III; IV: V; VI • (six volumes) 318
Aunt Kipp • 305, 311, 313
Austin, Jane 158
Austin, Jane G 74
"The Autobiography of an Omnibus" ("Living in an Omnibus") • 310, 311, 319
"An Autumn Song" • (poem) 303
Ayers, Gerald 184

"Baa! Baa!" (similar to "Merry's Monthly Chat   "; "A Beautiful Picture   ") • 314, 315, 317, 320
"Back Windows" • 305, 307
Baldwin, Sarah 162
Baltake, Joe 184
"The Bandit's Bride" • (unpublished; drama adaptation) 299
"The Banner of Beaumanoir" • 314, 320
Barnard, A M. (pseudonym of LMA) 65, 71, 72, 73, 95, 116, 205, 237, 302, 303, 307, 320, 321
Barnard College 227
"The Baron's Gloves" • 136, 305, 313
Barrie, Sir James 181
Bartlett, Alice 95, 281
Barton, Bruce 165
Barton, Clara 169
Basescu, Elinor 177
Bath Hotel (New York) 113, 282
"The Battle Hymn of the Republic" 56, 113, 212, 221, 222, 223, 270
Battle of Fredericksburg (Md) 61
Battle of Lexington and Concord (Mass.) 13, 111
Baum, Frank 168
Bazin, Henry 231
BBC (British Broadcasting Company) 183
Beach, Seth Curtis 232
"Beach Bubbles" • (poems) 300
"A Beautiful Picture Which Louisa M. Alcott Saw on a Hot and Dusty Journey" (similar to "Merry's Monthly Chat   ; "Baa! Baa!") • 315
"Becky's Christmas Dream" • 306, 312, 316, 317
Becky's Christmas Dream and Other Stories † (1895) 316
Becky's Christmas Dream and Other Stories † (c1902) 317
"Beds" • (poem) 68
"Beecher" 212, 213
Beecher, Charles 212
Beecher, Harriet *see* Stowe, Harriet Beecher
Beecher, Henry Ward 107, 108, 212, 273, 294; biographical sketch 265; works of 265

Beecher, Lyman 212
"Behind a Mask, or A Woman's Power" • 303, 320
Behind a Mask: The Unknown Thrillers of Louisa May Alcott • (anthology) 237, 320
Bell, Alastair 183
Bellamy, Edward 166
Bellevue Hotel (Boston) 89, 110, 116, 119, 120, 132, 235, 240, 282, 284, 285
Benary-Isbert, Margot 167
Ben-Hur 165
Bennett, Joan 178, 180, 181, 258, 260
The Bent Twig 165
Berkeley, Gertrude 174
Bernard, Dorothy 178
"Bertha" • 300
"Bertie's Box. A Christmas Story" • 313
"Beth Alcott's Playmate" 231
"Between Myth and Morning" 155, 192
"Bianca: An Operatic Tragedy" • 316
Bible 165
Bibliography of American Literature 238
Birch, Reginald 321
Birney, Meredith Baxter 182
Bishop, Thomas Brigham 223
Black Beauty 184
Blackwell, Henry Brown 273, 294
Blaidsell, Elinore 319
Blanck, Jacob N. 238
"The Blind Lark" • 315, 316
"The Blue and the Gray, A Hospital Sketch" • 305, 306
Bok, Edward W. 229
Bond, Louisa Caroline Greenwood 133, 137
"Bonfires" • 308
Bonner, Robert 81
Bonstelle, Jessie 174, 175, 229
Book of Nonsense 290
A Book of Song and Service for the Sunday School and Home 214
Books in Print 231
"Books That Separate Parents from Their Children" 150
Booth, Edwin 49, 75
Booth, John Wilkes 75
Boston, Mass 7, 33, 42, 43, 44, 45, 46, 49, 55, 56, 60, 75, 80, 89, 103, 110, 115, 119, 120, 122, 127, 128, 239, 240, 277, 278, 279, 280, 281, 282, 284, 285; fire 107
Boston Commonwealth 280
Boston Public Library 227
Boston University 227
Bowling Green State University 227
Boys' Best Book Stories, Poems and Sketches, by   Louisa M. Alcott † 316
"The Boys' Joke, and Who Got the Best of It" • 311
Brady, Alice 174
Brady, William A 174

Brazzi, Rossano 181
Brick-Ends (Still River, Mass) 24
Brigham Young University 227, 235
"A Bright Idea" ("Clara's Idea")• 312
"Brittany" (includes "Women of Brittany"; "Pelagie's Wedding")• 308
Bronson Alcott at Alcott House, England, and Fruitlands, New England† 318
Brontë, Charlotte 47, 290
Brontë, Emily 290
Brook Farm (Mass.) 21, 27, 29, 47, 85
Brophy, Brigid 154
"The Brothers" ("My Contraband")• 302, 318
Brown, Anne and Sarah 55
Brown, John 51, 52, 55, 218, 221, 272, 292; biographical sketch 266; daughters of 55, 266
Brown, Mary Hosmer 231
Brown University 227
Brownell, H H 221
"The Brownie and the Princess"• 315, 320
Buck, Pearl S 169
Buckley, R Bishop 217, 218
Bunyan, John 165
Burd, Clara M. 318
Burnett, Frances Eliza (Hodgson) 119, 120, 298; biographical sketch 266; works of 266, 267
Burnett, Swan Moses 266
"Buzz" ("My Little Friend")• 307, 312
By a Well Known Author (pseudonym of LMA) 302, 307
"By the River"• 310
Byington, Spring 178

C.H. 261
Calhoun, John C 165
"The Candy Country"• 130, 314, 315, 317, 318, 319
Cannes Film Festival 179
Cape May, N.J 239
Cape May Historical Museum 240
"The Captive of Castile; or, The Moorish Maiden's Vow"• 316
Carlsen, G. Robert 157
The Carol: A Book of Religious Songs for the Sunday School and the Home 213
Carpenter, Douglas 262
Carroll, Lewis (pseudonym of Charles Lutwidge Dodgson) 164, 287, 293, 295
Carson, Rachel 169
Cary, Joyce 175
Case, Nans 196
Centennial Exposition (Philadelphia) 115
A Century of Dishonor 129
Channing, Ellen Fuller 267, 269

Channing, Ellery *see* Channing, William Ellery, II
Channing, Mary *see* Higginson, Mary Channing
Channing, William Ellery, II 13, 16, 31, 46, 56, 64, 102, 243, 247, 269, 270; biographical sketch 267; as fictional character 106; works of 267
Channing family 27; children 13, 31
Charge of the Light Brigade 291
Charlotte's Web 167
Chatterbox Junior. "A volume of original stories by Miss Alcott and others† 312
Cheney, Ednah 149, 207, 216, 227, 228, 229, 232
Chesterton, G.K. 151
Chicago Tribune 173
Chickering Institute (Cincinnati) 173
Child, David Lee 267
Child, Lydia Maria (Francis) 8, 21, 51; biographical sketch 267; works of 29, 31, 267
Children and Books 167
"The Children's Joke"• 307
Children's Literature Association 167
"The Children's Song"• (poem and song lyrics) 216, 217, 300, 321
Children's Video Library 185
Chopin, Frédéric 224
Christian Science Monitor 237
The Christian Union 212, 265, 273, 294
Christina 197
"A Christmas Dream"• 313, 315, 317, 318; as play *Effie's Christmas Dream* 188
"The Christmas Elves"• (unpublished) 42, 43
Christmas Plum Pudding Stories by Louisa M. Alcott and Others† 313
"A Christmas Song"• 304
"A Christmas Turkey, and How It Came"• 314, 316
Cincinnati Historical Society 227
"Clams, A Ghost Story"• 311, 312, 319
"Clara's Idea" ("A Bright Idea")• 311
Clarke, Annie Lawrence 24, 75, 230
Clarke Historical Library, Central Michigan University 235
Classic Concord 231
"Clear the Stage for a Repeat Performance" 193
Clemens, Samuel 166; *see also* Twain, Mark
"Clover-Blossom"• 299
"Cockyloo"• 315, 318
Cohn, Mindy 185
Colcord, Mabel 178
Collodi, Carlo, works of 297
"Colored Soldiers' Letters"• 302
Columbia University 227
"Come, Butter, Come"• (poem and song lyrics) 225, 321
Comic Tragedies Written by "Jo" and

Index   337

"Meg" and Acted by the "Little
  Women"• 31, 149, 244, 286, 298, 316
Committee on College Reading 166
Common (Boston) 7, 8, 11, 44, 58, 110,
  130, 240
The Commonwealth Magazine 65, 67, 147,
  243, 270
Conan Doyle, Arthur 292
Concord, Mass. 12, 25, 33, 46, 49, 54, 55,
  56, 58, 64, 71, 83, 107, 111, 115, 119, 120,
  121, 125, 127, 128, 132, 216, 239, 240,
  243, 244, 277, 280, 281, 282, 284, 285
Concord Bridge 27
"The Concord Centennial: The Town Dele-
  gation" (pamphlet) ("Woman's Part in
  the Concord Celebration")• 310
Concord Dramatic Union 47, 279
Concord Free Public Library 227
Concord Historical Collaborative 248
Concord Lyceum 54
Concord River 13, 53, 74
Concord School of Philosophy see School of
  Philosophy
Concord Woman's Club 246
Constanduros, Denis 183
Conversations on the Gospel 9
"The Cooking Class"• 314, 320
Coolidge, Susan 193; works of 295
Cooney, Barbara 319
Cooney, Joan Ganz 169
Cooper, James Fenimore 166, 288, 289
Copus, E.J 165
Cornell, Katherine 175
Cornell University 227
"Corny's Catamount"• 314, 318, 320
The Cottage at Bantry Bar 167
"A Country Christmas"• 312, 313
"Courage and Patience"• (poem) 132
Cowan, Octavia 237
Crane, Stephen 166
Critical Essays on Louisa May Alcott
  233
Cromwell, John 174
"The Cross on the Old Church Tower"• 302
Cukor, George 178, 179, 180, 181
"Cupid and Chow-Chow"• 307, 308
"Curious Birds and Beasts" ("My May-Day
  Among Curious Birds and Beasts")• 307,
  320
"A Curious Call"• 305, 307
Current Literature 165
Currie, Cheri 184

Daisy Miller 166
"Daisy's Jewel-Box, and How She Filled It"•
  314
"Dandelion" ("The Little Boats")• 307, 319
"Dan's Dinner"• 305

Darwin, Charles 292
Daughters of the Puritans 232
Davenport, Carson 174
David Harum 167
"The Death of John"• 302
"Debby's Debut"• 301, 318
Dee, Frances 178, 180
The Deerslayer 288
De Forest, Marian 174, 175, 229
Delamar, Gloria T. 176, 214, 216, 224,
  225, 234
Delehanty, Thornton 180
Delman, David 161, 237, 256
"Despondency"• (poem) 23
Dey, Susan 182
"Diana and Persis"• 235, 236, 321
Dickens, Charles 78; works of 19, 31, 59,
  61, 62, 73, 80, 86, 110, 119, 120, 135,
  180, 229, 263, 288, 289, 290, 294
"A Dickens Day"• 304
Dix, Dorothea Lynde 9, 58, 63, 64, 165,
  267; biographical sketch 267
Dix, Lillian 174
Dobry 167
Dodge, Mary Elizabeth (Mapes) 104, 107,
  108, 119, 120, 128, 133, 137, 164, 189,
  229, 230, 293, 295; biographical sketch
  267; works of 268
"Does Little Women Belittle Women?" 160,
  183
"The Dolls' Journey from Minnesota to
  Maine"• 313, 317, 319
"Dolly's Bedstead"• 309, 316
A Double Life: Newly Discovered Thrillers
  of Louisa May Alcott• (anthology) 237,
  321
"A Double Tragedy. An Actor's Story"• 303
Down, Angela 183
"The Downward Road"• (poem) 198
Doyle, Arthur Conan 292
Doyle, Brian 193
Dreifuss, Arthur 188
Duncan, Isadora 169
Dunreath Place (Roxbury, Mass.) 113, 133,
  135, 137, 139, 242, 285
Dusenberry, Ann 182

"The Eaglet in the Dove's Nest"• 318
Earhart, Amelia 169
"Early Marriages"• 315
Eberle, Mrs. E A 174
Eddy, Mary Baker 169
Eggleston, Edward 166
Eight Cousins; or The Aunt Hill• 110, 115,
  148, 201, 282, 295, 310, 319; as play 187
Elbert, Sarah 236, 237
"Eli's Education"• 129, 313, 314
Elliot, Maud Howe 270

Elsie Dinsmore books 294
Emerson, Ellen 32, 38, 137, 277
Emerson, Lydian (Lydia Jackson) 27
Emerson, Ralph Waldo 7, 12, 13, 15, 18, 21, 25, 27, 31, 32, 46, 49, 52, 54, 55, 56, 67, 73, 74, 76, 88, 108, 120, 121, 122, 128, 166, 207, 212, 216, 218, 229, 231, 242, 243, 244, 245, 277; biographical sketch 268; as character in *Little Men* 100; as character in *Little Women* 89; death 127, 284; as fictional character 105; works of 268, 288, 289, 290
Emerson family 27, 46; children 13, 31
English Journal 157
"Enigmas"• 72, 302
Estabrook, Howard 174
"Eva's Visit to Fairyland"• 299, 315, 319
"An Evening Call"• 311

F , Maria 196
"F.A P."• (poem) 110
Faber, Leslie 175
Fadiman, Clifton 168
Fairfield, Flora (pseudonym of LMA) 36, 278, 299
"The Fairie Dell"• (unpublished) 299
"The Fairy Bird" ("Tilly's Christmas")• 307, 317
"The Fairy Box"• 315, 318
"Fairy Fire-Fly"• 304
"Fairy Pinafores"• 308
"Fairy Song"• (poem) 38, 299
"The Fairy Spring"• (poem) 223, 224, 315, 321
Fairy Tales 287, 290
"Faith"• (poem) 34
"Fame"• (poem) 105
"Fancy's Friend"• 304, 313
"The Fate of the Forrests"• 302, 321
The Father of Little Women 232
Faust 89, 116, 237
The Female Imagination 160
Feminist Studies 157
Ferber, Edna 165
Ferraro, Geraldine 169
Fetterley, Judith 157
Field, Anne 197
Field, Carolyn W 257
Fields, Annie Adams 55, 89, 126, 279; biographical note 268
Fields, James Thomas 38, 51, 55, 56, 66, 89, 102, 212, 242, 278, 279, 293; biographical sketch 268; death 126; as fictional character 97; works of 268
Fields, Kim 185
Finley, Martha 294
First Parish—Unitarian Universalist (Concord) 243

First Unitarian Church (Philadelphia) 114
Fisher, Aileen 233
Fisher, Dorothy Canfield 165
Fisher, Margery 159, 193
Five Little Peppers 244
The Flag of Our Union 71, 91, 205
"A Flower Fable" ("Queen Aster")• 315
"Flower Fables"• 32
Flower Fables• 38, 40, 42, 201, 203, 240, 244, 277, 278, 292, 299, 317
"The Flower's Lesson"• (poem) 299
"The Flower's Story"• 315
Fogarty, Thomas 319
"For a Grown-up Writers' (Re)Reading" 168
"For Johnny"• (poem) 77
"For the Attic Philosopher"• (poem) 41
Forbes, Ester 168
"Forest Green" 211, 212
Foster, Jodie 184
"France"• 308
Francis, Kay 187
Frank Leslie's Chimney Corner 205
Frank Leslie's Illustrated Newspaper 65, 71, 205, 270, 280
Fraser, Betty 319
"A Free Bed"• 135, 214, 235, 320
Freeman, Ethel Hale 187
French, Daniel 111
French Academy's Monthyon Prize 164
Friedan, Betty 169
The Frost King• 318
"The Frost King and How the Fairies Conquered Him"• 315, 319
"The Frost King; or, the Power of Love"• 299
Fruitlands (Harvard, Mass.) 17–24, 30, 46, 196, 230, 235, 242, 243, 277, 289
Fruitlands Museums (Harvard, Mass) 227, 242
Fuller, Ellen *see* Channing, Ellen Fuller
Fuller, Horace B. 80, 94, 234, 281, 294
Fuller, (Sarah) Margaret 9, 12, 13, 35, 108, 121, 231, 243, 267; biographical sketch 268; works of 269
Furness, Frank 114

Gardner, Margaret 24
Gardner, Sophia 24
Gardner, Walter 24, 75
Garland, Hamlin 165
A Garland for Girls• 136, 203, 234, 316, 318
Garrison, William Lloyd 8, 35, 44; biographical sketch 269; works of 269
Garson, Greer 182
"Geehale—An Indian Legend" 25
George, Jean Craighead 168

Index

Georgetown Union Hotel Hospital (Washington, D.C) 59–64, 71, 280, 293
Germantown, Pa. *see* Philadelphia
Gerould, Katherine Fullerton 152, 158, 190
Gibson, Flo 177
Gill, William 113
Gilliland, Richard 182
Glimpses of Louisa: A Centennial Sampling of the Best Short Stories by Louisa May Alcott• (anthology) 320
"A Glorious Fourth: No. 4 The Press Leaflets"• 315
Gloucester, Mass. 74
"Godfin and Silvertail"• 304
Goethe, Johann Wolfgang von 32, 76; as character in *Little Men* 100; as character in *Little Women* 89; works of, 89, 116, 237
Golden Bowl 166
Golden Horn 147
Golden Multitudes 166
"A Golden Wedding: and What Came of It"• 302
Goldstone, Bette 255
Good Housekeeping 174
Good Reading: A Guide to the World's Best Books 166
Gordon, Jayne 258
Gorsline, Douglas W 319
Gould, Elizabeth Lincoln 173, 187
Gowing, Clara 29, 230, 231
Gowing's Swamp (Concord) 29
"Grandmamma's Pearls"• 313
"Grandma's Story"• 313, 314
"Grandma's Team"• 307, 308, 318
"Grandmother's Specs"• 304, 312, 316, 317
Grant, Ulysses S. 75, 111
Gray, Robert 261
"The Greek Slave"• 316
Greele, Louisa May 6
Gregg, Virginia 182
Griffith, Richard 180
Grimm's Popular Stories 290
Gulliver, Lucile 238

Hackett, Walter 177
Haines, Jane 7
Haines, Reuben 5, 6, 239
Hale, Lucretia 296
Hall of Fame of Great Americans (New York University) 164
Halliwell, Leslie 182
Halliwell's Film Guide 180, 182
Hamlet 49, 75
Hammond, Lynn 174
Hancock, (Great-Aunt) Dorothy *see* Scott, Dorothy Quincy Hancock
Hancock, John 6, 13, 44

A Handful of Authors: Essays on Books and Writers 152
Hans Brinker 159, 164, 189, 230, 268, 293
Hanson, Hattie 175
"A Happy Birthday"• 308, 311, 319
Happy Days for Boys and Girls† 311
"Happy Women"• 81, 304
Hardy, Thomas 288
"The Hare and the Tortoise"• 314, 320
Harper's Magazine 154
Harper's New Monthly Magazine 148
Harper's Young People 129, 296
Harrington, Stephanie 160, 183
Harris, Alfred A. 175
Harris, Joel Chandler 296; works of 297
Harris, Julie 177
Harris, William Torrey 129, 229, 245, 285
Harrison, Bertram 174
Harvard, Mass 17–24, 196, 230, 242, 243, 277
Harvard University 227; library 235
Haskell, Alfred 24
Haviland, Virginia 192
Hawthorne, Hildegard (Mrs Oskison) 245
Hawthorne, Julian 53, 60, 66, 71, 90, 116, 172, 231, 245; biographical note 269
Hawthorne, Nathaniel 27, 46, 53, 67, 108, 127, 166, 231, 243, 244, 245, 271, 272, 291; as fictional character 106; biographical sketch 269; death 73; works of 269
Hawthorne, Rose *see* Lathrop, Rose Hawthorne
Hawthorne, Sophia Peabody 8, 27, 66, 245, 271, 272; biographical note 269
Hawthorne, Una 53
Heart and Voice 209
Heerman, Victor 178, 179, 181
Heidi 159, 167, 184, 189, 296, 297
"Helping Along" (included in "How One Sister Helped Her Brother")• 311
Hepburn, Katherine 177, 178, 179, 180, 181, 248
Hewitt, Henry C. 175
Higginson, Mary Channing 267, 270
Higginson, Thomas Wentworth 49, 54, 73, 173, 267; biographical sketch 269; works of 270
The Hillside (Concord) 25, 27, 30, 32, 46, 85, 244, 245, 277, 278, 290; *see also* The Wayside
Hilton, Florence 173
Hinds, Samuel S 178
Historical Society of Pennsylvania 227
Hogarth, Paul 320
A Hole in the Wall• 317
"A Hole in the Wall" ("Little Pyramus and Thisbe")• 315, 318, 320
Holiday 156
Holles, Antony 175
Holmes, Oliver Wendell 80, 119

Homeopathic Treatment Center (Dunreath Place, Roxbury, Mass) 133
Homolka, Oscar 177
The Hoosier Schoolmaster 166
"Hope for Housekeepers" ("The Servant-Girl Problem")• 308
The Horn Book 155, 159, 190
The Horn of Plenty of Home Poems and Home Pictures with New Poems by Miss Louisa M. Alcott and Others† 113, 311
Hosmer, Cyrus 12, 49, 58
Hosmer, Henry 12, 49
Hosmer, John 29
Hosmer, Laura *see* Whiting (Hosmer), Laura
Hosmer, Lydia *see* Wood, Lydia Hosmer
Hosmer, Mary *see* Brown, Mary Hosmer
Hosmer, Sarah 49
Hosmer Cottage (Concord) 12
"A Hospital Christmas"• 302, 306
"The Hospital Lamp"• 302
"Hospital Sketches"• 67
Hospital Sketches• 67–70, 70, 71, 73, 74, 82, 201, 204, 237, 280, 293, 301, 306, 319, 321
Hospital Sketches and Camp and Fireside Stories• 203, 294, 306
Hospital Sketches and War Stories• (working title) 81
Hospital Sketches; Memoir of Emily Elizabeth Parsons• 237
Houghton, Katherine 248
Houghton Library, Harvard University 227, 235, 237
"An Hour"• 302, 306
House of Seven Gables 166
"How I Went Out to Service A Story"• 36, 38, 242, 309
"How It All Happened"• 312, 313
"How One Sister Helped Her Brother" (includes "Helping Along")• 311
"How They Camped Out"• 312, 319, 320
"How They Ran Away"• 315, 318
"How We Saw the Shah"• 308
Howard, A P. 207, 209
Howe, Julia Ward 44, 104, 113, 114, 212; biographical sketch 270; works of 56, 270
Howe, Samuel Gridley 270
Howells, William Dean 166
"Huckleberry"• 308
Huckleberry Finn 158, 159, 164, 167, 168, 189, 260, 297
Hughes, Thomas 292
Hulette, Gladys 174
Hunt, William 90
Huntingdon House (Cape May, N.J.) 239, 240
Huntington Library 227
Hymns for the Celebration of Life 212

"In Memoriam Sophia Foord"• 314
"In the Garret"• (poem) 91, 302
Independent 174
Indiana University 227
Institute for Research in History (New York) 168
"An Interview with Jean Ingelow"• 313
Invincible Louisa 155, 233; as filmstrip 177; as recording 177
"Ion"• 316
Iowa State Historical Library 227
Irving, Washington 166
Island of the Blue Dolphins 168
"Italy"• 308
"An Ivy Spray and Ladies' Slippers" ("An Ivy Spray")• 315, 316, 320

Jack and Jill. A Village Story• 121, 122, 203, 296, 312, 319
Jackson, Helen Hunt 119, 165, 166; works of 129
Jambor, Louis 319
James, Henry, Sr , and Mrs. James 75
James, Henry, Jr 70, 75, 90, 91, 148, 166, 289; works of 70
Jane Eyre 290
Janeway, Elizabeth 155, 192
Jerome, Frank E. 223
"Jerseys; or, The Girls' Ghost"• 314, 320
"Jimmy's Cruise in the Pinafore"• 312, 319
"Jimmy's Lecture"• 315
Joan 196
"John"• 301, 306
"The John Brown Song"• (poem) 221, 222; lyrics to song 300, 321
"John Brown's Body" 56, 221
"John Marlow's Victory"• 312
Johnny Tremaine 168
"John's Sixteenth Birthday"• (poem) 126
Johnston, Alma 187
"The Jolly Fourth"• 312
Jones, Jennifer 181
Jo's Boys and How They Turned Out. A Sequel to "Little Men"• 128, 129, 132, 133, 148, 187, 201, 285, 298, 315, 319; as play 187
Journal of Black History 234
The Journals of Louisa May Alcott• (anthology of journal entries) 230, 321
Julia (Lulu's governess), as fictional character 133
Julie of the Wolves 168

Kagan, Marilyn 184
Karl, Jean E 256
"Kate's Choice"• 307, 308, 318, 319, 320

Index

Katy books 193, 295
Keller, Helen 165
Kellerman, Sally 184
Kimball, Ruth Putnam 187
"Kind Words from Miss Alcott"• 314
"The King of Clubs and the Queen of Hearts"• 300, 302, 306
Kings Chapel (Boston) 5, 44, 108
Kingsley, Charles 109, 295; works of 109
Kipling, Rudyard 293
"Kitty's Cattle Show"• 312
Kitty's Class Day (Proverb Stories)• 136, 203, 234, 297, 305, 311, 313
Kitty's Class Day (single story)• 305
Kitty's Class Day at Harvard (Louisa M. Alcott's Proverb Stories; Three Proverb Stories)• 311
Klein, Stacy 260
Knecht, Justin Heinrich 216
Kolba, Ellen D. 157
Kravitzky, Maya 197

L M A (pseudonym of LMA) 36, 299, 305, 320, 321
The Ladies' Home Journal 149, 168, 169, 172
"The Lady and the Woman"• 300
Lady of the Silver Skates: The Life and Correspondence of Mary Mapes Dodge, etc. 230
Lafayette, Marquis de 6
Landis, Jessie Royce 175
Lane, Charles 15, 16, 18, 21, 22, 23, 24, 28, 243, 277
Lane, William 15, 18, 21, 277
Larrick, Nancy 167
The Last of the Mohicans 166
"The Last of the Philosophers"• (poem) 138
"Last Years"• (poem) 136
Lathrop, George Parsons 244, 245
Lathrop, Rose Hawthorne 53, 119, 244, 245
Lawford, Peter 181
Lawrence, Annie *see* Clarke, Annie Lawrence
Lawrence, Rhoda Ashley 112, 133, 135, 248, 285, 286
"The Lay of a Golden Goose"• (poem) 97, 315
Leachman, Cloris 185
Lear, Edward 290
Leavitt, Mrs 173
Lee, Barbara 184
Lee, Gen. Robert E. 75
Lee and Shepard 149
Leigh, Janet 181
L'Engle, Madeleine 167
Lenyard, Addie 321
Lerman, Leo 156
Le Roy, Mervyn 181

Leslie, Frank 65, 206; biographical sketch 270
"Letter from Louisa M. Alcott"• (1876) 311
"Letter from Louisa M Alcott"• (1879) 312
"Letter from Louisa M. Alcott"• (1880) 312
"Letter from Louisa M. Alcott"• (1882) 313
"Letter from Miss Alcott"• (1883) 313
"Letter from Miss Louisa M Alcott"• (1884) 314
"Letter of Miss Louisa Alcott"• (1874) 310
'Letter on Amos Bronson Alcott"• 315
"Letter to Mr. Prang. Chromo-Lithography"• (advertisement) 303
"Letter to N W.C.T.U."• 311
"Letters from the Mountains"• 301
"Letty's Tramp"• 310
Lewis, Dio 54
Lewis, Elizabeth 6, 114
Liberator 51
Library of Congress 192, 194, 227, 234, 238
Lichtenstein, G. 261
Life Hymnal: A Book of Song and Service for the Sunday School 209
"Life in a Pension"• 303
"Lilybell and Thistledown, or The Fairy Sleeping Beauty"• 299, 315, 319
Lincoln, Abraham 62, 63, 75, 292, 293
"Lines to a Good Physician, from a Grateful Patient"• 307
Linn, Edith Willis 231
A Literary History of America 151
Literary Women 157
Little, Brown & Company 152, 162
"Little Annie's Dream; or, the Fairy Flower"• 299
"The Little Boats" ("Dandelion")• 306
"Little Boston"• 308
"Little Bud"• 299, 315
Little Button Rose• 317
"Little Button-Rose"• 316
"A Little Cinderella"• 309
"Little Genevieve"• 300
"A Little Gentleman" ("My Little Gentleman")• 306
"A Little Grey Curl"• (poem) 318
"Little Gulliver"• 304, 313
"The Little House in the Garden"• 314
Little House in the Big Woods 168
Little House on the Prairie 168
"A Little Kingdom I Possess" (poem and hymn lyrics) ("A Little Kingdom"; "My Kingdom"; "My Little Kingdom")• 210, 211, 320
"Little Lord Fauntleroy"• (review) 315
"Little Marie of Lehon"• 307, 319
Little Men; Life at Plumfield with Jo's Boys• 100, 101, 102, 148, 167, 187, 201, 281, 295, 307, 314, 317, 318, 319, 320; as film 187; as play 173, 187; as play *Daisy's Ball* 187

"Little Neighbors"• 309, 311
The Little Paradise of Pine Place (Philadelphia) 5, 115, 239
"Little Paul"• (poem) 300
"Little Pyramus and Thisbe" ("A Hole in the Wall")• 313
"The Little Red Purse"• 316
"Little Robin"• 315
"The Little Seed"• 299
"Little Things"• ("A Genuine Little Lady") 306, 313, 314
Little Women see *Little Women or, Meg, Jo, Beth, and Amy*•
"*Little Women*: Alcott's Civil War" 157
"Little Women" Clubs 110, 136, 171, 173, 226
Little Women Letters from the House of Alcott• 229, 318
"Little Women of Long Ago" 174, 231
Little Women or, Meg, Jo, Beth, and Amy (frequently just *Little Women*)• 3, 83, 90, 91, 94, 114, 119, 127, 128, 226, 233, 244, 247, 249, 252, 281, 312, 318, 319, 320, 321; adaptations 171–188; as cartoon-strip 172; copyright 88, 94, 135, 145, 149, 152, 162, 173, 196, 203; critical analysis of 145–163, 234, 253–263; feminism in 155, 156, 160, 161, 262; as film 178, 181, 248; as film (*Foxes*) 184; as film (silent) 178; as film (television) 182, 183; as film (television series: *Facts of Life*) 185; foreign titles 159, 190, 191, 192, 194–196; foreigners' comments 189–194, 196–197; forgery 162; income from 88, 94, 108, 145, 148, 149, 162, 166; modern readership 163, 249–252, 253–263; as play 172, 173, 174, 175; as play (Christmas scenes) 176; as play (excerpts) 173, 177; as play (operetta) 175; publication of Part I 88, 145, 162, 281, 294, 305; publication of Part II 93, 162, 294, 306; publication of Parts I and II 201, 306; as radio script 177; ranking of 164–170; as record 177; as record (excerpts) 177; religion in 147, 158, 159, 160; as television cartoon (*Tales of Little Women*) 186; titled *Good Wives* 148, 189, 193, 196; titles, other English 196; as video cartoon 185; writing of Part I 83–88; writing of Part II 89–93
The Little Women Society 173
"*Little Women*: Who's in Love with Miss Louisa May Alcott? I Am" 156
Livermore, Daniel Parker 271
Livermore, Mary Ashton (Rice) 112, 113, 114, 212; biographical sketch 270; works of 271
"Living in an Omnibus. A True Story" ("Autobiography of an Autobus")• 303, 311
Lodge, John Davis 177, 178

"London"• 308
"London Bridges"• 310
Longfellow, Henry Wadsworth 66, 242, 292, 293
"A Look at the Racier Side of Louisa May Alcott" 161
Looking Backward 166
"Lost in a London Fog"• 308, 311
"Lost in a Pyramid; or The Mummy's Curse"• 305
Lothrop, Daniel 244, 245
Lothrop, Harriet Mulford Stone (pseudonym: Margaret Sidney) 244, 245, 246
Lothrop, Margaret Mulford 244, 245
"Louisa Alcott" (by Chesterton) 151
The Louisa Alcott Reader; a Supplementary Reader for the Fourth Year of School• (anthology) 318
The Louisa Alcott Story Book Edited for Schools• (anthology) 318
Louisa Alcott's People• (anthology) 319
Louisa M. Alcott's Proverb Stories (Kitty's Class Day at Harvard; Three Proverb Stories)• 305
Louisa May Alcott (by Anthony) 154, 233
Louisa May Alcott (by Stern) 233, 238
Louisa May Alcott: A Bibliography 238
Louisa May Alcott: A Centennial for "Little Women" 238
Louisa May Alcott: A Reference Guide 238
Louisa May Alcott and "Little Women": etc. 234, 238
The Louisa May Alcott Cookbook 171
A Louisa May Alcott Diary 171
Louisa May Alcott, Dreamer and Worker: A Study of Achievement 232
Louisa May Alcott: Her Life, Letters, and Journals 207, 216, 228, 229, 232, 316, 318
The Louisa May Alcott Keepsake Diary 172
Louisa May Alcott Memorial Association 246, 247, 258
Louisa May Alcott, The Children's Friend 149, 227
"Louisa May Alcott Was Never Like This" 184
"Louisa May Alcott's Letters to Five Girls" 229
Louisa May Alcott's Little Women Paper Dolls 172
Louisa's Wonder Book—An Unknown Alcott Juvenile (Will's Wonder Book)• 234, 238, 320
Louisburg Square (Beacon Hill, Boston) 125, 129, 138, 242
"Love"• (poem) 139, 204
"Love and Loyalty"• 302, 306
"Love and Self-Love"• 51, 300
"Love Divine, All Loves Excelling" 212
"Lu Sing"• 133, 150, 318

Index

Lucas, E.V 180
Luce, Clare Booth 169
Lucy Stone Leaguers *see* Stone. Lucy
Lukas, Paul 177, 178
Lukens sisters (Carrie, Maggie, Nellie, Emma, Helen) 104, 108, 133, 229
Lulu's Library • (selections from series) 319
Lulu's Library • (series of three volumes) 136, 234
Lulu's Library. Vol. I. A Christmas Dream • 203, 297, 315
Lulu's Library. Vol. II. The Frost King • 137, 203, 298, 315
Lulu's Library. Vol. III. Recollections • 203, 230, 298, 316
"Lunch" • 312, 318, 320
Lyne, Adrian 184
Lynn, Diana 181

"M L " 51, 65, 234, 301, 319
"Mabel's May Day" • 300
"Madam Cluck, and Her Family" • 306, 307
Mademoiselle 156
"Magic Spell" • (poem) 87
Magid, Nora L 193
Maine Historical Society 227
Maltin, Leonard 180, 182, 183
"Mamma's Plot" • 308
The Man Nobody Knows 165
Mann, Dorothea Lawrance 190
Mann, Horace 27, 37, 51, 269, 272; biographical sketch 271
Mann, Mary Peabody 27, 115, 245, 269, 271, 272
"A Marble Woman: or, The Mysterious Model, a Novel of Absorbing Interest" • 303, 320
"March, march, mothers and grandmammas! . . ." • (poem) 300; *see also* "Young America"
Marie 197
Marill, Alvin H 182
"A Marine Merry-Making" • 306, 308
"Marjorie's Birthday Gifts" ("Marjorie's Three Gifts") • 311
Marjorie's Three Gifts • 317
"Marjorie's Three Gifts" ("Marjorie's Birthday Gifts") • 311, 317
"Mark Field's Mistake" • 300
"Mark Field's Success" • 300
Marmee: The Mother of Little Women 233
Marsella, Joy A 233
"The Masked Marriage" • 299
Mason, Sarah Y. 178, 179, 181
Massachusetts Historical Society 227
"A Masterpiece, and Dreadful" 154
"May" • (poem) 318
May, Dorothy Sewall 275

May, Colonel Joseph (Louisa May Alcott's grandfather) 6, 9, 10, 25, 102, 109, 247, 268, 275; as character in *Little Women* 85; death 14
May, Joseph (Louisa May Alcott's cousin) 114, 207
May, Mary Ann Cary 10
May, Samuel 6, 8, 15, 23, 35, 37, 52, 114, 207, 275, 277; biographical sketch 271; as character in *Little Women* 85; death 102, 281
May Alcott: A Memoir 231
"May Flowers" • 316, 317
Mayer, Arthur 180
McGinley, Phyllis 168
McGuffey's Reader 288
McGuire, Dorothy 181, 182, 183
McKeon, Nancy 185
McWhinney, Georgia S. 254
Meadow Blossoms. By L.M. Alcott and Others † 312
Meet the Austins 167
Meigs, Cornelia 155, 177, 233, 238
Melville, Herman 166, 291
Memories of Concord 231
"Mermaids" • 315
Merrill, Frank Thayer 127, 312, 314, 317, 321
"Merry Christmas" • (poem) 113, 311
Merry Times for Boys and Girls † 311
"Merry's Monthly Chat with His Friends" (September 1868; similar to "Baa! Baa!"; "A Beautiful Picture ") • 83, 304
Merry's Museum 80, 82, 83, 94, 145, 203, 234, 281, 294
Miller, Eli Peck 113, 282
"Milly's Messenger" • 306
Milone, Karen 171
Mind over Media 184
Minnesota Historical Society 227
"Miss Alcott on Mind-Cure" • 314
"Miss Alcott, the Friend of Little Women and Little Men" 117
"Miss Alcott's Letters to Her 'Laurie,'" • 229
"Mr Alcott's True Condition" • 313
"Mr. Emerson's Third Lecture" • 305
"Mrs. Gay's Hint, and How It Was Taken" • 313
"Mrs. Gay's Prescription" • 311
"Mrs. Podgers' Teapot, A Christmas Story" • 302, 306
Mitchell, E.T. 210
Moby Dick 166, 260, 291
"A Modern Cinderella: or, The Little Old Shoe" • 53, 54, 83, 300, 306, 318
A Modern Cinderella or the Little Old Shoe and Other Stories • 318
A Modern Mephistopheles • 116, 204, 237, 282, 296, 311, 321
A Modern Mephistopheles and a Whisper in the Dark • 316

A Modern Mephistopheles and Taming a Tartar• 237, 321
Modes and Morals 153, 158
Moers, Ellen 156
Monastery 219
Montgomery, Douglass 178
Moods (later *Moods. A Novel*)• 52, 55, 73, 75, 78, 148, 204, 237, 279, 280, 293, 302
Moods. A Novel (revision of *Moods*)• 127, 204, 238, 297, 312
Moore, Dickie 187
"Morning Glories"• 225, 304, 313, 318, 319
Morning Glories and Other Stories• 294, 304
Morning Glories and Queen Aster• 318
Morristown National Historic Park 227
Morrow, Honore Willsie 232
Moses, Belle 232
"The Moss People"• 308, 318
"The Mother-Moon" (poem, one of "Beach Bubbles")• 300
"Mother's Trial"• 306
Mott, Frank Luther 166
Mott, Lucretia 7
Mount Washington, N H 55
"Mountain-Laurel and Maidenhair"• 316, 318, 320
The Movies 181
Ms. magazine 172
"Music and Macaroni"• 316, 319, 320
"My Boys" (includes "My Polish Boy")• 307, 319, 320
"My Contraband; or, The Brothers" ("The Brothers")• 302, 306
"My Doves"• (poem) 304
"My Fourth of July"• 306
"My Girls"• 311
"My Kingdom" ("A Little Kingdom"; "A Little Kingdom I Possess"; "My Little Kingdom"; poem and song lyrics)• 207, 208, 209, 210, 211, 212, 310, 321
"My Little Friend" ("Buzz")• 304, 316, 317
My Little Friend and Other Stories† 316
"My Little Gentleman" ("A Little Gentleman") 307, 318
"My Little Kingdom" ("A Little Kingdom"; "A Little Kingdom I Possess"; "My Kingdom"; poem)• 35
"My Little Schoolgirl"• 310, 312
"My May-Day Among Curious Birds and Beasts" ("Curious Birds and Beasts")• 304, 307, 312, 316, 317
"My Polish Boy" (included in "My Boys")• 305
"My Red Cap"• 312, 313, 320
"My Rococo Watch"• 310
Myerson, Joel 230, 255
"The Mysterious Key and What It Opened"• 320

The Mysterious Key, and What It Opened• 304, 317
"The Mysterious Page or Woman's Love"• (unpublished) 299
"The Mystery of Morlaix"• 308

Nason, Janet 172
"Nat Bachelor's Pleasure Trip"• 42, 52
Nathan, George Jean 175
The Nation 146, 152
National Anti-Slavery Standard 148
National Congress of the Women of the United States 113
National Education Association 164
National Park Service 244
National Women's Rights Convention (Worcester, Mass.) 35, 291
Natwick, Mildred 183
"Naughty Jocko"• 315, 318
"The Nautilus"• (poem) 304, 307
Navias, Eugene B. 211, 212
"Nelly's Hospital"• 308, 318, 319
"Nelly's Hospital"• (pamphlet) 302
New England Hospital for Women and Children (Roxbury, Mass.) 135
New Theatre (London) 175
"A New Way to Spend Christmas"• 311
"A New Year's Blessing"• 299
New York (City) 33, 113, 114
New York Herald Tribune 180
New York Historical Society 227
The New York Ledger 81
New York Post 180
New York Public Library 162, 227
The New York Times 150, 151, 154, 155, 160, 193
New York University 227; Hall of Fame of Great Americans 164
Newberry Library 227
Newbery Medal 233
Newsboys' Home (New York) 113, 282
Niagara Falls, N.Y 113
Nieriker, Ernest 122; marriage 117, 284
Nieriker, Louisa May (Lulu) 125, 127, 128, 129, 133, 135, 137, 138, 149, 173, 223, 242, 284, 285, 286; birth 122, 284; death 286; as fictional character 133; marriage 286
Nieriker, May Alcott 235, 243, 281; as actress 31; as artist 28, 35, 45, 49, 54, 72, 80, 83, 90, 96, 102, 108, 110, 115, 247; as artist re *Little Women* 88, 147, 162; as author 244; biography of 231; birth 12, 277; as character in *Little Men* 100; as character in *Little Women* 3, 85, 86, 87, 91; courtship 283; death 122, 284; as fictional character 43, 53, 83, 236; illness 43, 71; life *1840-1847* 12-30; *1848-1855*

Index
345

31–42; *1856–1860* 43–54; *1861–1862* 55–63; *1863–1867* 63–80; *1868–1869* 80–94; *1870–1874* 95–110; *1875–1879* 110–122; marriage 117, 245, 284; as teacher 54, 55, 56, 279; works of 122
Nieriker, Sophie 125
"Night Scene in a Hospital"• 301, 302
Nightingale, Florence 60, 291
Niles, Thomas 38, 79, 83, 85, 88, 93, 97, 100, 102, 103, 115, 116, 126, 127, 129, 133, 145, 242, 281; niece 88
Nonquit, Mass. 128, 129, 284
"Norna; or, The Witch's Curse"• 316
The North American 148
"Not to Be Read on Sunday" 159
Note on Dickens (untitled)• 303
"Number Eleven"• 313

O'Brien, Margaret 181
O'Dell, Scott 168
O'Faolain, Sean 156, 158
"Off"• 308
"Oh, the Beautiful Old Story"• (poem and hymn lyrics) 212, 213, 214, 315, 320, 321
The Old Corner Bookstore (Boston) 38, 80, 129, 242, 278
An Old-Fashioned Girl• 95, 201, 281, 294, 306, 307, 317, 318, 319; as movie 188; as play 188
An Old-Fashioned Thanksgiving• 234, 312, 313, 319, 321
"Old Major"• 310, 311
Old Manse (Concord) 27
"Old Times at Old Concord"• 314
Olive Branch Magazine 36, 278
"The Olive Leaf" 34, 87, 104, 278
Oliver, Edna May 178
Omoo 166
"On Picket Duty"• 302, 313
On Picket Duty, and Other Tales• 73, 203, 280, 293, 302, 321
"On the Keel"• 316, 317
"Onawandah"• 313, 314, 320
Once Upon a Spy 209
"One Hundred Good Novels" 165
"Only an Actress"• 311
Optic, Oliver (pseudonym of William Taylor Adams) 291, 294
Orchard House (Concord) 46, 49, 83, 89, 103, 104, 107, 109, 115, 117, 121, 126, 128, 129, 172, 229, 240, 245, 246, 247, 258, 279, 284, 292, 297
Orchard House/Louisa May Alcott Memorial Association 227
"Ossian" 25
Ossoli, Marchioness *see* Fuller, (Sarah) Margaret
Ostrum, Barbara 260

"Our Angel in the House" (poem)• 48
Our Dumb Animals 230
Our Girls† 316
"Our Little Ghost"• (poem) 303, 312, 316, 317
"Our Little Newsboy"• 304, 307, 312, 316, 317
"Our Madonna"• (poem) 122
"Our Young Folks" 173
"Over-All Best Sellers in the United States" 166

Page, Anna 18, 21
"A Pair of Eyes; or, Modern Magic"• 302, 321
Palmer, Ada 175
Palmer, Joseph 18, 19, 23, 24
"Pansies"• 315, 316
Pansies and Water-Lilies• 318
Papyrus Club (Boston) 119
Parent's Guide to Children's Reading 167
A Parents Guide to Children's Video 185
Parents Review 189
Parker, Jean 178, 180
Parker, Lydia 44, 73
Parker, Theodore 21, 35, 37, 44, 47, 49, 52, 53, 128, 207, 212, 279; biographical sketch 271; as character in *Little Women* 85; death 279; works of 271
Parks, Rosa 169
"Parody on 'The Graves of a Household'"• (poem) 102; 204
Parsons, Emily Elizabeth 237
Patterson, Elizabeth 181
"Patty Pans"• 318
"Patty's Patchwork"• 307
"Patty's Place"• 308, 311, 318
Paul, Julian 319
"Pauline's Passion and Punishment"• 65, 280, 293, 300, 320
Pavey, Marie 174
Paxton, Sydney 175
Payne, Alma J. 238
Peabody, Elizabeth Palmer 8, 9, 27, 51, 55, 115, 121, 240, 245, 269, 271; biographical sketch 272
Peabody, Mary *see* Mann, Mary Peabody
Peabody, Sophia *see* Hawthorne, Sophia Peabody
Pease, Rae 255
"Peep! peep! peep!"• 304
"Pelagie's Wedding" (included in "Brittany")• 307
Pen Points 168
Perenyi, Eleanor 154, 158
"Perilous Play"• 305, 320
Perkins, Frances 169
Perkins, H.S. 207

Peterson's Magazine 36, 278
Phelps, Elizabeth Stuart 119
Philadelphia 5, 6, 7, 33, 100, 114, 115, 239, 282
Philadelphia Daily News 184
Philadelphia Fair 74
Philadelphia Female Anti-Slavery Society 7
Philadelphia Inquirer 161, 237
Phillips, Kate 175
Phillips, Wendell 35, 37, 44, 75, 218; biographical sketch 272; death 128
Philocalian Society of Chicago 173
"Philothea" 29, 31
Pickford, Mary 169
Pierpont Morgan Library 227
"The Piggy Girl"• 315, 318
Pilgrim's Progress 8, 27, 85, 86, 87, 131, 165, 244
Pinckney Street: #20 (Beacon Hill, Boston) 40, 55, 240
Pinkham, Lydia 169
Pitz, Henry 320
Planer, Franz 182
Plays, the Drama Magazine for Young People 177
"Pleyel" 214, 215
Pleyel, Ignaz 214
Plots and Counterplots; More Unknown Thrillers of Louisa May Alcott• (anthology) 237, 320
"The Ploughboy's Dream" 211, 212
Plumb, Eve 182
Poems by Louisa May Alcott• (pamphlet) 321
"Polly Arrives"• 311
Pollyanna 165
"Poppies and Wheat"• 316, 317, 320
"Poppy's Pranks"• 82, 304, 313
Port Royal, South Carolina 56
Porter, Eleanor H. 165
Porter, Maria S. 105, 109, 119, 121, 137, 230, 231
Portrait of a Lady 166
Potter, Beatrix 294
Potts, Cliff 182
Pratt, Anna Bronson Alcott 149, 173, 229, 242, 243, 285, 286; as actress 27, 31, 35, 42; re antislavery 34; birth 5, 275; as character in *Little Men* 100; as character in *Little Women* 3, 85, 86, 87, 91; as co-author 149, 245; courtship 47, 49, 53; as co-writer 31; death 286; as fictional character 43, 53, 83, 133; hearing 80, 108; home 115; illness 43, 107, 120; life *1831–1840* 5–14; *1840–1847* 14–30; *1848–1855* 31–42; *1856–1860* 43–54; *1861–1862* 55–63; *1863–1867* 63–80; *1868–1869* 80–94; *1870–1874* 95–110; *1875–1879* 110–122; *1880–1885* 123–131; *1886–1888* 132–142; marriage 52, 245, 247, 279

Pratt, Bronson Alcott (birth) 286
Pratt, Elizabeth Sewall (birth) 286
Pratt, Elverton Hunting (adoption) 286
Pratt, Eunice May Plummer Hunting (marriage) 286
Pratt, Frederick Alcott 77, 80, 104, 108, 110, 115, 119, 126, 129, 135, 149, 173, 242, 284, 285; birth 65, 280; death 286; as fictional character 133; marriage 286
Pratt, Frederick Woolsey (birth) 286
Pratt, Jessica L. Cate (marriage) 286
Pratt, John Bridge 47, 49, 53, 78, 95, 115, 127, 279; as character in *Little Women* 85; death 100, 281; as fictional character 53, 83; marriage 52, 279
Pratt, John Sewall 77, 80, 104, 105, 108, 115, 119, 126, 129, 137, 230, 242, 284, 285; adopted by Louisa May Alcott 135, 149, 173, 229, 286; birth 76, 280; death 286; as fictional character 133; marriage 286
Pratt, Louisa May (birth) 286
Pratt, Minot 47
"Preface to *Concord Sketches Consisting of Twelve Photographs from Original Drawings by May Alcott*"• 306
"Preface to Little Women"• (poem) 87
"Preface to *Prayers by Theodore Parker*"• 312
Pride and Prejudice 158
"The Prince and the Peasant or Love's Trials"• (unpublished) 299
Princeton University 227
The Promise of Destiny: Children and Women in the Stories of Louisa May Alcott 233
Proverb Stories (Kitty's Class Day)• 136, 203, 234, 297, 313, 316
"Providence. A Drama"• (unpublished) 299
Psyche's Art• 305, 311, 313
Publisher's Weekly 165, 191, 192
Punch 180
Pyle, Howard 168; works of 297
Pyle, Martha E 191

"Queen Aster"• ("A Flower Fable") 315, 318

"R.W. Emerson"• 313
Rabe, Olive 233
Radcliffe College 227
Rae, Charlotte 185
Ramona 129, 165, 166
Randall, David A 165
Randall's Island (New York) 113, 282
Rasim, Ernestine "Erni" (birth) 286

Index

Rasim, Ernst (marriage) 286
Rasim, Louisa May Nieriker *see* Nieriker, Louisa May (Lulu)
Ravold, John 187
Reading Roundup: Book One 177
"Recent Exciting Scenes in Rome"• 307
Recollections of Louisa May Alcott, John Greenleaf Whittier, and Robert Browning, etc. 230, 231
"Recollections of My Childhood"• 149, 230, 316
The Red Badge of Courage 166
"The Red Purse"• 318
"Red Tulips"• 310, 311
Redpath, James 67, 68, 73
Reid, Eliot 177
"Reminiscences of Louisa M. Alcott" 174
"Reminiscences of Ralph Waldo Emerson"• 313
Revere, Paul 44
Richard, Winston 186
Richards, Laura E. 270
Richmond, Virginia 75
Ricketson, Walton 132
Ride, Sally 169
Rimmer, William 72; as character in *Little Men* 100; as character in *Little Women* 89
"Ripple, the Water Spirit"• 299, 306, 315
Rise of Silas Lapham 166
"The Rival Painters. A Tale of Rome"• 36, 277, 278, 299
"The Rival Prima Donnas"• (short story) 278, 299
"The Rival Prima Donnas"• (unpublished drama) 299
Roberts, Victoria 172
Roberts Brothers 67, 79, 83, 88, 89, 100, 108, 116, 127, 130, 135, 145, 149, 152, 281
Robinson Crusoe 156
"The Rock and the Bubble"• (poem) 300
Rodnik 190
Rolfe, Abby F 246
Rollo books 149, 150, 151, 287
The Romance of a Poor Young Man 52
"The Romance of a Summer Day"• 307
Rookery Cottage (Philadelphia) 5, 239
Roosevelt, Eleanor 169
Ropes, Mrs. 63
"Rosa's Tale"• 312, 319
The Rose Family. A Fairy Tale• 71, 73, 280, 293, 302, 304
Rose in Bloom. A Sequel to "Eight Cousins"• 115, 203, 282, 296, 311; as play 187
Rosen, Phil 187
"Roses and Forget-Me-Nots"• 308, 311, 317, 319
Rossetti, Christina 295
Rostenberg, Leona 237
"Rosy's Journey"• 315, 318

A Round Dozen: Stories by Louisa May Alcott• (anthology) 320
Rowland, Eva 175
Roxbury, Mass 112, 133, 135, 242, 285
"A Royal Governess"• 305
Rudman, Masha Kabakow 184
Russ, Lavinia 159
Russell, William 5, 6
"Ruth's Secret"• 300

S , M.L 150
Sacajawea 169
Sachem, Squaw 13
St Louis Fair 74
St. Nicholas 107, 108, 119, 129, 130, 133, 150, 164, 203, 229, 268, 295
The St. Nicholas Anthology† 312
Salmon, Edward 189
Salyer, Sandford 233
Sanborn, Franklin Benjamin 47, 49, 51, 53, 55, 58, 67, 73, 100, 117, 120, 129, 174, 229, 243, 245, 279, 280; biographical sketch 272; works of 272
Sanger, Margaret 169
"The Sanitary Fair"• (poem) 302
The Saturday Evening Gazette 42, 43
Sauerman, Carl 174
Savitz, Harriet 256
The Scarlet Letter 166
"Scarlet Stockings"• 306
Schallert, William 182
Schechter, Harold 185
Schlesinger, Elizabeth Bancroft 229
Schlesinger Library, Radcliffe College 168
School of Philosophy (Concord) 120, 121, 245, 248, 284
"The School of Philosophy"• (poem) 121
The School Stage: A Collection of Juvenile Acting Plays 173
Schoolgirl 192
Scott, Dorothy Quincy Hancock 6, 13, 44, 111; as character in *Little Women* 85
Scott, Sir Walter 219
Sears, Clara Endicott 242
The Second St. Nicholas Anthology† 313
The Selected Letters of Louisa May Alcott• (anthology of letters) 230, 321
Selznick, David O. 178, 181, 183
Sendak, Maurice 167
"A Sermon in the Kitchen"• 307
"The Servant-Girl Problem" ("Hope for Housekeepers")• 308
"Seven Black Cats"• 308, 312
Sewall, Lucy 135
Sewall, Samuel 112, 135
"Shadow-Children"• 304, 313, 318
Shakespeare, William 150, 237, 263
Shannon, Monica 167

Shatner, William 182
Shaw, George Bernard 292
"Shawl Straps"• 307
Shealy, Daniel 230
Shields, K.D. 261
"Should Children Have Special Literature?" 189
Showalter, Elaine 236, 237
Sidney, Margaret see Lothrop, Harriet Mulford Stone
"The Silver Party"• 316, 319, 320
Silver Pitchers• 136, 296, 316
"Silver Pitchers A Temperance Tale,"• 310
Silver Pitchers: and Independence. A Centennial Love Story• 311
Singing Our History: Tales, Texts and Tunes from Two Centuries of Unitarian and Universalist Hymns 209, 214, 320
"The Sisters' Trial"• 43, 83, 300
"The Skeleton in the Closet"• 303, 320
"The Skipping Shoes"• 315, 318
"The Skipping Stones"• 319
Sleepy Hollow Cemetery (Concord) 49, 73, 117, 120, 127, 139, 243
Smith, C. Aubrey 181
Smith, Jessie Wilcox 317, 318
Smith, Nancy Stewart 258
Smith College 227
So Big 165
Solger, Reinhold: as character in Little Men 100; as character in Little Women 89
Solt, Andrew 181
"Some Anonymous and Pseudonymous Thrillers of Louisa May Alcott" 237
"A Song for a Christmas Tree"• (poem) 303, 311
"A Song for Little Freddie on His Third Birthday"• (poem) 77
"A Song from the Suds"• (poem) 86
"Songs from a Sea-Shell—The Patient Drop"• (poem) 300
"Sophie's Secret"• 313, 316, 319
Spacks, Patricia Meyer 160
Sparkles for Bright Eyes with Contributions by Louisa May Alcott† 312
Spindle Hill (Wolcott, Conn.) 5, 28
The Spinning Wheel Series• (four volumes) 316
Spinning Wheel Stories• 136, 234, 297, 314, 316
Spofford, Harriet Prescott 119
"A Sprig of Andromeda: A Letter from Louisa May Alcott on the Death of Henry David Thoreau"• 319
Spyri, Johanna 196; works of 297
Stapley, Richard 181
Stearns, Frank 67, 74, 81
Steffe, William 223
Stein, Harve 319
Stephenson, Henry 178

Stern, Madeleine B 145, 157, 230, 233, 234, 235, 237, 238, 257
Stevenson, Robert Louis 291; works of 297
Still River, Mass 24, 75, 230
Stone, Lucy 35, 79, 108, 111, 294; biographical sketch 273; Lucy Stone Leaguers 112, 273
Story of My Life 165
Stowe, Harriet Beecher 104, 107, 167, 169, 212, 242, 265, 291; biographical sketch 273; works of 273
"A Strange Island"• 304
Stroh, Kandice 184
Studying Art Abroad: How to Do It Cheaply 122
Success (unpublished)• 107, 279, 282; see also Work
Sulie, John 61, 70
Sumner, Charles 44, 54; biographical sketch 273; works of 273
"Sunlight"• (poem) 36, 278, 291, 299
The Sunny Side: A Book of Religious Songs for the Sunday School and the Home 207, 209, 213
"Sunset"• (poem) 22
"Sunshine, and Her Brothers and Sisters"• 315
"Sunshiny Sam"• 305, 312, 316
Swarthmore College 227
"Sweet One for Polly"• 311
"Sweet!? Sweet!"• (poem) 130
The Swiss Family Robinson 189
"Switzerland"• 308
Syracuse, N Y. 113

"Tabby's Table-Cloth"• 313, 314, 320
Table-Talk 117
Tablets 83
Taggart, Marion Ames 171
"Taming a Tartar"• 303, 321
Taming of the Shrew 237
Tanglewood Tales 291
Taylor, Elizabeth 181
Temperance Society (Concord) 126
Temple, Shirley 181
Temple School (Boston) 8, 9, 11, 12, 100, 275
Tennyson, Alfred 291
"Tessa's Surprises"• 305, 307, 318, 319, 320
Thaxter, Celia (Laighton) 89, 107, 119, 126; biographical sketch 273; works of 274
Theatre Book of the Year 176
The Theatre Guild on the Air 177
"This Is Your Life   Louisa May Alcott" 156
Thoreau, Henry David 13, 18, 21, 27, 49, 65, 66, 82, 108, 115, 121, 127, 216, 218,

Index

231, 243, 277; biographical sketch 274; death 56, 73, 280; works of 274, 291
Thoreau-Alcott-Pratt House (Concord, Mass.) 115, 120, 121, 122, 243, 282, 283, 285
"Thoreau's Flute"• (poem) 66, 74, 204, 301
"The Three Frogs"• 315
The Three Musketeers 156
Three Proverb Stories (Kitty's Class Day at Harvard; Louisa M. Alcott's Proverb Stories)• 203, 294, 305
Three Unpublished Poems by Louisa May Alcott• 318
Through the Looking Glass 164
Ticknor, Caroline 231
Ticknor and Fields 242
"Tilly's Christmas" ("The Fairy Bird")• 304, 307
Time 180
"To Anna"• (poem) 22
"To Father"• (poem) 37
"To Mother"• (poem) 16
"To My Brain"• (poem) 133
"To My Father on His Eighty-Sixth Birthday"• (poem) 131, 314, 316
"To Papa"• (poem) 318
"To the First Robin"• (poem) 14
Tom Brown books 294
Tom Sawyer 157, 158, 159, 164, 167, 189, 296
The Tombs (New York) 113, 282
"Touchstones: A List of Distinguished Children's Books" 168
Trail Makers of the Middle Border 165
"Transcendental Wild Oats"• 129, 243, 308
"Transcendental Wild Oats"• (pamphlet) 320
Transcendental Wild Oats and Excerpts from the Fruitlands Diary• 235, 320
Transcendentalism 15, 18, 20, 24, 35, 73, 235, 243
Transcript 42
"Transfiguration In Memoriam"• (poem) 118, 311, 316
Treasure Island 156
"Tribulation Periwinkle's Epitaph"• (poem) 68
"Tribulation's Travels"• 310
"Trudel's Siege"• 316, 319
Tsing-yung, Sung 191
Tubman, Harriet 169
TV Guide 182
TV Movies: 1983-84 Edition 180, 182, 183
Twain, Mark (pseudonym of Samuel Clemens) 167, 168, 287, 296; works of 297; *see also* Clemens, Samuel
"25 Most Important *Women* in American History" 168
"Two Little Travellers"• 312
Typee 166

Ullom, Judith C., 238
Uncle Remus books 296
"Uncle Smiley's Boys"• 306
Uncle Tom's Cabin 167, 212, 260, 273, 291
Under the Lilacs• 116, 117, 203, 208, 209, 284, 296, 311, 312
United States Postal Service 166
University of Florida 227
University of Michigan 227
University of Texas 227
University of Virginia 227; library 235
"The Unloved Wife; or, Woman's Faith"• 316
"Up the Rhine"• 303

"V V : or, Plots and Counterplots"• 72, 302, 307, 320
Vanderbilt University 227
Van Stockum, Hilda 167, 319
Vassar College 110, 226
Vaughan Williams, Ralph 211, 212
Vaux, Roberts 5
Venable, William Henry 173
Verne, Jules 295
"Victoria. A Woman's Statue"• 312
"Vienna" 215, 216
"A Visit to the School-Ship"• 306
"A Visit to the Tombs"• 311
Vowell, J. Maureen 260

"W.C T.U., of Concord"• 313
"Wait for the Wagon" 216, 217
Walden 291
Walden Pond (Concord) 27, 71, 120, 243, 274
Wallace, Lew 165
Walpole, N.H 42, 43, 46, 278, 279
Walpole Amateur Dramatic Company 42, 278
War and Peace 192
Warren Street Chapel (Boston) 55, 240, 279
Washington, George 6
Washington, Martha 6, 169
Washington, D C. 33, 58, 60, 61
The Water-Babies 109, 295
Water Cresses by L.M. Alcott and Others† 312
"Water-Lilies"• 316, 320
Watson, Henrietta 175
Watson, Lucile 181
Watts, Richard, Jr. 180
The Wayside (Concord) 46, 244, 245, 278; *see also* The Hillside
We Alcotts: The Story of Louisa May Alcott's Family as Seen Through the Eyes of "Marmee," Mother of Little Women 233

Weber, Nettie 319
Weber, Carl Maria von 209, 210
Wee, Aunt (pseudonym of LMA) 82
Welchel, Lisa 185
Weld, Anna 76, 77, 78, 79
Weld, George 76
Wells, Lizzie 42, 44, 85
Wells, Louisa 102
Wendell, Barrett 151
Wendte, Charles W. 207, 209, 213
Wesley, Charles 212
West, Beverly 174
Westcott, Edward Noyes 167
Weyn, Suzanne 172
"The Whale's Story"• 304, 313
"What a Shovel Did"• 310, 312
"What Becomes of the Pins"• 312, 319
"What Fanny Heard"• 306, 308
"What It Cost"• 315
"What Polly Found in Her Stocking"• (poem) 304
"What Shall Little Children Bring"• (poem and song lyrics) 214, 215, 216, 314, 321
"What the Bells Saw and Said"• 304, 313
"What the Girls Did"• 309, 311
"What the Swallows Did"• 304, 313
Wheeler, Roger 175
"When the Alcott Books Were New" 190
"When Shall Our Young Women Marry?"• 315
"Where Is Bennie?"• (poem) 304
Where the Wild Things Are 167
"A Whisper in the Dark"• 301, 320
"Whispers in the Den" 192
White, E B 167
The White Ribbon Birthday Book† 316
Whiting (Hosmer), Laura 102, 119, 133, 137
Whitman, Alfred 47, 55, 56, 58, 108, 126, 229, 279; as character in *Little Men* 100; as character in *Little Women* 85, 94, 108
Whitman, Walt 292
Whittier, John Greenleaf 294
Who's Who in Children's Books 159, 194
The Who's Who of Children's Literature 193
"Why Miss Alcott Still Lives" 151
"Wild Roved an Indian Girl, Bright Alfarata" 25
Wilde, Oscar 292
Wilder, Laura Ingalls 167, 168
William D. Ticknor and Co. 242
Willis, Frederick Llewellyn Hovey 24, 27, 36
Willis, Llewellyn *see* Willis, Frederick Llewellyn Hovey
"Will's Wonder-Book"• 234, 304, 307, 320
Will's Wonder Book (Louisa's Wonder Book)• 234, 235, 307
Windship, Charles May 42, 52
"Winter"• (poem) 28

Winterich, John T. 165
"Wishes"• (poem) 304
Wisniewski, Ladislas 76, 77, 78, 108, 117, 126, 229, 280; as character in *Little Men* 100; as character in *Little Women* 85, 94, 108
"With a Rose That Bloomed on the Day of John Brown's Martyrdom"• (poem) 51, 204, 300
Wolcott, Connecticut *see* Spindle Hill
"The Woman Who Wrote Little Women" 172, 231
Woman's Congress 113
The Woman's Journal 125, 129, 133, 230, 270, 294
"Woman's Part in the Concord Celebration" ("The Concord Centennial"; pamphlet)• 310
The Woman's Story as Told by Twenty American Women† 316
"Women in Brittany"• (included in "Brittany") 307
A Wonder Book for Girls and Boys 291
The Wonderful Wizard of Oz 167, 168
Wood, Lydia Hosmer 12, 49, 231
Woollcott, Alexander 192
Worcester, Mass. 35
Work: A Story of Experience (unpublished as *Success*)• 107, 108, 156, 204, 235, 279, 282, 295, 308, 320
"Work; or Christie's Experiment"• 308
Works of Louisa May Alcott• (anthology) 321
Works of Louisa May Alcott• (juvenile set) 321
The Works of Louisa May Alcott• (set) 321
The Works of Louisa May Alcott, 1832–1888• (set) 321
Wright, Catherine Morris 230
Wright, Henry 277
"A Writer's Progress: Louisa May Alcott at 150" 158
Wuthering Heights 290
Wyck farm (Philadelphia) 5, 7, 115, 239

Yale University 227
Yaron, Tamar 197
Young, Robert 182
"Young America" ("March, march, mothers and grandmammas! "; poem and song lyrics)• 218, 219, 220, 300, 321
Young Folks Library of Choice Literature: Louisa May Alcott 231
The Youth's Companion 147, 203, 230

Zakrzewska, Marie Elizabeth 135
Zundel, John 212, 213

Authors Guild Backinprint.com Editions are fiction and nonfiction works that were originally brought to the reading public by established United States publishers but have fallen out of print. The economics of traditional publishing methods force tens of thousands of works out of print each year, eventually claiming many, if not most, award-winning and one-time best-selling titles. With improvements in print-on-demand technology, authors and their estates, in cooperation with the Authors Guild, are making some of these works available again to readers in quality paperback editions. Authors Guild Backinprint.com Editions may be found at nearly all online bookstores and are also available from traditional booksellers. For further information or to purchase any Backinprint.com title please visit www.backinprint.com.

Except as noted on their copyright pages, Authors Guild Backinprint.com Editions are presented in their original form. Some authors have chosen to revise or update their works with new information. The Authors Guild is not the editor or publisher of these works and is not responsible for any of the content of these editions.

The Authors Guild is the nation's largest society of published book authors. Since 1912 it has been the leading writers' advocate for fair compensation, effective copyright protection, and free expression. Further information is available at www.authorsguild.org.

Please direct inquiries about the Authors Guild and Backinprint.com Editions to the Authors Guild offices in New York City, or e-mail staff@backinprint.com.